Inside War

INSIDE WAR

The Guerrilla Conflict in Missouri During the American Civil War

MICHAEL FELLMAN

New York   Oxford
OXFORD UNIVERSITY PRESS
1989

Oxford University Press

Oxford   New York   Toronto
Delhi   Bombay   Calcutta   Madras   Karachi
Petaling Jaya   Singapore   Hong Kong   Tokyo
Nairobi   Dar es Salaam   Cape Town
Melbourne   Auckland

and associated companies in
Berlin   Ibadan

Published by Oxford University Press, Inc.,
200 Madison Avenue, New York, New York 10016

Oxford is a registered trademark of Oxford University Press

Library of Congress Cataloging-in-Publication Data
Fellman, Michael.
Inside war : the guerrilla conflict in Missouri during the
American Civil War / Michael Fellman.
p.   cm.   Bibliography: p.   Includes index.   ISBN 0-19-505198-X
1. Missouri—History—Civil War, 1861–1865—Underground movements.
2. United States—History—Civil War, 1861–1865—Underground
movements.   3. Guerrillas—Missouri—History—19th century.
I. Title.   E470.45.F36   1988   973.7′478—dc 19
88–22690   CIP

1 2 3 4 5 6 7 8 9

Printed in the United States of America
on acid-free paper

PREFACE

Countless historians have written of the glories of battles like Gettysburg; few have depicted the grinding nastiness of the everyday Civil War. Boredom, aching feet, and dysentery, the daily realities for foot soldiers, do not make for stirring reading. The war of skirmish and of guarding supply lines and prisoners, the tasks which occupy most soldiers most of the time, is not a poetic test of men's souls. Guerrilla war, intrinsically ruthless and inconclusive, fails to please either the historian or the reader with much in the way of narrative clarity or a sense of man's honor enlarged. Real war assaults, diminishes, and embitters participants. It challenges them fundamentally—not to rise to triumph, but to survive brutal defeat, to maintain vestiges of their prewar selves. Guerrilla struggle, perhaps the prevalent form of war in history,[1] is also the most devastating challenge to any notion of civility or virtue in war. In this sense, guerrilla war approaches total war, the war of all against all.

Though understudied by historians, guerrilla war was quite widespread along the border between the South and the North during the American Civil War. From the hills of western Virginia, North Carolina, and Georgia, through the mountain hollows of East Tennessee and Kentucky to the wooded, hilly farmlands of Missouri, bands of guerrillas wandered the countryside striking terror in all those around them.[2] I have chosen to discuss Missouri not because it was unique but because of all regions it produced the most widespread, longest-lived, and most destructive guerrilla war in the Civil War. Missouri provides a horrendous example of the nature of guerrilla war in the American heartland.

It could well be that if the southern leadership had learned from the Missouri example and had chosen to fight a guerrilla war rather than a conventional one, they would have won. Such is one conclusion of the authors of the influential recent study, *Why the South Lost the Civil War,* who argue that the southern leadership was insufficiently inhumane even "to consider the guerrilla alternative [which] may be a major reason why the South lost the Civil War."[3] The landed gentry who ran the South were too concerned with Christian virtue and too afraid of the beastly and un-disciplined aspects of mankind and of the unruliness of their own lower social orders to sponsor a guerrilla war. They would not win the war at the cost of their conception of humanity, nor would they allow their lower orders to dominate combat, thus staking a claim to the reorganization of society at the successful termination of hostilities. Where they were in firm control, the Confederate leadership restricted guerrilla warfare.

One can gain more than a glimpse of what kind of civil war a general guerrilla struggle could have been by examining the events in Missouri. There, far behind Union lines, the behavior of pro-southern settlers was truly out of Confederate control, and there a guerrilla war raged for four years. Many Confederate sympathizers created an effective guerrilla war spontaneously and carried it on with little submission or even reference to Confederate authorities. This was a "natural," popular war rather than a planned, disciplined one. The rules of conflict grew directly out of local circumstances and bore little relation to the history and traditions of martial order or to the dream of a Christian Confederacy. Little remained under control, little remained forbidden.

Beyond being an episode of the Civil War and a view of what a general American guerrilla war could have resembled, the experience of Missouri gives us an especially clear picture of a yeoman, evangelical Christian culture undergoing a severe trial. Studying Missouri, we can extend our knowledge of the behavior of men in battle to include unorganized or, more precisely, self-organized combat.[4] We can also study the impact of war on civilian women and men, not merely those living in safety behind established military lines but those who are swept into the war itself. In part because of the richness of the archival sources for the American Civil War, we can study in Missouri not merely the institutional, strategic, and tactical elements of war but also the physical, emotional, and moral experiences of Americans fully at war with one another—the very inside of civil war.

Because the subject matter of this book was so trying, I owe a special debt to those institutions and people who helped me see it through. Grants from the President's Research Fund of Simon Fraser University helped me initiate this book. Dean Robert C. Brown, of Simon Fraser, provided timely support on several occasions. The librarians and archivists at all the institutions in my archival source list were extremely courteous and helpful. I would especially like to thank Richard S. Brownlee and James W. Goodrich of the Missouri State Historical Society for their generosity and interest. The Shelby Cullom Davis Center at Princeton University made me a Visiting Fellow, which allowed me time and a place to complete my research, ruminate out loud, and begin writing. The other Davis Fellows and the history faculty at Princeton helped make my year there stimulating and diverse. I am especially grateful to Lawrence Stone, Director of the Davis

Center, for his intellectual example, his company, and his unfailing encouragement that I follow my argument wherever it might take me. The Social Science Research Council of Canada provided me with a Leave Fellowship to help support my year at Princeton. A fellowship from the Huntington Library provided me, as it has so many other scholars, the perfect setting in which I could write much of this book. Brenda Code made the maps and Susan Weinandy the index with good cheer and thoroughness. I am grateful also for the enthusiasm and hard work of several manuscript typists, Anita Mahoney, Sharon Vanderhook, Jan MacLellan, Maylene Leong, and Bernice Henderson. Several colleagues took time out of their busy lives to read drafts of this book—Philip Shaw Paludan, John O'Brien, Martin Ridge, William Wiecek, Edward Ayres, Paul Dutton, and Richard K. Debo. Robert H. Wiebe and Michael Zuckerman offered me indispensable advice, critical analysis, and friendship from the beginning to the end of this project, for which I will always remain deeply grateful. The enthusiasm and good sense of Sheldon Meyer, Rachel Toor, and Scott Lenz of Oxford University Press have made the completion of this book a real pleasure. Finally, my wife, Santa Aloi, and my two sons, Joshua and Eli, always reminded me of the creative power of love which helped me keep a perspective on the destructiveness which this book documents.

Vancouver   M. F.
June 1988

For Joshua and Eli

CONTENTS

MAPS

ILLUSTRATIONS

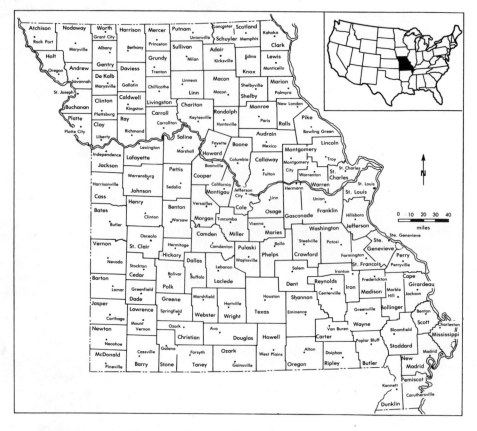

Political map of Missouri with counties and county seats

INTRODUCTION

The attack came at any Missouri farmyard, any night. "Two men dressed in Federal uniforms came and knocked at our door and said they wanted to warm. Tom told them to go round to the other door and then without thinking let them in. They jumped on Tom with their pistols and demanded his revolver. He told them he had none. They said there was one here and they would have it. Tom had to get Mat's which John had. I was very scared and sorry John had got up and let them in. They shot Mr. Jones through his door. But at Mr. Harmon they would not let them in and they went away."[1]

Pauline Stratton's description of this representative moment in guerrilla warfare is typical of hundreds I have read. Such war erased the line between combatant and civilian, between soldier and bandit. The moment occurred unpredictably. Often one had no idea of who was doing the attacking, both because southern guerrillas frequently wore Union uniforms as a disguise and because many Union soldiers, sometimes posing as southern guerrillas in Union uniforms, were entirely capable of free-lance skirmishing outside their shaky command structure. The terror of the attack was increased by the seemingly random degree of violence, as exemplified by these two men against the Strattons, Hammonses, and Joneses. Thus, should one cooperate or bar the door? Were two men outside, or twenty? Who were they, and which side should you appear to support? If you gave in, would you be robbed merely of a pistol or a horse, or would your house be ransacked and you be tortured to hand over your hidden cache of money? Would it stop there, or would you be burned out? If burned, would the men in your family be shot in the head? And would you be invaded again, and when? What would the neighbors think? What would the Union authorities think? Under such peril, how ought you to act? Who *were* they? Who were *you?* Pauline Stratton's dilemma was a cultural as well as a personal event. Her catastrophe, multiplied by hundreds of thousands, was the catastrophe of her society.

During the American Civil War, Missouri, a typical rural, industrializing, evangelical state was plunged into the worst guerrilla war in American history. Normal expectations collapsed, to be replaced by frightening and bewildering personal and cultural chaos. The normal routes by which people solved problems and channeled behavior had been destroyed. The base for their prior values—their "moral structure"—underwent frontal attack. Ordinary people, civilians as well as soldiers, were trapped by guerrilla war in a social landscape in which almost nothing remained recognizable or secure. The dislocations of their war pounded against all those cultural ligaments which tied people to one another and normally gave the security necessary for individuals to organize their psyches and their lives. Such war both exaggerated and undermined fundamental cultural structure.

The reams of diaries and letters, depositions to the military police, court-martial transcripts, and formal and informal military reports which form the evidential base of this study give a startlingly vivid picture of ordinary Americans caught inside the Civil War. We can learn of prewar expectations from the sense one gains of which values and rules for behavior were being violated during the war. There is a clear sense in the complaints and hopes voiced in these documents of the breakdown of well-understood boundaries, expectations, and standards.

Much had been undermined in frightening ways; people groped for means to re-establish norms in the midst of random violence and unending fear. These fears and prior norms were expressed throughout the society: many of the depositions were given by illiterates and semiliterates, people usually voiceless in historical reconstructions. Many accounts were verbatim reports of guerrilla words and actions, as well as of other dislocations caused by such warfare, by participants desperately trying to make sense of their benumbing experiences. These people lived in a storytelling culture; they were accustomed to narrating their experiences. In a psychological sense, they felt an urgent need to "tell their story" to someone in authority, less from expecting redress, which was usually unavailable, than from needing just to tell someone official about the wrongs done them. They knew that what had happened was illegal, and by their standards immoral as well, and they wanted duplicity recorded so that some day their travails might be known and the principle of justice might be reinvigorated. They did not accept violations as normal—they knew the difference between what they called civilization and barbarism, and they needed to believe that they at least had not descended into bestiality. They would not become nihilists, not in their hearts and minds, even if their culture had become a maelstrom.

This book is an attempt to understand something of the social and cultural meanings of such a war for ordinary Americans. It concerns the nature of terror and its personal and social impact, loyalty and justice as it had been expected and was reworked, the malleability of Protestant religious values in war and in peace, the cultural meanings of maleness and femaleness, the need to establish what I call survival lies during times of stress, the nihilistic tendencies and self-imposed limits of the young guerrillas and their Union opposition, the contradictory responses of regular armies and governments to waging this sort of war, the reworking of economic and racial relations, and the postwar reckoning with the guerrilla war experience.

I deal with anger and violence as intrinsic parts of cultural process rather than as separable topics. Violence is not outside "normal" culture, nor is it *the* dirty truth. Indeed, one can learn a great deal about the human capacity for cooperation by analyzing it in conjunction with the study of the equally human capacity for destruction. As part of the wider historical task of gaining greater understanding of this destructiveness, I discuss how ordinary Americans could create a landscape of desolation and at the same time display the often moving capacity for creativity which remained alive among these people.

Rural Missourians, the chief subjects of this book, were not monsters nor backwoods savages but family-centered, property-owning farmers, evangelical Christians, and lovers of law and order. They were in the midst of a rapid social transition from a traditional agricultural society to a more marketplace-oriented one. Most were operating within energetic local market economies which were becoming increasingly connected by new railroads to the booming industrial and trade center of St. Louis. Rural Missourians had long-term economic and social aspirations as well as fears concerning the economic revolution. But the Civil War was an unprecedented, enormous, immediate, and brutal invasion of their communities in transition. Whatever their peacetime adjustments might have been to the economic transformation of the mid-nineteenth century, rural Missourians were compelled to deal directly with a pervasive guerrilla war, which tore their society apart. They were the objects of hatred and destruction; they hunted and slaughtered. Their personalities as well as their bodies and their homes and farms were attacked. They struggled just to live, to make daytime sense of cultural nightmares.

I begin this study with an analysis of society and ideology in prewar Missouri as it underwent capitalist transformation. After a discussion of the demographic, economic, and political settings of Missouri in the 1850s, I analyze the events of "Bloody Kansas" of the 1850s. Missourians were ordinary yeoman farmers under cultural and political assault by free state settlers in Kansas, who characterized them as degraded and savage poor whites, and to whom they responded with similar, degrading characterizations. The deeply insulting slurs exchanged during this conflict prepared Missourians ideologically to respond with violence to the later "invasions" by Northerners during the Civil War.

Thus primed, Missouri exploded into a devastating, demoralizing, deteriorating guerrilla war in 1861. I begin by discussing the physical and psychological impact of guerrilla terror on civilian victims. They attempted to understand what was happening to them as violations of natural justice, a moral code in which they attempted to sustain their faith. Some clearly identified with one side or the other, maintaining a notion of loyalty of belief and behavior. Many more sought to be disengaged, neutral. Despite the stance people wished to assume, however, most were pushed into a web of lies in order to survive. With the collapse of security in the belief that good conduct mattered, that right and wrong were comprehensible, that one could build a life from day to day, many civilians became numb, separating their consciences from their actions. They also turned on each other, seeking revenge. Finally, overwhelmed with attacks and fear and chaos, many fled in panic.

Guerrilla warfare blew the cover off respectable society, and undermined official values. No official response could end or even deflect the self-governing engines of guerrilla war. The contradictory and inconclusive attitudes and orders of the civil and military commands, and their translation on the field of battle, are the themes of Chapter 3. I discuss the deep split at the top of the Union command between those urging punishment and those stressing reconciliation, the "hards" and the "softs." No sustained policy could come from such deeply divided leaders: they passed down conflicting and rapidly changing policies. Short of burning everything and killing everyone, which was tempting but morally impermissible, nothing worked. The southern command was also ambivalent. Proper Christian gentry leaders hated the illegal brutality of the guerrillas, but they also found them useful. Never fully licensing them, neither did they outlaw them. Official Union structure and authority disintegrated in the field. Small group actions, the basic antiguerrilla form of war, meant that the terms of combat were in fact negotiated on the one hand between Union troops and the guerrillas and on the other between Union troops and their junior officers, who were encouraged by their seniors to be duplicitous in the quest for "results."

The inner meanings of guerrilla war came not from above but from the guerrillas and counterguerrillas joined in combat. These actors played the internalized values of prewar culture against the unique wartime possibilities of acting out basic emotions. The first section of Chapter 4 is an analysis of the ideology and values of the guerrillas, both their assertion of manliness and honor and their desire to assume legality in their claims to social leadership. When captured, these young men quickly sought to resubordinate themselves to the dominant political society they just had attempted to destroy. Ordinary Union soldiers, like the guerrillas, were deeply embattled, torn between their prewar desire to become constructive, self-controlled men and the demands of their new wartime role as soldiers. Although most did not fall in love with destruction, almost all coarsened as the war went on. They felt attacked from all quarters and sought to lash out against their tormentors. In guerrilla war tactics and in the morality used by both sides, the natures of the combatants blurred as they reassembled their values and behavior into a guerrilla war-revised culture. Union soldiers increasingly resembled the guerrillas they were attacking. All shared a sense of blood sport as a test of manhood with humans as the game. At the core of the guerrilla war experience for all fighters was the deep need for taking blood revenge. Killing and mutilating the body of the male enemy expressed a Protestant-Manichaean sense of the good of one's own people and the evil of the Other.

Guerrilla war-revised culture also extended to women, primarily as victims but also as participants. Women were necessary as informers, suppliers, and sometimes fighters. The dialectic of restraint and rage toward enemy women by Union troops, gentility and menace by guerrillas, demonstrated the rubbing edges of repression and expression in male codes of behavior concerning women, reworked in a guerrilla war setting. "Woman" was the exalted shrine before which the Protestant-Manichaean warriors laid the sacrificed bodies of their male enemies. The nearly total absence of rape and murder of white women was highlighted by the acting out of violence on black and Indian women. During this war the spheres of women's roles and behavior expanded, testing the limits of the allowable and the forbidden. Guerrilla war also engendered desperate efforts on the part of both men and women to shore up loving, heterosexual relationships, the hope for peace in the face of so much inner and outer destruction.

I conclude with an analysis of the resolutions of guerrilla warfare in postwar Missouri. Widespread political and personal violence continued for about two years after the war, which lacked emotional resolution. The late 1860s also witnessed rapid northern-oriented economic development, fueled in the countryside by the extension of railroads and accelerating industrialization in St. Louis. Guerrilla war-revised culture had left a bitter and disruptive legacy, but by recombining familiar values with basic emotions, that culture also created the stuff for enduring, ennobling myths. In terms of popular memory, the guerrillas came to represent the best of the fading traditional society. The legend of the noble outlaw rose alongside that of the American Robin Hood, ex-guerrilla Jesse James. Heroic and comforting legends such as this were adopted by ex-guerrillas, masking memories of the actual guerrilla warfare I have described.

In all this analysis, my central concern is with the ways in which ordinary nineteenth-century Americans, civilians as well as soldiers, experienced war, not just in terms of behavior but also in terms of inner responses. I seek to present in primary colors the varieties of strong emotions—fear, hate, hope, love—which were aroused in war, one of humankind's primary activities. I define the container of all these emotions and the ideas through which they were articulated as moral structure. The battering and reshaping of moral structure in war instructs us about the nature of morality as it existed under more "normal" circumstances, much as the way divorce tells us about marriage. In addition, the quality of life during war in itself is an important subject.

I seek to describe, without romanticizing them but also without degrading or dismissing them, ordinary nineteenth-century Americans going through terrible times. Becoming contemptuous is a danger for peaceful academics deploying their cool medium to discuss violence. My subjects were neither heroic nor contemptible but ordinary people trying to sort out personal and cultural experience and meaning in an overwhelmingly stressful situation.

Inside War

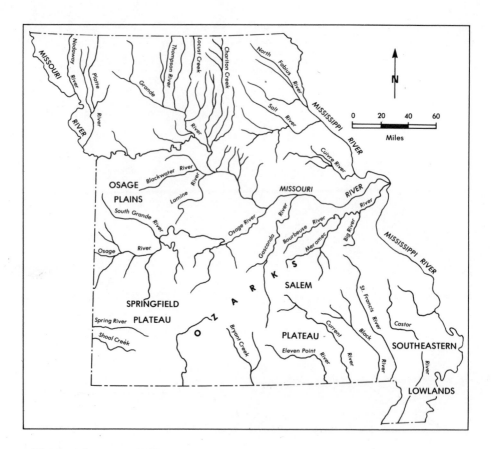

Physical features of Missouri

CHAPTER I

BEFORE THE WAR

Political Economy

As long as there was a sectional fence to straddle prior to 1861, most Missourians kept their perch on it. The northern tier of slave states—from Maryland and Delaware in the East, across the hill country populated primarily by smallholder yeomen, to Missouri in the West—joined two distinctive sections of the country and shared characteristics of each. They truly were border states. They were slave states, dominated by free white yeomen, where slavery was a real but marginal social and economic institution and where markets were being redirected toward the emerging manufacturing and trading colossus of the Northeast. However, just as there was resistance to the older, would-be aristocracy of slaveholders along the border—an opposition which had long distinguished that region from the deep South—so too was there resistance to the market economy spreading from the Northeast.

The new economic force was represented in the Missouri countryside most vividly by the banks and the railroads which suddenly linked traditional villages to the powerful hands of an unseen marketplace. In many respects, most Missourians wanted to be left alone on their farms in personal and economic liberty undisrupted by outside economic and ideological forces. They counterposed their personal freedom and private property, community cooperation and family honor to all "foreign" ideals and forces. Yet at the same time most Missourians would not have minded getting rich; they longed for profitable contacts with an outer world which interested them even as it repelled them. In their ambivalence about economic development and alien forces, Missourians resembled their rural brothers and sisters throughout the nation.

Missourians were not plunging from *Gemeinschaft* into *Gesellschaft*.[1] Indeed, for a majority of rural Missourians, and for a considerable time, there had been an increasingly active set of intermediary factors operating between them and the other world. Most crops traditionally grown for subsistence could also be sold into the local market economy. On the farms, household production decreased as purchases of finished goods and

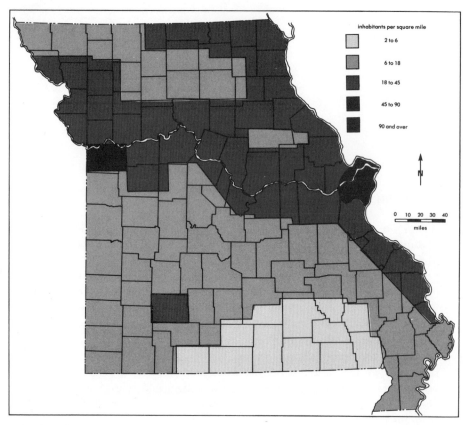

inhabitants per square mile

2 to 6

6 to 18

18 to 45

45 to 90

90 and over

0   10   20   30   40
miles

Population density in Missouri, 1860

of services like blacksmithing, milling, and wheelwrighting increased. Many of these exchanges with the developing small-town merchant class were conducted by barter, but cash values for deals were carefully recorded: farmers and merchants conducted what might be called semi-cash exchanges. Then merchants bought and sold into the larger commercial world with paper assigned cash value—if not actual money. Some rural historians have argued that this process of "proto-industrialization," as Steven Hahn has described it, "maintained the traditional family unit even as it was drawn into the sphere of commodity production under the auspices of merchant capitalism."[2] Family independence and localism and participation in the wider market could exist concurrently. Most Missourians were not subsistence farmers or peasants *cum* barbarians but established landowners already actively involved in the wider marketplace.

A general equality of condition characterized most of these farmers. Landless laborers and tenants, who tended to move on quite restlessly, did not become established economic actors. A few Missourians became well-off planters. Most were members of the broad yeoman class so character-istic of the upper South and the Midwest.[3]

Most Missourians were patriotic Unionists, believers in the libertarian revolution wrought by their sires. For them, liberty meant that their cher-ished Union should somehow compromise with the South, not coerce the southern states back into the Union. The presidential election of November 1860 demonstrated Missouri political predilections.[4] The most intensively slaveholding areas in Missouri voted strongly for the compromising upper South candidate, John Bell of Tennessee, perhaps hoping that he would prove to be the great sectional compromiser Henry Clay reborn; Stephen A. Douglas ran second in these areas, while secessionist John C. Brecken-ridge garnered most of his vote from poor white areas, where voters were perhaps attracted by his uncompromising argument for liberty and non-interference in traditional ways. Lincoln's 17,028 votes came almost ex-clusively from the German-Americans of St. Louis, a vote in part remark-able because it was a majority of the 27,000 votes Lincoln garnered from *all* the slave states. In the vote on a state secession convention four months later, amid the excitement of the departure from the Union of several southern states, Unionist candidates outpolled secessionists 110,000 to 30,000, or 73 percent to 23 percent. Most of these Unionist voters wished for some great new sectional compromise as well as for the preservation of the Union. In a few months' time, these conditional Unionists, as they were known, would have to make a hard choice. Some would go to one side, some to the other, but early in 1861 they all opposed secession. Most Missourians were conservative farmers of southern origin who voted as best they could to preserve the status quo.[5]

In Missouri, peacetime politics had mattered very much only to small well-organized factions within the dominant parties. Prior to the Civil War, the leading faction was the "Boonslick Democracy," a small group of slave-holding planters and their merchant allies along the rich bottomland of the Missouri River in the center of the state. This group, which controlled the governor's mansion and dominated the state legislature in 1861, de-fended slavery and believed Missouri to be a southern state—a part of the Confederacy. However, to win elections, they always presented themselves as committed Unionists and defenders of the Jacksonian version of the noble yeoman. They knew that they had to address a nonslaveholding white majority in terms more inclusive than their own material interests and ideological predispositions might suggest.

Such politicians aimed their appeal at an electorate that was overwhelm-ingly southern in origin. In the 1850s, approximately 75 percent of Mis-sourians were of southern ancestry, and many of the remainder came from regions in Ohio, Indiana, and Illinois which were settled earlier in the nineteenth century by Southerners.[6] The 1860 census data show that of

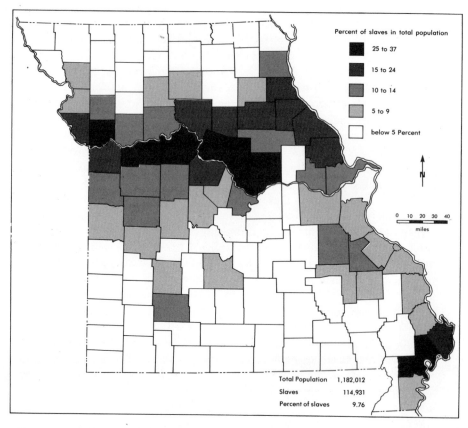

Percentage of slaves in the total population, 1860

the 431,397 Missourians born outside the state, 273,500 came from slave-holding states, nearly all of these from the upper South states of Kentucky, Tennessee, Virginia, and North Carolina.[7]

Most of the southern migrants who had slaves (a minority) settled along the Missouri River in the hemp growing areas of the west central part of the state and in the east central tobacco growing regions. Missouri was the second largest hemp producing state, next to Kentucky, and the sixth largest tobacco raiser. Both these crops were raised with back-breaking, labor-intensive work—work usually done by slaves. In addition, the market for hemp was a southern one, as both bagging and binding ropes for cotton bales were hemp products before the Civil War.[8] Yet this market was protected by a high Federal tariff on hemp, which bound hemp growers to the Union while the Confederacy argued for free trade. The slaveholding areas of Missouri, in the heaviest settled rural areas, were the Missouri River counties in the center of the state (see map above). They formed a slaveholding island cut off from the South by free states to the north, east, and west, and by the effectively nonslaveholding, thinly populated hill region of the southern half of Missouri, much of which was populated by southern mountain whites who were both bitterly negrophobic and haters of presumptuous southern planters and their Missouri counterparts.

Although they had their pretensions, Missouri slaveholders were not lords of the manor. The average number of slaves per slaveholder in 1860 was 4.66. About one Missouri family in eight (as opposed to one in two in the lower South) held slaves, nearly three-fourths of these holding fewer than 5, only 540 holding more than 20, and 38 more than 50.[9] Furthermore, as Table 1.1 demonstrates, slavery was on the wane in the 1850s, with only 9.8 percent of the population slaves, and with the proportion of nonslaveholding whites increasing yearly.

Ninety percent of Missourians lived on farms or in villages of less than 2,000 people. With the exception of St. Louis there were no cities in Missouri; only twenty-five towns had more than 3,000 people and none of these had as many as 10,000. Ninety-five percent of all churches were Protestant, two-thirds of these Baptist or Methodist. Statistically, the average Missourian was a Methodist from Kentucky who owned a 215-acre general family farm, owned no slaves, produced most of the family's subsistence, sold products and purchased goods within the local service economy, and was marginally but increasingly tied via cash crops and the purchase of machinery and consumer goods to external markets, primarily in St. Louis and the East. Cotton was not king, as it was in the deep South, nor was hemp or tobacco, except in a limited area; corn and hogs were. In 1860 Missouri was the second largest producer of corn and the fourth of swine.[10]

In the mid-1850s, markets for Missouri products in the East and Europe

Table 1.1.   Blacks in Missouri

Year	Total population	Whites	Free colored	Slaves	Percentage of slaves/blacks of entire population	Percentage of increase of slaves/blacks
1810	20,845	17,227	607	3,011	14.5	...
1820	66,586	54,903	376	9,797	15.4	239.4
1830	140,455	115,364	569	25,091	17.8	145.4
1840	383,702	322,295	1,478	57,891	15.5	132.1
1850	682,044	592,004	2,618	87,412	12.8	50.1
1860	1,182,012	1,063,489	3,572	114,931	9.8	31.0
1870	1,721,295	1,603,724	118,071		6.8	0.3

Adapted from Walter H. Ryle, *Missouri: Union or Secession* (Nashville: George Peabody, College of Education, 1931), 25.

increased dramatically. The railroad reached St. Louis in 1853, and the first 810 miles of track within Missouri were laid in the seven years after 1853.[11] The riverborne New Orleans market for farm products shriveled quickly, replaced by railroad links eastward via Cincinnati and Chicago. New markets led to intensified activity in local service economies. New markets also meant an economic spiral of new demand, larger profits for cash crops, considerable mechanization to increase farm productivity, the growth of banks and mercantile houses, and increased consumption of newly available consumer goods. This economic expansion led as well to an infusion of eastern capital backing railroads and to potential development by those same financiers of mines and industry.

At the hub of this development in the 1850s was St. Louis, one of the fastest growing industrial cities in the Union. St. Louis more than doubled in population in the 1850s to 166,773 persons of whom 60 percent were foreign-born, the highest percentage of foreign-born in any American city. This included 39,000 Irish and nearly 60,000 Germans. The existence of this powerful new city, peopled with so many immigrants, made St. Louis very strange indeed to the southern white, Anglo-Saxon, Protestant farmers of the vast Missouri countryside.[12] Strange too were the city dwellers' forms of work. By 1860 nearly 12,000 industrial workers were employed in 1,126 workplaces, producing nearly $28 million worth of goods—about 66 percent of the state's industrial output—making St. Louis the second largest manufacturing city in the Mississippi Valley, following Cincinnati.[13] All Missouri railroads led to St. Louis, and banking was heavily concentrated there as well, with much capital coming in from financial interests in the Northeast. The St. Louis agents of these interests reached out along the new railroad network for resources and crops to market and for customers to supply, drawing increasing numbers into the northern commercial network.

By 1860 it was apparent that Missouri was being integrated into the northern economy, leaving both southern economic ties and a primarily susbsistence economy behind. Significantly, Unionists campaigning against secession, seeking the most widely acceptable argument in the February 1861 special election, founded their campaign on just that economic development view of Missouri. Secession, they argued, would not only mean destructive war but an end to the building of the transcontinental railroad through Missouri. Prosperity depended on ties to eastern markets, and only eastern capitalists could finance resource and industrial development.[14] Eighty percent of Missouri's white male voters voted for the Union in that election, at least some because they saw the potential for a quick amassment of personal wealth, though voters responded as well to the symbolic value of the Republic and also out of fear of change. Yet many other voters, more than the 20 percent overtly secessionist, were still attracted by traditional notions of a nation peopled by independent, egalitarian small

Railroads in Missouri, 1860

farmers who owned their own land and lived in liberty and in voluntary relationships with other individuals.[15]

Many who cherished the values of self-sufficiency also entertained with pleasure the idea of becoming active players in the developing marketplaces spreading throughout the nation. The new forces were very confusing. But the traditional leaders were frequently seen as self-serving and deceitful; even while preaching the political theology of the common man, they often seemed rich neighborhood tyrants against whom economically ambitious farmers and merchants might well have wished to bring to bear new, external forces for their own, perfectly local reasons. It was possible to hold two seemingly conflicting ideals at the same time. Within both the more traditional and more modern senses of society and of self, the search for improvement based above all else on security was a central theme, and the issue during the Civil War became which version of society could offer this fundamental basis of comfortable and safe living.

By 1861 the St. Louis financial and industrial elite had become the new political force to challenge the dominance of the slaveholding elite of central Missouri. They made up in organization, discipline, and outside contacts what they lacked in numbers, tradition, or prior popular appeal. Perhaps more importantly in the short run, their strategy was planned by the astute Frank Blair, one of the Blair family so powerful in the Maryland and the Missouri Republican parties, as well as in Abraham Lincoln's innermost councils in Washington.

Blair pursued a two-pronged policy in the volatile early months of 1861 when southern sentiment was on the rise in Missouri. Within St. Louis—the only area of Republican strength in the 1860 election—Blair converted Republican "Wide-Awake" electioneering clubs into paramilitary Union clubs, primarily of Germans, 81 percent of whom had voted for Lincoln. These were the most committed Unionists in the state, and many of them had had prior military training in Germany. Blair used his contacts in the new national administration to arm these clubs and to oust the pro-southern commander of the St. Louis arsenal. The replacement was a staunch Unionist West Point man, Nathaniel Lyon, who was aided by an enlarged contingent of regular troops, which Blair linked to the armed local Union clubs. In the wider arena of Missouri politics and against the protests of his most committed Republican allies, Blair subordinated Republican goals to the broadest possible conservative Unionist appeal in order to win the February 1861 special convention vote with the smashing victory he achieved. He downplayed the slavery issue for economic arguments. For example, in St. Louis County the Constitutional Union clubs offered a moderate slate of seven Douglas, three Bell, and four Lincoln men. Blair then induced the convention to move from Jefferson City, which was in the middle of the slavery belt, to Unionist St. Louis, where in March it voted overwhelmingly against secession.

At this time a pro-southern state militia was organizing and gathering arms, some from the Confederacy. Its biggest camp was on the high ground above the St. Louis arsenal, and it was forming units as well in Jefferson City. Able to call on regular army troops, Illinois volunteer regiments, and his own relatively well-organized Union clubs, on May 11 Blair and Lyon stormed and captured the militia camp outside St. Louis, reinforced the armory, and put down the ensuing urban riot at the cost of thirty civilian lives. After this *coup d'état,* the state legislature might well have been able to declare secession on a wave of popular revulsion against such coercive government behavior spearheaded by hated "Hessians," but they had delegated that power to the special convention. Not strong enough yet to resist Union armed force, the state legislature sought to buy time by negotiating with Nathaniel Lyon on the issue of Union agreement to refrain from organizing troops in the interior of the state. Lyon instead issued an ultimatum and on June 15 seized Jefferson City. After a brief skirmish at Boonville, the secessionist state government fled to the southern part of the state. While Union troops from surrounding states began occupation of the important towns and railheads, the state constitutional convention re-convened, quite illegally, as a legislature and chose a provisional governor. Both sides then called for volunteers, neither meeting with much im-mediate popular response. Indeed there was never to be a *levée en masse* during the Civil War.[16]

The ensuing Civil War in Missouri was a fairly simple affair. The Union remained powerful enough militarily to maintain control of St. Louis, the railroads, and those towns and railheads they garrisoned, often with non-Missouri troops. Blair had both secured and narrowed the Unionist base through military action (not that the other side had given him other than tactical choices). The Confederacy, which gained in popular appeal when Missouri was "invaded" and occupied by often brutal military forces, was too weak to mount a sustained and organized military effort in the state after losing several battles in southern Missouri and northern Arkansas late in 1861 and in the spring of 1862. They did undertake several large-scale cavalry raids but could never establish permanent bases in Missouri. Tens of thousands of pro-southern families remained hundreds of miles behind Union lines, living next door to Unionists. Among these secession-ists, enraged by the mere fact of Union occupation as well as by its ex-cesses right on their doorsteps, were many young men of military age who had not gone south to join the regular Confederate army. A majority of Missourians were left confused and feeling caught in the middle of a battle they had wanted to avoid. They remained loyal to the Union yet deeply resentful of Federal force. They were to be whipsawed between the two organized poles of power; in the destruction of the ensuing guerrilla war, the everyday translation of ideology became the question of which side would enable them best to survive.

Popular Ideology

Another precondition to the Civil War in Missouri stemmed from the relations of Missourians to outsiders. Part of the power of the emerging American Northeast was expressed in the ability of the popular press there to create and broadcast images of Southerners and Westerners, particularly of poor whites, that attacked traditional smallholders for their supposed backwardness. Racing toward progress—defined as industrialization, ur-banization, education, and personal orderliness and accumulation—would-be cultural trendsetters disparaged the antiquated ways of folks like rural Missourians who, if they would not jump on the modernizing bandwagon, would be left behind as quaint relics of a passing and inferior culture. In many respects during the 1850s, slavery was painted as the chief example of cultural regress and personal corruption by an ever widening circle of northern popular writers. Slavery was a bond for whites to a discredited feudal agrarian past, a taint on all whites in a slave society, and a hindrance to be eliminated on the march to progressive development. All yeomen in such a society were debased into subhumanity by such an institution, or so the argument ran. Poor, ignorant, submissive to the slavocracy, they represented the fate of all whites should the slave conspirators rather than the forces of progress win the struggle between the sections.[17]

This popular northern ideological thrust against rural southern whites in the 1850s came to bear particularly on Missourians in the period 1854–56 in antislavery propaganda. Fighting the political question of the settlement of Kansas, abolitionists treated all Missourians as quintessential "poor white trash" in the race to settle the newly opened Indian lands just to the west of Missouri. They attacked not just the institution of slavery but the innermost character of all Missourians, living as they did in a slave state. Their honor impugned, many Missourians learned to hate Yankees with an urgent energy that would color their behavior during the Civil War. Analysis of what people said about one another in the press as well as in letters and diaries can give a flavor of the kind of sectional hatred and need for retribution which Missourians and their Kansas neighbors took with them into the Civil War.[18]

One can begin with the typical Yankee impressions of Julia Louisa Lovejoy, the wife of a New England Methodist minister, going west as an antislavery settler to Kansas. Even as her riverboat traveled up the Missouri River through the tobacco and hemp slave belt of that state in the spring of 1855, Lovejoy confirmed her preconceptions of the slave states. The very scenery was, "as we supposed, low and monotonous"; all the planters' dwelling places "dilapidated"; everywhere in Missouri she felt "the blighting mildew of *slavery*." How unlike this place was her native Vermont, with its "thrifty looking villages [and] stately mansions. . . ." If only her "energetic Yankee" brethren would leave the "sterile unproductive soil" of New England and "for a few years occupy these rich lands, how greatly would the fact of things be changed!"

At Jefferson City, Lovejoy was appalled by the appearance of the capitol building erected by the western slavestaters. "One thing seemed to us like *neglect* or *indolence,* the *rusty* appearance of the unpainted . . . cupola of the structure, that by heavy rains had soiled the exterior of the walls the entire height." In the very shadow of this contaminated statehouse, she was shocked to see a mule cart "being relieved from its contents of manure" by a colored woman, while her white male overseer supervised her "with an air of content . . . whilst he moved not a finger to assist the poor creature in her masculine task." Indignantly, she concluded, slavery was an accursed "unsexing demon." Further west in Kansas City she found only one church, "and this unpainted, uncarpeted, and . . . filthy" from the spit of tobacco chewers. In all of slaveholding Missouri "the inhabitants and the morals are of an *undescribably repulsive* and undesirable character."

In contrast to blighted Missouri, Lovejoy arrived in Kansas to find a spring garden. Untilled bottomland and rolling prairies "undulating like the waves of the sea" awaited human cultivation for good or for ill. The Lovejoy cabin along the Big Blue was in the middle of the town site of Manhattan, literally "in the centre of a garden of flowers of varied form and hue, surrounded with acres of rose bushes which when in blossom must perfume the air for miles around."[19] In 1855 Kansas was the Edenic West; it was the locale for the future of the small white farmer which simply had to be rescued from the possibility of becoming another slave-blighted Missouri.

The passage of the Kansas-Nebraska Act in 1854, through its popular sovereignty provision—actual settlers rather than Congress would determine the legal existence of slavery when the territory became a state—had guaranteed a sectional race to establish political hegemony in Kansas itself. From 1854 until 1858, Kansas became both the central symbol and actual battleground of the American sectional conflict. To deepen this struggle, all Missourians were depicted as degraded slaveholders by committed antislavery settlers like Lovejoy. A strong and growing suspicion of the South and a traditional and endemic fear of competition from black slave labor prepared northern settlers for conflict with southern settlers in the West. Given this background, the direct experience of physical contact and competition elicited an antislavery passion in northern settlers in Kansas.

Open conflict in Kansas was finally welcomed by many Northerners as a necessary cleansing event, a means to purge the vulnerable land and populace of those evil, presumably external forces that threatened them. Furthermore, blood sacrifice could apparently purge one's own people of the tendency to backslide into a degenerate moral state and could lead to self-regeneration. Publicists heightened the northern denunciation of an evil slaveholding southern race and juxtaposed it to the assertion of a heroic northern free people. Southern settlers in Kansas, almost all of whom were Missourians, also established their own opposing images of the people of God and those of the Devil. *They* would rescue the West from degradation. Compelled to think of themselves as defenders of southern slavery by the northern press, many white smallholder Missourians did strengthen a southern identity which they would carry forward into the big Civil War.[20]

For northern settlers, the enemy was neither the plantation owner nor his slaves but his by-products and minions, poor southern white trash—"Pukes" as Northerners came to call them.[21] These southern frontiersmen, primarily Missourians, were especially threatening because they represented to Northerners the degraded material and moral condition the slave system forced upon the independent white of modest means—people, in other words, of their own social position. Northern whites feared that they too could be compelled back into an impoverished barbarism, as had been the Pukes, away from the increasingly mature prosperity and moral tidiness by which northern freemen justified their individual existence and the purpose of their society. Perhaps at some unacknowledged level there was something enticing about a wilder, unstructured life; the guilt induced by this possibility, projected upon the Pukes, made all the more intense the necessity to conquer the southern foe.

To Northerners, it seemed clear that the Pukes were indeed savages, beasts who had to be expunged if free white civilization were to be implanted. Frequently the Pukes were defined as children of an earlier stage of civilization or as atavistic throwbacks, "men who cannot stand the control which civilization imposes upon every citizen," the *Christian Inquirer* asserted, "and who revel with delight in the license which frontier life holds out to all lawless tendencies."[22] The New York *Tribune* reporter comically described the average, repulsive Puke for his broad northern readership: "Imagine a fellow, tall, slim, but athletic, with yellow complexion, hairy faced, with a dirty flannel shirt, red or blue, or green, a pair of commonplace, but dark-colored pants, tucked into an uncertain altitude by a leather belt, in which a dirty-handled bowieknife is stuck, rather ostentatiously, an eye slightly whiskey-red, and teeth the color of a walnut. Such is your border ruffian of the lowest type. His body might be a compound of gutta percha, Johnny-cake, and badly-smoked bacon, his spirit, the refined part, old bourbon, double-rectified."[23]

Missouri Pukes were feared by their northern neighbors as dirt-wallowing, elemental brutes, suspended in a comatose state between bouts of primitive violence. They had never really left childhood, many northern settlers believed; hence their proclivity for, in Julia Lovejoy's words, "sucking whiskey," for a self-degrading, regressive orality.[24] Similarly, another northern settler believed that when Pukes were not fighting, they were "either whimpering with a desire to see their mothers, or complaining for the want of whiskey."[25] Childish and drunken, the Pukes loafed and blindly fought their way through life rather than constructing, through hard and persistent work, stable families and homes.[26]

Pukes were often described as being like animals rather than fellow humans. One midwestern journalist asserted, "They are a queer-looking set, slightly resembling human beings, but more closely allied to wild beasts."[27] The British journalist Richard J. Hinton wrote in his diary of a border ruffian leader whose face appeared "carbuncled and his nose 'rumblossom' of the deepest hue. Small piggish eyes looked out from his mass of gross fat."[28] Uncivilized, drunken, and unclean (as in Lovejoy's image of the stained copper cupola of the Jefferson City capitol), Pukes were

expected to act bestially.[29] Filthy language, torture, stabbings, and shoot-
ings in the back followed in northern depictions of Missourian behavior,
as did the most dreaded rape. "Think of this, my sisters in New Hampshire," Lovejoy wrote, "pure-minded, intelligent ladies fleeing from fiends
in human form whose brutal lust is infinitely more to be dreaded than
death itself."[30] Similar to the myth of the savage black rapist of the post-
Civil War South, this beastly Puke attacked every civilized value.

The beast must die, they ranted. Even Charles B. Stearns, perhaps the
only pacifist Garrisonian in the whole Kansas territory, could justify killing Pukes as subhumans sunk in a pit below the realm of humanity. To
Stearns these were "drunken ourang-outans," "wild beasts," and thus it
was his "duty to aid in killing them off. When I deal with men made in
God's image, I will never shoot them; but these pro-slavery Missourians
are demons from the bottomless pit and may be shot with impunity."[31]
Contact with such a monster race could turn even pacifist abolitionists into
outraged warriors.

Perhaps inevitably in this competitive arena, Missourians confirmed
northern preconceptions, but the more footloose among them may also
have been less than genteel measured by the northern standards of the
1850s. Nearly all Missourians were good, solid evangelical farmers, but
as in all western states, there was also a considerable floating population.
Some of these people, who were primarily tenant farmers, day laborers,
squatters, and, in some instances, drifters like Pap in *Huckleberry Finn,*
may well have drunk more whiskey, deserted more families, bragged
more, and worked less than most of their contemporaries. The undoubtedly
different mores of frontiersmen and farmers fed an intraclass agrarian conflict every bit as real and brutal as interclass warfare in an industrialized
society. This conflict was occurring all over the West as well as within Missouri society throughout the antebellum period, but for the purposes of
propaganda during the 1850s, northern antislavery writers represented the
cultural conflict as all civilized Northerners versus all Missourians—all of
whom were defined as atavistic primitives. Similar to modern red-baiting,
this was what one might call "savage-baiting." Every civilized Northerner
ought to reject regressive, barbarian types. One would identify such a type
in the Puke—some of whom doubtless existed. All Missourians could then
be tarred with this image in order to discredit them. This damnation of
Missourians as primitives encouraged rejection of them in the context of
the almost universal northern belief that American culture was progressing
to "higher," more civilized forms. We learn of the Pukes as losers in
cultural evolution. Northern writers meshed conflicts of cultural styles with
material struggles in the attempt to establish social hegemony in Kansas.
This was a central cultural event in preparation for the guerrilla war of
1861–65.

In defensive contrast to the threatening Pukes, Northerners in Kansas were compelled to create a heightened image of themselves. Reinforcing themselves with their lineage from their tribal Old Testament War God, evoking their heritage as Puritans, Yankees, and American revolutionaries, they sought, in combat with the Missourian servants of evil, to regenerate themselves morally, to reconstruct their class of freeholders, to save Kansas, and to serve as exemplars of freedom to the nation.

William Phillips, the *Tribune* man, satirized the Pukes as restless, whiskey-soaked illiterates who were passing frontier hunter types. "Deer-hunting was with them a science, coon-hunting a purely business affair." He felt that they were being forced further south and west, to be replaced by the solid, enrooting northern farmers. Of this succeeding class, "You can tell by the fences, and look of the houses, and by a thousand other things, that an industrious and calculating people are here."[32] Fencing in land would improve upon its use for deer-hunting; industry would replace vagrancy. In a similar vein, one Connecticut settler going west noted with abhorrence the violence done to baggage by Missourian railroad teamsters and wished that "some enterprising Yankee" could gain control of the Missouri line; "extraordinary carefulness" in baggage handling and a railroad timetable such as "to make arrivals and departures with a good deal of regularity" would follow inevitably.[33] Once settled on his homestead, this new Kansas citizen painfully felt the absence of "female society" and the protection of the cultural and legal institutions he had known back home and feared the "new temptations . . . new physical, mental and moral influences" of the unstructured, dangerous West. Almost immediately he and his friends set up a debating institute where the first two subjects were "Resolved: That a good wife contributes more to the happiness of a man than a fortune"; and "Resolved: That life in Kansas is preferable to that in Connecticut."[34] Here, the appropriate response to threatened values was to dig in one's heels and to attempt to re-create the secure underpinnings of civilization one had known in the East. Regression to a frontier stage of civilization would mean accepting Puke-like values; one had always to fight against any appearances of such degeneracy.

Yet, implicitly, industry and calculation, though good and reward-bringing, provided insufficient defenses against the environment and the enemy. Greed for land and pursuit of purely material gain could lead to worship of mammon, as northern settlers were well aware. To be morally sound, taking up the land and pushing off the Pukes (and Indians) had to be tied to a higher set of moral purposes, to serve God and to establish progressive civilization. This moral purpose was not merely a "rationalization" for "real" material interests and motives: truly serving the higher good would alone ennoble self-improvement and thus make regenerative the struggle against the Philistines in the land of Canaan. As the War God aided the Hebrews, so would he keep his covenant with his chosen people once more. "Jehovah will triumph and the people will be free," wrote one settler. Echoed another, "Jehovah is on the side of the oppressed, and He will yet arise in His strength, and His enemies will be scattered."[35]

The ethnic origins of the northern settlers gave clear evidence that they were a chosen people, the leading Kansas antislavery newspaper editorialized. "We know no State where the pure Anglo-Saxon Native American so thoroughly occupies the ground, as in this. So far as settlements are made, they are purely American. A few of the better class of foreigners are scattered here and there; but not enough to be objectionable."[36] The growing, polyglot eastern and midwestern cities like St. Louis were cluttered with seemingly unassimilable Irish and German Catholics and could not lead national reformation; in Kansas the homogeneous Anglo-Saxon American type could be re-created. Here, through such stock, would "Yankee enterprise" be "actuated by hallowed principle," a New Hampshire newspaper insisted. The Puritan spirit, which had "long since uprooted the upas tree of slavery" from northern soil, would, rekindled in "beautiful and fertile" Kansas, destroy the "dark plottings of the oppressor," represented by the slave forces of Missouri.[37] That ideal which had impelled the Puritans to flee to "their Western wilderness . . . a desire to plant the institutions of a pure Gospel on this virgin soil," a Massachusetts newspaper insisted was now being repeated by the heirs of the same stock in Kansas.[38]

The Puritan hero could indeed be reborn in Kansas. "Splendid faces" characterized the antislavery men of Lawrence, Hinton recorded in his journal. One was "a puritan brought back from the days of Cromwell or a vision of the old Revolutionary times, to show the world that all the fearless energy and strong integrity that characterized those epochs, has not yet faded out."[39] If the blood of these heroes would flow, it would be the sanctified blood of martyrs.[40] For William Phillips, Old John Brown was the very archetype of the Puritan hero: "He is one of those Christians who have not quite passed from the face of the earth." Brown, the Cromwellian patriarch writ superhuman, both thrilled and frightened the unqualifiedly antislavery man Phillips. "He is a strange, resolute, repulsive, iron-willed, inexorable old man. He stands like a solitary rock in a more mobile society, a fiery nature, and a cold temper, and a cool head—a volcano beneath a covering of snow."[41] Brown's otherwise socially dangerous nature, in its rightful time and setting, had become both heroic and necessary.

Eighty years before, many of those antislavery people engaged in the Kansas struggle believed, the American Revolution had called forth similar heroic qualities in the true American people. The freedom-loving moral manhood achieved in the American Revolution, subsequently gone flabby as unchallenged slavehounds desecrated that true national spirit, could now be regained in Kansas. As evocations of the American Revolution inspired antislavery forces in Kansas, so, through immediate action, could they now fire the first shot in the ever deepening civil conflict and build a new Bunker Hill monument for their descendants. "As the people of Kansas have been encouraged by the memory of their fathers' heroic struggle for right, so will the struggle in the future be strengthened by the remembrance of the Kansas contest," a Lawrence paper editorialized.[42] Such a vision counterposed to such a devilish enemy and in such a setting engaged vast numbers of northern settlers in Kansas, and masses of Northerners elsewhere by sympathy, in an antislavery struggle they had previously ignored or even condemned.

In this manner were northern preconceptions—ideal types of self and the poor white southern Other—confirmed and fortified in Kansas. The process occurred in an engagement, not a rhetorical or social vacuum, and proslavery settlers, almost all of whom were Missourians, had corresponding preconceptions and reactions. They naturally resented the Puke image imposed on them and fought against it and for the true morality which they felt they represented and Northerners violated. *They* were the good Anglo-Saxon stock. They too knew of the forces of the Devil and of the Lord and reversed the identities of the combatant forces.[43]

Proslavery settlers defined themselves as defenders of American institutions and of law and order. Coming by the wagonload across the Missouri border in 1855, proslavery voters had first organized the territory with a slave constitution. Some historians have suggested that there was a tacit understanding in Congress in 1854 that, popular sovereignty notwithstanding, the northern half of the territory, Nebraska, would be organized as a free state and the southern half, Kansas, as a slave state. Thus proslavery soldiers could construe their role as upholders of duly constituted authority against the invading northern rebel. "The crisis has arrived," a proslavery newspaper proclaimed late in 1855, "when it behooves every Law and Order man to aid in enforcing the laws. Resistance by force cannot be countenanced . . . we [must] aid in quelling the rebellion now existing." They stood for home, church, private property, familial and community honor, and male authority; they were the conservative party, guarding tradition from anarchic, invading northern radicals. Wrote a Leavenworth editor, "Every man must place a guard around his house to protect his distressed wife and sleeping babes, and dare not pass beyond the rounds of that guard or [he will] be shot down in cold blood."[44] Southerners merely defended what Northerners attacked.

To proslavery spokesmen, Northerners were "the foreign foe," committed to "the one idea of crushing us of the South as a people." The abolitionist ideas they imputed to all Northerners were bad enough; even worse, their proclaimed ideals masked their underlying moral corruption. Averring freedom and their own moral superiority, Northerners were really a pack of evil hypocrites—"Oh! those long-faced, sanctimonious Yankees!" one proslavery newspaper moaned.[45] Assertions of "Higher Law" served as an excuse and a cover for the destruction of positive law. "Who else would call Sharpes rifles moral weapons to be used in place of the Bible?" Lawbreakers who chanted the Higher Law—peace-lovers who emigrated armed to the teeth—Christians who sold good southern people out of the human race—"Surely none but the Yankee abolitionists could go to such heights and depths of duplicity, falsehood and hypocrisy. But these are the cardinal virtues in Abolitionism together with stealing."[46]

"Nigger-stealing" became the central symbol of all that was base in these northern invaders: not only would slave-stealing serve northern purposes by purloining southern property—it would reverse the natural, good order of society in general. To proslavery settlers, Northerners were not devoted to "the welfare of the country" but "alone to the one idea, sickly sycophantic love for the nigger," which led them to steal him and set him free. Underlying the ostensible purpose of destroying the institution of slavery raged northern white lust to couple with filthy black women. Northerners came to Kansas not to increase the area of freedom but "for the express purpose of stealing, running off and hiding runaway negroes from Missouri [and] taking to their own bed and their own arms, a stinking negro wench."[47] In this vision, Northerners wished to regress towards bestiality; desiring to have congress with creatures of the dirt, they became in southern eyes subhuman beasts of the earth, who claimed infuriatingly that they were saints.

In sum, Northerners sought to reverse the entire moral and social order, to enshrine the low and debase the high. If the nigger-stealers gained power, a proslavery newspaper insisted, "Our white men would be cowards, our black men idols, our women amazons." Those northern whites who were sent to conquer Kansas were Yankee abolitionists, or worse, the worthless minions of northern bosses, the impoverished northern urban slum-dwellers, "the filth, scum and off-scourings of the East and Europe [sent] to pollute our fair land."[48] This was the northern counterpart of the Puke. Here in southern eyes was the independent white degenerated to the level of worthless subhumanity. In the summer of 1856, an Illinois newspaper reported that "seventy-five drunken rowdies from the 'sands' of Chicago passed through our town, accompanied with a quota of *nymph du pavé* on their way to Kansas."[49] Proslavery settlers from Missouri thus believed that they were the repository of the independent yeoman ideal and that northern urban society, not slavery, had produced the threatening underclass of beastly and socially corrosive whites.

The appropriate analogue for the nigger-stealing abolitionists and their dirty troops was not the American Revolution, which the antislavery press had so freely appropriated, but the nihilistic French Revolution which had destroyed the entire social fabric in the name of freedom, and even then "the French Revolution itself affords no adequate picture of the startling scenes and horrors [the Yankee invasion of Kansas] unfolds." On the contrary, Southerners felt that *they* represented the true spirit of the American Revolution: "let us arise, buckle on the armor of our patriotic sires."[50] By the time that they sacked the antislavery bastion of Lawrence in May 1856, the proslavery forces were certain that they embodied American legal, moral, and social order against lawless, revolutionary northern invaders. Destruction of the nigger-stealing, filth-wallowing beast was a sanctioned act. "We simply executed to the letter of what the law decreed," wrote John H. Stringfellow, a Missouri Democratic politician who was the leading proslavery ideologue, "and left as though we had been to church— by the way, there is no church in Lawrence, but several free love associations."[51]

The roiling anger present in these contradictory conceptions of the Other was released into action by the friction of social contact. Free-soil and proslavery settlers would cluster together with their own kind on farms and in towns but formed antagonistic communities cheek-by-jowl throughout much of the territory. The inevitable arguments, endemic in the West, over defining valid claims for the best land, over rights of way, and over access to water and transportation were politicized along sectional lines in Kansas. When the competitor could be collectively targeted as a moral and social pariah, the explosions of violence against him were less sporadic and disorganized. Thus pushing and shoving in taverns, gang fights in the streets, and finally murder took on a sectional color. The weak forces of the law were also controlled by one side or the other, and so justice was not expected within the system and two vigilante organizations emerged, as did dual legislatures, governors, and constitutions.

When actual bloodshed began with the premeditated murder of an antislavery settler in December 1855, aggression was usually justified on the surface as defensive response to the allegedly systematic attacks of the beastly Others. Northerners had instituted "a system of highway robbery, and midnight plunder, worse than has ever been known in this country, and equaled only by the Bedouin tribes of the desert," wrote a southern defender of his New Jerusalem, while an antisalvery defender of *his* chosen land wrote that "human patience cannot long endure this system of terrorism and persecution." Defense of a sacred cause blended into and justified a crushing response to evil, encouraged, even demanded obliteration of the Other. "Our people propose acting only on the defensive . . . but when the issue shall be forced upon them . . . take care. A volcano is under your feet, and lightnings are overhead. Omnipotence is watching your every movement, and 'Those who take the sword shall perish by the sword.' "[52] In defending truth the sanctified people would come rightly to embody wrathful omnipotence.

When it came, fighting was welcome. In the absence of any agreed-upon over-arching authority and after months of unbearable resentment and tension, a just war would free morally sanctioned passion to render the issue into an open and conclusive test of force. "We are glad that the issue is thus finally reduced to one single, starting point, annihilation," an antislavery newspaper wrote. "We are ready."[53] At long last, cleansing conflict would demonstrate the muscularity of antislavery, Thomas Wentworth Higginson declared. "War only educates men to itself, disciplines them, teaches them to bear its fatigues, anxiety and danger, and actually to enjoy them."[54]

Each act by the other side demanded revenge. A small force of Federal dragoons rendered impossible most open engagements, but wide-ranging, vicious guerrilla actions of small groups were frequent. All means to intimidate the other side into capitulating or leaving the territory were used: crop and house burnings, theft of livestock and draft animals, tarring and feathering, torture, murder, and disfigurement of the slain. Reports of torture of captives and mutilation of corpses led to like responses. At Pottawatomie Creek on May 24, 1856, for example, John Brown cut off the hands of five captives (in perhaps acting out the Old Testament judgment on the theft of slave lives), stabbed them in the side, and then bludgeoned them to death with his broadsword. Vengeance demanded responding in kind. "Blood for Blood! But for each drop spilled we shall be required one hundred fold! . . . Every man shall be a law unto himself, adopting as his guiding star the 'golden rule.' "[55] In this eye-for-an-eye version of the golden rule, each side attempted the blood purge of the Other and those evils which the Other embodied.

Under these conditions no one could remain disengaged. Hundreds of northern and southern settlers were forced, whatever their prior position on slavery, to become openly proslavery or antislavery and to use violence as guerrilla war polarized the community. The diary of Samuel Reader, a young French-Canadian, records his being goaded into identifying himself as an abolitionist by mocking southern neighbors. In the summer of 1856, he joined a northern guerrilla band and marched around without seeing action. He was frightened and repelled by the Pukes. After one day of hard farm labor, Reader went to bed with a "kinky back" and that night "dreamed of getting a ball in the back by the Missourians of Topeka."[56] Charles Lines, a Connecticut pacifist who settled thirty miles from Lawrence, hoped as late as May 1856 that "prudent councils" would lead his neighbors to refrain from "unnecessarily involving themselves in trouble." However, in June the war came to them. Lines himself was particularly activated by the testimony of a "naturally very mild" man, much like himself, who had been tortured by the Pukes and left, tied up, to die. "Blood must end in the triumph of the right," Lines responded, and in anger took to arms.[57]

Antislavery forces won the Kansas struggle by continuing to settle at a greater rate than the poorly organized and under-financed proslavery Missourians. However, this conflict left wounds in its wake which were reopened far more violently by both sides in 1861. This was particularly true along the Kansas-Missouri border which was the ground of much of the most brutal fighting during the Civil War. Each side developed a Manichaean vision, with themselves cast as the people of Good, and the Others as the sub-people of Evil. In the wider context of the war, Northerners were prepared by the popular ideology broadcast eastward about Missouri rural whites to see all Missourians as Pukes fit only for destruction. In turn, many Missourians were ready to see all Unionists as invading Yankee devils served by a fifth column of Missourian proto-Yankees and Hessian mercenaries. Other Missourians were not so certain that they wished to identify themselves as what the outside world considered to be poor white trash.

Thus the fear of coercion and of the invasion of local communities by outsiders took on a special urgency in Missouri, due to the demography, the political economy, and the popular ideology through which Missouri came to be defined in the 1850s. The threat was not just to the institution of slavery but to the cultural identity of rural whites of modest means who lived in a slave society. In this light, the Kansas free-staters, abolitionists Frank Blair and the Black Republicans, St. Louis Germans, the banks, and the railroads were all agents of outside oppression. They did not leave Missourians to their liberty and their self-respect but banded together to discredit Missourians culturally and to destroy their institutions. If such an invader threatened freedom of choice and conscience concerning the institution of slavery, what communal or familial values or institutions would remain secure? A second question plagued these same Missourians: if the Union fell, what government would replace it to defend liberty, community, and family in the face of the chaos of a Civil War? Richmond was a very long way from the Missouri River, and the local pro-southern forces demonstrated at the beginning of the war that they were too weak to maintain power and provide security. Many Missourians recognized that they were party to the social and economic changes under way, which were northerly in direction, at the same time that they valued their southern origins and values. In principle, conditional Unionism best reconciled these opposing forces: guerrilla war, however, destroyed that middle ground and threw the unwilling as well as the committed into a maelstrom which surpassed understanding.

CHAPTER 2

TERROR AND A SENSE OF JUSTICE: CIVILIANS IN GUERRILLA WAR

Guerrilla Acts of Terror

No one, North or South, anticipated the duration or devastation of the American Civil War. At the start, Lincoln federalized 75,000 state militia troops for ninety days, long enough to defeat the foe in one glorious battle. Lacking standing armies and bureaucratic structures, both governments had to improvise the unexpected major war which ground into being.

Creating, manning, supplying, and transporting organized armies strained the resources of both sections. Yet these armies actually fought over only limited parts of the nation. Most of the long, shifting, and confused border between Union and Confederacy was wide open to attack and counter-attack throughout the war. These regions, of which Missouri was the most extreme example, were also bitterly divided internally. In this context, when regular troops were absent, the improvised war often assumed a deadly guerrilla nature as local citizens took up arms spontaneously against their neighbors. This was a war of stealth and raid, without a front, without formal organization, with almost no division between the civilian and the warrior.

In such a guerrilla war, terror was both a method and a goal. Guerrillas had a variety of ends—food, arms, horses, loot, information, ridding the region of enemy civilians, and above all, revenge. Through stealth and mobility, they sought to create moments when they were in total dominance and could exact what they wanted at the least possible risk to themselves. They sought to control their area through destruction of the enemy and his property and security. After their overwhelmingly violent, if temporary, assertion of power, they then relied on speed of movement, knowledge of the country, hideaways, a network of civilian abettors, and threats of renewed violence to intimidate unfriendly civilians into acquiescence, to keep Union troops at bay, and to continue their careers another day. This was not a stand-up war with uniformed, flag-carrying massed troops charging one another in open combat nor even the confusion of the typically disorganized battlefield; it was thousands of brutal moments when small groups of men destroyed homes, food supplies, stray soldiers, and civilian lives and morale.

In a typical incident on February 7, 1863, in Shannon County in southeastern Missouri, Thomas J. Thorp, Aleck Chilton, and John Smith rode up to the house of Obidiah and Nancy Leavitt. They had often bought groceries from Leavitt's store. This time, Smith shot into the front door. Leavitt grabbed his own gun, and as he rushed to the front door, Thorp and Chilton kicked in the rear door and shot Leavitt in the back. Nancy Leavitt later related that she put her wounded but still living husband down on their bed and "took up the shot gun and kept them out for about an hour." They told her if she would just give up the arms in the house "they would not bother me or my husband any more—and that they would not take my critters." Finally she gave in to their promises, and they re-entered the house. About five minutes later, John Smith "snapped his pistol at my husband's head," but the pistol misfired. All three men then went outside and caught the Leavitts' horses. They then returned to the house and Aleck Chilton "caught hold of me and held me in the middle of the room." Nancy Leavitt asked Thorp what they had against her husband. He replied, "he had enough against him to kill him . . . that he reported them to the Federals." Smith then went up to the bed and, with a pistol shot through the head, killed Obidiah Leavitt. Thorp took Obidiah's hat, his shoes, and his saddle, and the three guerrillas rode off on the Leavitts' horses.[1]

Such incidents occurred over and over again all over Missouri during the Civil War. Leavitt indeed may have reported these three men to Federal authorities or, more generally, he may have been known to guerrillas to be a Union man. Such "causes" of his being targeted may have been pretexts, believed or not by these three acquaintances of Leavitt, who may have disliked or resented him for other reasons or were simply intent on armed robbery. In a sense, analysis of the precise reasoning of the guerrillas is just academic: they had the power and, given the circumstance of a general war, reasons they deemed sufficient for shooting Leavitt. In addition, they did not have the slightest interest in a fair fight.

Guerrillas used a variety of methods to terrorize civilians. For example, threats made before the victim's wife by men known to be brutal often increased the fearsomeness of the moment, sending the couple into panic. James Hamilton, a well-known murdering guerrilla of southeastern Missouri, one night stole into Francis Tabor's house and said to Tabor's wife that it was "easy to draw a knife across [her husband's] throat . . . they intimidated her in that way," Francis Tabor testified at Hamilton's courtmartial. Later they had threatened to hang Edmund Shaw, who subsequently testified, "my wife was threatened very badly" by the proposal. Frequently guerrillas would string up a man to scare him into telling where he had hidden his money (a practice of most farm people in this rural pre-bank era). As guerrillas frequently killed civilian men by hanging, this prior knowledge and threat induced fear in the mind of the victim, which, when added to the pain of partial hanging, usually produced the desired results. There were many instances of beatings and widely broadcast stories of other forms of torture, such as pulling off toe nails with pincers.[2] Even if many of these tales were exaggerated or untrue, rumors of them carried terrifying powers.

In larger actions, guerrillas used similar terror tactics, albeit on a grander scale. In the most famous attack of the war, nearly 500 guerrillas gathered under William C. Quantrill to raid Lawrence, Kansas, on the morning of August 21, 1863. As Lawrence was fifty miles into strongly Unionist Kansas and the raid was totally unexpected, there were no organized defenses. Attacking at dawn, the guerrillas fanned out through the town. Small groups rode up and burst into houses like that of the Fitch family. There they called "for the man of the house," who, as he walked downstairs to them, "they shot in the presence of his young wife and three children." They then ransacked the house for money, arms, and jewelry and set it on fire, refusing to let Mrs. Fitch take the body of her husband or anything else from the burning house. Having killed at least 150 civilian men and boys and having burned most of the town, the guerrillas then raced back to Missouri, casting off most of their loot along the way in order to lighten their loads and dispersing in the dense Missouri woods to avoid the by now aroused and concentrating Federal forces.[3]

Even in such a large raid, the action was not on a battle line but was scattered. Lacking a disciplined battle plan, even the most calculating guerrillas acted more on the caprice of moments than according to any overall scheme. Those civilians they attacked could not know what response, if any, would reduce the destruction from the guerrillas. During the raid on Lawrence, for example, several groups of guerrillas called in turn on the Bissell family, who lived on the edge of town. The Bissells could see and hear the destruction of Lawrence, "the people running, black and white, young and old, and the *Fiends* dashing after them, firing as fast as they possibly could." The Bissells buried their silver and jewelry, their watches and money "and waited for them to come." Two guerrillas came to the back door and, as had been the case for the Fitch family, demanded to see the man of the house. When Henry Bissell came to the door, the guerrillas asked him if he had ever joined the Union army. When he answered he had not, one guerrilla said, "If you had told me you did I would have shot you dead." Henry gave them ten dollars, which satisfied them, and they rode off, telling the Bissells to take their goods out of the house, for they were going to come back to burn it. Another guerrilla came and asked for a drink of water "and said we were not agoing to be burned. . . . We took a little courage then and stopped to look towards town. We could see . . . the houses of our friends and acquaintances here and there all ablaze." Most of the guerrillas then rode past the Bissell house on their way back towards Missouri. "We began to take long breaths and think we were going to escape," when five mounted men, torches in hand, rushed toward their house. "Then we knew our time had come." They rode on up onto the porch, right to the front door. They ransacked the house, tore and stomped on clothes, searched for money, and fired the house. The guerrillas beat Henry with their gun butts, but they let him run for the safety of the cornfield instead of shooting him. "They tipped their hats" to the ladies "and bid us good morning. We returned the salutation."[4]

This final group of guerrillas ransacked and set fire to a house and beat a man savagely, but they spared his life and said goodbye to the ladies like gentlemen: the Bissells responded as if they had been paid a social call. Under these conditions, tipping hats and bidding each other good morning was a perverse reenactment of gentility—where the guerrillas demanded acknowledgment of their humanity for not killing a man but merely robbing and burning out his family. Earlier, another group had been willing to spare a life for ten dollars, where at other houses guerrillas from the same band, perhaps the very same men, shot the man of the house dead simply for being a grown male. Nothing that the Bissells did or refrained from doing determined their fate. They were at the mercy of the guerrillas. Henry survived on a series of whims, as others had died.

The general project in the Lawrence raid was to sack the town and kill men. Most guerrilla attacks, smaller and less ambitious than this one, were nevertheless terrifying in both damages actually inflicted and those threatened but withheld. Guerrillas operated among strangers and acquaintances, employing differing amounts of force to gain their ends.

The most frequent demand was for food: this might be the sole demand, or it might be the first of many. For example, on February 23, 1864, nine mounted men came to Ellen Brookshire's house near Rolla, demanding food. The next day, Brookshire reported to the local Union provost marshal that she had told the guerrillas "they could not have it except they were federal soldiers, they then stated that they belonged to the South and were passing through and should have food." They helped themselves. Mr. Brookshire then came home. Whatever events ensued, the Brookshires did not tell the provost marshal. Mrs. Brookshire said of her husband that "having bad eyesight he cannot identify them or any of them," and neither did she reckon she could.[5] The Brookshires had been intimidated into this inconclusive testimony, whether by specific threats or by a general fear of reprisal. Undoubtedly they feared more guerrilla visits from this band or from others. Some of the Federal troops to whom Ellen Brookshire was giving her deposition might be rebel spies who would pass on news of their activities to avenging guerrillas. Still, they did report to

Federal authorities, probably at least in part to cover themselves in case some unfriendly neighbor decided to report them as guerrilla supporters to the Union authorities, also a common occurrence in areas strongly garrisoned by the Union army. Ellen Brookshire insisted that she had fed the guerrillas only under duress, lest the provost marshal misunderstand her. In all these ways, the simple demand for a meal had terrifying possible meanings and consequences for the Brookshires.

In the middle of a September night in 1863 in Gentry County in northwest Missouri, Pauline Ellison, the widowed mother of five daughters, was awakened by two men pounding on her door. When she asked who they were, they shouted: "that it was none of my business—I must open the door or they would open it dam roughly." Entering, they asked for arms and searched for them. Ransacking a trunk for what "they guessed was a thousand dollars," they took only a small lead pencil. While searching the kitchen, "they put a candle to the ceiling and remarked that they wondered if the house would burn good, saying suppose we try it." They then gave Ellison seven days to leave the county. Ellison was so frightened by the incident that, though she asked for protection from the local Union garrison, it took a month for Federal authorities to persuade her to identfy the two guerrillas whom in fact she had known for nine years. Ellison had only been robbed of a lead pencil, but, particularly as she was living without any men to defend her family, she had felt badly threatened by these neighbors of long standing.[6]

Often guerrillas would threaten by anonymous messages those whom they considered to be Unionists. Near St. Joseph in June 1864, twenty ostensible Union supporters received a note which read, "you are hereby notified to leave here inside of three days or your life will pay the forfeit, you old Yankee. You voted for Lincoln, and I don't intend any such men to stay in this state."[7] None of the recipients of this note could have known how serious it was, but others had been killed for less, and they now knew that they were on some anti-Union blacklist. The curious legalese in which the note was framed, a kind of grandiose assumption of legitimacy by the unnamed attacker, suggested that, in his mind at least, he was the real authority who had judged these men to be Black Republicans fit for death. Which neighbor was this? Was he the friendly Virginian down the road a piece, or the mean, drunken Kentuckian who ran the grocery? Or was he some stranger who had been handed a list by some sly, pretended Unionist bent on secret revenge?

Often guerrillas were well-known local boys. In Reynolds County in southwestern Missouri in 1862 and 1863, the four Carty brothers were the local terrors. James and William were in the bush, but their teen-age brothers, Lafayette and John, who remained at home were the ones arrested: as they had plenty of cash and no work it was presumed that they were harboring their brothers' guerrilla band. Andrew J. Love testified at their court-martial that he had been robbed of his horses at gunpoint by the Cartys but that later Lafayette had come around to say "he has always been a friend to me, and did all he could to keep them from taking my horse." John also had held up an acquaintance at gunpoint, George Fitz-water, who testified later that John "said he had a damned notion to blow my brains out because I did not have more [money]. He told me if I ever told he would shoot me at first sight."[8]

The Cartys used both reassurance and threats to grasp for power among old neighbors in Reynolds County. Knowing a guerrilla did not mean that he would go easier on you; though, as in Lafayette's case, when arrested, in order to try to lighten their punishment, guerrillas would often claim that they had eased up on old friends and neighbors. In Lafayette Carty's case, a victim corroborated such a claim, apparently to lighten his attacker's punishment. In another instance Christian Chuck, a German-American living near St. Joseph, was shot by a group of guerrillas including his eighteen-year-old neighbor, Aaron Alderman. During Aaron's later court-martial, Christian's son, Jacob, was asked, "Didn't the two Alderman boys and Highsmith try to prevent the others from hurting any of you?" Jacob answered, "None of them three did."[9] If they had tried, they had been ineffective, and in any event in front of the court, power was reversed, and Jacob could gain a measure of revenge, whatever the mixed emotions the Aldermans may well have felt when their gang shot Christian Chuck. Perhaps Aaron Alderman had regretted the killing of Christian Chuck, as he claimed in his defense, but his partially willed action had in this case become a mortal matter for the victim and later for the captured guerrilla.

The face-to-face nature of a traditional rural society was no guarantee of social harmony, especially if a profound issue like political secession divided loyalties within an area. Frequently it was a matter of old scores being settled, but often new loyalties superseded an earlier, more tolerant attitude. Sometimes young men were swept into guerrilla actions against old acquaintances which they later regretted. P. A. Hardeman wrote her husband that when she had been away one day, a guerrilla band had stolen her clothing and jewelry. A few days later a local boy, Will Stearns, came by and "said he was in the house, but did not take anything."[10] Will had not stopped the robbery, despite the later regrets which he voiced to his victim, Mrs. Hardeman.

Terror could be enacted within a local community, or it could come from armed outsiders of unknown identity. Both guerrillas and militia often wore civilian clothes, and southern guerrillas frequently wore Union uniforms as a disguise. In October 1864 in Chariton County in northwest Missouri, a secessionist gang, including Frank and Jesse James, dressed in Union uniforms, lured Mr. Baynes out of his house, saying that they were Federals who had lost their way—they wanted him to show them the right route. When Baynes came out into his yard they shot him five times. They tried the same gambit down the road on the Rogers boys, who would not come out of their house, and so they just rode on.[11] It is possible that these guerrillas interpreted the Rogerses' failure to come out into the yard as a refusal to support Union troops, which made them secessionists if only by implication, and therefore men to be left alone. Perhaps the guerrillas simply did not want to risk a fight against an unknown number of fairly well-barricaded men. The pressure they put on the Rogerses and on Baynes was severe, and all of those men doubtless knew that Union troops might well burn out or shoot a man who did not help them, which they would take as an indication of secessionist sympathies. How was Baynes, peeking out of his window and seeing these Union-uniformed men in his yard, knowing that guerrillas frequently wore Union uniforms for cover, to guess their identities? One could trust neither old neighbor boys nor strangers nor even one's own eyes.

Guerrillas did not always stop to make loyalty tests. Frequently they attacked pro-Southern as well as Union families. Frances T. Bryan from North Carolina, who had a son in a Union military prison camp and other relatives in the Confederate army, was clearly southern in her loyalties. Yet her husband Charles, in Cooper County on the Missouri River, had by 1863 been "completely burned out" by repeated guerrilla raids. Other Missouri guerrilla bands attacked Confederate families quite frequently when they went behind southern lines for the winter. In the winter of 1864, G. M. Barker of Drew County, Arkansas, complained to A. H. Garland of Richmond, Virginia, who passed his letter on to President Jefferson Davis, that "These Missouri troops . . . represent themselves to be Yankees, and plunder just as bad." Guerrillas carried their adaptable form of war with them wherever they went, even into the Confederacy they were ostensibly defending.[12]

Union Acts of Terror

In Missouri, Union troops joined with Confederate guerrillas in destroying peace in the homes and minds of noncombatants. To take one example, at lunch time on November 16, 1864, four men dressed in Federal uniforms—pale blue pants, deep blue jackets, and pale blue overcoats—rode into Elizabeth Hawkins's yard and asked if there were any Federal soldiers about. "I told them I did not know, that they had all left the road and if they had returned I had not heard of it. I told them I thought they were Federal soldiers by being dressed in Federal uniforms. One of them replied that it was very common to dress that way, but did not say whether they were Federal soldiers." The four men, three of whom were "Dutch" (the nineteenth-century slang term for German-Americans), got their dinner and had their horses fed. One of them said to Elizabeth Hawkins, "I see you have plenty of clothes here, I will take a coat." The men then went out to the farmyard and took three horses, with bridles and saddles, and each man helped himself to a turkey.[13]

Robbery, menace, and threats of more to come were all forms of terror applied by Union troops as well as by guerrillas on Missouri citizens. As these four men implied to Mrs. Hawkins, not every Federal uniform was worn by a Federal soldier. Union soldiers could imply that they were Confederate bushwhackers pretending to be Union troops! In other words, Union troops could use their uniforms or civilian clothing as much of a disguise as could the bushwhackers. Sometimes they would be foraging under orders, sometimes, as seems more likely in this case, on their own. To civilians, it often appeared that, in the form of armed strangers or neighbors acting ostensibly for the Federal government, the Union was making war on them.

Unlike Elizabeth Hawkins who was attacked by strangers, Elizabeth Vernon of Lebanon knew her callers to be James Robeson and Samuel B. Stewart, privates in the Eighth Cavalry, Missouri State Militia. Coming into her home with pistols drawn, they said "they had orders to search for ammunition" and demanded that she unlock her desk drawers, bureaus, and trunks. They helped themselves to a gold watch and a silver watch, a gold pencil, a pocketbook containing twenty-five dollars in greenbacks, a black silk apron, a black ladies' belt, five yards of figured black silk, one black silk shawl, one blue Masonic scarf, and "diverse other small articles" but found no ammunition. "After they had a thorough rifling of the house, Stewart told me that I had never shown him any favor. I asked him what he meant by that? He said he wanted hard money, and if I would not give it to him, he would burn the house and every damned thing in it." Robeson said, "you need not think that you will lie us out of it." The Widow Vernon said she had no more money, and Steward and Robeson then said they would settle for ten dollars each. She told them the house "would have to burn, I cannot give what I have not got." They stomped out.[14]

The Widow Vernon's bluff worked, but under parallel circumstances her house might well have been burned. There were no rules for negotiations at gunpoint. Some civilians were more adept at reading their attackers than were others. And some groups of armed men were more malicious than others. Thus when a "parcel of men dressed in Union uniforms" rode up to the house of James Anderson of Livingston County in north central Missouri on the evening of October 16, 1863, after demanding whiskey and saying to Anderson's house guest, Mary E. Austin, "tell him to come out here, they wanted to see him," Anderson might well have expected to have been shot on the spot. Anderson refused to go out. The leader of the militia then said that if Anderson would give up his pistol they would leave. Mary Austin got the gun from him only "by hard begging." The armed troops then left "and did not come back."[15] This negotiation might have had far different results. Anderson might have been shot either if he had gone out into his yard or stayed in his house after he had given up his gun. He had no reason to believe the militia captain, who might have been a guerrilla, when he said that he would settle for Anderson's pistol. Anderson could not have prevented their entering, ransacking and burning his house, and shooting him. As it transpired, this event was relatively benign, and the militia leader kept his word in settling for the pistol, but the terror had been no less for the minor outcome—of course, the results of such visits were frequently much worse.

Indeed, Union soldiers often played dirty tricks to get what they wanted from civilians. Early in the war near Boonville, the captain of an Indiana company went into the house of one old man and told him they were Jeff Davis's men. "The old fellow was delighted and told them to take everything he had, so they took him at his word and seized thirteen horses and mules," telling the old fellow "that the Jeff Davis they alluded to was Jeff Davis of the Indiana [Union] Volunteers."[16]

Since local Union militia units frequently dressed in civilian clothes, they could be wrongly taken for guerrillas. They also could use mistaken identity to entrap civilians. On October 12, 1864, a detachment of James L. Chandler and five others of the Pike County Enrolled Missouri Militia were out pursuing Captain Woods's bushwhacker gang. A young man rode up to Chandler "and asked where the Captain was." Chandler asked him, "What Captain? He said Captain Woods. I asked him what he wanted with the Captain. He said he had some dinner for him. I told him all O.K. The Captain will be up directly. I then told him that we would take care of the dinner and him too." As Chandler dismounted, it suddenly dawned on William Banks, the young man, just with whom he was talking. He begged for his life, saying to Chandler that "he was forced to bring the dinner and was afraid that they would kill him if he did not." Chandler replied that "it was no use to beg—that when the Bushwhackers caught our men it was no use for *them* to beg." Chandler checked Banks's saddle bag, probably searching for arms or ammunition, and found two legs of chicken, some cold beef, pickles, pies, and bread—which amounted to one bushwhacker dinner, Chandler reckoned. For this degree of collaboration, Chandler wanted to shoot Banks, but "the Lieutenant would not let it be done," or at least not before taking Banks back to their post and asking their commander what response would be appropriate. Quite often such collaborators were shot "while attempting to escape," as the formula went. Banks may have been a willing collaborator, or he may have been coerced by the guerrillas. Chandler did not think it unfair to trick Banks this way— had Banks been shot rather than arrested, Chandler would have omitted to write such an account. Banks's death, if reported, simply would have been described as a guerrilla shot, and there would have been no repercussions. Banks doubtless knew that.[17]

Guerrillas could be dressed as Union troops, and Union militia often went around dressed as civilians, which made many like William Banks assume that they were guerrillas. Uniformed Union troops could pretend to be guerrillas dressed in Union uniforms and behave precisely as did guerrillas. Both sides had allies among the populace. In a guerrilla war where both sides wandered in small bands rather than marching in large columns, part of the terror for civilians was that they could never know for certain to whom they were talking and therefore could not trust anyone. Even old friends might have made deadly secret alliances. Despair at the confusion of identifying just who was the enemy led many rural Missourians to conclude as did J. L. Morgan, a North Carolinian tobacco merchant who left Glasgow, Missouri, in the summer of 1864 to settle in Brooklyn, New York: "Low lived men who claim to be Union or Rebel as occasion requires, [ride] the country destroying life & property, regardless of law & usages of regular warfare." Morgan described to his brother, a Confederate officer in prison in St. Louis, how "a band of armed men rushed out of woods, captured us. . . . We were ordered to . . . go into the dense woods where we expected to be murdered in cold blood as we were southern men," but just at this point "an opposing band came along & captured our captors," and Morgan's party fled under fire. Morgan did not derive much comfort from his rescue, as he thought the same sort of shiftless and cruel men on both sides would strike him again. He packed his bags and left Missouri. Thomas A. Peters of Bolivar concluded about this confusing state of affairs that in general "I think about one half the Bushwhackers seen is the enrolled militia," as all bands of mounted marauders dressed in civilian clothes tended to be reported as guerrillas. There was also great fluidity in both guerrilla and militia band formation, and some young men played it both ways. Civilians were terrorized by this uncertainty; caught in the middle of a chaotic struggle, they could never assume that the stranger at the gate—whom in peacetime they would have made welcome—was not their despoiler or even killer.[18]

Union troops were under some control as they operated to a greater or lesser degree within a command structure and were agents of a government, albeit a distant one. Certain constraints were thus placed on Union troops, and there were some forms of appeal to higher authorities for justice which were not possible against guerrilla depredators. However, it was also true that the forms of a legitimate army created opportunities for quasi-legal extortion from civilians, which were additional terrorist techniques not available to guerrillas. As well as haphazard freelance strong-arming, more clever Union troops could turn the screws through distortions of normal and legal military forms.

It was quite aboveboard to require a farmer to haul fodder, for example, but this means might be used to exploit and abuse someone an officer had singled out for special treatment for whatever reasons. Take the case of

Daniel Grant, whom a Union officer named Kinealy had decided to use. Grant complained to General Odon Guitar, Kinealy's commander, that Kinealy had "come to my house in time of the snow in the coldest weather" and ordered him to haul sixty barrels of corn to Bottsville. Before he had finished that task, Grant got another order to haul all the corn in his crib, amounting to 907 bushels, which took sixty-four loads over twelve days to deliver. Subsequently, Kinealy had ordered Grant to haul hay. "I went to Bottsville . . . and told him that I had done more hauling than any other man in the county and that I had to move and I had a house to build and that I had no hay frame on my waggon but he still told me that I must haul. I finly told him that it was no use to talk about it. I could not hall that. I did not belong to him. I went home." A few days later Grant was working down in the river bottom with his young son, hewing out doorsills, when four of "the Boys" from Kinealy's company came calling for him, demanding that he set to his task hauling hay for Kinealy. One of the soldiers "ast my little boy where I was. The little boy told him that I was attending to my business. He pulled out his revolver and . . . would have shot the boy if 2 of the boys had not caught up his pistol. He than went into the house, curst and swore that he would just as soon shoot me as he would a dam dog." Grant finally appealed to General Guitar, demanding to know whether Kinealy had the "rite" to so treat him. "If he has I have not a word to say if that is the law. I am a law abiding man and a union man" and a long-term sergeant in the army discharged only because of illness.[19]

As Missouri was under martial law, the Union military operated as the law enforcement agency during much of the war in most of the state, in effect superseding whatever civil legal structures remained in place. In such a position, the military had enormous discretionary power over civilians in the areas they controlled, unchecked by any truly effective appeals system. At times the command structure of an entire Union regiment would squeeze labor or property from anyone they targeted. Such was the case with the Eleventh Kansas Cavalry Regiment when it ran Jackson County, Missouri, during 1863. A. S. H. Crenshaw, livestock dealer in Independence and, according to the testimony of many neighbors, an heroic and outspoken Unionist in a heavily and violently secessionist county, fell into the clutches of the Eleventh Kansas for carrying two letters to Independence for a friend, one of which, unbeknownst to him, was addressed to a soldier in the rebel army. After his arrest, several Kansas soldiers stoned Crenshaw as he was being escorted to jail. The regimental quartermaster seized Crenshaw's corn and hay and burned his house. Crenshaw's jailer pointedly told him that another prisoner, H. L. Root, had been taken out and hanged the night before. Four days later without any charges being laid, four "detectives," acting on the orders of Major Plumb of the regiment who was also provost marshal of Independence, seized him, one by each arm, and with others at his back, pistols drawn, tried "to force him down into a deep ravine . . . where there were deep hollows." Having softened him up this way, they asked how many livestock he had, offering him one dollar per head. They then returned him to the guardhouse "as they said for *'this time.'* " Two days later the detectives took Crenshaw to a back room at the Commercial House in Kansas City where he was forced to sign several bills of sale. For one hundred cattle and thirty hogs the neat and legal appearing bill of sale was for $650; Crenshaw was offered $150 verbally and given nothing. For an additional thirty-one mules and horses the paper sum was $1,200, and again, Crenshaw received no payment. The same happened with another parcel of fifty-eight mules, the last of Crenshaw's property. Before leaving Kansas City, he appealed to Major Robert T. Van Horn, who was then acting provost marshal, not to let him be assassinated. Van Horn told him he would "never get to Independence alive." For some reason, probably because he had influential Union friends, Crenshaw was not then shot. In only slightly altered circumstances, the end of the story would have changed. Major Plumb would have written the local Union brigadier general that the notorious guerrilla informer Crenshaw had been shot attempting to escape his guard on his way back to Independence from Kansas City. Crenshaw clearly knew this probable end when he called out to the provost marshal for protection.[20]

Undisciplined Union troops, who frequently had personal scores to settle, often warred indiscriminately on local populations. In one area of endemic guerrilla terror in 1864, the provost marshal at Fulton wrote that the Union defense force, the Ninth Cavalry, Missouri State Militia, "are dreaded even by loyal men nearly as much as bushwhackers, as their officers seem to exercise but little control over them. They have very loose discipline on scouts as well as in camp," as their trail of looting and arson evidenced. Near St. Genevieve in 1863, Conrad C. Ziegler reported the plundering of his house by a company of foul-mouthed Union recruits. When three friends of Ziegler came to his defense, the troops seized them and marched them up the road. Captain Jennings, commander of the company, tried to rescue the three civilians from his troops who swore to him "that if he released them they would blow [the Captain's] brains out." Since officers elected by the militia were as unprofessional and untrained as the troops, rougher regiments developed "democratic" and undisciplined campaigning styles. Lawlessness was not true of all regiments, but it was far more characteristic than postwar regimental histories suggest. Citizens who expected protection were frequently attacked by these troops instead, as well as by pro-southern guerrillas.[21]

If indiscipline, extortion, and casual freebooting were Union army practices throughout the state, the war on Missouri civilians was policy for

Kansas regiments stationed in the border counties of western Missouri. Kansas troops had special accounts to settle with Missourians, dating from the days of "Bloody Kansas," the nasty border war of 1855–56. Certain regiments, notably the Seventh, "Jennison's Jayhawkers," were delighted at the opportunity to settle old scores. They asserted quite openly that Missourians should be punished for their secessionist, slaveholding sins, and they plundered, burned, freed slaves, and murdered with especial zeal. The counties they attacked tended to be strongly secessionist, as well as full of people who from the days of the border war had their own wrongs to right with Kansas and with those Missourians who might welcome such Union forces.

"Jayhawkers" was the term applied to Kansas raiders, and "jayhawking" became a term widely applied to free-form foraging by Union troops in the state and eventually nationwide. On November 12, 1861, Margaret J. Hayes was jayhawked on her farm near Kansas City. Her home was stripped of all valuable goods, and her team and carriage were driven off with her eleven slaves in it. She wrote, "It was very aggravating to see it drawn up to the door and to see negroes jump into it and drive off." Such actions were widespread in Jackson County and drove men either into the Union army or into guerrilla bands as the only places of proximate safety. Mrs. Hayes wrote her mother in 1862, "Times here are very hard: robbing, murdering, burning and every other kind of measure on every side. Every man has to join the Federal army or hide out in the country and have his property taken away from him. And if they are not shot on the spot they are banished from this country."[22]

Assuming all Missourians to be enemies, Kansas regiments believed it was their task to suppress them, to strip them of the means of resistance to Union authority as systematically as possible. Suppression was not in this case due to a failure of discipline but to an official policy of terror, which was justified as the only appropriate response to guerrilla terror. Guerrillas used the same analysis and the same methods. The cycle of violence could be endless. It was expressed in arson, looting, and shooting expeditions, associated with a spirit of spite meant to break the will of civilian enemies and their troops. Such events as I have already described were repeated thousands of times by Kansas troops, but the spirit of these attacks might best be illustrated by visits of two Kansas platoons. The first was to Thomas Shields's home in Lafayette County in February 1862. "They looked at their piano, and said that they had broken many of them since they left Independence. They must thank them if they did not break theirs. They forced Mrs. Trigg to play for them while they danced." The second visit was paid to a neighbor of E. A. Christie, "an old man who has but one arm to defend himself with." They strung him up twice and his son seven times, until they gave up their hidden cache of $1,150. "I saw the young man a few days afterwards and he had a dark ring around his neck," Christie wrote. When the sheriff arrested several suspects, an armed gang came over from Leavenworth, Kansas, and freed them.[23]

Kansas troops garrisoned in border towns would make frequent sweeps of the countryside, searching for guerrillas and punishing local residents who might have collaborated with the enemy—for them *all* Missourians

Daniel DeWitt, "My loss by Fedrels"

January 1861 by Capt Oliver's men	
1 blanket	$4.00
1 quilt	11.00
1 case of drafting instruments	6.00
Goodridg's Pictoral History of All Nations	8.00
2 pair drawers	3.00
4 Shirts @ 1.50 each	6.00
1 Black cloth coat	12.00
1 cloth coat	6.00
	$56.00

1st Sept 1862 Taken by Union Command to Lieutenant Col Tompson 5th Regiment Missouri State Militia	
1 grey mair 5 years old	$150.00
1 sett of Wagonharnis	$30.00
1 pitchfork	$1.25
1 singletree to wagon	$1.00
12 Wheat Sacks 50 ct ea	$6.00
	$188.25

Between 14th and 23 Sept 1862 Enrolled Militia under Col Coleman's command	
70 stacks of hay at $1.00 each	$70.00
6 loads of hay	$30.00
50 bushels of corn at 25 cts ea	$12.50
1500 bundles of oats at 3 cts each	$45.00
damage to meadow	$20.00
1500 Rails at $3.50 @ 100	$52.00
20 Bee stands robbed & destroy	$30.00
40 lbs bacon at 5 cts	$2.00
1 hand ax	$2.00
1 chopping ax	$1.25
2 or 3 chickins	$2.50
1 white sack	$ .50
1 year old calf	$5.00
1 3 year old steer	$12.00
	$224.35 [*sic*]

13 April 1863 Damage by Fedrels under Major Randall

1 horse	$50.00
mear	$40.00

May 1863 Damage by Col Penick's command

16 days worke on ditch at $2.00 per day	$32.00
	$122.00

25th August 1863 Damage by Cansas troops under Lieutenant Green

burning barn	$500.00
burning wagon	$75.00
D'o cariage	$60.00
burning 26 cu oats	$7.80
400 bushels corn	$100.00
5 tons hay	$40.00
wheat pan	$20.00
farming utensils	$50.00
taking 2 horses at $50 ea	$100.00
burning smoke house and contents, bacon, lard and salt	$200.00
Kitchen & contents	$300.00
house and contents	$1000.00
2 fields of wheat	$1500.00
1500 bushels	$500.00

Source: Daniel DeWitt Collection, Jackson County Historical Society, Independence

were by nature traitors. The harrowing list of losses calculated by Daniel De Witt of Jackson County gives a sense of the results of repeated raids. De Witt was raided six times between January 1861 and August 25, 1863, when he was burned out, the visits being paid by Missouri as well as Kansas Union troops. De Witt kept careful account of his losses (see table) which were typical in this region.[24]

Civilians' losses were guerrilla and Union soldiers' gains and were consumed on the spot or sold elsewhere. Kansas soldiers could sell into a relatively secure, flourishing market behind their lines back home. A good deal of money was to be had in the resale of stolen goods. From just one raid in 1861, Lieutenant Colonel Daniel R. Anthony's Seventh Kansas Cavalry took back 150 mules, 40 horses, and wagon loads of furniture and clothing. As the commander of the expedition, Anthony took the lion's share. Later he wrote to his brother-in-law back East, "Don't you want a captaincy or a majorship in the army—or dont you want to come out here and speculate in cattle—horses and mules—there is a good chance to buy cheap—and stock a large farm here at little expense—There is money in it to any one who will attend to it—I would advise you to come out and try it. Why wont you come?"[25]

Individual enterprise and maximum gain at minimum costs were the great traditional yeoman economic values. All the costs in this case were borne by traitorous Missouri guerrilla sympathizers, who according to Union soldiers richly merited such Union treatment. As far as guerrillas were concerned the invading Yankee troops and their conniving, anti-communal Missouri allies deserved to be stripped of every vestige of property. Guerrilla and Union terror cowed civilians and also effected a primitive redistribution and counter-redistribution of wealth from the traitorous to the deserving. However, even the sharpest trading in peacetime was another order of behavior, as these citizens well knew. They had been secure in title to their property and in the peace of the neighborhood. If clever trading was rewarded during normal times, it was presumed to be mutual and voluntary: extortion was agreed to be criminal behavior. Everyone knew the difference between honesty and dishonesty, peace and violence. Though in peacetime some relationships were dishonest and violent, most were not, and bad behavior was against the law and against moral standards and would when possible be punished by the community and law-enforcement agencies. Now civilians were isolated and ravaged from all sides; for them, violent attacks punctuated endless days and nights of anxiety. What did loyalty and justice mean to them now? How could they respond to such chaos? Where could they turn for protection?

A Sense of Justice

The most direct and spontaneous response to an attack was to fight back. However, when the attacker held the upper hand, even if only temporarily, fighting back most likely would lead to disaster. If one's neighbors and community opposed disturbances of the peace and violation of property, one might rally these immediate allies. However, in most of Missouri during the Civil War, communities were usually divided and fought among themselves. One might appeal to outside authorities—either guerrilla chieftains or Union military leadership—who might be able to provide temporary aid but could not guarantee security. All these responses, relying upon self-help, enlisting community aid, or appealing to outside authority, shared an ideological basis—a belief in natural justice. Terror was simply wrong, and should never be allowed to displace fair dealing and Christian forbearance. Such a sense of justice, basic to the social contract as Missourians conceived of it, was the most internalized form of resistance to terror, a core belief never discarded entirely even by the guerrillas and Union attackers themselves. Yet terror was designed, whether intentionally or not, to strike directly at this communal tap root; the horror of guerrilla war lay in part in its turning a normally disputatious rural society, filled with verbal abuse, occasional physical fights, and endless law suits, into the locale of war of all against all.[26]

Individual resistance to guerrillas most frequently meant instant death, but sometimes anger at being assaulted overcame whatever calculation a person might have made in calmer circumstances. Occasionally, resistance was effective. Mrs. Susan Hornbeck reported that on May 13, 1863, John Herd and several others, two of whom she knew by their surnames, "broke a pane of glass out of the window, presenting a pistol," demanding to see Mr. Hornbeck, and then battered the door open. When she asked why they wanted her husband, Herd said she "should damned quick see." Threatening to "blow hot lead through her" should she interfere, John Herd "started swearing he would kill my husband." To this point, this was the standard scenario for the killing of a presumed black Republican, but when John Herd got to the top of the stairs, Mrs. Hornbeck later reported, "my husband took a board and knocked him down, after which the rest of them left the room. John Herd layed in the room a while after which he got up and went out."[27] This strange anticlimax was atypical; normally the other guerrillas would have come to their captain's aid and killed Hornbeck. Most civilians would have killed a threatening guerrilla they had downed. One can only speculate about the social dynamics behind this story, but it demonstrates that some people physically resisted their attackers despite the probable outcome.

Some individuals who resisted guerrilla attacks did so by continuing to call upon neighbors for help, as was common before the war. Jessie Chrisman of Maries County, in central Missouri was plowing in oats during the planting season in 1864 when three mounted men rode up "and asked me if I did not want to trade horses. . . . I told [their leader] that I would not swap him at all, that they had the power to take them, but that I did not think they would. At last he said he guessed we would swap" and drew his pistol, demanding that Chrisman change the horses and plow on down to the far end of the field. When Chrisman had done so, he looked back and saw the riders were gone. He then jumped on his other horse "and collected [five] of my neighbors," tracked and found the raiding party and, driving off the rest, captured the leader, a returning Confederate captain, whom they turned over to the military authorities.[28]

Such stories of traditional community resistance to outside invaders were not uncommon though much less frequent than reports from individuals who had been attacked and felt they could not turn to trustworthy or concerned neighbors. Of course, it may also have been true that in some areas no one reported problems because neighbors pulled together, successfully repelling attackers throughout the war, and felt no need to report to outside authorities.

German-Americans were one group singled out by guerrillas as enemy Unionists. Most southern-born Missourians coupled nativism to politics, targeting Germans, the largest immigrant group, as the greatest foe. This had been true at least since the mid-1850s when the Know-Nothing party had made strong inroads among Missouri voters, riding on widespread anti-German feelings. Whatever their internal ideological differences, Germans knew what their pro-southern neighbors thought them to be and were more unified in a collective unconditional Union response than any of them. One Illinois infantry private, Henry Marsh, wrote in his diary of the "dutch town" of Hamburg, where 300 men had organized a home guard. They had requested ammunition from Marsh's colonel, who had refused them, but many of Marsh's fellow enlisted men did give it to them.[29] If all civilians had been so united politically and so well organized, there would have been no widespread guerrilla war. Such was not the case.

From time to time, citizens would agree to disregard their differences, supporting the South when guerrillas came to town and changing protested loyalties when Union troops were resident. Such was the case at Marshall in central Missouri in the spring of 1862. Union troops encircled the town, capturing several armed men who were on their way south to join the Confederate army; but when Union soldiers actually entered the town, as Abiel Leonard reported, "I never saw such a complete change in so short a time. . . . When the troops came, the citizens were all Union. There was not more than two or three Secessionists here that would be candid enough to tell it. The troops expressed great surprise at finding so many Union men here."[30]

Appeals to Union authorities often stemmed from a belief that external forces had disrupted the naturally peaceful order of the community. The very idea of appealing for redress to Union forces, the basic substance of most of the military records I have analyzed, in itself was evidence of the belief that local relationships had to be maintained. Outside authority should be brought to bear not as a permanent draconian military government but to cleanse local communities of injustice and return them to antebellum status, where right was right and wrong was wrong.

In civilian testimony at courts-martial and in depositions and petitions to Union authorities, an outraged sense of justice betrayed was the central theme. The victim would testify not only to destructive acts done to him or her but to the unjust and malevolent spirit which animated the attackers. John A. Bean, a leading Unionist farmer living near Macon City, had known the guerrilla Henry A. Griffith from boyhood. Bean testified that the other guerrillas who accompanied Griffith on a ransacking visit to Bean's home called him lieutenant and added that Griffith "appeared to be very active in shoving things around, appeared to be a young *convert.*" Griffith stole Bean's Union League documents, and burned a photograph of Bean's son-in-law, a Union officer, saying, "boys did you ever see a God Damned Federal Officer burn before?" Bean continued, "Well, they just danced jam bone, sung rally round the flag boys [a Union anthem], while burning the Stars and Stripes." In another case, four men who had known John Nichols before the war, testified at his court-martial that Nichols was "the terror to [Pettis] county." William Sharp said that "He was very bad before this rebellion. He is a bushwhacker." Edmund Kean, Nichols's uncle, testified that Nichols had shot at him and had stolen his horse, bragging that "he had killed many Union men." F. W. Gresham pointed at Nichols in the courtroom, saying, "you killed Gay's negro George which you do not deny" for George's having informed Union officers of Nichols's whereabouts. Gresham was looted at gunpoint by Nichols and his band. "When they were leaving Nichols said I ought to think I had come off very well, that if they [the band] would treat me right they would take me out and hang me like a dog. My wife being weakly was very much frightened and has scarcely got over it."[31]

When they had their day in court, an unusual opportunity during a guerrilla war, these victims all testified not only to the bad results of the acts of terror but to the evil moral intention which animated such terror. Missouri may have had rough and ready qualities before the war, but such testimony is evidence that a code of natural justice was generally believed to be the basis of normal, nonthreatening relationships, and that terror was *not* seen as a means to legitimate self-service.

Even in the face of rampant and seemingly random violence many victims believed that justice would be reasserted. The hope for some later, true redistribution of justice may have lain behind Daniel De Witt's complete list of losses at Union hands. Someday, when normal justice had returned to the land, he would file a claim and be compensated. Even if he himself very much doubted this hope, it was significant that he wrote out his list, for that act itself was evidence of his faith that in all justice he ought to be compensated, that in a proper and attainable peaceful society such wrongs would be righted. Americans had courts and civil procedures—there was no need to resort to brute force to resolve conflicts. Thus one husband requested of his wife, who had been raided by Quantrill's gang in 1862, "Write immediately and please send me a list of things taken by the bushwhackers and their value as I wish to lay a claim."[32]

Since civilian authority had collapsed in much of Missouri, military provost marshals were often the only available agents of the law; petitions and appeals went to them or to their superiors in the command structure. Thus the Callaway County provost marshal received copies of a string of frightened letters which Henry Barnes had written to his father. "The woods [are] alive with Bushwhackers," Henry wrote. He had been taken out into the woods one night to listen to a debate over whether or not he should be hanged. His house had been looted, and when the guerrillas had demanded his wallet and had seen that it contained "only about a dollar, they had handed it back and swore they would not take such a little amount." Henry's father, John, wrote to the authorities that the Union outpost nearest to Henry was eighteen miles away, that "a man's safety in that country, at present, is to be a friend of the rebels," and that "the good Union people of that district are entitled to the protection . . . a very few troops" would provide.[33] The traditional American fear of a standing army and military-based law was overriden by this form of warfare for many men like Barnes—only the army could give the countryside some semblance of the rule of law.

Placed in a position of authority, acting as police, judge, and jury with military power unencumbered by the checks of ordinary civil law, many local provost marshals nevertheless attempted to distribute their conception of justice in an even-handed way, to respond directly and openly to civilian demands, to weigh evidence, and to mete out punishments fairly. The monthly report for November 1864 of Captain Gustavas St. Gem, assistant provost marshal in St. Genevieve on the Mississippi River south of St. Louis, was fairly representative for a not especially violent period of time. During the month he made thirty-four arrests of men accused of being guerrillas or southern sympathizers. Upon examination of each man, he released twenty-one under oath of loyalty and peace bond and sent thirteen on to prison and further examination in St. Louis. All the prisoners claimed that they had been conscripted, and St. Gem tended to believe them in those instances where testimony against them was not conclusive or where they were not widely reputed to be guerrillas. St. Gem released one prisoner who had been arrested on the word of a neighbor, after which St. Gem wrote, "said testimony [was] not . . . found positive and reliable." In another case, James Miller earned his release in part by naming James Cozens and Dudley Horn as the culprits who had conscripted him and kept him under surveillance in a guerrilla encampment. In nearly every case, arrests followed accusations by civilians. St. Gem seemed to have known how unreliable such testimony often could be under chaotic wartime circumstances, and he discounted evidence for the spite he well knew it might contain.[34]

In April 1863, Conrad C. Ziegler, a wealthy farmer residing near St. Genevieve, petitioned Provisional Governor Hamilton R. Gamble and also brought suit in the county circuit court asking compensation for $10,000 worth of damage he claimed had been done to his orchard, fences, and house by the First Wisconsin Cavalry Regiment, who had encamped on his land near a steamboat landing. The person sued was none other than Assistant Provost Marshal Gustavas St. Gem, who, Ziegler maintained, had directed those troops "to quarter on me for food and forage [because] he was a personal enemy of mine." St. Gem's colonel responded that Ziegler was a "notorious secessionist" who only wished "to annoy a faithful and energetic officer, to insult Union men generally and to enlist the sympathies of the ignorant and unwary in behalf of Secession." In his own defense St. Gem replied that Ziegler had never filed a complaint with him "in my office," the local provost marshal being the proper authority to contact in such a case. St. Gem claimed that he had no authority over a Wisconsin colonel in any event; that he had never suggested depredations; that as a Federal officer under military orders, he was not answerable in any event before a civil court; that charges by persons of known disloyalty should not "for a moment be entertained" by military or civil authorities; and that Ziegler should be arrested for filing his petition, which in itself was an act of disloyalty and treason. In the last entry in this file, Ziegler's lawyers withdrew from the civil case.[35] St. Gem's defense was a succinct summary of many of the dangers of abuse present in military government, if and when a civilian wished to complain about the behavior of these authorities. Whatever the merits of Ziegler's case, there was little recourse to either civil or military authorities against possibly capricious, selective, and discriminatory behavior of military authorities in the field. This provost marshal behaved fairly in most instances, but if he chose to persecute someone, he could.

On the Kansas border, many Missourians believed with good reason that they were the objects not of a random distribution of justice but of a concerted policy of plunder and destruction at the hand of Kansas and Missouri troops and from thieves invited into the state by Union forces. Such is the gist of a letter Austin A. King of Independence wrote to General John M. Schofield in St. Louis in 1863. Whereas the Kansas colonel in charge of Independence had reported to Schofield that he had killed thirty guerrillas during a recent sweep of Lafayette County, King wrote, "truthful and loyal" Union men of that county all knew that only unarmed civilians had been killed. One hundred and fifty horses reported confiscated from secessionists were in fact stolen from peaceful, law-abiding citizens. The pernicious effects of such raids were augmented by provost marshals who had been planted in each county and "who seem to think it absolutely necessary to commit a certain amount of oppression in order to render their authority respectable."[36]

Many soldiers were themselves sickened by the violence done to the concept of justice by their comrades. In a letter to his wife written early in the war, Illinois Private John Higgins despaired of the "very disrespectful and disgraceful" behavior of Union troops. The "Dutch" in particular were a "perfect set of devils," but his Illinois company too was leaving behind a "perfect reign of terror, starvation and hatred . . . on the part of the people." Everything that could be stolen was stolen. His comrades would wantonly shoot 100 sheep and eat just a few, leaving the rest to rot. "There may be a day of reckoning and severe punishment meted out to those who do such things, which I hope to God there be by our higher officers, and I don't care how soon that time may come for if it is not soon done, our Army will be a disgrace forever."[37] Everywhere he looked, Private Higgins saw the army servicing the gods of annihilation; for him, the time of judgment, when good and evil would be weighed, seemed a distant prospect in some place beyond Missouri.

Loyalty, Neutralism, and Survival Lies

Some Missourians, the unconditional Unionists, supported the military oppression of secessionists which so frightened Private Higgins, even as they
acknowledged the attendant dangers of misrule. In July 1862 in a letter
sent to St. Louis authorities co-signed by seven neighbors, G. O. Yeiser
of Mexico spelled out the desires of many staunch Unionists. It was absurd to try to coax traitors back into the Union fold by light punishments
like bonds and oaths, Yeiser wrote—rebels would only "laugh at" such
slaps on the wrist, taking them as evidence that "the government was
afraid" to execute them. "To bargain, temporize, bear with, counsel, persuade & talk soft to traitors is like using the same on water to persuade
it to run uphill." Reason would work only on morally sound men, and
turning traitor was evidence of moral collapse. "Experience teaches us that
so soon as a man turns against his Government,—then he becomes a
liar, deceiver, defrauder and murderer." Such evildoers could never be
reconverted through forgiving means. They could be brought to submission only through fear of naked authority. "What can you expect to
make of such characters—particularly if they are ignorant & prejudiced
& bigotted—by anything short of a summary and terrifying punishment."
Bridgeburners, destroyers of public property, and bushwhackers should
all be shot down when caught, and the army should live off rebel sympathizers. "Disarm them entirely . . . leave them destitute. . . . Let them
feel the force of the law & the power of the government." Yeiser understood that with such a policy "some innocent men must suffer," but he
would have the army err on the side of too much punishment rather than
too little, requiring each suspected traitor to prove that "he *is, was and
ever has been* true and loyal," corroborated by the unambiguous word of
"known and unflinching Union men of the . . . neighborhood," such as
himself.[38]

Intense loyalism and hatred of the enemy were the means to keep alive
a sense of moral and cultural shape in the atmosphere of guerrilla war
terror, yet they were developed at the expense of charity and toleration.
Justice without restraint was a perversion of American Christian values
and could easily lead to despotism and injustice. This unrelenting position
grew during the war as Unionists forced their neighbors to choose sides
in order to reduce the frightening ambiguities of never being sure where
anyone stood and how they might behave. If mercy no longer flowed,
justice would have to be imposed.

Unconditional Unionists were infuriated when exiled secessionists were
allowed to return home to live in peace and prosperity, while Unionists
continued to suffer at the hands of marauders. In February 1863, eighty-
eight Boone County residents petitioned the St. Louis military commander

to stop a policy of allowing leading pro-southern families "to return here to exert the influence their wealth gives them to again plot treason and delude the ignorant with their false teachings." These eighty-eight Unionists believed that rich Confederates had misled poor Southerners from the start, causing the guerrilla war to begin—"the poor deluded victim of these fine coated Rebels [who were] driven into the brush by their pernicious counsels are not rich enough to bribe anyone to petition for their pardon."[39] Why should wealth be allowed to purchase freedom? At least the poor men among the Southerners took up arms rather than pretending loyalty while in reality sponsoring and profiting from treasonous warfare. This was a Unionist echo of the common complaint voiced by southern poor whites that the Confederacy was sponsoring a rich man's war and a poor man's fight.

In many places avowedly Unionist farmers were a despised, attacked, and beleaguered minority who paid dearly for their openly professed loyalty. Part of their anger grew from their sense that not only secessionists but moral trimmers who walked both sides of the road led easier lives than they did. Indeed, some Unionists could acknowledge that sometimes they were tempted to become chameleons themselves. In this vein, A. J. McRoberts of Saline County wrote to his wife, who had gone back home to Ohio, "I am obliged to either leave or turn secesh. I am a Union man by nature. I thought when I came back here this spring I would play secesh but it is against the grain so much that I could not make it work well."[40] McRoberts, who had a safe place to move to in the North, did leave Missouri that summer, choosing exile, poverty, and loyalty over staying in relative safety in Missouri in disguise or in danger in open Unionism.

Some pro-Confederates also openly professed their loyalties, even when captured and questioned by Union authorities. They were prepared to bear a potentially high price for maintaining stated loyalties. In 1863 C. Percy Rawlings, a forty-six-year-old Howard County farmer, was arrested after hauling corn to William Jackman's guerrillas. Although he deposed that he had only aided the guerrillas because he "was compelled to do that" (the usual defense of arrested guerrilla abettors), Rawlins refused, when asked, to make the usual stock acknowledgment of Unionist sympathies. "I am a Southern sympathizer," he declared. "I do not desire to see the South put down in the rebellion nor do I desire to see the authority of the U.S. Government re-established over the South. I have one negro. I have some nephews in the southern army."[41] Rawlins was exceptional in professing southern loyalties under such circumstances. Almost every guerrilla and sympathizer became a verbally loyal Unionist when asked these same questions while under Union arrest.

On occasion pro-southern groups would reassert their loyalties when provoked by Unionists. In Williamstown in the northeast corner of the state, northern and southern Methodists shared a church building, the Northerners holding services in the morning and Southerners in the after-noon. One June Sunday afternoon in 1864, some northern Methodist young bloods decided to hold up the Stars and Stripes over the church door through which the southern Methodists customarily exited. R. J. Ander-son later wrote to the district military commander, "Some of the ladies would not go out under the flag, but got over the center railing, in order to pass out of the other door." Another Union boy held a second Federal flag over that exit. "One of the ladies, Miss Martha Palmer, knocked the flag out of his hand and into the street, and passed out. Mr. Oscar Chappel, in passing out, stamped it with indignation, and several times since has boasted of giving the Union flag a good stamping, coupled with the remark that he would do so again. Others have done and said the same."[42]

Until midsummer 1864 the Unionists and secessionists of Williamstown had been able to live together fairly peacefully. The split in the Methodist congregation reflected mutual forbearance, even if only in this sector of life, although it likely reflected a wider agreement to refrain from provoca-tive or violent activity. On this Sunday morning, the Union boys smoked out explicit southern allegiances and resentments from their neighbors, who when put to the test, would rather have been overtly disloyal to the Union flag than symbolically submissive. The immediate issue was petty, though the longer-term outcome may have been less so.

If they chose to do so, Union authorities, where they had military forces, could destroy the lives of professed southern supporters. Mrs. Margery J. Callahan and her niece, Miss Lulu Kinkead, were arrested in St. Louis on June 4, 1863, for sewing rebel flags and uniforms. Evidence against them came from intercepted letters Callahan had written to her husband, away in the Confederate army. When she was questioned on June 17, after two weeks of imprisonment with no charges being laid and after be-ing threatened with banishment, Kinkead was asked, "Are you loyal or disloyal?" to which she replied, "I suppose I am disloyal." She refused to take a Union loyalty oath and was banished. Yet on the same day and under the same threats, Callahan betrayed two southern spies and the underground southern mail network in St. Louis and took the oath. The provost marshal told the hearing officer that Callahan "has done her part of the bargain" and that he had given her his word; she was released.[43] It is my clear impression that there were more Margery Callahans than Lulu Kinkeads in Missouri, more survivors than heroes—if maintaining loyalty under these circumstances would be the appropriate test of moral probity.

As was the case with Callahan, one way to prove Union loyalty was to betray others. Groups of professed Unionists frequently would petition military authorities concerning the disloyalty of certain groups or individ-uals, and individual citizens would write or make oral depositions against disloyal neighbors. Four Audrain County farmers testified in a military hearing which led to the forfeiture of the bond of Abel Crawford for aiding and abetting the rebellion. All four called Crawford a "bitter secessionist," a "warm Southern man who always talked against the Government." One said that he "had the reputation of giving aid and comfort" to guerrillas, that "he had every reason to believe" that Crawford aided guerrillas, and that "he was known to associate with the worst characters in the county." When Phinneas McCarty had been attacked by three guerrillas, McCarty's son had succeeded in driving them off. The guerrillas had fled in the direction of Crawford's house, where three horses were seen the following morning. John Cunningham concluded that Crawford's "general reputation in the neighborhood [was as] a busy secesh and has been all summer."[44] Perhaps Crawford was not punished more severely (he was placed under oath and bond) because of the circumstantial nature of the evidence, but hearsay and guilt by association were often the basis for charges of disloyalty, some of which led to capital punishment.

It is also significant that Abel Crawford openly disclosed his southern loyalties to neighbors he knew to be Unionists. Of course he would have wished to intimidate them and, if possible, force them to leave the area. However, as Federal troops were stationed nearby in Mexico, he ran risks even in cheering on the secessionists, if that is all he did.

Loyal secessionists who wished to act for the rebellion in their area could either take to the bush or aid those who did. During the entire course of the rebellion, many effectively erased the line between civilian and combatant. Some may have merely lent verbal support to the Confederacy and associated with politically like-minded people. However, if there were men professing southern sympathies and if there were also guerrilla attacks in the region, Union neighbors linked disloyal sentiments to contiguous disloyal actions. Their loyalty would be reaffirmed at relatively low risk by their naming names to the authorities; if their own loyalty had ever been called into doubt, secret impeachment of neighbors could be a means of clearing their names. This was the context for witch hunts. It also meant that bearing false witness bore fruit, though such an act violated values of honor, democratic freedom, and truthfulness.

The Reverend William Powell, in a deposition signed by ten others who lived near St. Joseph, named the Brinton family, the Richie family, Mr. McDaniel, and Squire Powell—none of whose first names he knew—as well known to have been in complicity with guerillas. Joe Johnson deposed that "Old Man Brinton told me about two years ago that myself and all men of my principles had got to leave this country in a few days." Suggesting they be banished, N. J. Allison, U. S. military detective, named the Burness family, Mr. Neil, and Mrs. Bennett, the wife of a Methodist minister in the southern army, as guerilla supporters according to Unionists around Waverly. Mr. Neil told Detective Allison that he never complained of or informed on the bushwhackers, that he "did not want to have anything to do" with informing, out of fear that the guerrillas would "find it out and kill him"; but Allison concluded that Neil "cultivates [the guerrillas'] friendship." For this Union detective, feeding guerrillas and then not informing Union authorities that one had done so amounted to disloyalty worthy of banishment from the state.[45]

In other petitions, however, known Unionists attested to the good character of suspected guerrilla supporters who had been arrested by Union forces. Thirty "loyal citizens" of Knox, Scotland, and Clark counties in northeastern Missouri appealed for the release of George Staniford from the military prison at Alton, Illinois, where he was being held without charges. They claimed that he had never borne arms against the United States nor aided those who did and "that he will conduct himself as becomes a loyal and peaceable as well as Union loving citizen and will not give aid or comfort to those in arms against the government." Twenty-four loyal citizens of Boone County petitioned for the release of L. D. Coon and his son Enoch, "quiet and peaceable citizens [who] if they have committed any crime it was no further than compelled to do." These signatories assumed that the Coons had in effect been taken hostage by Union troops to be exchanged for two Union men kidnapped by rebels, who had since been released. Now, in fairness, the Coons should go free.[46]

Loyal citizens in both these instances basically claimed that these neighbors were peaceful and not willingly disloyal. For the unconditional Unionists, however, disloyalty meant anything less than explicitly committed Unionism. Both sorts of petitions were common during the war. It is possible that some of the more gentle petitions were bribed or extorted from Union men, as unconditional Unionists often claimed. Doubtless, petitions were written differently according to the reputation of the subject of petition. Some petitioners may have believed forbearance was the more useful social policy, while others believed forgiveness would be interpreted by rebels as contemptible weakness and that only the application of the iron rake would be effective. For shifting sets of reasons, some local communities were more cohesive, defending even the politically suspect, while others were subject to mutual recriminations and purgings. If we get some of them, the feelings may have run, they will get some of us. Therefore, forbearance could be a somewhat more sophisticated form of self-service than revenge. Forbearance could also have been a means to maintain honor and self-respect.

Loyalty was not the safest and most common presentation of self during this guerrilla war; prevarication was. Frankness and directness led to destruction more often than did reticence and withdrawal. Not letting on, telling the questioner—from either side—as little as possible but enough to placate him, became the safest avenue of escape. I would call that political technique of trying to live on through terror *survival lying* and would not judge it as anything but necessary. It made more sense to be a living liar than a dead hero, and the stakes were that great. At the same time, tellers of survival lies were aware of the moral ambiguity of their actions. Survival lies were a means of adapting to war, one way in which character was "doubled" through the creation of a wartime alter-self. This alternative self was purchased at a great price, the sacrifice of integrated, fair-playing membership in the community, yet paradoxically it was necessary for self-preservation when people were under such relentless attack. Some, like A. J. McReynolds, attempted playing secesh but found they could not, as it went too much against their Union "nature." Though eventually most rural Missourians did become war refugees, the majority tried to do whatever was necessary to stay at home, including sacrificing their honor.

Abraham Allen of Crab Orchard in west central Missouri raised a volunteer Union militia and tried to gain information from his neighbors concerning guerrilla activities, which he believed threatened the whole community. When he asked civilians on the road if they had heard of guerrillas thereabouts, he wrote to the district commander, "Invariably their answer was no, with as much astonishment as if they live in St. Paul, Minn[esota]. The rebels have in this country double protection. They are protected in the daytime by the Federal arm, and protected at night by the jayhawkers. Just look; the Union [men are] here without either."[47] To Allen, all the citizens of Ray County, except for the few armed and active Union men, appeared to have adopted the same mode of lying in order to gain as much protection as possible from both sides.

When they were arrested and interrogated by Union authorities, most guerrillas and guerrilla sympathizers lied about their involvement. The formula for denying or downplaying involvement was to claim that one had been coerced and threatened into giving aid or had been involuntarily conscripted into guerrilla service. When asked whether he had aided guerrillas, Richard Alexander, a farmer from Wayne County in southeastern Missouri, replied, "Only when I was compelled to." When in the spring of 1863 seven men of Burbridge's command "come demanding dinner and forage, [I] refused to give it to them. They took what fodder they wanted and ordered my wife to get dinner for them. She did so . . . They asked me for nothing more." In this testimony, Alexander was denying that he gave food or fodder willingly or that he supplied information on Union troop movements. "What were they doing?" the provost marshal asked. "I don't know. I did not ask them," Alexander replied. This may well have been true as he would have wished not to have been viewed as being informed about guerrilla activities. At least as far as a Union provost marshal might be concerned, he knew nothing, and indeed he may have asked nothing from the guerrillas, as a form of contingency planning for possible Union questioning. In July 1863, six men of Jim Reeves's band had ridden up to Alexander's yard. "They asked me if I had any news. I told them I had none." They stole three yards of calico, a hat, and dinner. In June 1864, two men in civilian clothes "came to the fence and asked my wife if there had been any bushwhackers there . . . while these two men were there 4 men came up and run them off. No one was killed. I was not at home at the time. . . . I don't know whether my wife gave either of them any signal that the Militia were coming." Alexander denied knowing the two men or whether they had been guerrillas or Union militia. His wife had probably been accused of tipping the two men off about the arrival of the militia, and Alexander sought to exonerate himself by blaming her but hoping not thereby to cause her any undo harm. Alexander admitted feeding the guerrilla McMillan three or four times. When one Jackman came to his home, helped himself to fodder, and swapped saddles, Alexander said Jackman had told him he was a "travelling picket," an official sounding army-like title. "What do you think he meant by being a travelling picket?" the provost marshal asked Alexander. "I did not think anything about it." "Did you know he was a Rebel spy?" "No, Sir." "Why did you not report this man to the Federal authorities?" "I had no means. There was no Federal post within 45 miles." And what about the four or five barrels of salt Alexander traveled 45 miles to Pilot Knob to purchase?—He just bought them for neighbors, as the permits he held up at that point demonstrated. "Are you a Southern sympathizer?" "No, Sir." "Do you desire to see the South put down . . . ?" "Yes, sir, I do and am willing to help to do it."[48] Richard Alexander's involvement in a damning string of incidents—making him appear a guerrilla sympathizer—he explained as harassment at guerrilla hands. Playing dumb, minimizing involvement, denying that they gave out information on Union activities, insisting that failure to comply with guerrilla demands was overridden by guerrilla robbery, stressing the fear of destruction, and all the while professing active loyalty to the Union were standard defense ploys of sympathizers caught in Alexander's position, even when the evidence of aiding the guerrillas was quite clear.

The process of survival lying is further illustrated by the testimony of W. E. Brassfield, a thirty-seven-year-old Clay County farmer, who was the chief witness in Silas Best's court-martial. In July 1864, Best and three others rode up to Brassfield's farm, demanded supper, and took Brassfield's horse and gun when they left. Brassfield had employed Best from time to time as a farmhand before the war. Testifying that Best had made no threats, Brassfield added, "I had reason to believe that [the others] would have made me [cooperate] if I had refused." Other guerrilla parties had come calling in the past and had made similar demands. When the court asked Brassfield whether he had cooperated in these instances, he replied, "Well, we just went along and gave them their suppers." While the guerrillas were eating, Brassfield told the court, he had said to Silas Best, " 'I am sorry to see you in this fix,' and he said, 'so am I and I would like to get out of it.' "[49] Brassfield's testimony demonstrated shrewd abilities at survival lying. He made it clear to the court that he had only aided guerrillas when compelled to do so and that he had been victimized in this case as in the others. Yet despite losing his horse and saddle, he also lied for Best, a neighborhood boy of his acquaintance. Brassfield said he had been coerced by the group rather than threatened by Best. Brassfield then repeated—or perhaps fabricated—a conversation which demonstrated to the court the involuntary nature of Best's guerrilla participation and his eagerness to get himself out of the trade. Clearly, Brassfield wanted to aid Best in court but did not want to implicate himself. His testimony demonstrates the resignation but also the courage and empathy that could be involved in telling survival lies.

From time to time, the terror of guerrilla war compelled nearly everyone to choose sides for the immediate occasion, and sometimes these temporary alignments could become future millstones. When suddenly under the power of the other side, one might honestly believe that an earlier alliance had been the result of coercion rather than free will. This would lead to the earnest plea that terror had displaced normal peacetime conscience. Clever men like W. E. Brassfield and Richard Alexander could maneuver in these minefields with less personal risk than others, but the everyday politics of guerrilla war confused and frightened ordinary people who were struggling just to survive and trying to maintain some semblance of security.

If they had had a truly free choice, most Missourians would have remained neutral during the war. The 1860 election, when 71 percent of the electorate voted for the middle-of-the-road candidates, Douglas and Bell, was a fairly accurate representation of rural Missouri public opinion, and throughout the war, neutralism remained the generally preferred if often untenable position. Men of good will simply should not rob and butcher one another, they believed, and many felt that the correct stance was to refrain if at all possible from any form of participation. Some even wished to reclaim neutralism after having made a choice earlier in the war. For example, in 1863 Confederate deserter George W. Carter wrote from his hiding place somewhere in St. Charles County requesting a pardon, "That I may be allowed to renounce a soldier's life and remain the balance of this war quietly with my little family." He also wanted an exemption from Union military duty and in exchange promised to go to Illinois and maintain "a neutrality as strict as that of a tree of a forest."[50]

As the war evolved, neither guerrillas nor Unionists permitted neutralism, seeing it as service, however meekly given, to the enemy. At the start of the conflict, a St. Louis politician, Barton Bates, wrote about the contents of a letter he had received from an acquaintance in

St. Charles. "He says secession is wrong but it is also wrong to oppose it. There are *a heap* of fellows like him—mere dishrags—whose influence operates in favor of Secession, while in their heart they are opposed to it, but have not the decision to manifest their opposition." Later in the war, James O. Broadhead analyzed the same survival lying situation with more compassion when he wrote that *"timid* citizens, be they ever so loyal . . . pretend to favor bushwhacking when they believe themselves in the power of the bushwhackers."[51] Broadhead realized that honor was more easily maintained in safely Unionist St. Louis than in the war-wracked countryside.

As the war ground on, unconditional Unionists lost patience with would-be neutralists. (The same was probably true of guerrilla responses, though the archival records do not contain their reactions.) Many Kansas troops drove the point home as their central war aim. Joseph Trego, surgeon for the Fifth Kansas Cavalry wrote that for his commander, Jim Lane, "Neutral men are just about all of them secessionists in principle [and that] he meant the secessionists in Missouri to *feel* the difference between being loyal and disloyal citizens and he is doing it. We have camped where there was secession farmers on one side and Union farmers on the other, when we would leave the secession were stripped of everything like crops and fences while the others remained untouched." One can only imagine the guerrilla reprisals against those farmers left untouched and thus in effect targeted by Lane—many of whom doubtless stressed their southernness or neutrality to the bushwhackers. Neutralism was disallowed by the Union military authorities at Waverly during the summer of 1862. An avowed Unionist reported that the military demanded that all loyal men between the ages of eighteen and forty-five enroll for militia duty and that "all who do not enroll their names are to be considered as spies and traitors and are to be treated as such." Such policies intensified both resistance and the need to tell survival lies. If you were not actively demonstrating your loyalty, you were presumed disloyal. The deeper and longer the war, the more the middle ground of neutralism was undercut. There were fewer and fewer hiding places. John Johnston wrote to his sister and brother from Kansas City in 1863, "Secesh are leaving the city and this section of the country like rats from a burning house. . . . The times are growing more radical in the border states. This issue is [either] 'the *Union,* right or wrong the *Union,*' or sympathy with the rebellion. And men are being forced to show their hands."[52]

Collapse of the Sense of Security: Taking of Revenge

Guerrilla terror disrupted life most dramatically when an armed gang invaded a farm or town, but it also created deep fears and destruction in everyday life. The presence of guerrillas in the neighborhood eroded any

sense of security for those living there. Holdups and raids on lines of supply in regions dominated by guerrillas destroyed business confidence, for
example. "In all the small villages the Union merchants have closed or
are closing out and leaving," a merchant of Pisgah in central Missouri
wrote to General William S. Rosecrans, "while the secure traitor smiles
surreptitiously as he counts the gain he thereby enjoys." Guerrillas repeatedly robbed mail routes, cutting rural and small-town Missourians off
from their only links to loved ones and to the outside world in general
and deepening the normal isolation of rural life. P. Harlan wrote to her
sister, "If you thought anything of me, how lonesome I am here and all
alone you would write oftener but I don't think that is the reason that I
do not get any letters for surely you do write and the letters do not come
through for there has not been any mail here for several days."[53]

These disruptions of village business and of the mails also implied that
there were much greater threats just outside of town. Because guerrillas
could be anywhere in the countryside, they seemed to be everywhere.
Thus George Gresham of Lexington in west central Missouri noted that
mail on the main stage line southeast to Sedelia was frequently robbed and
that the local citizens believed themselves threatened by Quantrill and his
"considerable force" who were marauding about somewhere nearby. "There
is but few [Federal] troops here, only 70 men, I am told, and they hold
the town and the Bushwhackers and Murderers the Country." In his letter
Gresham presented the atmosphere of lurking menace that guerrillas created even when they were not actually present. The countryside was a
hostile sea surrounding and threatening to swamp one's insufficiently garrisoned island. Farmers often lost the will to carry on, as they could neither predict an invasion of their farm nor prevent it. Major George S.
Avery of the Third Cavalry, Missouri State Militia, observed in 1863, "If
the war had not swept its devastating hand over the country, the farmers
here would be as prosperous as in any country. The farmer here has nothing to encourage him. Today he may have plenty. Tomorrow he may have
nothing. His produce all consumed—his buildings injured—his fences destroyed—his stock driven away, to receive no remuneration. His principle
and actions are what save him and again they may cause him to be destroyed—he has no security."[54]

Even the presence of Union militia was not always a guarantee of security, for many of them were of dubious loyalty. Paw Paw regiments, as
they were known, were composed in large part of returned southern soldiers and sympathizers who had taken the oath of allegiance to the Union.
Amounting to a rebel fifth column, they often appeared to Unionists to
have cut bargains with guerrillas, dividing Unionists' spoils between them.
George S. Park wrote of the region around Parksville in 1864, "The
military power is now entirely in their hands, locally. No unconditional
Union men went into the Paw Paw militia. A few soft Union men were

taken in for a blind." After Park's home had been ransacked by guerrillas, the Paw Paw captain, a former guerrilla, refused to investigate. "They can trump up charges at any time and have things all their own way. Union men are not safe to report, for fear of secret vengeance. We are in their power."[55]

The collapse of the sense of security, a result of the infiltrations of guerrilla warfare into everyday life, multiplied by rumors and experience of guerrilla horrors, often produced panic. Frequent violent attacks and threats of more, when coupled to an insufficient or unreliable Union force, could tip the psychological balance toward sudden group flight. Union authorities were anxious to keep news of large-scale panic quiet, lest citizens in huge areas of the state flee and thus allow the guerrillas to win their war. This was a real danger. In July 1864, describing a situation true in much of the state that summer, three leading citizens of the village of Huntsville in central Missouri wrote to General Rosecrans, "There is a perfect panic here. People are leaving their homes and have lost all hope. . . . All parties share the panic alike. The people are without organization and cannot resist such large bands. Please do not publish in the papers."[56] Unionists, both civilians and members of the military, undermined the security of secessionist and would-be neutralist citizens as well. Doubling the effects of guerrilla terror tactics, their counter-terrorist activities spilled widely over the populace, further undermining the security of citizens of all political persuasions.

Federal authorities often admonished local Unionists to form self-protective home guards. Frequently, in the vigilante tradition of armed self-help, they did so. However, unlike the peacetime vigilante tradition—where the entire community, or at least the representatives of the mainstream of the community used vigilantism to discipline outsiders or people who were widely believed to have transgressed community norms—in the internally divided communities typical of rural Missouri during the Civil War, such groups were expressions of a fragment of the community acting against other fragments. Though they had the color of officially sanctioned legitimacy, local Union units resembled guerrilla bands in making war on civilians they deemed disloyal.

During 1863 in Andrew County in northwest Missouri, a group of perhaps eight Unionists formed a vigilance committee which determined which citizens were "obnoxious" and, under the signature "Colorado Boys," ordered several of them out of the county. One day they went gunning for Finley Dysart who, the Colorado Boys' leader told local farmer Robert Pollard, "Would never make a good Union man and deserved death." When they arrived at Dysart's farm, Pollard later deposed, "They saw a little boy there and they asked him who that was, pointing at Ed Burns who was there. The boy said it was Uncle Finley and he was fired at and killed thinking it was Finley Dysart." Robert Pollard then fled the county, as he had received the same Colorado Boys' notice as had Finley Dysart.[57]

Undisciplined Union volunteer troops—frightened by the guerrillas who sniped at them and bored with garrison duty in little towns away from the controls of home—frequently behaved in ways which made peace, property, and life insecure for local citizens. Such troops were always hungry, always thirsty for whiskey, and often seeking ways to vent their energy, resentment, and frustration.

"The town was in a state of confusion that a lot of drunken soldiers could only produce," wrote the provost marshal at Chillicothe on November 8, 1863, and so he issued an order shutting down the local saloons. That night "a lot of soldiers came in and called for whiskey" at Sherman and William's saloon. The bartender, Leo Manning, told the boys they could not have it, taking out and reading the provost marshal's order. "They remarked that they were going to have whiskey as long as the [saloons] were left open that they had as good a right to have whiskey as a citizen. One of them then took hold of me," the bartender deposed, "and forced me to the door while another said he was a good bartender and went around and set out the whiskey when they all drank." The troops were cursing out civilians in general and getting drunker when a local resident named Barton came in and began arguing politics with the men. "The soldiers slapped him on the jaws and then [one] got into a fight with Barton, knocking him down over the stove and drawing his revolver on him. The pistol snapped and did not go off or else if it had Barton would have been killed." The soldiers went back to drinking. Manning, the bartender, told them he would have to report them. "They said that was all right that I had used them right. If I had not they would have shot the damned saloon all to pieces." Manning wrote down their names but ripped up the list the next morning after a conversation with the soldiers' officers, Captains Brown and Barnes, who told him "to say no more about it, that probably it would breed more trouble." Manning kept his mouth shut until the provost marshal approached him.[58]

Frequently troops were garrisoned in civilian houses or just took them over, often from citizens who had fled. In December 1863, the Eleventh Kansas Cavalry occupied Independence—to them the very center of secessionist sentiment which had spawned the Lawrence massacre a few months earlier. The Kansas troops used most of the good business blocks as horse stables and stayed in local homes, which they proceeded to tear up. Transients accompanying the army also squatted in unoccupied houses. W. L. Bone wrote to the absent Professor Mims of Independence, "An Irishman is now in your house—treats it tolerable well—pays no rent. The Stegall brick house, near ours, is now occupied by an old man, who cut up some 10 or 15 hogs in the parlor room last Sunday." Mims had asked if he could secure compensation for damage done his property, to which

Bone replied, "I doubt it. If property is used by a command as a necessity, and it is destroyed, then the government will pay for it, I believe; but when it is torn to pieces by private soldiers without orders, I do not think the govt will pay for it."[59] Many civilians felt themselves under attack from Union soldiers and also believed that there was no likely legal redress for what was being done to them. The military frequently appeared to be their persecutors and subsequently their judges and juries, beyond whom there was no effective appeal.

Union troops destroyed lives as well as property. In 1864 Charles Sheppard wrote from Springfield (the locale of the largest Union camp in southern Missouri) to his brother Henry, "You are lucky to be away—I would advise you to stay away." Captain Boardman's artillary company was nearby, and "Our gardens suffer terribly—part of his Co. are Dutch—they dug up all my sweet potatoes in one night—and the cabbage go constantly—they are stealing your plank—they have killed all your pigs but three—two of them are lamed." What was worse was that some of the troops were murdering civilian men fingered by local Unionists. "Friday night old man Marlow, a Mr. Morrow and a brother of Jasper McDaniel were murdered at their homes by radical militia—the week before Jim Thompson was murdered between this place and his home—I don't know who is safe—Philips and Hardin have been threatened and are pointed out to soldiers as Copperheads and Rebels. We are in a worse state than was before."[60]

By no means was the situation in Springfield an isolated or unusual case of army behavior. Union troops frequently upset the security of the civilians they were supposed to be protecting. Federal officers themselves often reported being driven frantic by the mob-like activities of the troops ostensibly under their command. The lieutenant colonel who had just taken command of the garrison at Warsaw in August 1863, wrote his commander that "our soldiery" had committed "six [murders] within the last ten or twelve days. . . . There is a feeling of insecurity universally prevailing with the peaceable citizens . . . all in this place that can get conveyance express an intention of leaving. There is no discipline whatever exercised over the soldiers here, which, added to the indiscriminate sale of liquor, renders the soldiers fiends rather than soldiers. The best citizens here have been menaced with death by the soldiers."[61]

Often the clashes of Union and rebel forces also undermined civilian security. If part of a community panicked, the rest were also affected. In addition, sharp dealers could take advantage of the weakened morale produced by Union-guerrilla conflicts to exact additional costs from civilians caught in the middle.

In St. Joseph, Charles Monroe Chase, a shrewd newspaper reporter, pointed out early in the war that local business collapsed due to divisions within the town. "When the war broke out rebels ruled the town. More 'than half of her citizens were genuine Secesh, and it was only after the severest military discipline that Unionism triumphed. Hundreds of her citizens left for the South in hot haste and between days." The property they abandoned sold for as little as one-eighth its prewar value, driving general property values down by two-thirds. Business was deranged and personal relations embittered. "If a man in St. Joe knocks down a neighbor that neighbor forgets the other cheek injunction and proceeds to return the compliment. This custom . . . helps the law business . . . to say nothing about the pugilistic discipline it affords the parties."[62] Though rendered with humor, Chase's description captured something of the material impoverishment and mutual recrimination characteristic of Missouri small-town life during the war. The bitterness of guerrilla conflict infiltrated everyday social contact, even in towns free of overt guerrilla war.

It distressed both citizens and Union commanders that dishonest speculators and merchants could profit from the huge illegal trade guerrilla war offered, exploiting ordinary people in yet another manner. Brigadier General Richard C. Vaughan, commander of the Kansas-Missouri border district, decried those practices which were stripping the region of working stock. "It is impossible for anyone not living in this country to imagine the extent to which horse stealing in every imaginable shape is carried on. Men claiming to be loyal . . . can travel safely all over the country, and can pass into the guerilla camps . . . without danger. The truth is they are in league, the guerrilla steals the horse, & the loyal trader buys him." In addition, some traders "impose upon the credulity of the simple & uninformed people by telling them that it is the purpose of the government to confiscate all their property & in order to save what they could. They sell it in many instances for one fourth of its real value to those men, who then turn them over to the government contractors at full price."[63]

Black-marketing of stolen goods such as clothing, jewelry, and home furnishings reached an impressive scale. Brigadier General Benjamin Loan in Jefferson City in 1862 offered a clear analysis of illicit commerce. Either "good society" or economic double-agents "claiming to be Government contractors and with provost-marshal's passes in their pockets," would contact guerrillas directly, purchase their stolen goods, warehouse them, and transport them, generally by riverboat to St. Louis, reselling them through merchants who either were secessionists or did not ask probing questions. Loan was particularly incensed that in the end government contractors often repurchased Union horses stolen elsewhere in Missouri. That "good families" of southern sympathizers had gained permission to take their goods with them to St. Louis so infuriated the Unionists of Brunswick that at one point they burned down the riverboat company warehouse rather than see what were to them all those doubtlessly stolen goods taken off like honestly earned property.[64]

In addition to St. Louis as a trading center for stolen goods, Kansas provided a relatively secure place for resale. Illinois (especially Quincy), Iowa (especially Keokuk), and Kansas City were the other usual market places. Kansas Union Private W. W. Moses, for example, wrote his sister in 1862 that he had "Jayhawked some silver cupps and sent them to Illinois" and left instructions that on event of his death, his sister should keep one and send the rest to their mother in Minnesota.[65]

The poorest Union private and the well-heeled merchant joined guerrillas in what amounted to a system of exploitation, doubtless with many bribes made to higher military authorities, corrupting them along the way. Attacked from all sides, civilians often felt paralyzed by these attacks coming in so many forms and from so many directions. W. A. Brannock, who lived near Pleasant Hill close to the Kansas border, wrote to his son in the spring of 1865, "we was rob last fall of three hundred Dollars worth and all for the brush men. And they are here a gain one of their wives are here. I hav told them that I could not coock for them, that the Feds had swore vengeance againstes us if we ever fed them a gain. What are we to do?"[66]

So much general insecurity undermined morale, frequently producing bursts of panic, survival lying, and desperate lashing back. No civilian response was "right"; none could amount to clear and consistent "strategies." All the power was in the hands of guerrillas and various partially disciplined Union forces; civilian victims felt a variety of conflicting responses and moved to and fro among them, depending on the vicissitudes of circumstances and their varying states of mind. There was no uniform or general response characteristic of all or most Missourians; indeed one cannot generalize too much about the emotional results within any individual. No adaptation to war could be complete for essentially powerless civilians. They bounced around alternative possibilities, surviving, if they did, at the cost of inner disintegration.

Under prolonged pressure, guerrilla war terror often led to psychic numbing in its victims. Senseless destruction could overwhelm the required personal and cultural security to such a degree that people felt emptied of inner meaning. In many letters, one reads of what appears on the surface to be an almost matter-of-fact acceptance of violence as a new, accepted norm. In the summer of 1864, J. W. Woods, a schoolteacher from Newton County in southwestern Missouri, wrote to his favorite aunt that horse stealing and robbery had become ordinary experiences "at night and by day" and that the young men were out fighting, preying on the "Old Men, and boys," who were the only males left on the farms. "Things are in such a commotion here & if no one is killed we think it is not of much interest & we hear of some outrage almost every day. There is a great excitement here but I don't know if it is for anything or not." Civilians "are the prey of both parties. . . . Now and then [guerrillas] kill a man. There have been two or three such characters brought in and shot—informally of course." In these letters, Woods also discussed crops and offered his aunt condolences on her sister's (his mother's) death from natural causes. Another Missourian wrote a friend from Bolivar in south central Missouri in 1864, "Times are about as usual in this county. Occasionally we hear of a man being shot or a horse stolen. No houses have been burnt recently. Recently we have begun to think times tolerably quiet. Old Man Staley was shot a few days ago, since has died. I have enquired in regard to Hy Litton but hear nothing of his being killed. He is reported in the neighborhood of home." From the Kansas side of the border, Samuel Ayres wrote a friend in 1863, "The most we have to complain of is the operations and depredations of the bushwhackers and the Red Legs. They pay us a visit occasionally and levy a tax to the amount of one or more horses—Sometimes plunder houses—run off cattle—kill a few men and burn some houses."[67]

These letter writers may have been adopting a stance filled with bravado and coolness in order to defend themselves against the strong emotions guerrilla war aroused in them. By this point in the war they simply may have adjusted to the violent new norms and so were just reporting the facts on war as they would on crops, gossip, and the weather. It is of course possible that both these responses were going on simultaneously in these men. However, I also believe there was a note of black humor and ironic understatement beneath the intentionally muted sense of horror expressed here. In part they seem to be saying: times have become so terrible that a death on my doorstep is neither abnormal nor novel any more. Violence no longer provokes a response. Peace is unimaginable, and old standards of justice and loyalty are now meaningless—referring to them as values would only frustrate me and deepen my hurt. If I can harden myself to the mayhem and death surrounding me, perhaps the inside of me can survive, to be revived if peace ever returns. It is entirely within "their" power to come and destroy me physically, but until they do, I will surround myself with a desensitizing shell to keep my essential self intact, even when the world as I knew it has gone mad and force has become all.[68]

Accompanying this psychic numbing was a bottomless greed—for food, for clothing, for ornaments, for self-service at the expense of all others, and above all, for money. A Missourian exiled to Paris, Texas, commented, "I have gotten to believe that there is a kind of madness taken possession of or giving them a great propensity for lying. . . . Everybody is run mad after money. Money is all they care for or think about."[69] It does not seem implausible that the instability and deprivation of such a war would produce an obsession with security. Nothing or no one out there could be trusted. A desperate shoring-up process often ensued, as if money and material things could fortify the self and compensate for the enormous threats the surrounding world now offered in such abundance.

Numbing and a sense of personal isolation were related to real and imagined fears that one was being targeted for destruction by hostile individuals and gangs "out there." Arrests and rough treatment frequently followed some process of being singled out by someone unknown. One can see from petitions to higher authorities written by some victims that they had guessed the probable identities of their accusers. In 1863 H. L. Brolaski of Kinswick near St. Louis was disarmed by a militia detachment while his neighbors were not. He knew why this had happened, and he wrote to the militia commander. "The reason arises from the personal enmity of a man by the name of Zeigler, keeper of a drinking saloon at this place," and the long-term, malevolent leading Unionist of the region. "He has made false statement," to the lieutenant who arrested Brolaski, just as "he has attempted to influence other former comrades of this post. . . . The whole thing is done to annoy me and drive me away. He has openly threatened to do so—or harm me if he can."[70]

A former friend or even family member sometimes carried on a personal vendetta by informing Union authorities that the object of his grudge was traitorous. Emma Tizer of Arrow Rock in central Missouri appealed to the Missouri provost marshal for the release of her husband who had been jailed seven months without a trial. The cause of his imprisonment was clear to her: "Last Fall my husband and my Brother-in-Law William Foddree . . . fell out in a settlement and came near fighting and Foddree being a coward was afraid that my Husband would whip him some day for his abuse—so he thought that the best way for him to do was to go to Huntsville and swere fauls against my Husband," accusing him of being a sometime guerrilla.[71]

In other instances, the person charged with disloyalty had been named by a source unknown to him. In some respects this form of accusation must have been even more frightening than one coming from a known source, for the victim only knew that someone had denounced him or her, often for unknown reasons, making it all the more difficult to fight back. Which of one's many actions was the fateful one? Which person out there bore such hatred? In October 1863, Thomas E. Birch received a circular in his mailbox denouncing him as a traitor; he realized that he must have been placed on some Unionist blacklist. He had continued to be an open Democrat while in the militia, and in every other way he was a loyal Unionist. "We have a class of men that declares every man to be disloyal who disagrees with them or who disagrees with the administration of Mr. Lincoln." Although Birch agreed that in wartime "captious opposition" to the government was wrong, he continued to believe "temperate criticism" of political policy was the very demonstration of American liberty.[72]

L. H. Rogers, a medical student and returned Confederate soldier who had taken the oath of allegiance to the United States, escaped from a military prison and wrote from his hiding place to the Union district commander, Brigadier General Odon Guitar, "I did not escape because I was perpetrator of some dark crime and was trying to evade the justice of the law, but because I was imprisoned for nearly a week without letting know the charges you had against me and without giving me a fair and impartial trial or allowing me to meet my accuser face to face. I have not the remotest idea what I was arrested for. The oath I had taken I have never violated." Rogers offered to surrender if General Guitar would tell him the charges and trial procedures which would be followed.[73] Rogers knew his civil rights and due procedures in criminal cases. However, under martial law the military operated under other terms—basically a citizen would be arrested if someone of sufficient military authority believed evidence against or rumors about him. Any faceless personage could destroy one's reputation or land him in jail. Guerrillas also produced their blacklists, formed in just the same haphazard manner. Appeal against their lists was even more difficult.

It seemed to many beleaguered citizens that there were not merely individual vendettas being carried on but also large criminal conspiracies unfolding which might at any time overwhelm the whole community. Suspicious of would-be elites, nineteenth-century Americans were prone to find conspiracies everywhere even in peacetime. Of course both guerrillas and the Union military had circles of supporters, and each side appeared to the other to have well-oiled secret organizations aiding combatants and ferreting out enemies. The captain of the home guard of Miller County in south central Missouri in 1864 was convinced that a pro-southern Masonic lodge gone underground had designated seven of his men, all members of the Union League, for capture and execution by the guerrillas. "We have noticed some secret moves as though there was meeting somewhere in the country. We do not know of any Union men who have taken a part with them. Their meetings often last all night."[74]

Civilians and soldiers were frequently shot by guerrillas who then melted back into the civilian population. Guerrillas clearly could exist only with widespread civilian aid. Therefore there must be, the logic of deep fear went, some general criminal conspiracy of which sporadic crimes were but the most obvious expression. Thousands of everyday behavioral quirks by one's newly suspect neighbors seemed to add up to a stealthy larger plan, which one day might burst into a victorious rebellion. G. O. Yeiser, who wished Union methods to become more draconian in central Missouri, noted all the signs: "What means the riding through the country at all hours of the night—in moonshine & *darkness*—in rain & shine as well as in clear weather? What means the numberless squads passing in every direction through the country, shunning and avoiding the public roads and towns? What means the many bands of armed men encamping at the various points—appearing and disappearing as if by magic?—What means the stealing of horses all through the country? . . . What means the quietness—self-satisfaction, good humor & pleasant mien and bearing of the

Secesh (traitors) in the community? & their insolence? What means the number of secessionists when they threaten to express themselves in a manner to indicate that they will get the upper hand in our midst?"[75] A cheerful manner might foreshadow rebellion. Presumably a scowling face would also be an indicator of insurrection, which meant that every man Yeiser did not know for a fact to be loyal would appear disloyal to him, so anxious had he become.

For Yeiser and many men like him, all these furtive little signs added up to a potential popular uprising, when the southern conspirators would rise as one to destroy the Union. Some Southerners hoped that Confederate invasion would lead to such a rising and were surprised when it did not occur during General Sterling Price's 1864 invasion. Indeed, during that summer several thousand men joined in the rebel cause, including several Paw Paw militia units in the area around Kansas City. But in general, fears of organized conspiracy were widespread, dividing the community and leading to reprisals designed to nip rebellion in the bud. The smallest tic in speech or glance, which normally would not be noticed, now might be taken to mean something terrible. This heavy freighting of ordinary interaction was one more way terror undermined peacetime culture.

In response to the fear of conspiracies and vendettas in this setting of widespread terror, many citizens lashed out in vengeance after suffering at the hands of attackers. Their responses rounded the circle of violence begetting violence. Brigadier General Clinton B. Fisk, commander in the badly divided St. Joseph area, put the matter clearly when he wrote in 1864 about the inversion of the Golden Rule: "There is scarcely a citizen in the county but wants to kill someone of his neighbors for fear that said neighbor may kill him."[76]

Citizens would turn on each other, often anonymously, as in the case of "A Friend" who wrote to the provost marshal in St. Louis, "This is to inform you of the disloyalty of the Clerk of the steamer Nebraska. He is seen to carry the rebel mail down on the boat every trip. . . . They are all rebels on the boat except the Pilot. I hope it will be tended to. He is doing the government more harm than twenty men could do."[77] It is impossible to discern the motive of "A Friend" of the Union or to know whether the provost marshal followed through on this missive. Whatever private wrong or political act might have led to this complaint, "A Friend" was using the wartime situation to get even for some real or imagined grievance.

Many Missouri militia troops joined the armed forces or used their military status to get even for wrongs done to them and their families. Guerrillas would frequently attack farms, specifically when they knew that the men were away in the Union forces. These attacks added more fuel to the anger of the militiamen. Lieutenant Colonel T. A. Switzler concluded about the Union garrison in Warsaw in 1863: "Many of the soldiers are in the neighborhood of their homes, and all have private wrongs to avenge, and it is plain to see the effect."[78]

In 1859 F. F. Sheppard and Tom Whelan of Independence had a fight. On the morning of April 28, 1862, Lieutenant Whelan and his Union cavalry unit entered the Widow Hudspeth's house where Sheppard (also a loyal Unionist) lived. Sheppard later deposed that Whelan had said at gunpoint, "get-up here Sheppard God damn you and dress yourself God damn you I am agoing to kill you. I asked him what he was agoing to kill me for. He said for shooting him. I told him that I would never have shot him if he had not come at me with an axe. . . . I told him not to kill me but if I had done anything wrong to take me up to town and deliver me up to the Officers. He said no by God the Officers had no use for such men as me, that he was agoing to kill me. Tom then made me get down on my knees and ask his pardon. They then took me out into the yard." While Whelan was organizing the firing squad, Sheppard ran round the house and escaped, about twenty-five shots being fired at him as he fled.[79]

Unionist civilians could often manipulate the anger of local militiamen, directing them into settling personal scores. Brigadier General Egbert B. Brown in Jefferson City in 1863 made a clear analysis of this amplification of vengeance. "Prompted by feelings of revenge in the soldiers, and by the counselings of the citizens, who do not fail to use whisky if necessary to make soldiers more reckless, the most heartless murders have been committed."[80] One can almost hear the drunken late night conversations of resentful citizens who worked on equally resentful soldiers to take their shared grievances out on those goddamn secesh down the road.

At times the desire for revenge was expressed in a partially sublimated form. David B. Braden wrote both his desires for revenge and his failure to act on those desires in his diary on January 26, 1864. "Last night Jacob Wilson of Company E of a Union regiment stayed with us. I believe he deserves killing. He acknowledge that he had robed Union familys and I think that he was one of the Devils that helped rob Father in July. I felt very much like shooting him. It is still very warm."[81] Even in his diary, Braden censored the desire to kill in revenge, because he had not become a killer, even of a man who had probably wronged his own family, and even in a society in the midst of war.

Notwithstanding the grief and anger of having had family members killed by guerrillas, many men could not openly seek vengeance. Something restrained them from destroying as their loved ones had been destroyed. Sanford Bullock, a militia private who lived in Howard County on the Missouri River, wrote of his grief to the general of his region. His brother John, a fine Union man, "was captured some few days since by a band of guerrillas who shot him all to pieces & threw his body into the Missouri River." They took all his money, "leaving a mother & two sisters to live upon the charity of the public," Sanford's salary as a private being insufficient to keep them. "You may think it strange of one who occupies such a low station in life as myself for writing to you," Sanford wrote to the exalted general. But what he sought was permission to exact revenge on his enemies. "There are many in this County who are daily feeding the bushwhackers & I feel that I ought to take a horse from some of them in retaliation for [their] horrible deeds of carnage." Sanford then placed his desire to avenge a personal wrong in a larger context of legal and moral legitimacy. Bushwhackers and their abettors "say there is no law and where there is no law they say there is no transgression. I long to see the day come when the principles involved in the constitution will be carried out to the letter," and all those who are guilty of treason "exterminated." Sanford asked his general to sanction revenge for him. "Give us the priviledge we pray you to make the rebels who have brought this civil war upon us to feel all the horrors of the same. Ask yourself the question that if it was your Bro. what would you do? I dare say you would avenge the death of the Bro. with the blood of at least one hundred Rebels."[82]

Here is the agony of a young man caught between his desire for vengeance growing from personal rage and his desire to live in a lawful "civilized" community. In rural Missouri, blood revenge was the dominant mode in which military participants viewed their personal relationship to guerrilla war. Yet Sanford Bullock and others still expressed the desire for a just war as at least in part the proper response to wrongs done to one's kin. Bullock sought to square his wishes for redress by acting as a disciplined and properly subordinated soldier, appealing to his general— the grandest authority figure he probably had ever seen—to mandate a personal act as part of the larger, legitimized struggle for the Union. Not uniquely, Sanford was caught between a view of the vendetta as a means to settle scores in a traditional community and membership in a modern army which should provide the avenue for redress. Rather than responding lawlessly, he asked his general to suspend the rules or at least bend them enough to make legal what he knew to be illegal retaliation against civilians for acts committed by specific, unknown guerrillas. The general had no such independent legal power, though in a *de facto* sense local commanders did alter concepts of legality in their everyday orders. However, Sanford did not know this, and he appealed to General Guitar as *the* paternal authority, asking him for something he might have guessed could not be granted by any mortal man. In his grief, Sanford had to appeal to some such figure in order to externalize and gain some control over powerful emotions. I do not know how Sanford behaved subsequently. At some time in the war he had the power to avenge his brother against someone he construed to be the enemy. Whether he continued to sublimate these feelings or acted them out is something we will never know.

Most often vengeance seems to have come far more simply to most civilians and citizen-soldiers—*les talionis* continued to apply, the golden rule, the Constitution, and brotherly love notwithstanding. Yet Missourians were wracked with internal tensions as to appropriate responses, and they desired to maintain a framework more abstractly just than an eye for an eye. Not everyone who killed became a cold-blooded killer.

The Death of the Peculiar Institution

In 1861 slavery was an organic and accepted if increasingly marginal part of Missouri society; by 1865 it was dead. Put more positively, by 1865 sláves were liberated. The most politically and socially revolutionary aspect of the Civil War, emancipation served as a marker of the social transformation of Missouri from a southern-leaning society to a northern-tilted one. Slaveholders were stripped of their most valuable capital goods, slaves became active in determining their own futures and white Missourians had to adjust to a new set of race relations. Emancipation was a potent symbol of the disintegration of prewar Missouri society.

Attitudes toward the peculiar institution divided Missourians during the war. Conservative Unionists as well as secessionists supported slavery, while unconditional Unionists opposed slavery as well as secession. At the start of the war, Abraham Lincoln, himself something of a conservative Unionist (if mainly for tactical reasons), sought to placate conservative Unionists in the border states by not attacking slavery where it existed in order to retain their loyalty, critical to the preservation of the Union. He long refrained from joining forces with radical Unionists who from the onset of the war had attempted to make antislavery a test of true Unionism. This division among Unionists was especially bitter in Missouri, leading to much internecine fighting. For example, J. H. Ellis of Chillicothe in north central Missouri bitterly complained in 1863 that the local commander, Brigadier General Odon Guitar, was enforcing slavery, "playing the devil at St. Joe." Guitar had "a guard unit stopping negroes who attempt to cross the line into Kansas—arrest them—sends them back to their masters," and he had "had a negro shot *in the river*" who had free papers. If Guitar was presuming to "dictate" for the district, Ellis concluded, "there are some people would prefer removing to that America whereof Mr. Lincoln is President."[83] Ellis doubtless exaggerated, but he represented a growing number of Unionists in 1863, emboldened by the issuance of the Emancipation Proclamation, although it did not apply to Union slave states, who believed that actively defending slavery was tantamount to fighting for the South. Guitar held a traditional and by then deeply challenged position on slavery. If the war was a national one, Ellis wished to align the local aspect of it to the broader war aims rather than having Missouri defended for traditional but by now outmoded purposes.

In 1861 the vast majority of Missouri Unionists were traditionalists on the slavery issue. By 1864, judging from the state elections that year, the radicals had won the majority of the white population to their side. The radical state government officially emancipated Missouri slaves on January 11, 1865. By then antislavery had become a much more widely accepted test of Unionism. Accompanying this shift in attitudes toward slavery were glimmerings of alterations of white attitudes toward blacks, which earlier were unanimously racist.

Right from the start of the war, the institution of slavery was undermined, both by military action and by slaves freeing themselves. On August 30, 1861, in declaring martial law over the entire state, General John C. Frémont, then commander in St. Louis, declared all slaves free. Though Lincoln compelled Frémont to rescind the order and though the Unionist provisional governor declared that no Union action would ever interfere with slavery, Frémont's action articulated a previously unthinkable proposition concerning the survival of the institution in Missouri.[84]

Also at the start of the war, Kansas troops began raiding the western border counties of Missouri and encouraged slaves to follow them to freedom in Kansas. On November 15, 1861, in Kansas City, Illinois Private Dan Holmes recorded in a letter the speech given by the ideologue of Charles R. Jennison's regiment, John Brown, Jr. "He said he was going to take all the negroes he could from the secessionists, arm them and form regiments of them and set them to fighting, and if the government won't sustain him he will go on his own hook. He is a bold, rash, impetuous desperado. He has a flag being made at Boston with a life size portrait of Old John Brown upon it." Ushered by Kansas troops, perhaps as many as 2,000 male slaves fled to Kansas during the first six months of the war, enough men to fill two colored regiments. The First Kansas Colored Infantry, commissioned on January 13, 1862, was one of the first black regiments in the Union army. Thousands of other slaves ran off, wandering the countryside, often in the train of Union troops who both cared for them and exploited them.[85]

Union officers and men, even negrophobic ones, generally believed, though not always correctly, that slaveholders were their enemies and that depriving enemies of their labor force would injure them economically and psychologically. Indeed, following the lead of Ben Butler, they commonly referred to escaped slaves as contraband—supplies of the belligerents. In the context of this guerrilla war where bushwhackers blended into the citizenry and so few whites could be counted on to help fight the bushwhackers, Union soldiers learned that blacks provided the most trustworthy military information. Soldiers understood that the *quid pro quo* for black informers was freedom and some protection, and therefore they usually sought to protect their valuable new sources. The ironic fact that Union soldiers could trust those black slaves they despised and not their white brothers and sisters also caused them to raise their estimate of the black character. This process amounted to a lesson in practical abolitionism for many Union troops.

A. J. McRoberts, a Saline County Unionist, wrote his wife that their neighbor, Mr. Manfrew, recently "came very close to losing his scalp." General Benjamin Loan's men "would have killed him if they would have found him. He caught a negro that was on his way to Loan to report on the rebels, and gave him a thrashing, he must have hit the negro a hundred licks & they say you'll tell the demn feds will, you, & Loan's men got hear of it and it made them desperate mad." Giving information, which they knew was their most valuable possession, was for many slaves the route to self-liberation. As the war progressed, more and more Union commanders provided protection as a matter of course to black informers, and the exchange of information for freedom was institutionalized. One can see this transition in the request of Lieutenant Colonel Arnold Krekel to his commander on March 10, 1862. His men had just broken up a guerrilla band, killing three including "the notorious Tid Sharp. . . . A negro boy gave valuable information in conducting the command, and I would ask for permission to retain him until the war is over, as he cannot safely return."[86] Later in the war, field commanders like Krekel would simply assume authority to free slaves they encountered.

As the war deepened, increasing numbers of Union soldiers came to see slaveholding as treason, morally as well as practically taking the side of blacks. Ephram J. Wilson, a slaveholding farmer who lived near Palmyra in northeast Missouri, complained in the summer of 1863, "About ten days ago a hired negro man in my employ left my premises without any cause whatsoever and carried away with him by force a small boy, a slave belonging to me." Wilson took his revolver, a family keepsake, and unsuccessfully went in pursuit of his property, who he heard later was in Colonel Edward A. Kutzner's camp. A few days later, at 2 A.M., about one hundred Federal troops rode up to his house demanding his pistol, ransacking his house, and "threatening to search my wife's person unless the pistol was produced." He was certain, probably correctly, that the Negroes had informed on him. Feeling outraged, wanting the return of his pistol and his slave, Wilson then called on the provost marshal in Hannibal "to make complaint and he bluntly remarked to me that 'any man would hold a slave with very few exceptions is neither a Christian, a patriot or a loyal citizen.' "[87] The obtuse Wilson wrote up this recital of complaint and sent it to the district commander, still hoping for redress from a higher authority. He continued to believe that any honorable man would share his outrage at this blatant military theft of his private property and the besmirching of his honor. He did not comprehend the general shift in Union attitudes from seeing blacks as someone else's property to re-envisioning them as holders of valuable information and of their own personhood.

Union troops often found enjoyment in their role as protectors of escaped slaves. In July 1862, Wisconsin Cavalryman Stanley Lathrop wrote his parents about his regiment's march into northern Arkansas. "We are the first Federal troops who have ever been in this part of the state. Almost all the rich plantation owners have fled as usual, and their negroes are beginning to come to us, often riding to us, often riding a mule or horse of their master. Some of the owners have tried to get them back but it was no go. Col. [Edward] Daniels says he did not persuade them to run away and he will not return them as the Fugitive Slave law privilege of *habeas corpus* etc are suspended."[88] For this Union colonel, slaves were no longer objects of property law. By coming into Union lines they acted as free men and women, and he would not return them against their wills to a status of unfree property.

Also relatively early in the war, Charles E. Cunningham, sheriff of Johnson County in west central Missouri, was informed that a large number of slaves were going to accompany Federal troops when they withdrew from Warrensburg by rail. Cunningham reported this to Major Charles Baunzhaf, the Union commander, who told Cunningham to retrieve the slaves by coming out four miles from town where the train would stop. Cunningham gathered a posse of six men and rode out to the train. Accompanied by the major, the sheriff gathered up a group of the slaves, had his posse act as their guard, and rode on looking for more. "I found one more and was taking her back to the others, when I met them released from the guard. The men who I had left as guards informed me that the Major after leaving me told the slaves in their hearing and that of his men that if they did not want to go back I could not make them. I undertook to catch one of them when a large number of guns were drawn on me and the negroes released, with threats made against my life as well as that of my men with me. This was done without the Major attempting to quiet the men although I had gone out at his own request."[89]

Sheriff Cunnningham represented the good citizens of Johnson County in a straightforward, traditional manner: many of them were slaveholders and he was simply protecting their property. He appealed to H. R. Gamble, the provisional governor, a conservative Unionist who had sought in his official pronouncements to protect both the Union and the institution of slavery, thus sharing Sheriff Cunningham's position. Cunningham had come up against military forces who, as was typical of the organized military units as opposed to local militias, were more committed to antislavery than was their major. It is possible that Major Baunzhaf had sought to prevent a riot in Warrensburg by misleading Sheriff Cunningham, inviting him with duplicitous intent to reclaim the slaves four miles outside of town. Baunzhaf might have been entrapping Cunningham with a plan designed to deceive him and hurt him. It is more likely, if Cunningham's report was accurate, that Baunzhaf changed his mind about allowing the return of the Warrensburg slaves, responding to the overwhelming opinion of his men. Certainly the troops vigorously opposed the sheriff; when they saw what was happening, they drew their guns, making the return of the slaves impossible whatever their major might have intended.

For the slaveholders, the world was being turned upside down. They were losing their property and their means to future wealth; they were losing their traditional control over blacks who were, they believed, potentially dangerous insurrectionaries; they were losing their sense of their own standing in their communities as men of station and property. They responded with a combination of exasperation, resignation, fear, and anger to what they saw. For them, as the old country expression went, the top rail was going to the bottom and the bottom rail was going to the top.

Exasperation and bitter humor characterized the manner in which James L. Morgan, a tobacco merchant who lived in Glasgow on the Missouri River, dealt with the gradual loss of his slaves. He had come to Missouri from Virginia in 1859 and in 1863 wrote back to an old friend, encouraging him to pay a visit. "We have plenty to feed you on—and at present have servants enough to wait upon you. Don't know how long we will have them, however, we had 8 to run off last week—the negroes are leaving this section fast—when I came to this state I sold most of my negroes and of course my Father thought it a very bad move—I am satisfied now that the only bad part of it was that I did not sell them all."[90] Morgan was proud that he had been shrewd enough to have cut his losses in slaves before the war. He also regretted the possibility that soon he might not have enough "servants" (so much more genteel a word than slaves) to be able to guarantee his Virginia gentleman visitor a gracious reception. He dealt with his loss in a refined manner, using humor rather than outright anger.

Margaret J. Hayes described the Kansas jayhawking of her property in 1861 in Westport near Kansas City in a similarly measured tone. The Kansans filled her carriage with loot and her slaves and drove off west. "It was very aggravating to see [the carriage] driven up to the door and to see [my slaves] jump into it and drive off."[91] The slaves seemed so eager to depart; that did rub salt into the wounds.

Some slaveholders were swept with fear of retaliation from their ex-slaves. Rumors of impending raids pushed some of them toward panic. In October 1862, J. B. Henderson from Louisiana, a Mississippi River town, wrote to James O. Broadhead, the conservative Unionist U.S. district attorney in St. Louis, "Many people are shuddering over negro insurrections and the terrible outrages of negro freedom." In 1863, further west on the Missouri River in Lafayette County not far from Kansas City, Richard C. Vaughan wrote to Broadhead about the widespread fear that Negro regiments were being formed in Kansas for the express purpose of invading and devastating Missouri slaveholding areas like Vaughan's county. "Our wives and daughters are panic stricken, and a reign of terror as black as hell itself envelops our county." That terrible fear of slave rebellion, accompanied by fears of the violation of white women which white males projected onto black men, now seemed to be in the process of actually unfolding in the form of the onward march of black Union regiments.[92]

Some former slaveholders greeted the threatening new racial scheme of things with anger and violence, taking revenge on the slaves they were about to lose or on former slaves. On January 28, 1864, Jim, now a Union soldier, with his squad of six men, approached William C. Reynolds, his mother's former master, asking for her clothing and for tobacco he said was due her. According to two white witnesses, "Mr. Reynolds talked very friendly" and then without provocation, seized his gun and called out to his three sons, who stepped out of the house and began firing their shotguns. The other black soldiers fled, but Jim fell. Reynolds and his sons then went up to him and shot him twice in the head, finishing him off.[93]

Lynching of blacks commenced in Missouri at the end of the war. If blacks were to be free, many whites believed they had to leave the region or else be hanged, as they were impermissible in the community as other than utterly subordinated slaves. A bushwhacker, James H. Jackson, sent "general orders" to one farmer in Ralls County in northeast Missouri, "my garrilis is heard that you have a cople of famallely of negros settle on your plase. . . . If you dont make dam negroes leve there ride away I will hang the last negro on the plase and you will fair wors for we cant stand the dutch and negros both."[94] Germans, generally considered the worst "nigger lovers," were themselves considered foreign elements to be purged from the properly American community. But free blacks were the greatest threat, and lynching was one immediate response to their appearance in large numbers at the end of the war.

The maintenance of clear color lines in public places, particularly in cities, was another means to attempt the reassignment of black freemen to their properly subordinate place at the bottom of the social scale. One can read of what might be called proto-segregation in St. Louis during the war. On the morning of November 16, 1864, S. F. Aglar, a railroad agent, boarded a streetcar with his wife and the wife and daughter of a Union colonel in order to attend an orphans' fair. "We found a squad of soldiers on the platform and several negro women in the car. The ladies of course objected to ride in the same car with negroes" and they upbraided the conductor, who "said he would make them ride on the platform." Aglar, the ladies, and the conductor agreed on what would be appropriate new racial protocol. However, the captain of the soldiers, characterized by Aglar as German and drunken, did not agree with racial segregation, "saying that the colored woman had as much right in the car as white people." The captain finally consented to the displacement of black women but "appeared greatly exasperated at us because our ladies objected to ride with colored women." Arriving at the corner of Broadway and Franklin, the captain suddenly ordered his men off the car and dragged Aglar down to the street by his coat collar, took his name, and threatened him with future arrest. Aglar wrote this story to General William S. Rosecrans, commander in St. Louis, expecting him to punish this offensive German.[95]

Segregation, reinforced with physical intimidation and lynching, would triumph in the long run. However, in 1864 there was no consensus among whites that this would be the appropriate institutional reconstruction. There was justification for black liberation in the eyes of some whites, and former slaveholders and negrophobic whites, no doubt numerically dominant, had not yet put the Negroes back into their "place."

Whatever the eventual postwar outcome, for blacks themselves fleeing a master, actively joining the Union cause by providing information, and aiding or entering the army could be, if frightening, an exhilarating act of self-liberation. One can imagine the pleasure it gave sixty-seven-year-old escaped slave Paris Bass to swear in a deposition to Union authorities against his longtime master, Eli Bass, that the notorious outlaw Bill Anderson, not once but many times, spent the night on the Bass farm in Calloway County. "He always rode a sable horse. I knew the horse & could tell his nicker."[96] Eli Bass surely was punished severely because of Paris Bass's testimony, and the former slave was able to enjoy a revenge unavailable to slaves before the war.

On August 8, 1864, at Jefferson City, a former slave named Jackson took the stand as the sole witness for the state in the court-martial of his former mistress, Fanny Houx of Lafayette County in west central Missouri, who was being tried for entertaining and feeding guerrillas. On a Monday morning five weeks earlier, Jackson had been out plowing when he noticed "a parcel of horses around the well." When he went down to the house for breakfast he observed "some wash pans and a couple of towels in the yard." As he sat by the kitchen waiting for his meal, his mistress "came down the steps out of the dining room and observed to me that I had better go and watch for the 'feds.' She said they might come and get to fighting and some one or other get killed. Says I to her I don't care if they do. She says you don't? I says no Madam I don't. She (the accused) says I will tell the bushwhackers directly they come what you said right before your face. I said I dont care if you do, tell them." The twelve bushwhackers then came up to the house, and Fanny Houx told them what Jackson had said. "One stepped up and said God damn your black soul what do you mean talking that away. I said nothing." A second guerrilla said, "who is talking that talk. The other says the old nigger setting there, the Lady says. So he stepped up and drew his pistol and struck me on the head, and says the first thing you know you will be taken out and have your brains blown out." Fanny Houx then sent her son up the hill to watch for Feds "and said to the bushwhackers come up to breakfast, gentlemen. Come up to breakfast." After breakfast, one of the same guerrillas dragged Jackson to the center of the yard, stripped off his shirt, and took a hickory pole in both hands—"he just tip toed to it and come down on me the same as if he was beating an ox. He said to the others standing around, boys you've got nothing to do but cut hickories and fetch them to me as fast as I can wear them out." After the hickories, the guerrilla continued beating Jackson with a lap board. "He wore that out on me. He turned me loose [saying] I want you to go to the feds now, God Damn you so that I can slip in at the dead hour of the night and shoot you."

Jackson stuck to his story, even under cross examination by Fanny Houx's lawyer. In her deposition to the court, Houx claimed that Jackson harbored "a malicious spirit of revenge" toward her for her interceding earlier when Jackson had been beating his wife. Asked at the trial by Houx's lawyer if "you and your wife had not had some serious difficulties before those bushwhackers came . . . and whether Mrs. Fanny Houx did not interfere in favor of your wife," Jackson answered, "Yes sir, we had some words four or five weeks before. I slapped her twice with my hand. I thought she needed it. There was no bushwhackers there then and that had nothing to do with the bushwhacking scrape." Did Jackson bear hatred towards Mrs. Houx for her interference? "No sir." Houx also deposed that she opposed bushwhacking and had only fed the guerrillas when compelled to do so. Also in Houx's defense, Jacob A. Price, the sheriff of Lafayette County, then testified at the court-martial that he had known Jackson for eighteen years and would not believe him under oath. He also testified that Houx was a vocal opponent of bushwhacking. Price was also Houx's brother.

The panel of seven Federal officers believed Jackson and convicted Houx. They took the word of a black man, five weeks prior a slave, against the word of a white lady and an elected law-enforcement officer.[97]

The importance of such victories, which happened quite often when blacks went to Union military authorities, should neither be downplayed nor romanticized. Jackson and other slaves may have believed that there would now be equal justice for them. In the long run, this would not be the case; segregation and lynch law would soon enough become the agreed-upon method of racial domination in the white community. Yet for a tantalizing historical moment under the pressures of guerrilla war, the white power structure was indeed divided on the issue of race, and slaves like Jackson could deploy one party against the other. The violence of slavery had made it something of a training ground for surviving guerrilla wars: beatings were nothing new for Jackson. The most revolutionary social change in this war was the destruction of the slave system, and many slaves took their own freedom in acts of self-liberation which also debased and punished their former masters. Missouri blacks were the single group of civilians to gain something so positive during the guerrilla war. For many white Missourians, black gains were one more indicator of the collapse of their culture.

Flight

Unlike blacks who had little to lose when they ran to their freedom and the start of self-determined lives, most rural white Missourians lost a great deal during the war—male kin, property, security, decent communal relations—all the building blocks of a normal life. They had to lie and cheat and bear false witness just to survive. If there was enough terror applied and if the terror worked sufficiently on them, many Missourians could not sustain their compromised, fear-ridden lives; suddenly they fled their homes in panic. Sometimes by ones and two or by families, often by regions, hundreds of thousands of Missourians became war refugees, at times leaving whole counties desolated and depopulated. Some returned home after the immediate panic subsided and some at war's end, but thousands never returned.

News of the approach of large guerrilla bands or the Union army was sufficient to drive many potential victims away, at least until the immediate threat passed. In July 1861, Philip Welsheimer wrote back to his family describing the flight of many of the inhabitants from Mexico, Missouri, which took place in response to his Union regiment's march into town. He estimated that 500 or 600 of the 1,500 inhabitants remained. Many houses, especially the finest ones, stood empty, and in others only women, children, and Negroes remained. "You inquire for the men and the reply is that they have gone from home. The Union men here say that there is at least three hundred men from this town that are out in the brush skulking around like sheep-killing doggs for fear of some of Uncle Sams boys will get ahold of them."[98]

Wild rumors of Federal depredations, many of which were exaggerations of what was indeed very nasty Union troop behavior, preceded advancing units, frequently causing panic and flight in anticipation of their arrival. Wisconsin Private Stanley Lathrop wrote to his family of his regiment's march from Missouri south into Arkansas. "The inhabitants of Gainsville had almost all fled in terror from the approach of the 'Northern Hessians.' Here we first heard of those stories which have preceded us during all our hitherward march—that we were burning and robbing houses, destroying property, imprisoning or killing all males from twelve years upwards—and much more of the same trash."[99] Many Kansas and Missouri Union troops did reach the level of destruction unfairly attributed to this Wisconsin regiment. Rumors, coupled to a greater or lesser degree to actual threats, evoked panic in many people. Panic was an emotional reaction to perceived threats, not a measured analytic response to reality.

It was fearsome to flee, especially for those who had no kin to join elsewhere. One could carry little, and the roads were infested with bush-whackers waiting to rob loaded down passers-by. Leaving almost every-thing behind meant instant poverty as well as homelessness. Only enor-mous fears could fuel flight, and many stayed put, fearing leaving even more than staying. At the start of the war, one young Unionist wrote to his brother from heavily secessionist Independence, "All the people are leaving here that are for the Union *that can get away*. If I could get away from here I would go in a minute but there is no chance. I cant sell nor trade my property. I would sell it for half of what it cost me if I could. God only knows what these times are coming to. If I could raise a team, I would start from here tomorrow. Property is not worth anything." This young man could not sell his land to raise enough money for a wagon and team to carry his movable goods. If he left, he would have to leave all his wealth behind. "A friend of mine started for Iowa this morning— he wanted me to go with him very much—but no go. I expect I shall have to stop here and see it out."[100]

In many locales, most of the residents fled, and though the data are vague, it appears that some went back East and South to previous homes, if they were not in an active war zone. Some, of all political persuasions, went west to Texas, Colorado (a new territory attractive to Missourians from the end of the 1850s), California, Oregon, and during the gold rush of 1864 to the Idaho Territory. Others, a larger number, secessionist and Unionist alike, fled to Illinois and Iowa; while still larger numbers fled within Missouri to towns made relatively safe by sizable Union garrisons, especially to St. Louis, physically the most secure place in the state. How-ever, if they were without kin or good friends or a great deal of liquid capital, these refugees remained propertyless and homeless. Very large numbers spent weeks and months wandering the countryside with insuf-ficient food, shelter, and clothing. The towns and farms they left behind quickly became wastelands.

The grind of guerrilla war, coupled to the flight of politically like-minded neighbors, frightened and depressed those who remained. One young pro-southern woman, in a letter she left unsigned lest it be inter-cepted by vengeful Unionists, wrote her aunt, "nearly all of the southern families have left: Bettie Brown has gone but it is not known whether she went to her father or whether she went with Sarah Brown and Lee Cooper to Denver; it is supposed she went to her father. There have been various reports got out about your leaving so suddenly. . . . Amanda had started to go to Mrs. S. [but has] been taken prisoner, and [has] written you to come to her immediately. I would write you some other things—but I think it is best not in this letter at least." Another secessionist woman wrote to her husband in a Union military prison that she was thinking of going back to her family in Kentucky. "Times are gloomy, the Southerners have left and are still leaving this part of the country & are nearly all gone."[101]

Women and children who had been left behind and were frequently victimized when their male kin had gone off to the army or the brush fared worse as refugees. Armed bands of men could travel in greater safety and could take more with them. One Unionist from Montgomery County in east central Missouri noted in the spring of 1864 that "immigration to Idaho has commenced, and the class that are passing through here with few exceptions are all of the Southern sympathizing class, most of them being young hearty men. . . . They are armed with rifles & revolvers & have plenty of good mules, stock & money."[102] These may well have been guerrillas who were getting out of Missouri while they were still in good condition.

Other southern sympathizing Missourians joined Unionists in seeking out towns protected by sizable numbers of Union troops. P. J. Bond of Bolivar in southwest Missouri wrote from the safety of Columbia, a fortified Union military district command center, to a friend he called a fellow "exile" that he now was in a safe haven. In Bolivar, the local Union militia had been carrying on widespread reprisal raids against presumed southern sympathizers in response to guerrilla killings of their comrades. Amid more disciplined Union troops, Bond was relieved in his change of scene. "I feel considerable more like a free man (not a nigger). I walk the streets here *in broad open daylight*."[103] The release from continual fear which he had found in a well-protected Union army town where he was not known as a sympathizer was liberating for the moment, however much Bond had left behind.

If they re-established themselves comfortably, exiles often felt a certain smugness that they had made the right move. The tobacco merchant James L. Morgan wrote to his brother from New York City in 1864, offering him money. "Don't think we will ever want to live in Mo. again. Our information is that about all of the best people have left the county, our town Glasgow is nearly all burnt up—& many of the best citizens have been killed."[104] However, Morgan never did establish a business in New York and eventually returned to Missouri.

If one were not entirely coarsened by his or her experiences, flight became a part of war rather than an escape from it. Reports of war continued whether or not one went or stayed, refreshing terrible memories. From St. Louis, the southern sympathizer Sarah McDonald wrote her children early in 1865 that all the southern men were selling out and leaving, "some going one place and some to another." Whole regions "are being depopulated" of Union men who "are afraid to stay there and Rebel [who] are afraid also." She had heard of soldiers "killing [southern] men almost every day." Though she felt secure personally in St. Louis, she still shared the urge to flee. "I some times feel like I would like to be at Denver or some where else but when I reflect there is no place I can go that will make me forget this terrible war."[105] McDonald believed that the destruction visited upon her was an example of the violence visited upon all good citizens. In the final analysis, terror was an internal experience caused by external events. Even in the safety of St. Louis, even if she were to flee to Denver or the Sandwich Islands, she would not be able to escape the damage done to her by the guerrilla war. Through this personal damage, she was able to empathize with fellow refugees.

Soldiers on the march frequently commented on the desolation left behind where civilians had fled in panic. The vacated houses of a town just deserted held an eerie emptiness. Philip Welsheimer wrote his family about the strangeness of his regiment's march through northeast Missouri, "a fine country but nearly forsaken. The Rebels first drove off the Union men and since the troops have got in a great many rebels have left." In several towns "but two or three families" were left; everywhere were "fine brick houses & fine frame houses standing empty and some with the furniture in and one [with] dinner standing on the table."[106]

In long-abandoned rural areas and towns, guerrillas, Union troops, and wandering scavengers had devastated the land: dozens of soldiers recorded in their diaries and letters the scorching of vast deserted areas. For example, Private H. C. Crawford of the Third Missouri State Militia Cavalry wrote his mother from southern Missouri in 1862: "this is one of the roughest countrys I ever saw. . . . Uncle Sam would have made a good bargain to let the Secesh took this part of Missouri off his hands. There is a good many buildings bernt about here. I do not herar any talk about any secesh about here. In fact this country is about deserted."[107]

Frequently, in describing ravaged towns, soldiers compared former prosperity to current devastation with a moral lesson about war attached to the narrative. John A. Martin, a Kansas officer originally from Pennsylvania, wrote his sister about one town near Kansas City, "Westport was once a thriving town, with large stores, elegant private dwellings and a fine large hotel. Now soldiers are quartered in the dwellings and horses occupy the storerooms. The hotel was burned down three days ago. The houses are torn to pieces, plastering off, the mantles used to build fires, and doors unhinged. I presume the place will be burned as soon as the troops leave." Marching out of town, Martin observed the countryside, "crops ungathered, houses deserted, barns & stables falling to pieces, fences torn down and stock running loose and uncared for, are all around . . . I have been all over the country about here without meeting with a half dozen habital dwellings." Martin concluded that this destruction was the central meaning of civil war "terribly portrayed."[108]

As humans had built, so had they destroyed. What had been abandoned was then ruined. J. Freeman wrote in 1864 about Clay County, a long burned-over Kansas-Missouri border region, "this once beautiful and peaceable land is forsaken and desolated, ruined, and only fit to bats, owls, & cockralls to inhabit." Observers such as Freeman and Martin were also participants in the destruction. They would not have willed to have been so, and they wrote as if they were not personally engaged in the destruction, perhaps wishing to distance themselves from responsibility for their army's handiwork. They knew that the appropriate task for good people was to cultivate, build up, and then prosper from good works—which they expressed when recalling how fine this now war-ravaged countryside once had been. Now the cultivators had fled, and only scattered guerrilla and Union units remained to roam the burned-out country, dodging each other, picking each other off. An Iowa soldier wrote to his hometown newspaper about Salem, a "once pleasant country village" in south central Missouri: "Around us, we see the ruins of buildings, despoiled of doors, sashes, and everything movable. Others, among them the Court House—pierced with loopholes, evince former apprehensions of attack. Bands of guerrillas prowl about the neighborhood, committing occasional depredations. They are, however, kept in wholesome terror by Co. Q. 3rd Mo. Cav., stationed here, who make it a point to take as few prisoners as possible." This writer expressed both his horror at destruction and his acceptance of counter-terror as a normal mode of Union participation in guerrilla warfare. This was a new territory peopled by a set of actors with revised morals, a whole new world.[109]

When the terror began to subside, some citizens moved back to their old homes and began to rebuild. W. A. Wilson, who returned to Marshall at the end of 1864, wrote his wife that "the town looked like desolation itself, only 2 or 3 men could be seen in the place. Occasionally you could see a lone woman moving about or a child. The men had left the country, or were hid in the woods, or gone to Dixie. The future prospects of quiet in some parts of Missouri are anything but flattering." Though Wilson had returned, this town was no longer as he had once known it. "I am quite lonesome here. Most of my old aquaintances have left the place, and strangers have come in. There are 2 companies of soldiers here."[110] Soldiers and stragglers lived in the shell of Marshall.

Refugees on the roads and near Union camps were often literally in shock. After William C. Quantrill's blood-drenched sack of Lawrence on August 11, 1863, the citizens of the Missouri border counties knew terrible reprisals were both inevitable and imminent. A. Comingo wrote from Lexington on August 20, "the people are crazy from fear and terror with which their lives are filled . . . weeping and wailing like children." On August 25, General Orders #11 proclaimed that four of the Kansas-Missouri border counties were to be evacuated and burned. The citizens were ordered to move to resettlement areas next to Union military posts, where, the state provost marshal's agents reported, they were crowded into "delapidated outhouses" or in tents or in huts "constructed from the boughs of trees. . . . They are huddled together in the little villages at which posts have been established and are suffering from the want of food and the other necessities of life."[111]

Eighteen months later, some of the citizens of this district had returned home only to be continually battered by both guerrillas and Union soldiers. The district commander reported to St. Louis of their psychological state: "The worst feature in the country is the cowed and dispirited state of the people. All manhood appears to have gone out of them. Alike in fear of the soldier and the bushwhacker, all they ask is military protection of provost-marshals and the privilege of neutrality."[112] These war refugees were numb, depressed, and defeated by the massive dislocations of their lives and seemingly resigned to dark fates. In their despair they had turned to the Union, not out of a change of faith but as the only possible source of protection.

All over the state, refugees streamed toward Union troops for aid and protection. In February 1863, when the Nineteenth Iowa Infantry Regiment marched south through the Ozarks to Forseyth, civilians from Arkansas fled north to them. Private Timothy Phillips wrote in his diary about his reactions to the refugees. On February 22, he noted, "A large number of families from Arkansas have sought protection in our lines and as they are in a destitute condition arose of necessity, we furnished them with provisions." On February 25, "Refugees continue flocking to us and dare not return to their homes." On February 28, "Plenty of women in camp begging for rations." By March 19, "We have now here some two dozen women and not less than a hundred children—more or less—varying in age from two weeks to 15 years." On March 5, "Refugees are coming in daily. An order has been given to build a stockade around the court house. Large quantities of timber have already been got cut for the purpose." The Union regiment tried to offer protection against guerrilla attacks as well as to provide shelter. They were afraid of a Confederate attack on themselves. Phillips also wrote in his diary that every two or three days the Iowa troops would find a body floating in the river. There were dangerous enemies out there. As more and more refugees came into camps, Phillips, doubtless sharing the resentments of his regiment in general, began feeling put upon, particularly as he doubted the loyalty of many of the refugees. Referring to secessionists by one of their nicknames, he wrote, "Butternuts continue to flock in to us under various pretenses and draw rations for themselves and horses. It may be right but I do [think] our regiment is liable to be imposed on by these representatives of Arkansas." How could Phillips and his fellow soldiers know who was a friend and who a foe? Perhaps hidden secessionists would take Union bread and then organize an uprising from within the Forseyth stockade. After all, the Iowa troops were deep in enemy land. When a company of "Arkansas Rangers," Union guerrillas in Confederate Arkansas, arrived, Phillips remarked with great relief, "they are fine looking men and will make their mark." However, there were also Butternut spies in the midst of the refugees, two of whom the Iowa regiment found out by placing a counterspy in the guard tent with them. It was hard to ferret out the truth. "Several men and women . . . who have been loud in praises of the Union it is now ascertained beyond a doubt have been keeping up a regular communication between the rebels and our camp."

Whatever their prior loyalties and the state of his own fears, Phillips believed the refugees should be aided. After all, if they were helped, they might desert rebel principles and come back to the bosom of the Union. Phillips noted one reconversion: "Five rebel deserters from Little Rock came to us today and enlisted in Company K of our regiment. They were a different looking set of men after shedding their dirty butternuts and putting on a suit of Union clothes."

In April, receiving orders to join the Vicksburg campaign, the Nineteenth Iowa pulled out of Forseyth, burning the town, stockade, courthouse, and all. Phillips made no more mention of the refugees. Receiving them was less important than joining large-scale operations in Mississippi. In June, Phillips's regiment was at the railhead in Rolla, the district Union camp, awaiting transportation eastward. Phillips contrasted life in this safe garrison town to life as he had seen it in the Ozarks. "There is little here to indicate the desolation and misery that is sweeping over the entire state. Its streets are thronged with people each seemingly bent on his own thoughts or schemes of gain or emoluments. The business portion of the place is a crowded mart with throngs of eager purchasers or those wishing to dispose of their merchandise." For Phillips, greed-laden Rolla stood in absolute contrast to Forseyth. Out there in guerrilla land were bodies in the river and hungry, homeless refugees, killing and fearing being killed. Phillips had responded with fear and resentment but also with compassion to that condition. Here, at a railhead well protected by Union troops for strategic reasons, was an artificial boomtown which disgusted Phillips. For him, business as usual in these wartime circumstances was corrupt. Individuals in this haven only served themselves: having by accident escaped the horrors Phillips had seen, they refused to identify with the sufferings of nearby civilians so much like themselves, who had been ravaged by guerrilla war.[113]

During the summer of 1863, the Tenth Illinois Cavalry was also stationed in the Ozarks, at Cassville, fifty miles over the mountains to the

west of Forseyth, receiving large numbers of refugees. On July 30, the
Reverend Francis Springer, the regimental chaplain, set down on paper his
thoughts about "Incidents" of life in this refugee camp. "Refugees from
secession come into camp nearly every day . . . chiefly women and children. . . . Their wagons are usually loaded with bedclothes, wearing apparel, provisions, a few cooking utensils and such other articles of family
convenience as they could pack on or tie to the wagon. On getting within
our lines, rations are usually furnished them from the ample commissariat
of Uncle Sam. For want of houses, they either live in their wagons or in
tents made by spreading a few quilts over a pole resting at each end or on
forked stakes planted in the ground." Springer was appalled by the condition of the children. "Unwashed, half-clad & shoeless boys and girls are all
in pitiable abundance." Refugee women worked at chores until they were
exhausted. Springer was especially struck by several women driving crude
ox carts into camp, loaded with cakes and pies to sell to the soldiers. And
just outside "thievish brigands and secesh spies are hovering about our
encampment."

Earlier that week, "A wild man . . . was seen descending the adjacent
hill densely covered with trees. He seems an apparition suddenly revealed.
He is barefoot, hatless, scratched with briars & with no covering for his
nakedness but a coarse dark gray homespun blanket over his shoulders and
reaching halfway down his thighs. . . . His countenance is expressive of
extreme dejection." Since his arrival, "He refuses conversation, takes but
little food, & seems alike careless of the attention of friends & the threats of
foes. His constant posture from morning until night is sitting or crouched
on the floor of the guard house."[114] If bodies could flee, so could reason.

CHAPTER 3

OFFICIAL ATTITUDES

Official Union Policy

This guerrilla conflict truly was a spontaneous creation of the people, by the people, for the people, and against the people. It sprang up in Missouri and elsewhere in the border states right from the start of the Civil War and became a military and social fact. It gained importance sufficient to compel both the Union and Confederate governments to respond to it. Handed the conflict, both governments sought to define and limit guerrilla fighting, a form of war for which they had great contempt. Despising guerrillas for their wild lack of discipline, leaders on both sides also understood that such fighters had their uses, and when it was in their interest, both sides permitted and even encouraged them. Caught up in their own ambivalence, never in control of the fighters, the authority and credibility of official leaders crumbled. In guerrilla-infested areas the external, officially defined order they offered dissolved, and with this dissolution went popular faith in established values.

Military men and politicians in both Richmond and Washington tried to establish guidelines concerning guerrilla war. Missouri military headquarters in St. Louis attempted to construct policy from general pronouncements in Washington and in conjunction with promptings from the Missouri state government. On the Confederate side, those Missouri militia units which had defected from the Union and had gone south to join the regular Confederate army and the pro-southern government-in-exile worked in conjunction with the Trans-Mississippi Department Confederate command. Union departmental headquarters gathered information and advised the brigadier generals and colonels who attempted to direct the activities of scattered regiments in their districts through junior officers actually patrolling with men in the field. Most of the time, the Confederate military command was several hundred miles to the south of the guerrillas and could exercise no control whatsoever over them.

As this was a war without fronts or pitched battles, almost all of the fighting was done by units of men—from five to one hundred—operating essentially on their own, detached from higher military authority. Officers in the field had difficulties controlling their men, and when the lack of a clear policy became the basis for an inter-unit struggle, the problems were hammered out on the spot, and the outcome was relayed up the line of command. The commanders themselves were profoundly ambivalent about remaining within the law to fight the lawless, unconventional guerrillas, and their uncertainty was sensed by the men under them. They often gave conflicting signals, and the exigencies of immediate situations and the temperaments of the fighters led to a living, changing "policy," one which frequently lapsed into utter chaos.

National Union policy on the fighting of antiguerrilla war, promulgated in 1863 through the office of General Henry W. Halleck, general-in-chief, was written primarily by Francis W. Lieber, the German-American legal scholar. Halleck had been frustrated and disturbed by his experiences with guerrilla war as commander in Missouri over the winter of 1861–62. Somewhat of an intellectual, before the war Halleck had published a treatise on international law and war, in which he discussed guerrillas in only a vague and general way. Unsettled by the experiences he had had with bushwhackers in Missouri, wrestling with a variety of Confederate guerrillas, Halleck wrote to Lieber on August 6, 1862, requesting his advice on how to create a legal framework for guerrilla war in America.

Halleck was concerned with the spontaneous, disorganized guerrillas of the Missouri type, who also populated much of the upland country of the border states. He was also confronted by the larger and more disciplined detached Confederate cavalry units operating in northwestern Virginia under the command of John S. Mosby. Mosby's raiders usually operated independently of higher Confederate commanders, often behind Union lines. After a raid they would scatter and resume their civilian lives. However, unlike the Missouri bushwhackers, they had Confederate commissions and lines of command, wore Confederate uniforms into battle, took Union soldiers prisoner rather than executing them, and sometimes disciplined their appetites for the destruction of civilian lives and property.

In response to Halleck, Lieber attempted to construct a historically based typology of guerrillas, suggesting that different sorts merited different treatment. According to Lieber, the term "guerrilla," defined as a "party of light troops for reconnaissance, and opening the first skirmishes," came into use to characterize rural Spanish resistance to Napoleon during the Peninsular Wars. However, Lieber did not want Napoleon's behavior used as a precedent when responding to American guerrillas, for the Corsican "frequently substituted the harshest violence for martial usages." Napoleon considered all such fighters, whatever their association with a regular army, and whatever their degree of discipline, to be brigands fit only for immediate death.

For his part, Lieber sought to distinguish "regular partisans—distinctly authorized by their own governments . . . and of the main army of a belligerent," from irregular guerrillas—"small parties of armed country people . . . who resort to occasional fighting and occasional assuming of peaceful habits, and to brigandage . . . devastation, rapine or destruction." In this construct, Mosby was a "distinctly authorized" partisan, while the Missouri boys were mere brigands. Lieber described as "irregular" the Missouri-style bands which were "either self-constituted or constituted by the call of a single individual" and not under some general military law. "Its disconnection with the army as to pay, provisions and movements . . . and permanency" was representative of the "term guerrilla as now used." Other characteristics which made these bands outlaws included pillage, "intentional destruction for the sake of destruction, because the guerrilla chief cannot aim at any strategic advantages or any regular fruits of victory," spying, "necessitated murder, because guerrilla bands cannot encumber themselves with prisoners of war," and "general and henious criminality," because the fundamental disorganization of the band and the dependence of the leader upon the men of the band meant "little discipline can be enforced."

Often in history, Lieber wrote, when they had flourished uncontrolled, guerrillas had created such slaughter fields as those of the Thirty Years War and the religious wars in France, wars far more savage than the more delimited "regular wars in modern time." If not stopped quickly by harsh measures taken by regular armies, the "destruction, relapses and degeneracy" of a guerrilla war would proceed in a manner "fearfully rapid. It requires the power of the Almighty and a whole century to grow an oak tree; but only a pair of arms, an ax, and an hour or two to cut it down." Regular partisans, when "captured in a fair fight and open warfare," ought to be treated as other prisoners of war while "the so-called bushwhackers are universally considered, if captured, brigands and not prisoners of war." These savages were an offense to modern civilization and the cultural evolution of warfare and should be shot rather than taken captive as befitted proper, modern soldiers. However, for the good of the civilian population, this harsh universal law of punishment might undergo "relaxation or mitigation," if so decided upon "by the executive power, civil and military, or possibly by the legislative power."[1]

Following receipt of this learned discourse, Halleck asked Lieber to draft general instructions for Union armies in the field, which were reviewed by a board of officers and then issued as General Orders #100 on April 24, 1863. These instructions were an attempt to define martial law within the framework of modern war. "Military oppression is not martial law; it is the abuse of the power which that law confers." Sheer tyranny was wrong. "For the very reason that [the soldier] possesses the power of arms against the unarmed," he had every reason "to be strictly guided by the principles of justice, honor and humanity" and not by "cruelty." Soldiers should always recall that "Peace is [the] normal condition; war is the exception. The ultimate object of all modern war is a renewed state of peace." Lieber deeply believed that "civilization had advanced" and that Union soldiers were fighting a just war, not employing *lex talionis* but using decent, civilized means to obtain the higher end of an honorable peace. For example, private property could only be seized by dint of military necessity, and then proper receipts had to be given so the pillaged owners later could obtain indemnity. As for guerrillas, in these General Orders Lieber incorporated his distinction between uniformed Partisan Rangers, who when captured were to be treated as all other prisoners of war, and irregular guerrillas, who were "not entitled to the privileges of prisoners of war, but shall be treated summarily as highway robbers or pirates." In addition, Lieber defined civilians who gave military information to the enemy or voluntarily guided them as "war-traitors," whose punishment was to be death.[2] If he followed General Orders #100, the good Union officer would be draconian only toward guerrillas and their abettors and honorable toward everyone else.

In letters to Union civilian and military leaders in Missouri during the war, Abraham Lincoln generally demonstrated a shrewder and more subtle understanding of the scope of the problem concerning Union forces than did Lieber and Halleck. On May 27, 1863, giving general instructions to Major General John M. Schofield whom he had just appointed commander in St. Louis, Lincoln wrote, "Let your military measures be strong enough to repel the invader and keep the peace, and not so strong as to unnecessarily harass and persecute the people." Realizing the difficulty of that Solomonic task, Lincoln added, "It is a difficult *role,* and so much greater will be the honor if you perform it well."[3]

Lincoln knew that only a general who was a masterful actor could maneuver successfully among strife-torn Missouri Unionist political factions, not to mention deal with the unending guerrilla warfare in the countryside. With many of its citizens sympathetic to the South, many more neutralist, and almost none Republican, Missouri institutions replicated this shattered polity. In October 1863, writing a long letter to calm Missouri radicals, in the exasperated black humor so characteristic of him, Lincoln noted that the American Civil War presented a "perplexing compound" of stances toward the Union and slavery which had produced at least six identifiable Unionist factions in Missouri—"Thus, those who are for the Union *with,* but not *without* slavery—those for it *without,* but not *with*—those for it *with* or *without,* but prefer it *with*—and those for it *with* or *without,* but prefer it *without.* Among these again, is a subdivision of those who are for *gradual* but not for *immediate,* and those who are for *immediate,* but not for *gradual* extinction of slavery." Lincoln was not exaggerating—slavery was an immediate and divisive issue in itself among Missouri Unionists, and it was also a metaphor and example of a wide range of views on just what sort of society Missourians ought to build.

All these conflicting and committed views were for the Union, but, Lincoln added, "by reason of these differences, each will prefer a different way of sustaining the Union. At once sincerity is questioned, and motives are assailed. Actual war coming, blood grows hot, and blood is spilled. Thought is forced from old channels into confusion. Deception breeds and thrives. Confidence dies, and universal suspicion reigns." He continued, "Each man feels an impulse to kill his neighbor, lest he be first killed by him. Revenge and retaliation follow. And all this . . . may be among honest men only. But this is not all. Every foul bird comes abroad, and every dirty reptile rises up. These add crime to confusion. Strong measures, deemed indispensable but harsh at best, such men make worse by maladministration. Murders for old grudges, and murders for pelf, proceed under any cloak that will best cover for the occasion."[4] In this his closest analysis of wartime Missouri, Lincoln captured the bitterness of the guerrilla war. However, he did not deal with Missouri guerrillas or pro-southern civilians in any significant way, merely dismissing them as bad men who used the cover of rebellion for their evil, personal ends. For him, Missouri was one big factional battle run by men who let their ill will work its poison through their minds and their society.

Lincoln's advice to every succeeding general and political figure in Missouri was that good men ought to come to their senses. This or that policy change would be far less germane than a change of heart. Near the end of the war, Lincoln wrote to Thomas C. Fletcher, the new radical Unionist governor, "It seems that there is no organized military force of the enemy in Missouri and yet that destruction of property and life is rampant everywhere. Is not the cure for this within easy reach of the people themselves? It cannot but be that every man, not naturally a robber or cutthroat would gladly put an end to this state of things. A large majority in every locality must feel alike on this subject; and if so they need only to reach an understanding with one another. Each leaving all others alone solves the problem. And surely each would do this but for his apprehension that others will not leave him alone. Can not this mischievous distrust be removed?" Lincoln then called for old-fashioned town meetings. "Let neighborhood meetings be every where called and held, of all entertaining a sincere purpose for mutual security in the future, whatever they may heretofore have thought, said or done about the war or about anything else. Let all such meet and waiving all else pledge each to cease harrassing others and to make common cause against whomever persists in making, aiding or encouraging further disturbance. The practical means they will best know how to adopt and apply. At such meetings old friendships will cross the memory; and honor and Christian Charity will come in to help."[5]

The war was nearly over and Lincoln was tired. He had long believed that bad men and the badness in mankind had caused the strife in Missouri society and that Christian forbearance ought to pave the way for a social cure. Lincoln was internally divided. On one side was his deep melancholy, which reflected his fears of innate human evil. On the other side was his passionate hope for the potential of Christian charity, good will, and democracy, which for him made America the world's last best hope. In response to Lincoln's letter, Governor Fletcher replied that he would "diligently, faithfully, and honestly try the policy you support, letting none know my utter want of confidence in its success." Responding to the demands of his constituents, sharing their bitter rage towards the guerrillas and their civilian supporters, Fletcher wrote Lincoln that he was also preparing "the only other policy," he believed was available to him. "I have to say: That the destruction of life and property in every part of Missouri which has been going on for nearly four years and which is yet going on, is not the result of the immediate action of men who can be reached by any amicable propositions. The State being infested with thousands of outlaws who are naturally 'robbers' and 'cut-throats,' no good man desires to reach any understanding with them. . . . It would but madden the true men of this State to talk to them of reliance on the 'honor' and 'christian charity' of these fiends in human shape. . . . I am satisfied, Mr. President, that if you could see and fully understand what we have done and suffered in Missouri . . . you would agree . . . that we want no peace with rebels but the peace which comes of unconditional surrender to the authority of the law."[6]

In their private communications to St. Louis officials, national authorities were closer to the spirit of Fletcher's letter and Lieber's General Orders #100 than they were to Lincoln's forgiveness. For example, on July 24, 1862, the conservative Republican attorney general of Missouri, Edward Bates, wrote to the equally conservative Governor H. R. Gamble that Lincoln's cabinet had just discussed the question of the execution of guerrillas. They had agreed that they wanted quick courts-martial and executions, as otherwise "few or no courts martial would sit . . . but that the guerrillas which hereafter, for the most part, disappear (without specification). I shrewdly suspect that your best officers are already acting on the idea. And upon the whole, I am not sure that it is not the best; for I am persuaded that *speed* is quite as necessary as the *fact* of the punishment of such marauders."[7] Although expressing himself unclearly, whether from the desire to cover up his actual intentions, from uncertainty, or from fear of what he knew he meant, Bates, the nation's legal chief, was suggesting that guerrillas be shot on the spot when captured rather than be arrested. Wise field commanders would follow this practice, which neither they nor their superiors would ever declare in so many words to be policy. The ambiguity in orders from the very top suggests that the authorities knew that the policy they believed to be most efficient they also knew to be illegal. Such ambiguity was the heart of the signalling process from Washington, Lincoln's personal kindness notwithstanding.

Those who were shot on the spot were men whom Union soldiers declared to be guerrillas. This punishment was inflicted for many reasons, often on men who were neither guerrillas nor their supporters. Gradually, the ever increasing level of military brutality in Missouri became widely broadcast, by 1864 provoking the Union command in Washington to send out R. B. Marcy, inspector-general of the army, to report on the impact of the no-prisoners policy in Missouri. "These bushwhackers undoubtedly deserve the most severe chastisement for the atrocities they have committed," Marcy reported, "but when they surrender, it seems to me that they should be speedily taken before a competent tribunal and given the opportunity to prove their innocence before being executed. The existing practice enables evil-disposed soldiers to rob and murder loyal and inoffensive citizens under the plea that they were acting as bushwhackers, and it unquestionably tends greatly to demoralize troops." The practice of widespread executions had compounded guerrilla activities, making much of Missouri unsafe for citizens of any persuasion. "Many of the soldiers and their families have suffered from the depredations committed upon them by rebels, and they have their enemies whom they desire to punish, and they are very prone to use the power which their military positions give them to accomplish unwise purposes." Marcy would have preferred to replace local with better trained out-of-state troops who did not have three years worth of grudges to avenge, but as he doubtless knew, without any large-scale, active Confederate military presence such troops were needed elsewhere, and local militia would be the ones to carry on the war. Marcy, though, had no suggestions about how to put local militia rage back under discipline.[8]

In 1864 Marcy still believed in a war of honor in spite of what he actually saw—a no-prisoners policy on both sides of the guerrilla war that had spread arbitrary execution deep into the civilian population. General directives from Washington had in effect licensed this no-prisoners policy, in part by offering only pallid remonstrances against it, based on mild declarations about conducting a just and honorable war, an ideal which presumably still existed.

As Lincoln had observed in St. Louis, both the military and civilian leadership were badly divided over what general stance to take towards guerrillas and hostile civilians. Some officials were "softs"—reconciliationists—and others "hards"—punishing law-and-older advocates—while many others vacillated between these two positions, as the blood continued to flow whatever the ascendent policy in St. Louis at the moment.

General Henry W. Halleck had been just as ambivalent in issuing orders when he was commander in St. Louis. As he had made clear in his prewar treatise on the international law of war, Halleck had no hesitation about shooting captured guerrillas as brigands rather than treating them as prisoners of war. On March 13, 1862, he had issued an order proclaiming that "every man who enlists in [a guerrilla band], forfeits his life and becomes an outlaw." Such men fell outside the rules of war; honorable treatment was reserved for disciplined soldiers. Therefore he declared, "All persons are hereby warned that if they join any guerrilla band they will not, if captured, be treated as ordinary prisoners of war, but will be hung as robbers and murderers."[9]

Though this order was clear enough, Halleck knew that its application could not be so straightforward. His own soldiers were disorderly and vengeful and could not be counted on to apply the policy in a disciplined manner. Halleck wrote to General McClellan from St. Louis, "This, General, is no army, but rather a military rabble." In addition, Halleck learned that in this kind of war, soldiers could rarely find guerrillas let alone distinguish them from the surrounding population. On New Year's Day, 1862, Halleck wrote to General Thomas Ewing concerning a rash of railroad-bridge burnings. "This is not usually done by armed and open enemies, but by pretended quiet citizens, living on their farms. A bridge or building is set on fire, and the culprit an hour after is quietly plowing or working in his field. The civil courts can give us no assistance, as they are very generally unreliable. There is no alternative but to enforce martial law. Our army here is almost as much in a hostile country as it was when in Mexico."[10] If you could not confidently identify the enemy, all civilians became enemies. But Halleck believed he was fighting for the Union, fair-play, military honor, and Christianity, and so he ordered his troops to look closely at the civilians to try to establish their guilt or innocence. Advancing troops should protect the lives and property of civilians unless they were enemy abettors. "Women and children, merchants, farmers, mechanics, and all persons not in arms are regarded as non-combatants, and are not to be molested either in their persons or property. If, however, they aid and assist the enemy they become belligerents, and will be treated as such. If they violate the laws of war, they will be made to suffer the penalties of such violation."[11]

It was up to field officers to interpret this policy, to decide who was a true noncombatant and who a belligerent outlaw. Halleck was a logical and relatively humane general who wished to treat soldiers separately from noncombatants. In guerrilla war there was no such line, and Halleck was asking his subordinates to make theoretical distinctions on lines erased by the facts. He wanted both a vigorous prosecution of the war and fair treatment for the innocent. In these circumstances, Halleck's sensibility resulted in deep ambivalence about all potential military behavior, which meant that there was no clear policy he could establish.

Such ambivalence was characteristic of the military leadership in St. Louis, whoever the commander at the moment. General Orders #100 were reformulated and reapplied as directives to martial law enforcers in Missouri as General Orders #30, issued in St. Louis on April 22, 1863.

These demanded "strict adherence" to laws against spying, guerrilla activities and aiding guerrillas, with application of the "strictest punishment," as the only avenue to restore peace. "We are at war with those who were brothers, friends, neighbors. They are now enemies." Yet commanders were to remain discrete, impersonal, and just in their punishments. "While we show them the severity of military power, we must not forget that it is our object to bring them back again to the relations enjoyed in past times, and all inflictions are only designed to subdue the rebellion."[12] Commanders must be calm judges, sifting the bad from the good citizens in a spirit designed to convert the hidden bad into the good. Without this spirit, the tendency to indiscriminate slaughter would grow. Above all, however, the bad had to be punished. With all civilians under suspicion, attempted distinctions between friend and foe, civilian and guerrilla, could only prove illusive and frustrating, most easily dealt with by an increase in action and a decrease in speculation.

One more cause of the ambivalence of the military commanders in St. Louis was their effort to conciliate the bitterly factionalized civilian élites which Lincoln described so accurately. Some of these men wanted to punish civilians who were enemies in the wildest definition of the term, while others wished to welcome back as many errant sinners as possible to the bosom of the Union. Others wandered between these two stances, which were temperamental as much as political. The hards (radicals) and the softs (conservatives) demonstrated a fundamental division, not about their shared goal of preservation of the Union but about the means by which it might be accomplished.

The softs tended to believe that both the rebellion and the guerrilla war were extrinsic to the true Missouri community. Really left alone, Missourians would choose the Union and reassert natural and traditional social harmony. The softs, tending to blame bad men, outlaws, and aliens from both sides for their troubles, could not believe that many of their countrymen had turned traitor in their hearts.

At the start of the war, H. R. Gamble, provisional governor and leader of the softs until his death in 1864, believed, as did the vast majority of Missourians, that misbehaving Union troops were causing the growth of the rebellious spirit. In his letter of August 26, 1861, to President Lincoln, Gamble wrote that Union forces were officious and insensitive to local needs. Out of control, they caused trouble for believers in the Union. Missouri "had become the theatre of a desolating war and is in danger of assuming an attitude of hostility to the Union." Men like Gamble feared that Union troops already had helped turn a majority from the Union to the secessionist cause.[13]

Gamble's letter was written in a kind of code. German-Americans from St. Louis numerically dominated the first Missouri Union regiments, and rural white Anglo-Saxon Protestant Missourians resented them as "Hessians"—alien military oppressors. Nineteenth-century Americans were generally xenophobic, and they also deeply resented the notion of a standing army and the idea that the national government might determine local life by force of arms. Viewed from this widely shared ideological perspective, any Union troops would have been resented as invaders of local liberty. None of this suggests, however, that these troops were any less officious and arbitrary than any other armed force sent to quell civil insurrection.

As late as 1863, Gamble continued to believe that undisciplined Union troops were as much the cause of disorder as guerrillas. He emphasized that he wished to exterminate guerrillas but stressed at the same time that misbehaving Union troops continued to enable the secessionist cause to flourish. He formalized this sensibility in a call to the legislature for the creation of a dispassionate court for the trial of captured guerrillas and their civilian cohorts. "I think the establishment of such tribunals would be the foundation of a proper restraint upon soldiers, by taking away all excuse for punishment by them, except in the single case of punishing men actually taken in arms, and it would have a better effect in restraining those who are tempted to join such bands when they discover certain but regular punishment before them."[14]

Gamble was reiterating his belief in the rule of law and not men at a time when the judicial system had in effect been destroyed. He continued to believe that normal, average men had an intrinsic sense of justice and that they would be good, loyal Unionists if they could but choose freely to be so. Guerrillas were outlaws to be punished, but Union troops were often invaders to be neutralized. If both sets of bad actors ceased their evil impositions on the people, natural and traditional loyalties would return to normal.

A more focused version of this belief of the softs in the essential externality both of the rebellion and of the Union army was the explanation that the guerrilla war was basically the second round of the 1855–56 events of "Bloody Kansas." Dressed in Union blues this time, Kansans were invading Missouri to settle old scores, where they were met head on by bands of low-life Missouri toughs. Both these sets of bad men warred against the true and good Missouri community. The rebellion of the South had nothing to do with it. In May 1862, Major General John M. Schofield stated this widely shared opinion in a letter to Secretary of War Edwin M. Stanton. Schofield wanted to replace all Kansas Union troops in Missouri with those from other states. "This appears to me to be a necessity, resulting from the bitter feeling existing between the border people, which feeling is the result of old feuds, and involves very little, if at all, the question of Union or disunion. . . . The chief difficulty now in the way of the speedy pacification of Missouri is the disposition of lawless bands . . . on either side to . . . violence [and] destruction."[15] Remove these Kansas troops and you would remove the central irritant causing Missourians to go to the bush.

Schofield, Gamble, and most other softs shared Abraham Lincoln's continued democratic faith in the essential goodness of ordinary men and women in their communities. Therefore, by definition, this guerilla war had to be an external visitation of evil; it could not flow from the inside of American society. In late 1864 in his biennial address to the legislature, Willard Preble Hall, who had become governor following Gamble's death, admitted that "the authorities" had been unable to quell the guerrilla war. Only "the people themselves can rid the State of these pests of society, if they will but do their duty." Guerrillas "infested" only those counties "in sympathy with the rebellion"—when they rode into counties known to be loyal they were quickly expelled or destroyed. The solution to guerrilla war was clear and simple: "the inference is, that if counties known as disloyal would cease to sympathize with treason, and become earnest supporters of the Government, guerrilla warfare would soon cease to exist." The spontaneous reassertion of positive Unionist communal sentiment and not military force and suppression would end guerrilla war. This was a civil version of the evangelicalism of the frontier, which stressed human freedom and individual conversion. Ordinary humans had the capacity for knowing and finding the right end. Converted individuals then would freely gather into the true community. In the civil as well as the religious aspect of this evangelicalism, corrected states of mind could not be forced into existence; only if force (to the softs, that of both Union extremists and guerrillas) were removed, could the mind of each individual cleanse itself.[16]

For the Missouri hards, evil had become intrinsic to the Missouri community and could be extirpated only by the hardest means. This was a more neo-Calvinist or, more precisely, Manichaean version of man and society. The same Protestant tradition which emphasized human freedom also stressed human depravity with its other face. Methodists and Baptists could derive either message from their backgrounds. Temperamental predisposition, when forced by harsh circumstance, was finally the determining factor in which Christian version of dealing with evil a person chose. For the hards, those who had gone outside Union loyalty and the law of the state were evil monsters who had to be uprooted and exterminated in order to rescue the good people and overarching law and order from the powerful clutches of evil.

At the start of the war, on September 8, 1861, Barton Bates wrote to his brother Edward, the attorney general, that one could fight a war of honor only with an honorable belligerent and deal with guerrillas only as evil forces below the pale of honor. "If we treat the regular confederate army as honorable foes, we will be justified in treating the irregulars as spies and assassins and shoot them promptly." Bates, like most hards, would have wished to act swiftly and incisively, cutting away the cancerous evil before it infiltrated and destroyed the entire community. Fearing "an efficient enemy in the rear," Bates believed that only a "terrible bloody lesson" would halt guerrillas in their tracks. "They should be *summarily shot by thousands.* They have well earned their fate, and the example made of them may be of great value elsewhere in deterring rebels within the lines of the army, from following their example as robbers, spies, & assassins."[17]

Union officers at the St. Louis headquarters tended to broadcast a no-prisoners policy; for them leniency and observance of legal limits were applicable only to good and loyal persons and not to outlaws. Thus one Union officer wrote in 1864 from St. Louis to his subordinate commanding the post at Cape Girardeau, further south on the Missouri River, "these rebels are not to be captured under any circumstances, but to be killed when found." This general admitted that such a policy would be unclear when applied to captured men suspected of guerrilla activities unless they were actually caught in arms. "If a man is not known to be a guerrilla and taken without arms, and afterward proves to be a guerrilla, he must be regularly tried. Such trials, however, only result, where the prisoner is convicted, in putting the Government to the expense of boarding and lodging him during the war, as the President rarely approves a sentence of death." One ought to serve the law and the Union despite the wishes of even the President, who was the chief soft. The general's conclusion was quite clear, even if not stated explicitly: when in doubt, shoot. "It is . . . best to take few prisoners."[18] The evil ran deep, and the response must cut even deeper, despite the risks of injuring a few of the innocent.

The hards believed that leniency, limiting the war against noncombatant sympathizers, had not worked, and therefore the only option was to make war on the whole enemy population. General William T. Sherman reached the same conclusion by 1864, and the army command in St. Louis often preached the line of total war. In July 1864, Major General Samuel R. Curtis wrote to a Missouri congressman that that harshness of Napoleon toward belligerent civilians, which had so disturbed Henry Halleck and Francis Lieber when they had constructed the official Union antiguerrilla policy, ought to be copied in Missouri. If civilians raised the rebel flag, their town ought to be sacked and burned; if an enemy regiment broke parole, they should be disarmed and shot. That was Napoleon's policy, and the Union forces had best follow it. "It is time that communities in this country understood that such breaches of public confidence are to be followed by such terrible consequences as to deter the people from their repetition. We must end the war as we go, either by parole or devastation; and where paroles are rendered useless the alternative is the terrible military necessity."[19]

Sacking a city was Curtis's metaphor for exterminating active civilian rebel sympathizers as well as guerrillas. Neither Curtis nor any other St. Louis commander sponsored genocide, but their stance toward the war took them in that direction and led them to indicate quite clearly that shooting selected civilians ought to be part of the war against guerillas. They did not agree with the softs that the guerrillas were extrinsic to the community, and at times they believed that they had to destroy the community in order to save it. They drew back from this annihilationist conclusion, but they did not condemn those sporadic outbursts of the shooting of civilian men that did occur. They sensed nothing less would work but also recoiled from the implications of the position they half wished to pursue.

Given these conflicting and contradictory general postures, the directors of the war attempted to be pragmatic rather than doctrinaire and thereby added one expedient to the next, not out of a sense of strategy but out of desperation that something ought to work better. Constantly pressed to send their best troops to the grand campaigns east of the Mississippi River, they never had enough relatively well-trained and disciplined troops for a massive antiguerrilla force and had to rely primarily on ill-disciplined, furious, local militia troops. They had to carry on as best they could.

The basic Union tactic was to fortify strong points from which to launch antiguerrilla sorties. On June 1, 1862, General John M. Schofield outlined this program to his new commander in northern Missouri. He wanted Brigadier General Prentiss to occupy at least one town in each county with combined infantry and cavalry units. From these posts, the men were to launch quick strikes to demoralize rebels and disrupt their ability to organize among the local citizens. They were also to identify and arrest the most prominent secessionist spokesmen. In 1863 Schofield wrote to a commander in the same district to try selective banishments of civilians from the state in order "to make an example. . . . And let it be generally understood that the policy will continue to be pursued until the guerrillas are driven out." In 1862 Brigadier General Benjamin Loan wrote Schofield that he had arrested several secessionist leaders in St. Joseph. "I have no doubt but some of them will be convicted of the highest crimes by the most conclusive evidence, and will be condemned to death—if they are ordered to immediate execution and are executed it will have a most tranquilizing effect."[20]

In addition to strong points, small unit strikes, and selective banishments and executions, in 1863 the St. Louis authorities codified a system of oaths and bonds which had been developed in various forms in the field. When a suspected guerrilla sympathizer was arrested he would take the following oath. "I solemnly swear that I will bear true allegiance to the United States, and support and sustain the Constitution and laws thereof; that I will maintain the national sovereignty paramount to that of all State, county or Confederate powers; that I will discourage, discountenance, and forever oppose secession, rebellion, and the disintegration of the Federal Union; that I disclaim and denounce all faith and fellowship with the so-called Confederate armies, and pledge my honor, my property, and my life to the sacred performance of this my solemn oath of allegiance to the Government of the United States of America." Generally an arrested suspect taking the oath also had to post a performance bond, guaranteeing that he or she would "abstain from all words or deeds tending to aid, encourage, or promote the existing rebellion . . . and shall not, directly or indirectly, furnish information, arms and money, provisions, or any other commodity whatever to, or hold communication with, any person or persons engaged in hostilities," against the United States.[21]

Almost all arrested sympathizers willingly took the oath and posted a bond, claiming at their hearing then (as they would if rearrested) that they had been coerced into aiding guerrillas against their will. The oath was based on the principle of personal honor—a good person kept his word. The authorities too believed in at least their own honor and thus could not conclude that everyone else was inevitably a liar. Indeed, personal honor was at the root of American rural society, especially in the South. However, as honor and loyalty were undermined by guerrilla war, the oath and bond had no systematic basis in fact, and the false word of violators could be determined only on an individual and sporadic basis. Similarly, establishing fortified bases, sending out small strike forces, employing selective banishment, and carrying out executions were haphazardly adopted defensive tactics which might at best partially contain a guerrilla war but could never uproot it.

The St. Louis command made two notable efforts to develop more powerful and concerted antiguerrilla policies during the war. The first was a general assessment—a special war tax levied on purported guerrilla sympathizers. The second was the depopulation and total destruction of a guerrilla-infested region.

Assessments began at the start of the war on the local level. In August 1861, Brigadier General John Pope, commander in the northern Missouri district, ordered disloyal citizens of Marion County to surrender the guerrillas in their midst or else pay special levies, which his troops soon began to collect by confiscation. In December 1861, General Halleck issued orders setting up a Board of Assessment to levy war taxes on disloyal St. Louis residents, a policy pursued vigorously by the Board for the next six months. On June 23, 1862, General Schofield, as commander in St. Louis, extended this policy to cover the entire state, to be administered by civilian county boards acting under the district commanders. These boards frequently acted on unproven suspicions and out of a desire for revenge, as well as from economic self-interest. There were also rumors of private bribe-taking and extortion. Under the cover of enforcing assessments, militia troops often ransacked local citizens. At times, guerrillas responded with war levies themselves.[22]

The softs, led by Governor Gamble, believing that assessments only furthered social discord and created more guerrilla sympathizers, expressed sympathy for the appeals of those families assessed by the boards. Both the softs and the hards (led by General Samuel R. Curtis, who at the end of 1862 had replaced Schofield as commander in St. Louis) appealed directly to President Lincoln. Lincoln, exasperated, replied to Curtis concerning assessments, writing that "one class of friend believes in greater severity, and another in greater leniency. . . . As usual in such cases, each questions the other's motives." Lincoln wrote that Gamble stood accused by hards of "hunkerism, and a wish for political influence," which supposedly mattered more to Gamble than his Unionism; while the softs declared that the hards acted "more for private malice, revenge, and pecuniary interest, than for the public good." Lincoln then told Curtis that he had spoken with an honest Missourian who claimed that in one instance a man was told his assessment was $30,000, of which $10,000 went to the government and the remaining $20,000 into the pockets of the collecting agents. Evidently, Lincoln believed this sort of story, for he supported the softs and, not listening to Curtis's subsequent defense of the system, ordered the suspension of all assessment procedures on January 20, 1863. From time to time local commenders issued levies in special cases, but never again was this a general policy.[23] Applied unevenly and revoked in haste, the aborted assessment policy became a Union defeat.

In response to the furious public opinion aroused by Quantrill's raid on Lawrence on August 21, 1863, the Union army tried a more drastic antiguerrilla policy along the western border of Missouri. Issued in Kansas City by Brigadier General Thomas E. Ewing on August 25 as General Orders #11, this policy called for the depopulation within fifteen days of the northern half of Vernon County and all of Bates, Cass, and Jackson Counties, the strong guerrilla areas from which the Lawrence raid had been launched. Residents had either to leave the area or move to within one mile of the Union military posts in the region. Approximately 20,000 people were forced to evacuate their homes, almost all of which then were burned by Kansas troops. In the face of a huge public outcry, execution of this order was suspended by November, and those who could obtain certificates of loyalty were permitted to return home the following March. Most did not come back until the war was over.[24]

This was the most drastic measure taken against civilians during the Civil War prior to General Sherman's march to the sea. But unlike Sherman's action in Georgia, this policy was implemented in a Union state. General Orders #11 did not distinguish between the loyal and the disloyal —all became war refugees. The order quickly gained an odious reputation in the North, as well as in Missouri and the South. Various Union officials involved in issuing the order later constructed elaborate rationales for their actions. Yet it seems clear that it was in fact something of a compromise measure. Immediately after the Lawrence raid, Senator Jim Lane worked up a crowd in Leavenworth, preparing them to charge into Missouri and slaughter the enemy. Responding to these threats as well as sharing Lane's rage, Ewing nevertheless had sought in the immediate aftermath of the raid to employ regular military means to punish nearby Missourians.

General Schofield in St. Louis affirmed General Orders #11 at the same time as he employed all his authority to stop Kansas mob action. On August 29, he wrote to Kansas Governor Thomas Carney concerning Lane's proposal, "if this vengeance could be limited to those who were actually guilty there would be no objection to it; but it is a simple matter of course that the action of such an irrepressible organization of enraged citizens would be indiscriminate retaliation upon innocent and guilty alike. You cannot expect me to permit anything of the sort. My plainest duty requires me to prevent it at all hazards. A few days of reflection will show [you] the folly and wickedness of such measures and cause them to be abandoned."

Two weeks later, Schofield publicly attacked Lane as an unprincipled demagogue who falsely claimed "an entire confidence" to control a mob. Schofield justified depopulation as the best possible response, one which was limited to destruction of property rather than including taking of civilian lives. In this region, "all the inhabitants [were] practically the friends of the guerrillas," with the few remaining Unionists intimidated into complete silence. Therefore "the utter impossibility of deciding who were guilty and who innocent, and the great danger of retaliation by the guerrillas upon those who should remain" led Schofield to back the order.

In his annual report of November 1863, General-in-Chief Halleck defended Schofield to a point, arguing that depopulating and laying waste the region were "within the recognized laws of war" and had historical precedent. "They were adopted by Wellington in Portugal and by the Russian armies in the campaign of 1812." Yet Halleck had backed down from the policy. "They should be adopted only in case of overruling necessity. The execution of [the] order . . . has been suspended."[25]

In the heat of the fury in Kansas over the Lawrence massacre and in the context of the guerrilla war in Missouri, General Orders #11 had been a measure intended to moderate and channel public revenge. In a national context, even in the middle of a Civil War, this policy appeared to be a wildly punitive attack on noncombatants in a Union state. Rapidly retreating from the order, Union authorities suffered another defeat and abandoned a harsher direction they might have taken antiguerrilla policy in Missouri. In any event in the spring of 1864, the guerrillas just moved their activities to other portions of the state, where they continued to have both many sympathizers, and Unionists, and Union troops to attack. It was unlikely that Union authorities would have depopulated and burned the entire state. Even immediately following the Lawrence raid, devastating four counties was clearly not a policy acceptable to most Unionist citizens of Missouri or of the Union. As in the case of assessments, there were political limits to the level of destructiveness of antiguerrilla tactics. Not permitted by public opinion to exterminate whole populations or to burn all the means of subsistence; not allowed to confiscate all the property of vast numbers of rebel supporters; limited in their military means; torn between softs and hards; uncertain about the appropriateness and effectiveness of all imaginable policies; their soldiers pinned down in their posts in a countryside dominated by guerrillas, making their men as much the hunted as the hunters; diffused by their own ambivalences and uncertainties, Union military authorities would never construct a satisfactory policy to respond to this guerrilla war.

Official Confederate Policy

To the gentlemen in Richmond, southern guerrillas fought a dishonorable and inefficient yet doubtlessly often useful war. Bands of bushwhackers had sprung up spontaneously all along the border among Southerners trapped behind the Union lines. Because they could not eliminate guerrillas, the Confederate authorities tolerated their existence. In 1862 the Confederate government sought to license and therefore control these bands under the Partisan Ranger Act, an expedient they abandoned two years later. Yet in a *de facto* sense, the Confederate army always used guerrilla bands as detached cavalry, and they also appreciated and rewarded guerrilla exploits which served to keep large numbers of Union troops stationed in areas far behind the front. Guerrilla bands were also useful at harassing the fringes and communication and supply line of Union armies, impeding their advance. As well as being a threat to humanity and Christian civilization, guerrillas were a threat to the enemy.

In Richmond, official Confederate army and governmental awareness and ambivalence about guerrillas—and their policy formulation toward them—grew almost entirely from their concerns over the bands which operated in the mountains of Virginia and North Carolina, the most famous of which was the outfit led by Colonel John M. Mosby. Mosby's men were effective at keeping Union forces disorganized and on the defensive in the Shenandoah Valley. It was of Mosby's band (and half a dozen like it in the eastern theater) that Confederates thought when the word "guerrilla" was mentioned.

In the typically distended and decentralized manner of the Confederate experiment, the leaders in Richmond had little knowledge or interest in what was going on west of the Mississippi River. Therefore, policy for the West was constructed almost entirely by the Trans-Mississippi command, which wrestled independently with the devil of western guerrilla welfare. Military leaders in the West shared the gentlemanly Christian values of the commanders in the East, and they too disapproved morally of a form of warfare they also found militarily valuable. In any event, they had little control or influence over the behavior of self-proclaimed Confederate guerrillas hundreds of miles north of their lines, and they could attempt to orient guerrilla behavior only when guerrillas visited them during the winters in Arkansas and Texas or when they organized one of their periodic cavalry raids up into Missouri.

Seeking to bring already existing guerrilla bands under their umbrella and to channel their future growth, on April 28, 1862, the Confederate War Department proclaimed the Partisan Ranger Act. Nowhere in this brief law did they define "Partisan Ranger," except through an accompanying provision prohibiting any "Guerrilla Service" other than the commissioned Partisan Rangers. In effect, they commissioned already existing guerrilla bands, bringing them under official aegis, and empowered the President to license more. Partisans were to operate under the same terms and regulations as regular troops, except that they were offered bonuses for any enemy arms that they could capture.[26]

Almost immediately, some higher military officers, particularly in the Shenandoah Valley, and certain civilian figures, most notably North Carolina Governor Henry T. Clark, began lobbying for the break up of the newly licensed guerrilla bands. Most of the anti-Partisan Ranger arguments were couched in practical terms, but underlying these complaints was a repugnance for that sort of low military behavior.

In July 1862, Clark began badgering Secretary of War G. W. Randolph about the negative impact of the Partisan Ranger Act. Their existence as a legitimate alternative to the regular army was "intefering sadly with the enrollment of conscripts." The idea of groups of freebooting men on horseback was contrary to discipline and undermined the morale and the manpower of the regular army. "The idea of being mounted is agreeable to the habits of our people," but unless they were well trained and closely monitored, such troops were militarily useless except as couriers and pickets. They were expensive to equip, draining the already thin resources of the countryside. "Partisan rangers have a kind of separate and independent command, which is another attraction and, I might add, source of detriment." So many companies were forming in North Carolina "claiming to be partisan rangers" that Clark feared the whole regular enlistment process might collapse and be replaced by self-enlisted bands operating outside of the army chain of command. One could not win an honorable battle for national independence through this degree of military disorganization. The free spirits of the South had to pull together within disciplined military forms.[27]

In his annual report for 1863, James A. Seddon, Randolph's replacement as secretary of war, elaborated on the deepening objections to Partisan Rangers. Their usefulness had been "very partially realized, while from their independent organization and the facilities and temptations thereby afforded to license and depredations grave mischiefs have resulted. They have, indeed, when under inefficient officers and operating within our own limits, come to be regarded as more formidable and destructive to our own people than to the enemy." In addition, they existed under "lighter bonds of discipline," which served to demoralize regular soldiers who were both subject to "greater perils and privations" and deprived of similar "indulgences." This was the general gloomy picture to which there were a few "daring and brilliant" exceptions—Seddon meant Mosby, who had been careful to cultivate powerful Confederate sponsors. Seddon wished to disband the partisan units and absorb their men into the regular army, to repeal the Partisan Ranger Act with exceptions made for the valuable few.[28]

Civilian objections to the system of licensed guerrillas were seconded by the upper echelon of the army early in 1864. On January 11 of that year, Brigadier General Thomas L. Rosser, commander in the Shenandoah Valley, wrote to General Robert E. Lee that, with the exception of Mosby, these irregular fighters were a "nuisance and an evil to the service," ought to be disbanded, and the men placed in the regular ranks. "Without discipline, order, or organization, they roam broadcast over the country, a band of thieves, stealing, pillaging, plundering, and doing every manner of mischief and crime. They are a terror to the citizens and an injury to the cause. They never fight; can't be made to fight. [Most] have engaged in this business for the sake of gain." Rosser was more expressive than either Seddon or Clark had been about the moral evils of guerrilla warfare. Men who wished to become irregulars were not patriotic and self-sacrificing like regular enlistees but greedy and cowardly. Their behavior tended to be downright criminal; they undermined recruitment and encouraged desertion. "They cause great dissatisfaction in the ranks from the fact that these irregular troops are allowed so much latitude, so many privileges. They sleep in houses and turn out in the cold only when it is announced by their chief that they are to go upon a plundering expedition."[29] War ought to be noble sacrifice not illicit pleasure, Rosser argued, quite aware of what to him and clearly to the enlisted men in his army were the immoral (and tempting) gratifications of the freebooter's life.

Rosser's letter of condemnation took effect. It was endorsed by J. E. B. Stuart, head of the Confederate cavalry and by Lee who, on January 22, 1864, passed it on to the War Department with his recommendation that the Partisan Ranger Corps be abolished. In response the secretary of war sent out a circular on the disbandment of Partisan Ranger units, to which Lee replied, "Experience has convinced me that it is almost impossible, under the best officers even, to have discipline in these bands . . . and even where this is accomplished the system gives license to many deserters and marauders, who assume to belong to these authorized companies and commit depredations on friend and foe alike." With the single exception of Mosby, who had done "excellent service" and was "strict with discipline and a protection to the country in which he operates," Lee recommended that these units be disbanded immediately. The Confederate Congress did just that on April 21.[30]

The Confederate leadership, consisting of Christian gentlemen fighting for lofty principle, could not continue to license or ignore what was to them degenerative warfare, even if quite effective—a possibility they usually sought to deny. They would not win the war by any and all means. Indeed, Lee rejected guerrilla war as a way of carrying on the cause in 1865 when the regular armies had been defeated, a means which at least would have prolonged the war. Officers and soldiers with civilized values would become lesser men by skulking in the bush. They could not re-envision themselves as naked destroyers. They also feared poor whites, even Confederate ones, upon whom they projected their fears about the totalist, morally degenerate warrior. They would rather lose the war than wage unrestricted war, which in their defensive, relatively impoverished but geographically extensive context would have meant guerrilla war.[31]

Guerrilla activities in Missouri appeared to have made little impression during the Virginia-centered dispute over the Partisan Ranger Act. However, there were Confederate Missourians in the government in exile in various placs in the South who lobbied Richmond about the guerrilla war in their state. Most voiced fears of guerrilla barbarity similar to those articulated by the eastern high command.

What was the appropriate response to the abuse done loyal southern men by the Union occupying army in Missouri, queried the lieutenant-governor in exile, Thomas C. Reynolds, of Jefferson Davis in 1862? Reynolds opposed *lex talionis*. "I have found that our friends within the enemy's lines were generally anxious to have our government confine retaliation within very narrow limits. They considered their dangers rather increased than diminished by it, as they furnished subjects for revenge much more numerous than any surplus of soldiers we may capture." Rather than a policy of revenge by guerrillas, Reynolds proposed seizing enemy civilians as hostages against future Union barbarities done loyal citizens. Similarly, Thomas A. Harris, a member of Congress from Hannibal, wrote the secretary of war in 1862 of his desire not to carry on or abet guerrilla war in Missouri. Loyal citizens already "writhing under the yoke and oppression of the enemy" were subject to daily guerrilla "acts of unprecedented oppression and barbarity, in violation of all the principles of civilized warfare." Either the southern troops in Missouri should be upgraded to match Confederate regulars elsewhere, Harris argued, or President Davis ought to express his public disapproval of the guerrilla warfare carried on in Missouri in the name of the Confederacy.[32]

Much to the despair of such Missouri gentry in exile, the guerrilla war ground on, unaffected by their protests to distant Richmond. Late in 1863, Colonel C. Franklin wrote to President Davis complaining not only about actual guerrillas but about regular cavalry generals like J. O. Shelby and John S. Marmaduke, who behaved like "old jayhawking captains" on their raids into Missouri. They "adopt the pirates' law of property. Mankind are considered but objects of prey, and, astonishing and painful as the knowledge must be, they rob indiscriminately friend and foe." Especially vexing to Franklin was his belief that such abusive behavior had alienated the Missouri populace. They had "transferred to the Confederate uniform all the dread and terror which used to attach to the Lincoln blue. The last horse is taken from the widow and orphan, whose husband and father has fallen in the country's service. No respect is shown to age, sex, or condition. Women are insulted and abused." Even more galling, Union General Steele, campaigning in Arkansas, was "winning golden opinions by his forebearance, justice and urbanity." Those were the characteristics of an officer and a gentleman, one who would always oppose piratical ways. Franklin believed that he did not have the power to discipline his own regiment and could not employ his untrained and often drunken junior officers to discipline untrained men, as all of them acted like social "equals" and some as the "superiors" of the officers. "I resigned rather than command a regiment in a mob." Franklin would never allow plunder. "Private property must be respected" and paid for if taken with a receipt "binding the Govt." Having rescued his honor and beliefs from the Missouri rabble, Franklin closed his letter to his esteemed President, "May the great Head of the Church guide and guard you." Colonel Franklin still stood on the rampart for Christian civilization and the Confederacy, though without Missouri soldiers.[33]

Of course most Missouri Confederate officers did not resign this way but continued to fight for their social and moral vision, which they adjusted to fit the circumstances. Perhaps more clearly than practical officers, Franklin shared the genteel values of the Confederate leadership in Richmond. The horror of the Missouri guerrilla war as portrayed by Franklin could only have added to its disrepute in Richmond.

Nevertheless, other voices addressed this elite, telling them that guerrilla fighting was the only possible manner of war in occupied Missouri. Particularly in response to Union "outrages" like General Orders #11, these others insisted that *lex talionis* was the only law which could strike back at the Union leviathan in Missouri. In response to that expulsion of civilians, the Richmond *Daily Dispatch* editorialized on September 1, 1863, "The savage and inhuman measures adopted by the Yankees to put down guerrilla warfare proves that this mode of defending a country otherwise unprotected is more annoying and more dreaded by them than any other. . . . Let the guerrilla system . . . be thoroughly carried out, and if the barbarous retaliate . . . let the guerrillas, without waiting for orders exact an eye for an eye and a life for a life."[34] Violent self-defense and appropriate revenge for dishonorable attacks were also the gentleman's prerogatives, ones often in conflict with his other more measured and pacific values. Guerrillas often conceived of themselves as duelists on the field of honor. In Missouri they set the tone of the conflict—responding in the way the writer of the Richmond *Daily Dispatch* affirmed publicly. No doubt many southern leaders at least understood the desire for blood revenge.

Given the distended nature of the Confederacy—poor communications, insufficient logistical support, manpower shortages, mistrust of bureaucracy and of centralized authority—the Confederate government ignored the Trans-Mississippi Department, which was drained of manpower and resources but otherwise left alone to run its own war. Although able to defend themselves, Confederate armies in the West were singularly unsuccessful in taking the offensive, suffering major defeats in southern Missouri and northern Arkansas in 1861 and early 1862, as well as reverses on expeditions in Arkansas and New Mexico later in the war. They responded with some vigor to Union attacks but were on the whole ill-organized, under-equipped, and demoralized. One senses defeatism in the communications within the Trans-Mississippi command at least as early as June 1862, reflected in the general report of the commander in the West, Major General Thomas C. Hindman. Federal and Confederate stragglers were marauding in northern Arkansas, Little Rock had nearly fallen, and many Arkansas militiamen resisted being reorganized within the Confederate army. There was a shortage of all war material. A lack of feed corn for horses threatened the cavalry. Pay was slow in coming. The desertion rate had shot up, which had led Hindman to shoot some deserters as an example to the rest of the troops. Under these conditions, Hindman needed all the help he could get, and thus he considered the "numerous guerrilla parties" in Missouri and Arkansas as essential parts of the southern army and praised "Captain Quantrill," among others, for his "zealous and useful" help, particularly in enrolling and organizing troops.[35]

Fearing marauders but appreciating any and all active military anti-Unionism, Hindman sought to bring Missouri guerrillas into the Confederate service. On June 17, 1862, eleven days before the Confederate Congress passed the Partisan Ranger Act, apparently acting independently, Hindman issued General Orders #17, an even looser guerrilla enrollment act for his department. In his orders, he recognized explicitly that these troops would be self-constituted and would remain in their home areas behind Union lines. He urged such troops to report their organizations to his headquarters and lent their existence a Confederate meaning. "For the more effectual annoyance of the enemy . . . all citizens of this district who are not subject to conscription are called upon to organize themselves into independent companies . . . arming and equipping themselves, and to serve in that part of the district to which they belong." The men were to elect their own officers and were "to commence operations . . . without waiting for special instructions. Their duty will be to cut off . . . and to kill [Union parties] attacking them day and night and using the greatest vigor in their movements. . . . All such organizations will be reported to these headquarters as soon as practicable." Captains of these independent companies were to be held responsible for the good conduct of their men, were to keep records in order to draw pay, "and will report to these headquarters from time to time."[36] In the context of Union-occupied Missouri, Hindman was recognizing the facts and attempting to gain some measure of control over guerrillas. He was also sanctioning parties who were engaging the enemy, killing and pinning them down in a part of the South which was nearly paralyzed in terms of regular military activity.

Guerrillas, if useful to the Confederacy, were also fearsome, and Hindman was ambivalent about them. One of their fighting qualities was their tendency to make war not just on Union troops—this Hindman valued—but also on noncombatants. And when guerrillas operated within Confederate lines, they behaved the same way against southern civilians as they did against citizens in the North. On November 28, 1862, Hindman wrote to Colonel W. P. Thornton in northern Arkansas, commanding him to arrest each and every Missouri guerrilla in his region, to enlist them in the regular army, or to dispatch them southwards. Just six months after issuing General Orders #17, Hindman was contradicting them. "One hundred straggling Missourians . . . are committing daily depredations upon the citizens. . . . Wandering to and fro, from camp to camp and scattered all over the country, doing no good, but much harm, in every way."[37]

Usually Missouri guerrillas were outside Confederate lines and Confederate control. Whatever they thought of the bad news they heard about guerrilla behavior, the Trans-Mississippi command could do nothing about it and so were officially silent. One exception to this general situation occurred during the winter of 1863–64, when several hundred Missouri bushwhackers, having lost their ground cover and hence much of their security, rather than disbanding, rode south into Texas to winter. For this period the Confederate army command and southern civilians developed direct relationships with Missouri guerrillas on vacation.

Fresh from the destruction of the escort of Union Major General James G. Blunt, including the killing of nearly one hundred cavalrymen at Baxter Springs, Kansas, on their march south, W. C. Quantrill and about 350 guerrillas were welcomed by the Confederate military leadership. From

Bonham, Texas, Brigadier General Henry E. McCulloch greeted word of the Baxter Springs attack by "Colonel" Quantrill as "Very good news from our front," praise which Major General J. B. McGruder in Houston broadcast to his army by a general order, adding that the news also gave him "much pleasure" for the "brightening of our prospects." Major General Sterling Price wrote about the glorious victory at Baxter Springs, adding the news of the arrival of the Missouri guerrillas in Texas. "Colonel Quantrill has now with him some 350 men of that daring and dashing character which has made the name of Quantrill so feared by our enemies, and have aided so much to keep Missouri, though overrun by Federals, identified with the Confederacy." Price wrote to Quantrill that he took "great pleasure in congratulating you and your gallant command upon the success attending it . . . against despotism and the oppression of our State." Price wanted Quantrill to help present the true facts about the "murderous and uncivilized warfare which [the Union] inaugurated" so that together they could show the world that all guerrilla actions were but "just retaliation," measure for measure.[38] Three regular army generals were eager to reward noted Missouri guerrillas for their actions and to help them explain as legitimate self-defense any excesses they may have committed.

Stories preceding the Missouri guerrillas, as well as their behavior in Texas, soon convinced these generals that they were not dealing with Christian gentlemen. General McCulloch, in whose district of north Texas the guerrillas were camping, was the first to be disillusioned. By October 22, he was writing to the Trans-Mississippi headquarters about Quantrill, "I appreciate his services, and am anxious to have them; but certainly we cannot, as a Christian people, sanction a savage, inhuman warfare, in which men are to be shot down like dogs, after throwing down their arms and holding up their hands supplicating for mercy." Quantrill had not reported to McCulloch as he ought to have done out of courtesy to the military district commander. McCulloch did not know firsthand about Quantrill's mode of warfare, but rumors made it sound to him that his behavior was "little, if at all, removed from that of the wildest savage; so much so, that I do not for a moment believe that our Government can sanction it in one of her officers." Quantrill's status was unclear. If he held a Partisan Ranger commission from Richmond, as he sometimes claimed, he should be officially reprimanded, and if he did not, his conduct should be "disavowed" and he invited to absent himself from all contact with the regular army. McCulloch became increasingly convinced of bushwhacker evil, a week later writing that he had "little confidence in men who fight for booty," who battled like "the uncivilized Indian," and who refused to obey his orders or join the Confederate army.[39]

At the Trans-Mississippi headquarters in Shreveport, Louisiana, Lieutenant General E. Kirby Smith, Hindman's replacement, had been prepared to believe the worst about Missouri guerrillas, accepting the opinion of Lieutenant General Theophilus Holmes that the methods of the Missouri guerrillas had only served to "entail additional persecution and distress upon our friends, without advancing our cause in that State . . . one jot or tittle." However, at the end of October, Quantrill paid a visit to Smith and charmed him, convincing him that he was indeed a well-bred and misunderstood soldier of honor. Smith wrote McCulloch that the guerrillas "are bold, fearless men, and . . . are under very fair discipline. They are composed, I understand, in a measure of the very best class of Missourians." Having accepted their status as proper gentlemen, Smith took their word about their honor on the field of battle. "They have suffered every outrage in their person and families at the hands of the Federals, and, being outlawed and their lives forfeited, have waged a war of no quarter."[40]

Subjected to more than a guerilla chieftain's sweet talk, McCulloch could not control the Missouri guerrillas, the "brush crowd," as he began to call them, in his district. Many had deserted, some of these to the Union army. "Quantrill will not obey orders," and his men had caused "so much mischief" that McCulloch was determined to arrest the lot and ship them to Shreveport or Houston. "This is the only chance to get them out of this section of country, which they have nearly ruined, and I have never yet got them to do any service." Sent to seize some whiskey at a distillery, they had instead plundered, shot up, and burned it, killing one man and intimidating the neighbors into silence concerning the incident. "They regard the life of a man less than you would that of a sheep-killing dog." They had robbed scores of farmers. They were dishonorable cowards not soldiers. "They will only fight when they have all the advantages and . . . run whenever they find things too hot." McCulloch tried to fob off these scoundrels on Brigadier General H. P. Bee on the Texas gulf coast. To this end, he had promised Quantrill that he could keep his men together in "the independent partisan service," accepting Quantrill's word that he had "his commission from the President." He wrote that Bee should disregard all the nasty rumors about Missouri guerrillas. "There is no doubt about their being true Southern men . . . they have been bad behaved in some instances, but have not been guilty of a fourth of what has been charged against them." In April 1864, after two more months of robbery and murder in north Texas, frequently done by mounted men wearing Union cloaks, a favorite Missouri guerrilla disguise, McCulloch wrote Captain E. P. Turner of Smith's command, "I assure you the Captain Quantrill command had been a terror to the country and a curse to our land and cause in this section, and I have never been able to control them, because I have not had troops that had the moral and physical courage to arrest and disarm them."[41]

If the Confederate military with its resources could not subdue Missouri guerrillas in their midst, civilian authority was even less able. Such authority was represented in the person of the Missouri governor in exile, Thomas C. Reynolds, who had established his "capital" in Marshall, Texas. In September 1863, Reynolds wrote to the Missouri Confederate cavalry commander, J. O. Shelby, that he was "utterly opposed to the mode of warfare known as 'bushwhacking,'" and that Shelby should draft such guerrilla parties as he found into his regular corps. Shelby should always accord the enemy and insist from him "the rights and courtesies due to a recognized belligerent." When several guerrilla bands showed up at Sterling Price's headquarters demanding pay, Reynolds wrote him that money should be given only if the men's captain followed military prescriptions, presenting "proper and necessary" returns, rosters, muster rolls, "forwarded through the proper channels. . . . To obtain pay, these rules must be observed." Undisciplined irregulars should not have the privileges of regular soldiers. Reynolds wrote to another Missouri Confederate officer that guerrillas had "either to submit to conscription within our military lines or return to Missouri to carry on a precarious warfare, without legal organization, means of support or protection under the laws of war." One was either a regular soldier or an outlaw, and Reynolds was not prepared "to give anyone authority in the name of the State of Missouri to carry on mere predatory warfare." Reynolds knew he was powerless to limit the guerrillas in any way, but he would at least withhold his meagre legal sanction from them.[42]

Apparently, the Missouri guerrillas gone south for the winter behaved in Texas as they had in Missouri. With the leaves back on the trees, they departed the Confederacy to carry on again in their home state. They never submitted to the military discipline of the regular army or curtailed their mode of war. They set the terms. The Confederate army and government could not influence guerrillas operating independently in Missouri; neither could they control them when the guerrillas were among them. And when regular officers observed their vacation behavior, all their worst fears about the savagery of guerrilla warfare were confirmed. If these men were portents of a democratic postwar Confederacy, they wanted nothing to do with it. They could never completely disavow these brutal enemies of their enemies, but when they saw them up close, they realized that they could not embrace them either.

The guerrillas themselves were confused about their outlaw status. They knew what the Confederate command thought of them, and they valued legitimacy as well as action. They intended by all means to remain independent of the regular army, and they clearly resented pretentious officers who presumed to have the authority to order about real fighting men like themselves. It was altogether consistent with their prior record for them to have behaved just the way McCulloch claimed they had in Texas, and with the spirit he described. However, they did believe they were fighting for the southern cause, and they did not conceive of themselves entirely in apolitical terms. They were ambivalent about their near-outlaw status in southern eyes. Guerrilla double-mindedness can be seen in their thieving careers combined with their occasional attempts at defining themselves as regular soldiers rather than as bushwhackers. They would sometimes let the Union military know that they wished to be treated as regular soldiers and dealt with as such.

In July 1863, several mounted men fell in with John Thrailkill, who told them he was a Confederate recruiting officer looking for guerrilla Captain Hart, in order to persuade him to join the regular service. One of the mounted men remarked to Thrailkill, "Well, I have been burned out and I want to join Capt. Hart or somebody that will kill them wherever they find them." Thrailkill replied, "if you are that kind of man I dont wish you to join me. There are two arms of the service to which I am opposed, one is bushwhacking and the other is jayhawking. There are regular confederate officers and if you want to join the service, I would advise you to join someone that has proper authority to recruit you." At this point the mounted men, who were Union spies, arrested Thrailkill as a Confederate belligerent rather than shooting him on the spot as a guerrilla.[43] Thrailkill had defined the line between bandit and soldier in a sufficiently clear way to convince these Union agents. He showed them he intended to operate within the implicit rules of war.

The clearest demarcation between outlawed guerrilla and legitimate belligerent was whether or not prisoners would be taken. On the evening of August 4, 1864, Union teamster Mike Kelly was captured by fifty armed guerrillas on a highway not far from the big Union base at Rolla in south central Missouri. They took his saddle and showed off their cavalry riding prowess. Two of the guerrillas asked Kelly "if he thought they could go fast enough to catch a Yankee, and galloped [their horses] leaving the reins loose," the horses running in place in a line like well drilled cavalry horses. One of the two officers then told Kelly that these were regular soldiers just arrived from west Tennessee and instructed Kelly to tell General McNeil, "If the Gen'l shall take my men prisoners of war, I shall take the Feds so. But if he don't take my men as regular prisoners and kills them I will serve his men the same way."[44] These guerrillas knew that the difference between a regular and a guerrilla lay in the kind of military discipline they had demonstrated. Doubtless, the Missouri guerrillas who tore up Confederate Texas in the winter of 1863–64 knew the same rules. They were eager to command themselves and to destroy everything in their way, but they also wished to be proper soldiers—as they saw that role. They fell far outside Confederate definitions of the ruly soldier, but within their own code, they thought they were proper Confederates. During most of the war, they were indeed the only active rebel soldiery in Missouri.

Four times between 1862 and 1864, the regular Confederate army launched large-scale cavalry raids north into Missouri; the largest in September and October 1864 was led by Major General Sterling Price. During these expeditions, the Confederate cavalry utilized local guerrillas as part of a larger effort to rally all the good southern people of Missouri to support the rebel military. They presumed that the guerrillas would join them and that the people would rise, throw off the chains of their captivity, and join the noble Confederate cause which they had always championed in their hearts. Price dearly hoped that what began as a temporary raid, diverting some of Sherman's army and gathering supplies, would turn into a full-scale invasion and even occupation.

Great hopes alternated with deep fears in the South in 1864. Price's raid was but one expression of the increasingly desperate desire for a smashing victory which would totally change the tide of war. After the major defeats at Vicksburg and Gettysburg in 1863, despair and war-weariness grew throughout the Confederacy. General Robert E. Lee's stubborn and brilliant defense in northern Virginia kept Grant's army at bay, inflicting huge losses on it. Yet Grant pressed on, relentlessly grinding away at the limited human and material resources of the South. Even under these conditions, Confederate cavalry under Jubal Early raided northward, nearly reaching Washington as late as July, 1864. Commanders like Early and Price hoped for an almost apocalyptic reversal in the fortunes of the Confederacy, touched off by their raids, which many in the South confused with invasions.

Price and the 5,000 to 10,000 Missourians in his army had long believed that there was a hidden, oppressed majority of Missourians restlessly awaiting the day when they could free themselves. They were reinforced in their faith by the letters they received from their families back home. Price also sent out spies to gather information about conditions in Missouri in order to form a prognosis for the outcome of an invasion. Late in 1863, Colonels John H. Winston and John C. Calhoun Thornton reported on their recent mission to west central Missouri. They found "the great body of the people true to the South in all their energies and sympathies. The galling yoke put upon them has been worn most restlessly & we believe that with a reasonable prospect of success they will attempt to throw it off." They believed that an invasion might well trigger "a simultaneous universal uprising." If Price were to come into the state, 75,000 to 100,000 men would join him. This spontaneous army would outflank and threaten the rear of the huge Union army in Tennessee, trapping it between the new Missouri Confederate army and Braxton Bragg, crushing it or compelling it to retreat back to the Ohio River, "thus reducing not only Missouri but Tennessee and Kentucky." Winston and Thornton advised that whatever the effect further east, the Union would lack sufficient "spirit & resources" to drive Price's naturally enlarged army out of the state. Price replied to the two sanguine colonels that he could "not doubt the fact" that all those good southern men in Missouri were "content in their loyalty" to the Confederacy and "anxious for an opportunity to take up arms in the support [of the South] for I cannot believe that men, who *have been* free, can be made to submit to that abject slavery which the North is attempting to impose upon the South, nor that they can be so cowardly to surrender without a blow to their liberties, their property & their honor."[45]

Not all Missourians, however, had such great expectations for Price's project. On July 18, 1864, Governor-in-exile Reynolds wrote to Price, asking him to make "powerful diversion" into Missouri. "Even if compelled to return, it might gain time for us" further east, forcing the Union to send troops to defend Missouri. "If successful in maintaining itself" in Missouri, Reynolds suggested that Price would be reinforced from Arkansas, but the "main point" was to divert Union troops and energies.[46]

Price would have none of Reynold's defeatism. Responding to news of a sizable Confederate uprising in Platte City, Price replied to Reynolds that the people "are ready for a general uprising, and that the time was never more propitious" for an invasion. "Our friends should be encouraged and supported promptly. Delay will be dangerous. Unsustained, they may be overwhelmed by superior numbers, become dispirited, and, finally, disheartened and hopeless." In his enthusiasm—coupled with great fears— Price was seconded by the experienced and usually hardheaded cavalry commander, J. O. Shelby, who wrote to the Trans-Mississippi headquarters on August 9, 1864, "news from Missouri still continues glorious. If General Price, at the head of 5,000 cavalry, could penetrate the State he could light such a fire of opposition and enthusiasm that 50,000 loyal Missourians would spring to arms."[47]

In a letter to Price, General E. Kirby Smith advised him to attempt to seize St. Louis, both for its supplies and toward the end of "rallying Missouri to your standard."[48] However, Smith also discussed in some detail a route for retreat and the precise supplies Price ought to gather to bring back south. Smith was a realist, but he also responded to the energy and high hopes expressed by Price and his Missouri entourage. Smith wanted very much to believe that the conquest of Missouri was possible.

Price's 1864 raid was thus the culmination of a Missouri-in-exile revitalization movement, part of the huge revival which swept the Confederate army at that time. Knowing the war had not gone well, sensing their limited power, fearing the moral cause was nearly lost, these Missourians, like other Confederates, looked for portents of a revival of the heart among their southern brethren back home. At the edge of despair, they had a compelling need to rekindle their faith and that of the truly loyal Missouri citizens in cleansing, apocalyptical action. "Delay will be dangerous," Price wrote in great urgency. If the uprising did not occur soon, it might be forever subdued.[49]

All historians have agreed that the raid was a fiasco. In his analysis, Stephen Oates insists that Price misunderstood cavalry raid tactics, moving far too slowly, traveling far too heavily. However, it seems likely that Price used this deliberate pace because he was waiting for the general uprising to gain force and to come to him for a huge assault on St. Louis. The people did not rise as one. Perhaps 5,000 men joined the raid, but most of these deserted after the first military defeats. On October 23, Price's army was crushed at Westport near Kansas City, and it disintegrated during its subsequent panicked flight back south.[50]

This invading army had lost most of its fervor long before defeat at Westport. Gradually it dawned on them that the *levée en masse* was not taking place, that the people of Missouri had failed them and had failed the noble cause. Never a well-trained or disciplined army, the troops turned on the citizenry and began to plunder. Ever the believer in law and order, Governor Reynolds, who accompanied the expedition in order to attempt to reinstate the lawful government, turned on Price for failing to discipline his troops. Whereas the project presumably had been for the re-establishment of justice, Reynolds observed only the violent spread of injustice. Everywhere he saw "the wholesale pillage of horses and mules as of stores and dwelling goods in the vicinity of the army." The Confederate army had destroyed everyday order. "In fact, in an expedition designed to reestablish the rightful authority of Missouri to the Confederacy, the Governor of the State cannot even purchase a horse or a blanket, while stragglers and camp followers are enriching themselves by plundering the defenseless families of our own soldiers in Confederate service."[51]

An expedition meant to redeem Missouri and prove the nobility of the southern cause had instead devolved into a chaotic, large-scale reenactment of the war on civilians which the guerrillas had developed. Ironically, one of Price's purposes had been to bring the guerrillas under his command, to discipline and reduce them as part of the larger cause of revitalizing Missouri society. He quite openly used guerrillas as scouts and on raids against enemy communication and supply lines. In turn, the guerrillas were eager to serve him as long as they rode in their own independent units.

Price gave various guerrilla bands direct orders to carry out sorties in conjunction with his larger cavalry aims. For example, on October 11, he ordered "Captain" Bill Anderson to cross to the north side of the Missouri River to "permanently destroy" the railroad there. He also ordered Anderson to report on his operations at least every two days. Several guerrilla units attached themselves to Shelby at this time, though some took time out to rob a bank on October 14.[52]

Price's use of guerrillas infuriated the Union command and caused them to fear that a no-prisoners policy would take hold and that, in general, the lawless behavior of Price's troops would increase through contact with bushwhackers. "Permit me also, general, to express my surprise and regret that you have allowed to associate with your troops bands of Missouri guerrillas," wrote Union Commander William S. Rosecrans to Price in western Missouri on October 22 in one of those exchanges of letters between enemies surprisingly common during the Civil War. These bushwhackers were men "without principle or feeling of nationality, whose record is stained with crimes at which humanity shudders." Rosecrans feared that through incorporating bandits, Price's army would turn outlaw. "You and I, general, have tried to conduct this war in accordance with the highest dictates of humanity and the laws of war among civilized nations. I hope the future will make no change in this respect."[53] Of course, by this means Rosecrans was assigning the blame to Price in advance for any excesses in their struggle, but Rosecrans also testified to the horror and fear guerrillas induced in most regular army officers. They wanted rules and limits in war lest they turn savage in suppressing wild men.

As it happened, it appears that Price had some restraining influence on the guerrillas, who rather admired him and were willing at least at times to alter their behavior to a degree. For example, on October 10, the day after Price captured the Union garrison at Boonville, Union militiamen John S. Price and his company were marched into the courthouse square and lectured about the evils of the Union by Sterling Price. A large group of Bill Anderson's guerrillas surrounded the disarmed Union militia, "yelling like so many wild Indians [and] called out, 'we had better shoot the Sons of Bitches,' " but Price ordered them paroled and so the Union men lived. Two weeks earlier, in a raid that attained infamy throughout the nation, Anderson's band had executed twenty five unarmed Union soldiers they had pulled off a train at Centralia: they meant what they shouted at Boonville.[54] However, at least in front of Price during an organized Confederate operation, the guerrillas were compelled to respond to prisoners within the context of traditional rules of war.

After his army had fled, Price was arraigned by the Confederacy for gross incompetence and dereliction of duty. Preparing himself for the court-martial that was to follow, Price sought to distance himself after the fact from the guerrillas. He admitted that he had used them and that they had done "some damage" to the railroad, but "none of any material advantage." They had "totally failed" to take out the large railroad bridge further to the east, which would have stalled the Union counter-attack from forming against him.[55] For the higher Confederate authorities who would try him, Price wanted to downplay the importance of the guerrillas, to minimize his relationship with them, placing it entirely within a proper military context, and to deny that his men in any way were tainted by guerrilla modes of warfare.

When they raided northward and when guerrillas came south to winter, the regular Confederate army leadership kept a great distance from these men they knew to be extra-legal and uncivilized in their approach to war. They never commissioned them as military squads, though they did address their leaders with honorific officers' titles. They sought to use the guerrillas for their own military purposes, and therefore they never literally outlawed them. But they could not control the guerrillas, could not curtail their war on civilians (even within the Confederacy), could not conscript them into the regular army, and could not persuade them to follow orders. The guerrillas continued to fight on their own hook, as they put it, when there was no Confederate command around, which was most of the time. Basically, they set their own terms of warfare, to which regular officers had to adjust. The gentlemen at Shreveport and Richmond abhorred them and hated the notion that guerrilla methods might be useful and that their own honor might be a military impediment. They also knew that unchristian guerrillas harried and damaged the enemy. In terms of policy, official southern attitudes cancelled each other out—they could have no policy, and the guerrilla war continued until at the end the guerrillas were the last Confederates to surrender.

Union Policy in the Field*

For most of the war, the Confederate command was missing from the Missouri field of battle, and each band of guerrillas ran an independent war. The Union, which had at least a semblance of lines of command throughout the state, tried to work according to some general principles of military regulation. District and regimental commanders attempted much of the time to coordinate the activities of their troops according to their notions of a correct and just war. Field officers shared the ambivalence, fears, and uncertainties of the officers in St. Louis and Washington. In

---

* There was a hodge-podge of different sorts of Union troops in Missouri during the war. Some were volunteers in the regular Union lists, primarily from Iowa, Wisconsin, Illinois, and Kansas. Most of the approximately 50,000 regularly enrolled troops from Missouri were sent East. Fourteen cavalry regiments, approximately 10,000 men, comprised the Missouri State Militia. These men were paid with Federal funds, provided Federal officers, and kept on active duty in the state. The vast majority of Missouri soldiers entered the Enrolled Missouri Militia. They were unpaid troops under local officers, who served when called to meet emergencies. There were over 50,000 such soldiers. In addition there were many loosely organized, often self-constituted groups called citizen's guards or home guards. Local troops were expected to subsist off the enemy.[56]

practice they were allowed wide latitude of behavior by their superiors who understood that men in the field had to grapple with the elusive foe in varied and changing ways. Given the enormous frustrations of antiguerrilla warfare, field officers varied in their methods according to their values and temperaments in leadership and in the boundaries of behavior they attempted to set for the soldiers in their command. They fully understood the vagueness of the line between civilian and guerrilla and brought conflicting hopes and fears to bear on just who the enemy was, and how he was to be treated.

Different commanders employed different military techniques. Whatever regimental or district commanders attempted was filtered through the majors and captains in charge of the outposts and fighting patrols, and these junior officers responded to their own varying sets of imperatives. They often had desires and beliefs of their own to act upon, and in addition, they frequently lost control of their men, who set their own unit's policy of revenge and destruction. To some extent, the whole issue of authority is best looked at from the bottom up, as the men in the field—responding directly to the guerrillas—set most of the daily policy in actions which often left their officers the tasks of sorting out accomplished military facts and of negotiating the practical terms of combat with their own men.

Like the gentlemen in Richmond, Washington, and St. Louis, Union commanders in the field believed that the purpose of war was to achieve victory with honor; they were agents of a government which sought peace based on social justice and the union. They were serving higher civilization and the Union in order to re-establish justice. The problem was in the means to this end: should they exterminate or reconvert bad men in order to rebuild the good society? This was the practical military restatement of the Unionist elite's disagreement between the hards and the softs, radicals and conservatives.

In 1864 from his post in north central Missouri, Colonel J. H. Shankling represented the hard position: guerrillas "are not only enemies of our country, but of Christianity and civilization, and even of our race, and the only remedy for the disease is to kill them." Because the threat was so profound, the response must be also. Other would-be exterminationists stressed that the Missouri guerrillas were waging war against the possibility of a civilized American democratic society. Complaining that those in the eastern United States misunderstood the stakes of the war in Missouri, Palmyra's provost marshal, William R. Strachan, wrote to the *New York Times* in 1862, "we think we are fighting a battle for the world, for humanity, for civilization, for religion, for the honor of our forefathers, for republics," for the future. These highest possible ends had to be served by the most stringent means, which in this case meant that General John McNeil's recent execution of ten guerrilla prisoners in retaliation for another guerrilla band's killings of Unionist civilians was justified. "What is war? Is it anything but retaliation? Must we allow our enemies, the enemies of liberty and republicanism, to outrage all laws of war, and not take some steps to show them the propriety of adhering to those laws?"[57]

Other Union field officers and local provost marshals, believing that they too were serving noble ends, felt compelled to impose limits on the means they employed, lest they themselves become monsters of destruction. Writing to his superior at district headquarters in south central Missouri, Provost Marshal Samuel N. Wood stated that he was sending on two "Notorious Characters," who would doubtless be shipped on to St. Louis, where they would likely be released on parole only to return south to take up thieving again. "If we do justice and shoot them it would not be sanctioned, not even by our own Sense of Right." Wood's sense of retributive justice was similar in ferocity to the exterminationists, but he counterposed his conscience to the absolutist definition of justice. As only God could judge finally and as men had to base their actions on their fallible knowledge, society had to be based on forgiveness and not merely retaliation if it were to be a higher Christian civilization. Employing the most brutal means would demean and diminish the possibility of reaching that social goal. It would be better long-term policy to limit the means, for eventually men would have to re-establish communities based not on absolute truths but on diversity, independence, and toleration. Thus Major General Samuel R. Curtis reaffirmed to the colonel commanding at St. Joseph in 1864 that though many "old rogues" in that town "deserve hanging" it would be better policy to forebear. "Bringing up old scores would only open old sores, and it is better that such wrongs should go unredressed and the rogues unwhipped of justice than to trouble society with the bother of their trial, conviction, and punishment."[58]

One can hear in the language of these Unionist softs expression of forgiveness, a basic principle of the warmer side of the evangelical Christianity in which nearly all rural Missourians were bred. Some field officers believed that men and women gone to bad principles of secessionism could be converted back to Unionism and true Christian social relations. These were souls imperiled rather than unredeemably evil people. Thus one day in March 1864, Major Henry Neill gave a "little talk" to the men of Clinton, Missouri, as he enlisted them in the local militia, regardless of their prior commitments. "I told them that we could not fight always; that we had now warred until we were all ruined . . . the past must be forgotten; the dead must bury the dead; by-gones must be by-gones. . . . Peace and prosperity . . . stood before them if they would in good faith stand one by the other for the future in the observance of the laws and each other's rights." The results of his sermon were very gratifying to him. "Colonel, I have never had the honor to spend such an hour. The old men wept like children, and I do really believe that every man on the ground in good faith dedicated himself to his country."[59]

In this Christian ritual of rededication to social justice, much like that proposed by Abraham Lincoln to Governor Fletcher in his letter of January 20, 1865, one can hear the softs' appeal to mutuality, a spirit absent in the language of the hards who would save the Union by a blood purge. This was the fundamental disagreement in Unionist discourse which undermined any possibility for policy consensus toward prosecuting the guerrilla war, even on the local level. If all believed in the democratic Christian commonwealth, all disagreed on the means to attain it.[60] Moreover, many officers were divided within themselves on the question of appropriate actions. They knew that in the rules of war the soldier respected the distinction between armed enemies and noncombatants. They knew that guerrillas and their supporters breached that distinction, thus gaining a military advantage over scrupulous Union officers. Therefore the daily issue was whether they should follow or transgress what they knew to be the legal forms of warfare. Receiving contradictory signals from above and urgent, fury-prompted demands to eradicate the enemy from below they clung out loud to legal forms, all the while whispering their desire for an antiguerrilla war without limits. Knowing that they ought to maintain discipline by enforcing clear rules, they also wanted to destroy the enemy by any means available. Willy-nilly, they employed a moral and legal double standard, both sides of which they passed down in their orders.

At times, soldiers requested a completely free destructive hand from their superiors. They desired a license to use all possible means of battle, including those they understood to be extra-legal. For example, on June 4, 1864, Captain Eli J. Crandall, Linn County militia captain, wrote to his district commander, "I have [civilian] victims spotted for hostages to retaliate on. I will have at least 15 men to start out on a scout by this evening, who will not take bushwhackers prisoners." Crandall announced his intention to kill all suspected guerrillas and suspicious civilians as well. Just what enemy actions justified the retaliatory killing of civilian hostages was not clear. Crandall declared his intentions to his commander, indicating that he sought approval, at some level recognizing the possible illegality or immorality of his proposal. The St. Joseph headquarters replied by return wire that Crandall ought to maintain the distinction in meting out punishment between guerrillas in arms and other enemies. "Well-known thieves or bushwhackers engaged in their hellish work will be pursued and killed, but prisoners disarmed will be treated in a legitimate manner. Reports and returns must be rendered promptly to these headquarters." Headquarters disciplined Crandall, reminding him that controlled, properly subordinated behavior was the mark of the civilized army. Crandall should follow "the design of the general commanding" in his overall policy, "to exterminate the desperadoes," but at the same time he should remember that Union soldiers had to be "held in the highest state of discipline," lest they convert themselves "into a party of murderers and plunderers under Federal patronage." Any lawlessness by Crandall's men would be detrimental, "and offenders will surely be severely dealt with."[61] Officially, this headquarters refused to sanction open-ended destruction in the name of the Union.

Stressing limits on antiguerrilla activities served two central purposes: it reassured civilians that the army was not warring on all of them indiscriminately, and it reminded soldiers that they were not a mob but authorized and obedient governmental agents serving legally and morally defined ends. For these reasons behavior should always contain the appearance of legal correctness.

Early in the war, responding to secessionist "characterizations" of Union actions in western Missouri as "vandalism," a Union captain at Ft. Leavenworth requested that Missouri militia Major Robert T. Van Horn issue a proclamation, "to satisfy the public mind," declaring that the United States would not recognize or tolerate unlawful acts. This might not stop lawless Union soldiers, but it "will at least place the responsibility of any further depredations of that nature where they properly belong," on the heads of the erring soldiers.[62] Because depredations were clearly not state policy, the public would be reassured. Even more significantly for the ends of social justice, an army would cohere only if it were composed of ruly soldiers.

Due subordination was insisted upon over and over again by local commanders, which corroborates other evidence that indiscipline was rampant. On August 20, 1862, headquarters in Macon City in northeast Missouri issued a typical order concerning the taking of supplies and horses from local rebel sympathizers. Taking material from them could be done only by order of senior officers who would be held responsible for the behavior of their troops. "Nothing so soon or so strongly demoralizes a body of soldiers as license to pillage or plunder, and any unauthorized taking of property or any waste or wanton destruction of the same will be punished with the utmost rigor of a severe code."[63]

There was no general license to plunder, but plundering was to be both permitted and limited by license. Soldiers might misbehave, but when they did, they were disavowed as agents of official policy. If lawless activities were altogether too flagrant, higher authorities might step in to establish limits. This might be true for a whole unit. To give the best known example, Jennison's Jayhawkers were sent to Louisiana in 1863 after tearing up much of western Missouri. In addition to the punishment of whole units, some individual soldiers were court-martialed for illegal activities. Such was the case of Kansas Captain Orrin A. Curtis, expelled from the service and sent to the Missouri state penitentiary for hanging three civilians near Cane Hill, Arkansas, on November 12, 1864. In July of that year, Curtis had already been reprimanded after his company had burned most of Harrisonville, Missouri. Leaving that town, the reportedly drunken Curtis asked a local man "who gave him the privilege to farm there" and lit at least seven farms on fire as his unit headed west. After his conviction for murder, Curtis appealed to Missouri Governor Thomas Fletcher, "as a radical man and a brother," not to deny hanging the men but to insist "that I was justifiable," as he had acted under orders and had taken these men in arms in the bush (an assertion which was untrue judging by his court-martial record). "If I had of stoal anything or of murdered a singel man I would of said that it was right for me to be punished for it but I dont think it wrong to cill bushwhackers but I hav to suffer for it." Curtis had been imprisoned by the authorities for his excesses, but equally significant, his appeal worked. Fletcher forwarded it to General Grenville Dodge who pardoned Curtis.[64]

It was unusual for even the most egregious offender to be soundly punished by his military superiors. If an incident of Union misconduct appeared outrageous to a local commander, he might order an investigation or at least demand a justification from the responsible junior officer, but these demands were almost never followed through. Such a case occurred in Cameron in northeast Missouri in May 1862, when Brigadier General Benjamin Loan received word of the death of Asa Davis and his father, Ambrose. Following the shooting of a Union cavalryman in an ambush, Asa ("of whose guilt there seems to have been no doubt," Loan concluded) was arrested and shot while attempting to escape. Ambrose came to the camp of the unit who had shot his son, requesting that he be allowed to attend his son's funeral. The Union troops turned him away, and about a mile out of camp, he was shot dead. Ambrose's death appeared to Loan to be "a case of deliberate assassination under circumstances that will not be tolerated." Loan required an explanation from the colonel of the regiment involved, "with a definite statement" showing who in the unit should have guarded Ambrose rather than permitting his death, even if the colonel could not uncover the names of the actual trigger men.[65] There is no record of subsequent replies or actions. Loan's main intent probably was to limit repetition of such acts.

The knowledge that their guerrilla enemies generally took no prisoners and warred on civilians all the time weakened local Union commanders' demands for good conduct from their subordinates. If the Union army failed to respond in kind, it would risk destruction at the hands of the enemy. It was also contrary to their sense of equitable justice to obey an honorable set of rules disregarded by the other side. Occasionally, Union officers would send missives to regular Confederate soldiers they knew to be in the neighborhood, requesting that both sides fight hard but according to rules of decency. In July 1862 Brigadier General Egbert B. Brown wrote to Confederate States Colonel John C. Tracy, telling him that he was eager for a scrap and that if Tracy's soldiers fought openly as soldiers and fell captive, "we shall treat you so well that you will regret that you could not always be a prisoner." However, if Tracy's soldiers "in the guise of citizens steal into our lines and shoot down our soldiers from the bush they will receive, as they deserve, no mercy." Brown concluded that his men did not wage war on "peaceable citizens," even those of enemy sentiments, and carried on "none but an honorable warfare against legitimate combatants."[66] I do not know how Colonel Tracy responded, but usually in Missouri there was no responsible, commissioned Confederate officer to whom a Union field commander could make an offer like Brown's to Tracy.

Like the frightened and angry officers and men in garrisons and on patrols, local commanders were frustrated and infuriated by their rarely seen but deadly foe. Contrary to their desire to preserve law and order was their need for violent retaliation. Reporting the killing of one Holden, Brigadier General Benjamin Loan, who had been riled by the Union assassination of Ambrose Davis, wrote in this case that Holden had deserved to be killed by the militia, though he stressed that this was not an officially requested murder. "It was a mild punishment for the many outrages perpetrated on Union men."[67] Privately, Loan at the least accepted and even relished a death he knew he should not sanction in public. Like many field officers he vacillated between mercy and a desire for retributive mayhem.

At times, local commanders quite explicitly articulated this double standard about treatment of enemy noncombatants. On August 1, 1864, Colonel J. T. K. Hayward, whose regiment was stationed at Brookfield in north central Missouri, wrote his district commander, Brigadier General Clinton B. Fisk, "I think all who are proved to be in a civil complicity with bushwhackers should be shot. When a known disloyal man feeds and harbors bushwhackers and can't show that he did all he could to prevent it, and to give the most speedly notice of it, burn him clean." Hayward then made clear his knowledge of his use of a double standard, "This may not look well in a published order, but I think it would work well in practice."[68] All over Missouri, regimental and regional commanders wrote one set of propositions for the record and at the same time either explicitly or implicitly approved of activities they knew were illegal, suggesting in effect—do as I imply, not as I say. This was the field officer's equivalent of what I have called the survival lies of civilians. They implicitly requested that junior officers do whatever had to be done but then report their activities to their superiors not as they had actually happened but as they ought to have happened. Junior officers, pressed to extreme action by their men, by their own urgings, and by an implacable foe, hardly needed encouragement to act outside legal limits. Few felt that their superiors were pushing them into actions they did not wish to do. All acted in an inferential concert of slaughter, knowing that one could not fight guerrillas with legal niceties

Odon Guitar, Union brigadier general and guerrilla hunter. As was true of General Benjamin Loan and many other field officers, he vacillated between mercy and a desire for retributive mayhem. Many Civil War generals affected the Napoleonic hand in the bosom. (*State Historical Society of Missouri*)

and yet that an officer of the Union could never officially affirm that his actions were outside the law.

The style of command of Brigadier General Clinton B. Fisk, who was in charge of the guerrilla-infested district of north Missouri in 1864–65, presented a clear example of this double standard. The ambiguity of Fisk's orders, his subordinates' confused attempts to respond to his mixed commands, and his subsequent whitewashing of those illegal activities he had demanded implicitly, were made evident in several incidents during the last, brutal year of the war.

On February 6, 1864, Colonel J. B. Rogers wired Fisk that a mob had seized the captured guerrilla John F. Bolin and had lynched him. This telegram crossed one from Fisk to Rogers, written in response to an earlier message from Rogers announcing Bolin's capture. Fisk's wire read, "It will hardly be necessary to give Bolin a trial," by which he meant that a quick drumhead court-martial would satisfy legal necessities. Alarmed that it would later appear that he had followed an order from Fisk which he had known to be illegal and that Fisk was ordering Rogers to turn Bolin over to the mob, Rogers immediately wired back to Fisk, "While I think the hanging of Bolin just, I still regret that it was done by violence, without trial. Your telegram to me will be misunderstood as winking at it. I apprehend further violence. I will be obliged if you will give me a reprimand or a hint to allow no more violence, so I may the better be able to restrain my men." Fisk complied with Roger's request, wiring back, "I would prefer that no such villains be taken prisoners, but after they have been captured and imprisoned within our lines, law and order and the well-being of the community imperatively demand that they receive a proper trial and be punished for their crimes in the manner prescribed by law."[69]

Fisk continued to give ambiguous orders to his subordinates, perhaps not fully comprehending their scarcely concealed ferocity. In January 1865, for example, he wrote Major Samuel A. Garth commanding the small garrison at Glasgow, "Hesitate not to burn down every house where it can be demonstrated that the occupants harbor and conceal the murdering fiends. Do it by an order and destroy everything on the premises. Deal summarily with the parties who harbor and conceal. They are equally guilty with the bushwhacker and must share his fate."[70] How was Major Garth to read this directive? Did not "deal summarily" mean to kill on the spot? Such military euphemisms suggested an obviously illegal actual intent, while at the same time they covered such an intent on the literal level. Local commanders like Fisk could insist that they had never actually commanded through illegal orders the excesses committed by soldiers under their charge.

Receiving directives like these, pushed by their own anger and that of their men, it is little wonder that many junior officers in the field summarily executed civilians. There is no way of learning how many civilians were killed under this regime, as most deaths were either not reported or were reported as guerrilla deaths. Since guerrillas were usually dressed as civilians, such reports were incontrovertible. However, from time to time a rather dense junior officer would report the execution of a civilian in an undissembled manner, believing that he had been licensed to kill by his superior.

On January 25, 1865, Cavalry Captain R. M. Box reported to his colonel the killing of civilian Allen McReynolds near Warrensburg in west central Missouri. Box sent several men disguised as bushwhackers to this suspected guerrilla supporter's house. McReynolds willingly fed the men and gave them information, though he told them he would not carry provisions to the bush for them for fear of Federal reprisals. When arrested, McReynolds admitted to Captain Box that he had harbored William C. Quantrill and other bushwhackers several times. After consulting with the two other junior officers in his platoon, Box shot McReynolds on the spot and issued a written report of his action to Colonel John F. Phillips. On the request of Major General Grenville M. Dodge, the commander in St. Louis, Phillips passed on Box's report, noting that McReynolds had been a "prominent" southern civilian abettor in a bad secessionist territory. Phillips believed this incident had been a justifiable and salutary "warning lesson" for the rebels of Warrensburg, "by executing summarily the chief among its citizens." Phillips neither affirmed nor denied that he had given Box a direct order to execute this civilian. In turn, Dodge enclosed these letters in a report to the adjutant general's office in Washington, which forwarded it to Secretary of War Edwin M. Stanton. Dodge added that he had investigated the incident thoroughly and had concluded that "as it was clearly proven that McReynolds defiantly and openly assisted bushwhackers under a guise that deceived us, I took no action, though I do not approve of unlawful acts." Dodge disapproved of such actions done by officers as they "sometimes tend to bad results," which he did not enumerate. Dodge concluded, "I have given such orders as will prohibit any such action recurring. Hereafter men caught in arms will have no mercy shown them."[71]

In effect Dodge condoned this particular action while disapproving of it in principle. But he then undercut the principle both by the vagueness of his disapproval and by his forceful approbation for increasingly vigorous antiguerrilla actions in general. Colonel Phillips had seconded the actions of his subordinate without even a formularized reprimand. Box had not been punished, although he probably had learned to censor his future reports. Indeed, if he read Dodge's position clearly, he would know enough to simply record about any similar future case that another prominent southern guerrilla had been shot as he resisted arrest.

In March 1865, the month following General Dodge's ambiguous directive reminding local commanders that shooting unarmed civilians was illegal, militia Captain John D. Meredith in Glasgow on the Missouri River made the mistake of fully and honestly reporting his antiguerrilla activities to Clinton B. Fisk. Meredith had sent out five of his men under Lieutenant Self, disguised as bushwhackers to uncover guerrilla sympathizers. At their first stop, Mr. Drane had told them that he was "a Southern man from the ground up" and then had given the supposed guerrillas breakfast, new socks, and advice concerning Federal troop movements. Later when Union-uniformed Captain Meredith called, Drane denied ever having seen any guerrillas. Meredith burned Drane's house. Meredith then went on to Mr. Graves's house, where the disguised Self had elicited the news from Graves that "he had always been a Southern man, and that he had had no cause to change his principles." The pretended guerrilla Self asked Graves if he had seen any bushwhackers lately. Answering that he had not, Graves then said that he would not have reported them to Union authorities had he seen any, "as it might get him into trouble." Lieutenant Self then asked, "Would you feed guerrillas and not report them to the authorities?" Graves had answered, "I would not report on anybody." When he arrived, Mere-dith arrested Graves and after more conversation concluded that this man was a "quiet, determined, and dangerous man; a man of some influence and one who could and would do more harm by his acquiescence and aid (unarmed though he was) than if he were in the bush with his revolvers belted around him." Meredith executed Graves. On his return to his post in Glasgow, Meredith reported to General Fisk. Meredith wrote Fisk that his colonel "told me I need not make any report to him, and he therefore does not know what I did." Meredith did not seem to understand that his colonel had abandoned him. Fisk, recently reminded by General Dodge that illegal shooting of civilians was prohibited, arrested Meredith. Fisk then wrote to Dodge for instructions. For his investigation, Fisk had concluded that Meredith had made a truthful report, that the burned dwellings "were simply of the lowest class of bawdyhouses" where guerrillas "did congregate most," that at least one hundred families in the Glasgow area "ought to emigrate or die," and that local Unionists of "high positions of honor and trust will, for a fee" certify the total loyalty of any of their southern neighbors, even of "the devil himself." Under these circumstances death was deserved, and yet Fisk also insisted to Dodge, "No order for the destruction of property or the killing of an unarmed citizen ever emanated from my headquarters."[72]

It was not surprising, given what we have already seen of Fisk's orders, that junior officers like Captain Meredith might have misapprehended the full flavor of the general's message—that one ought to burn out and kill civilians, but then cover one's tracks. Meredith missed this crucial point, and his regimental and district commanders, scrambling to whitewash their own records and reputations, pinned all guilt on him. Insisting on results from their subordinates, local commanders covertly instructed them both how to widen their latitude of behavior and how to write correctly limited reports of their actions. Meredith's behavior was quite typical of anti-guerrilla practice during the war. It was his honesty in writing an accurate and full report which was unusual. Meredith was either too eager to please his superiors or too slow mentally to understand the reportorial task of the efficient junior officer.

As the war continued, increasing numbers of men shot civilians with decreasing compunction, but specific conditions and responses changed from moment to moment, undermining any consistent policy formulation. On one point, official Union policy appeared to be clear: active guerrillas were outlaws and were to be executed when captured in arms on the field rather than to be treated like regular prisoners of war. Following General Halleck's legal pronouncements on this issue early in 1862, Brigadier General James Totten, district commander for central Missouri, issued Special Orders #47 in Jefferson City, which read in part that "all those . . . who are known familiarly as guerrillas, jayhawkers, murderers, marauders, and horse-thieves, will be shot down by the military upon the spot when found perpetrating their foul acts." In May the St. Louis command made this a general policy.[73]

Throughout the war, most units acted in the spirit of this order, though officers continually reiterated and justified it, which suggests continued doubts as to its moral if not legal legitimacy in the minds of Union soldiers. As late as the Fall of 1864, Major General Samuel R. Curtis was quite defensive about enunciating his belief in taking no prisoners. "Our troops everywhere now consider it right to kill bushwhackers, even after they surrender," he asserted, demonstrating a certain unease about shooting even an armed guerrilla if he actually gave himself up. The "barbarous butcheries" committed by guerrillas, "the tortured bodies of their victims, and the scalps and ears worn on the bushwhackers' bridles, will evince a disregard of all rules of war, and even savage barbarity." Therefore guerrillas "deserve hanging or any other sort of butchery," as they had defined their appropriate punishment by the nature of their warfare. Thus a totally brutal Union response was merely recognition that guerrilla war in itself "is butchery" which justified "horrors" in putting it down. History also demonstrated that "Brigands have no rights, and Napoleon had them shot down by regiments." It was a great effort for General Curtis to internalize this imperative law of extermination, as part of his conscience continued to rebel at becoming a butcher, even when he believed that the enemy had put his men in the charnel house.[74]

Given the exchange of slaughter for slaughter, it was little wonder that guerrilla chieftains and Union field officers gave verbal commands to take no prisoners. It was the brutal killing of one of his men at guerrilla hands that first led General Curtis to his no-prisoners stance. He wrote to St. Louis in May 1862, "A set of assassins are prowling about Little Red

River. One of our men bathing in that river was shot and beaten to death with clubs. I have ordered such villians not to be taken as prisoners." For many units this policy was stated as a simple matter-of-fact. "We take no prisoners," Colonel James Ford wrote to the St. Louis command. George Wolz, a German-American private from St. Louis, wrote back to his parents from Springfield in 1862, "there are strict orders against taking any more prisoners that is found in arms or as bushwhackers but to leave them on the ground we found them on."[75]

As Wolz seemed to indicate, when enraged by the execution of comrades, a no-prisoners policy seemed both natural and just, yet actually shooting an unarmed man was still horrifying; sometimes men needed orders to fire from their officers to actually pull the trigger. Many officers expressed themselves to their subordinates as did Lieutenant Colonel Bazel F. Lazear, who responded to the capture of the "counterfeiter and nigger thief" Bradaway and several of his guerrilla companions by writing, "I am sorry they are prisoners on my hands, as they should have been shot on the spot."[76] This formulation suggested both that Lazear encouraged a no-prisoners policy and that his men sometimes could not bring themselves to be cold executioners. Once officially made captives, it was difficult to rationalize the immediate execution of guerrillas.

Given the ambiguity of instructions from above and a personal, terrible ambivalence in wanting both to exterminate all guerrillas and to remain honor-bound gentlemen in their own actions; and given the uncertainty about exactly which captives were committed and deadly guerrillas, many soldiers found it difficult to be as ruthless as they felt they ought to be. They often employed verbal and legal rituals to justify executions—to themselves as much as to outsiders. One such device was a quick "trial." For example William C. Long wrote to his children from the field in 1862, "We captured a bushwhacker yesterday. . . . He has been tried by drumhead court marshall and condemned to death. He will be executed in about one hour. His grave is now digging." Courts-martial, even cursory ones, legitimated executions as acts of reason and not passion, with evidence rather than wrath forming the basis of action. An even more condensed, quasi-legalized execution was the widely used formula expressed by cavalry Captain Thomas Thomas in his official report from the Ozarks in 1864 concerning the capture and fate of Jacob Rustin and John Inman, two "notorious" bushwhackers. "On the march to camp the prisoners attempted to make their escape by running, and were both instantly killed."[77] It was perfectly all right to shoot prisoners attempting to escape, as it was to execute them after a "court-martial." These formulas became the conventional euphemisms for reporting the execution of guerrillas.

Even the soldiers in the most ferocious Union regiments were sufficiently ambivalent about violence to be erratic in their application of the injunction to take no prisoners. One of the few reports to reveal much about these mixed attitudes was by cavalry Major F. W. Reeder, written in dime-novel bravura. One February afternoon in 1863, Reeder's men surrounded several of McGee's guerrilla band. "My men now were in their element, and whilst others quickly tore down the fence of the corn-field, the rest surrounded it, and within fifteen minutes we had exterminated the whole band. We take no prisoners from amongst them, as I had previously given the order not to do so." To this point in his report, Reeder seemed clear enough: the good guys had wiped out the bad guys. The balance of the report was more temperate, however. Reeder counted nine killed, twenty "mortally wounded and 3 slightly, the latter of whom we brought in." Three prisoners were taken, despite the no-prisoners policy Reeder had declared in the previous sentence of his report. Furthermore, his men did not execute the wounded. "Not having time . . . to attend to the crippled and dying, I left them to the tender care of their good friends, of whom there are plenty close by."[78] In his bitterly ironic words, Reeder indirectly revealed that his normal impulses would have been to nurse the wounded. He left them to be cared for, perhaps to return to battle one day. All his bravado only partially succeeded in reinforcing ruthlessness. Reeder had not succeeded in obliterating all his recognition of guerrillas as humans. Of course, this was of little help to the men Reeder's unit had killed. Sparing some prisoners as the exception to the rule of execution served primarily to relieve the consciences of the executioners, who could thus demonstrate to themselves that they had remained human, even when they also had proved that they were as hard as warriors ought to be.

This self-serving mode of making exceptions to a no-prisoners policy also characterized the report of militia Lieutenant John W. Boyd, who wrote from southern Missouri in November 1863 that his unit had burned twenty-three houses of guerrilla sympathizers and had killed ten bushwhackers, sparing only one, Samuel Jones, "on account of his extreme youth and apparent innocence." Of course, in a guerrilla war many young boys became efficient killers, but Boyd could not bring himself to kill every possible enemy. As it was, operating under a regular army command in Rolla which sought to impose more constraints on militia behavior than did other Union commands, Boyd was investigated by the local assistant adjutant general. In response, he amended his original report, adding that the ten guerrillas were "shot when trying to escape houses when surrounded." Pressed to justify himself, Boyd added, "whilst I was endeavoring to live a peaceable citizen of the county, they have hunted me like a wild beast and tried to kill me for my principles. . . . Were I again placed in similar circumstances I would do as I have done."[79] Boyd himself made what he doubtless considered to be his own compromise with his no-prisoners desire—he also operated in an area where the no-prisoners policy was not readily accepted by the local command, regardless of what had been articulated as general policy in St. Louis or elsewhere.

As well as differing on the issue of taking guerrilla prisoners, Union units in the field also varied widely in their treatment of civilians they believed to be guerrilla sympathizers. In addition to execution, local Union leaders often took civilian hostages and banished some from the state.

On a less than formal level, local Union commanders let it be known to selected rebel sympathizers that they were on a Union blacklist, and would be attacked in retaliation should local Union soldiers or civilians be harmed. Union post commanders frequently threatened to make civilians pay for guerrilla wrongs. Such was the case of Captain W. T. Leeper who wrote to the St. Louis command, "Those who feed and conceal them are as mean as [guerrillas] are, and I will kill them, if the thing does not stop. . . . If they kill a loyal man, I will kill five of them." At times, post commanders took civilians hostage and threatened publicly to kill them. In August 1864 at Marshall in central Missouri, Lieutenant Colonel Bazel F. Lazear wrote to his district headquarters, "I have arrested several women that I will send in in due time [for imprisonment], and have arrested several of the worst rebels that I am holding as hostages for the lives of Union men." In 1863 Brigadier General Egbert B. Brown, commander of the central district in Jefferson City, went so far as to publish a general order concerning his secessionist prisoners: "if further acts of lawlessness are perpetrated by bushwhackers in Saline County they will be executed. . . . They will be furnished with facilities to notify their friends of the sentence passed upon them."[80] The St. Louis command ruled this order illegal. The antiguerrilla war never reached the point where civilian prisoners were executed as a matter of official policy. Many Union officers issued threats such as these and sometimes carried them out, knowing that the higher authorities would rule out an explicit policy to execute civilians. However, the higher command would be willing to turn a blind eye to a wide range of retaliatory measures, and so field officers learned what they could get away with and how to report it.

In their official reports, frustrated local commanders frequently fantasized about hunting through the countryside and banishing every possible guerrilla supporter. This escalation of war was tried once on a large scale in 1863 as General Orders #11, but public opinion forbade total destruction and depopulation of areas still ostensibly in the Union. Often, however, considerable areas were burned out and civilians banished.

Full of rage over having nine of his men killed, three wounded, and six missing in one week, the local regimental commander stationed in Independence in 1863 wrote to St. Louis headquarters that, as always, the guerrillas had split up and blended back into the civilian population. He believed it would be impossible to exterminate them "unless the government can afford to send ten soldiers for one guerrilla." The only way to cleanse the country would be to employ overwhelming force to "destroy all subsistence [in] the country and send off their wives and the children" of all guerrillas and civilian sympathizers.[81] Colonel Penick, the author of this report, and other officers like him knew the Union could not afford to commit such a large army to Missouri, and they knew that they would never have the means or the license to destroy the country and its civilians.

In a limited, almost random fashion, many local Union commanders banished families whom they considered to be the most ardent Confederate sympathizers. Writing to his wife from central Missouri in the summer of 1864, Colonel Lazear told her he was in the "worst rebel country I was ever in," where he knew for certain the loyalty of just one man. "I have several women under arrest and will send them out of the country," he wrote, knowing he could not banish all but one family and hoping that selective banishments might serve to deter other sympathizers. In the summer of 1863 near the Kansas border, chasing guerrillas unsuccessfully, Colonel James McFerran asked his superiors for approval of his order banishing seven families of known guerrillas. "I hope this move will meet your approval, because it will be impossible to rid the country [of guerrillas] and protect the loyal people when these notorious and influential families remain to feed and comfort them."[82] Such limited banishment served more to reassure Unionists than to undercut guerrillas, but at least it gave Union officers a sense of taking some action against the civilian base of guerrilla fighters.

Other than the aborted General Orders #11, the most thorough banishment was in the southern Kansas-Missouri border counties. On January 1, 1865, Brigadier General John Sanborn banished 147 families (26 headed by women), 79 individual married women and widows, and 18 unmarried women. Sanborn was the only officer I have found who attempted an extensive banishment policy after 1863.[83]

The uses of banishment and hostage-taking, like the question of capturing or shooting prisoners, and the level of violence in general continually changed from place to place. Much depended on the desires of the private soldiers in relation to the local style of command. One Iowa infantryman, writing for his hometown newspaper from Houston, Missouri, in 1863, made it clear just how important the overt and covert signals of the local commander were. When they had been stationed in Rolla, all assignments were "morbid, routine like, hen roost guarding duties enforced upon us." Now at Hamilton, the "policy adopted by the commanding officer [was far better]. Here the old General says, 'boys, take what you can and keep what you get,' " while at Rolla the orders had been " 'not to infringe upon the property of any of the surrounding population,' under the pretext that they are all union loving citizens." This soldier believed that "the kid glove policy . . . encourages rebellion . . . whilst the iron hand laws . . . create quite a different effect." At Houston where foraging expeditions "take from all," the village storehouses were full, and vigorous pursuit of guerrillas meant that "the Missouri and Iowa Cavalry boys dot the hills and vales of [this part of] the State of Missouri with the carcasses of the vile traitors."[84]

The behavior of enlisted men was not merely passed down from those in command nor did soldiers simply maximize violence when given the opportunity. Rather, officers and men responded to one another through mutually felt, conflicting needs. All were frightened, angry, and confused and operating in the context of very ambiguous general policy and muddled orders from above. Actual struggle with the guerrillas and enemy civilians was a chaos of contradictory, half-considered, haphazardly applied actions which incorporated only fragments of whatever policies troops actually absorbed from their commanders.

Ordinary soldiers had a central role in combat in guerrilla war, fighting in small units often far away from military command. In addition, the Union army, like the Confederate, was a people's army with officers elected from the circle of hometown boys who grew up in communities where rough and ready individualist egalitarianism was the prevailing ethos. There was every reason for officers not only to know their men but to understand and share their values, especially when all were equally exposed to great danger.

The primary community for soldiers was their own platoon or company, thirty to ninety men stationed at a barely secure outpost, surrounded by a dangerous countryside where guerrillas laid in wait to pick them off and where many of those friendly-acting farmers were agents of the enemy. It is no wonder that field officers identified with and defended their men against all outsiders, which tended to mean everyone—the guerrillas, the Union brass, and all local citizens. This hostility to outsiders was frequently expressed by plundering. In 1864 James A. Price, a farmer living in Weston near Kansas City—also a major in a Kansas cavalry regiment—wrote to the Union commander in Kansas City that he had complained to Major John Jennison, commander of the 138th Illinois Volunteer Regiment, that Jennison's men were "continually committing depredations and thefts . . . indiscriminately" against the citizens, "most of undoubted loyalty," around Weston, including Price himself, to whose fields they came every morning, buckets in hand, "and milked my cows" dry. Jennison had replied to Price that he "was God damn glad of it."[85] When Major Price, in his role as a local farmer in a hostile area, defended his neighbors and himself against plundering, he became one of "them" to Major Jennison's men and hence to Jennison himself, who identified completely with his men, even against a fellow officer from outside his company.

Regimental and district commanders were chary of overriding extra-legal behavior of ordinary soldiers dealing with secessionist sympathizers in matters of widely agreed upon Unionist concern. For example, one February Sunday in 1863, a militia soldier nailed a United States flag over the entrance to a church in the heavily secessionist town of Lexington in west central Missouri. Many of the worshippers refused to pass under the portal and requested the local colonel to remove it. He ordered some off-duty soldiers to take down the flag. They refused to obey orders and the flag remained. Hearing of the incident, the colonel's commander, Brigadier General Benjamin Loan, decided not to question the colonel unless the St. Louis command insisted. "If the knowledge of these facts came to me officially I should feel compelled to place Col. McFerran under arrest," Loan concluded, and such an arrest would be an "injudicious" act. In ordering the flag lowered at the request of "disloyalists," he was "betrayed into an indiscretion of which he is now heartily ashamed."[86] General Loan did not back the colonel by punishing the men for disobeying orders. Rather, he affirmed the popular understanding of Unionism, the policy the men had insisted upon when they had disobeyed their colonel.

Missouri militiamen had a great need to exact revenge against their rebel sympathizing neighbors, and they knew which scores they wished to settle. In the summer of 1864, Captain Eli J. Crandall of Brookfield in north central Missouri analyzed for his district commander the mentality of the men in his company. He explained that although he tried to limit violent reprisals by his men against guerrillas, he also understood and sympathized with their need for revenge. At Crandall's post there were forty Union refugee families who had fled from the surrounding countryside, "while their rebel neighbors were at home in peace and making money." As the Union imposed rules and limits on its soldiers which the other side did not maintain, the guerrillas had the advantage in the war for control of the land. "Our men . . . have left their homes from fear . . . leaving their crops planted and going to ruin, as they know they cannot remain at home safe. Then when they go through the country scouting and find the country full of bushwhackers, and at the same time find rebels attending their farms, enjoying the blessings of their homes and protected by the Government . . . and we, through their acts, liable to be killed at any moment, I only wonder that more devilment is not committed by them."[87] Crandall strove to curtail excesses committed by his men, but he also shared their need for getting even with the rebels they knew, the very men who had deprived them of peace, security, and wealth.

The same attitude—a junior officer sharing anger with his company while wishing to restrain them—was expressed by militia Captain Banner in 1862 in an outpost near Rolla. A local farmer named Lett had a hog which one day had gone into the tent of Private Hays, one of Banner's men, and had eaten Hays's provisions and torn his clothes. In the ensuing shouting match, Lett was branded disloyal. A few days later, the unit got drunk on a half-barrel of beer Captain Banner bought for them, and when an equally drunk civilian named Wolf seized the moment to call them names and brandish a knife, the soldiers shot at him as he fled on his horse towards Lett's house. Not catching Wolf, the pursuing soldiers settled for

Lett, and as an investigator reported later, "There had not been a good feeling beween Lett and the soldiers on account of the hogs. . . . The men were enraged at Wolf but as he could not be caught they vented their old malice on Lett, but they did not fire on *him*."[88] Captain Banner, who had encouraged his men to fire on Wolf, rescued the badly beaten Lett. Such cases were typical, though death was often the result.

Crandall, Banner, and many other junior officers attempted to fight the guerrilla war inside what they understood to be the Union umbrella of rules and limits on their behavior. Other local Unionist combatants did not actually join an official command but operated independently. Doubtless, some units were "entirely made up of thieves and robbers," who subsequently sought a Union license for their activities, as Brigadier General Egbert B. Brown characterized several groups he was attempting to purge from his district in 1863. Other professedly Unionist groups refused to join the Union army at all, operating as a brotherhood or posse against those whom they considered "Secesh." In 1864 Lieutenant William McIlwrath warned his regimental commander about a Unionist reign of terror in Grundy County. Local citizens who had taken a loyalty oath, had voted the Conservative Unionist slate, or "even if they merely refuse to halloo for Jim Lane" were being "waited on by a party of men at night" and told to get out of the county. This Unionist gang included about twenty men who called themselves an "independent militia" under the leadership of circuit Judge DeBolt. McIlwrath had offered them rations, which the judge had refused, saying "that if his men could not find rations for themselves they had no business with him." McIlwrath had remarked that he did not know these men were enrolled in the Missouri militia, to which the judge had replied, "that they were not; that he was here in command of an independent company of jayhawkers, out upon a jayhawking expedition." McIlwrath reported, "This conversation occurred on the public street, and in the middle of a crowd of some fifteen or twenty of his men, who seemed to relish the idea of being commanded by such a captain."[89]

Many enrolled militia units, as well as avowedly "independent" bands, approached this counterguerrilla model, acting in the name of the Union as guerrillas acted for the Confederacy. On a local level, northern and southern activities tended to mirror each other. In the fall of 1864, the Fiftieth Regiment, Enrolled Missouri Militia, cut a swath through 100 miles of northeast Missouri, which led to so many complaints that the case was investigated four months later by Union authorities. The militia systematically plundered everyone in their path of horses, mules, wagons, bed clothes, and wearing apparel, not issuing receipts for anything. They also "burned houses contrary to orders" of the district commander, Brigadier General J. B. Douglass, who complained of their actions, "not from sympathy for the Rebels thus robbed, for I believe that a man that refuses to fight for his country ought not to be allowed to live here." Rather,

Douglass worried, "To allow our soldiers to rob and plunder in this way and apply the proceeds to their own use is ruinous to discipline and good behavior." Douglass believed that the Fiftieth Enrolled Missouri Militia was not an exceptionally bad regiment: "this is only a sample of the conduct of our troops all over the country."[90]

In guerrilla war, the guerrillas set the actual policy to which enraged local Union units responded in kind. The more remote levels of command attempted both to set limits on behavior and to encourage their subordinates in their struggle. Ambivalent themselves, higher authorities were unable to formulate or implement a consistent policy, which would not have led to much success in winning the war in any event. Official policy was muddled and incoherent, army bureaucratic controls were loose and tending to disintegration, and policy was mainly set in the field by ordinary, frightened men who acted out of their loathing but also from their embattled humanity and their inhibitions. Even much more modern, ostensibly disciplined and technologically advanced armies than those in Missouri during the Civil War have proven unable to impose an official policy in a hostile countryside during guerrilla wars, where the guerrillas dictate the terms of the struggle.

CHAPTER 4

BROTHER KILLERS:
GUERRILLAS AND UNION TROOPS

Guerrilla Self-Conceptions

"I am a bushwhacker and a guerrilla," the manacled, nineteen-year-old Marion Erwin shouted in defiance at his Union guard, "and I am proud to be one." Erwin was being transported on a Missouri River steamer to a court-martial where he would be sentenced to be hanged. While en route to his trial, he claimed that both Lieutenant Colonel D. J. Stynes and Lieutenant Simmons of the Seventeenth Illinois Cavalry, who held him captive, had insulted him, and he swore to kill them in revenge. Later, prisoner Erwin apologized to Stynes: "You treated me like a gentleman and therefore I respect you [but] I am going to find that Lieutenant and am going to kill him as certain as God. I thought you were him and that was the reason I pitched into you in such a manner." The colonel then told Erwin that the lieutenant had been killed in action. "Good," Erwin said, "For so help me God, I would have killed him." Then Erwin added, "I just want to tell you, I am not a bushwhacker nor a guerrilla. I said so down there blowing."[1]

On July 13, 1863, Joe Hart, the eighteen-year-old guerrilla chieftain of Gentry and Andrew Counties in northwest Missouri, wrote his parents about the death of his younger brother, John. "Don't weep over him. He fell like a hero . . . he never flinched amid the shower of balls which fell so thickly around him, but led the charge on the enemy with the coolness and gallantry of a veteran." Joe reassured his parents that he had already taken a measure of revenge against the enemy, killing three Union militiamen who had "attempted to shoot whilst in the house where they were killed in the presence of women. I could not help it." Their deaths were "their own fault—they should have surrendered." Besides, "they helped to murder George Breckinridge and Holdon Mason, and shot Mrs Mason in the arm." Joe had avenged John with these three Yankee heads;

in addition, they had had it coming as punishment for injuring a woman. Now Joe Hart intended to carry on his vengeance as a principle, one which would grow into a famous career. "I am going to . . . kill off Andrew County—every last devil, and they know it. You bet they fly where they hear of me up here—they say I am a d——d sight worse than Quantrill." Hart censored swear words out of this letter his mother would read, as he knew he ought to on account of the good manners she had taught him, while bragging to her of his reputation as a cold-blooded killer. He was shot and killed by Union troops on July 24, 1863: his unmailed letter of July 13 was found in his pocket.[2]

Almost all Missouri guerrillas were very young men. All fought outside of regular military units, roaming the countryside in shapeless, temporary groups, lurking, striking, vanishing, and terrorizing everyone they consid-

W. A. Depriest, a guerrilla chief of Missouri. This photograph was taken on January 1, 1863. (*Iowa State Historical Society*)

John McCorkle and J. B. Harris, guerrillas. These two guerrillas of the
Missouri-Kansas border region sometimes rode with Quantrill, and are here
"got up" in their best outfits. (John McCorkle, *Three Years with Quantrill,
A True Story* (Armstrong, Missouri, n.d.))

Bill Anderson, known in legend as "Bloody Bill." He was W. C. Quantrill's second in command; by 1864 his replacement. Anderson was in the band which destroyed Lawrence, Kansas, on August 20, 1863, killing more than 150 civilian men and boys. On September 27, 1864, at Centralia, he led the guerrillas who killed, mutilated, and scalped 150 Union soldiers, thirty-five of whom were dragged unarmed off a train. (*State Historical Society of Missouri*)

ered their enemies—until they themselves were shot to death. They set their own rules of war, a war in which little mercy was shown or expected. Although their methods were robbery, arson, and murder—terrorism— they believed that they were noble American revolutionaries fighting for the liberation of Missouri from the Yankee invader and his lowly Missouri minions. They were the defenders of helpless women and children. They were the blood avengers for their brothers and comrades and civilian supporters killed by the Federals. They were free men on the hunt for justice, killing evil, bad-principled men in the name of traditional American liberty. They would obliterate the enemy, every last devil, or die in glory.

Unfortunately, very few personal letters or diaries of guerrillas remain, and so evidence of guerrilla self-conceptions comes mainly from the threats they made to Unionists who later reported them to military authorities. However, several did write letters either to the press or directly to Union commanders, and in these missives, one can read proclaimed guerrilla self-justifications. Here the guerrillas asserted the legitimacy and nobility of their cause—their sense of power and authority, written while they were riding high. Yet from a second body of material, the statements of those few who were captured rather than summarily executed one reads of desperate young men who had gotten out of their depth in an overwhelmingly violent society and who were now humbled and wishing just to survive. Reversal of fortune led to reversal of self-conception. These contradictory sets of self-images were both "true" pictures of young men caught up fighting a guerrilla war.

Guerrilla manifestoes were usually signed with an official-sounding Confederate title, despite the fact that these troops were irregulars and rarely in contact with the distant Confederate army, much less under its control. Indeed, guerrilla bands included many Confederate deserters. Thus in 1863 in another unmailed letter found on his body, Joe Hart of Jackson County signed himself, "Joseph L. Hart, Captain and Recruiting Officer Frontier Line Brigade, C.S.A." in a letter addressed to the Union garrison commander at Liberty. A year later the Liberty *Tribune* in Jackson County heard from "Fletcher P. Taylor, Captain Commanding the County." William Coleman signed a letter, "By Authority of Major General Earl Van Dorn," who must have been at least 300 miles to the south at the time. Clifton D. Holtzclaw called himself, "Captain, Confederate States"; and twenty year old Bill Anderson named himself, "W. Anderson, Commanding Kansas First Guerrillas," in a letter in which he proudly proclaimed, "I have killed many. I am a guerrilla. I have never belonged to the Confederate Army, nor do my men."[3] Such title adoption was not merely boyish pretense but was one means by which guerrillas, who were also proud of their extreme extra-legal behavior, assumed political legitimacy.

Though many like Joe Hart and Marion Erwin learned to enjoy killing and destruction, there were purposes external to and "higher" than making havoc which they believed they were serving. A few of them might have become outlaws whether or not there had been a war, and after the Civil War, several did become famous bank and train robbers, although almost all who survived surrendered at the end of the war and lived out peaceful lives as farmers. But during the war, most hoisted the black flag as part of what they conceived to be an intrinsic part of the Confederate revolution, naming themselves official Confederate soldiers when none held regular Confederate commissions.

S. Cockerill, who called himself, Colonel, C. S. Army, wrote to Union General Samuel R. Curtis from the bush in Jackson County, from what he called Camp Morgan on February 7, 1863, protesting the burning out, banishing, and killing of "defenseless men . . . for no other cause than being opposed to the negro-thieving policy of the Administration." Cockerill said that Union extermination was carried out "under the pretext that your troops have been bushwhacked. I will let you know that there is not a bushwhacker in this county . . . though I believe it is true that there are 100, more or less, Confederate soldiers in Jackson County that are often, to use Federal phraseology, 'compelled' to ambuscade your troops to save their lives, as there is no disposition to show them any quarter." Cockerill had heard that poison rather than medicine was given to jailed guerrillas who fell ill, while others were shot without trial. "Now, Sir, if this is permitted, I will not only hoist a black flag . . . but I will fight under it, and show no quarter to any claiming protection under the Stars and Stripes. If this is your mode of warfare, you will please inform me, by the publication of such orders in the *Republican*."[4]

Cockerill claimed that he and his fellow guerrillas were regular soldiers fighting war by standard rules. He, a colonel exchanging public views in polite, learned language with his fellow officer on the other side, was demanding improvement in the level of military legality employed by the Union. By attacking defenseless civilians for their political views, by abusing or shooting "Confederate" prisoners rather than according them the fair treatment of normal war, the Union was disturbing the peace of the community and compelling Cockerill and his comrades to defend the people. Union policy had created guerrilla resistance as the only means to communal self-defense, and now Cockerill as the true colonel had to instruct his fellow Confederate soldiers, honorable men all, to reply in kind to the illegitimate Union invader.

Wrapping themselves in high-sounding legal language as well as in the Confederate flag, guerrilla leaders sought to demonstrate that they knew the difference between proper and improper military conduct and that it was the Union side which had deprecated the standard. With regret and only in response to Union ill-usage, Confederates had now to apply *lex talionis* in clear self-defense. Thus the well-known central Missouri guerrilla leader, Clifton D. Holtzclaw, calling himself, Captain, Confederate

States, wrote to the post commander at Keytesville, "I wish to inform you that you must restrain your troops or I shall be compelled to retaliate for every violation of the rules of civilized warfare. I am determined to kill two Union for every So. sympathizer that you or your party may kill (that is, peaceable citizens), and also will kill a Radical for every house that is burnt. I regret that these things are necessary, but you or the men with you give me no choice. . . . I will state that I am only repeating my instructions from the Confederate Government." In a similar tone of finely phrased threats of vengeance, Joe Hart warned the nearest local Union commander that if Union men burned a house "in consequence of my having received comfort therein, I shall immediately cause two for one to be burned"; for every Southern sympathizer murdered "in consequence of my having been about," Hart would have two Union citizens put to death; and for every guerrilla killed, he would take the lives of five Union soldiers.[5]

At times, assuming the same moral high road, guerrilla leaders would propose a truce to their Union opponents. Fletcher Taylor wrote Captain Kemper in Liberty that he had left Clay County on the understanding that "the Radicals" would also leave, terms he said had been negotiated by a "Peace Committee" of civilians which had gone between Kemper and himself. Then Taylor had learned that one Coffman had been killed by Union forces. "I immediately returned to avenge his death, and I did by killing the two Bigelows." Taylor had left again "according to promises," but now he had once more returned, this time for good or until all of the radicals would leave. "If all the citizens are to be sufferers by you, I will make the Union party suffer as much, if not more—for by your interruption of them it recruits my company." Taylor's terms for a truce were that all civilians he believed Radical had to leave and that all the remaining citizens, rebel sympathizers by definition, were to be left alone by Union troops. In the same letter, Taylor proposed peace not through a truce but by both sides setting the civilians aside, as it were, and battling it out hand to hand, warrior to warrior. "If you and I would let them alone, we could fight one another and we will be fighting men who have put themselves out for that purpose, and not fight the unsuspected citizen who is not in arms." It was up to the Federal captain. If he let secessionist citizens alone, "I will be equally as kind," and if the Union warred on citizens, "so be it, *I will retaliate*," and if soldiers would be willing to fight guerrillas directly, "I will return the compliment."[6]

One Wedington, calling himself, Lieutenant, Confederate Guerrillas, wrote to Union Colonel Clark in 1863 at Harrisonville near the Kansas border, that he had captured two of Clark's soldiers and had considered executing them "in accordance with the custom heretofore." Instead, he was releasing them with a letter to convey to the Union post, in part because they were just boys but also out of a desire to change the threshold of violence. "I heartily regret the inhuman treatment of prisoners here on the border; but I, by this act, propose carrying it on in entirely a different way. I have released your men, and am willing to do it hereafter. Now let us conduct the war in a way in which we will not be ashamed of in after years."[7] This remarkable act of conscience looked beyond the immediate struggle to a postwar reassertion of prewar norms. At least in this message, Wedington consciously demonstrated that he had kept peacetime elements of cooperation and mercy alive. His was the only such statement I found.

In all the other manifestoes, revenge was the obsessive theme, as in guerrilla estimation mercy was a quality which had been destroyed by the Union. Vengeance was the theme which tied together the tattered bits of self-justification these guerrilla boys assembled in their public proclamations. Thus Bill Anderson, known in folklore as "Bloody Bill," wrote to the citizens of Lexington in July 1864 that the Yankees had killed his father and sister. "I have fully glutted my vengeance. . . . I have tried to war with the Federals honorably, but for retaliation I have done things, and am fearful will have to do that which I would shrink from if possible to avoid." Anderson's was a personal war of vengeance against a personal enemy. Yet he had a semi-conscious political stance as well. He asserted that he was protecting the people against both thieves and Union troops. "My command can give them more protection than all the Federals in the State." He was the bastion of traditional liberty and security. He would "let the Federals know that Missouri's sons will not be trampled on." He was the true defender of the virtue of women. "I will have to resort to abusing your ladies if you do not quit imprisoning ours." He warned citizens that if they heeded Union appeals to take up arms against guerrillas, "I will hunt you down like wolves and murder you." Bill Anderson then half apologized to and half taunted Colonel James McFerran about killing fifteen of McFerran's men: "they refused to surrender and I had them to kill. I regret having to kill such good Southern men, but they are fit for no service but yours, for they were very cowardly. Myself and two men killed nine of them. . . . They are such poor shots it is strange you don't have them practice more." To Captain John T. Burris, an old acquaintance, Anderson wrote in guerrilla humor, "Burris, I love you; come and see me. Good-by, boy; don't get discouraged. I glory in your spunk, but damn your judgment."[8]

Infantile narcissism and a sense of omnipotence characterized Anderson's missive, giving it a surreal quality. He was playing a lethal form of king of the mountain—and was himself killed in October 1864. In his way, Anderson displayed much of the grandiosity which characterized publicly declared guerrilla self-conceptions. Bursting in on the enemy, guns blazing, they saw themselves as noble knights, cunning and daring, rescuing damsels in distress, saving desperate civilians just in the nick of time, slaying the foe, avenging wrong, defending the southern cause. The nasty means they usually employed were forced on them by a barbarian foe. Inside, they were pure.

In 1855 at age eighteen, W. C. Quantrill went West for adventure and to make his fortune. He drifted from one school teaching job to another, dallied with the ladies, rode and hunted. He wrote back to his mother, whom he resented for never answering his letters, that he was sorry he had left her and that one day soon he would come home and settle down. He wrote her during the winter of 1856, "In the Spring I will come home not to seek an asylum, but rather to make one." In 1860 in a letter to his mother, he talked about his wandering ways. "I can now see more clearly than ever in my life before, that I have been striving and working really without any end in view. . . . One thing is certain: I am done roving around and seeking a fortune, for I have found where it may be attained by being steady and industrious. And now that I have sown wild oats for so long, I think it is time to begin harvesting; which will only be accomplished by putting a different crop in different soil." Two years earlier, Quantrill had written to his chum, William Scott, bragging about his prowess at hunting and with the girls, stating a preference for Indian-white half-breeds. "You and the rest of the boys there must attend to the girls well while we are here in Kansas & tell them that we are all going to marry squaws & when they die we are coming to old Dover for our second wives so that they must not despair."

As well as writing about his personal ambivalence concerning appropriate forms for the good life, Quantrill discussed social and political life out West. In 1858 he was a staunch defender of the honor of the Kansas free-state forces against the "D——n lies" told about them in the Democratic press. Of Jim Lane, the leading Kansas radical Republican politician from the 1850s through the Civil War, Quantrill said he was "as good a man as we have." By 1860 he had reversed his position, writing his mother that although "you have undoubtedly heard of the wrongs committed in [Kansas] by the southern people, or proslavery party, but when one once knows the facts they can easily see that it has been the opposite party that have been the main movers in the troubles and by far the most lawless set of people in the country." He hated antislavery Kansans for their defense of John Brown. "May I never see a more contemptible people than those who sympathize for him. A murderer & a robber, made a martyr of; just think of it." Quantrill had a political sensibility; for whatever reasons, he had switched positions. He was not unthoughtful, and had consciously chosen the southern side before the war commenced.

In 1859 Quantrill had joined an expedition to the Pike's Peak gold fields. His party had gotten lost during a Rocky Mountain blizzard. Many of the group had died, and the survivor Quantrill wondered obsessively why he had lived. He wrote his mother when back in Kansas, "I often think that there must have been something else for me to do, that I was spared; for my companions were all strong, healthy men & endured no more hardship than myself, still the greater part of them have seen their friends for the last time on this earth; all of this has had a tendency to rouse me & let me see what I have been doing." As he had been chosen to live by fate, he had to give his life a purpose, to find an "asylum" of meaning, yet he was also possessed with a sense of isolation and internal emptiness. In July 1857, he wrote his mother, "I have but one wish, and that is that you were here, for I cannot be happy here all alone; & it seems that I am the only person or thing that is not happy along this beautiful stream."

Quantrill related his sense of cold isolation, both inner and outer, which was driven home to him by reflection on his Pike's Peak winter experience, to an awareness of warmth and abundance unavailable to him personally, which he observed in springtime Kansas. In the spring of 1860 he wrote, "The prairie has a carpet of green, variegated with innumerable flowers," each forest "branch is set with shoots of tender green," which, along with the springtime songs of birds "enliven the farmer & he joins with them as he turns over the rich loose soil from which he is to reap his harvest for the support of his family." In contrast, Quantrill had no family and did not work the land, the central means through which to enter a full, natural life. Instead, there he sat "in my schoolroom [contemplating] these scenes," his mind drifting back to memories of the "desolation" of the Pike's Peak journey, where "nothing [was] to be seen but snow and sky; and no animated objects but our little company, and they struggling hard to be merry and full of joy." How different the Kansas spring was, "everything here appears rife with life . . . all teaming with animation . . . and all mankind, [with] dreams of the future and building up their prospects. . . . I think everything and everybody around me is happy and I alone am miserable." For him, happiness would forever remain an unobtainable potentiality, which he would always see but never grasp, "for God intended that this earth should *be earth* and not *heaven* for mortal man."[9]

It is tempting to dismiss these sentiments as the maunderings of an ordinary young man steeped in a watered-down literary romanticism. However, something in Quantrill's writing is quite authentic and disturbing. Quantrill felt both an inner deadness and a desire to do something not ordinary but great, and so it is not impossible to understand that he might, if the occasion permitted, turn savagely on life with, in Glenn Gray's words, the "Mephistophelan cry that all created things deserve to be destroyed."[10] Quantrill expressed a deep longing for purposeful action; he had a political sensibility; and he lacked affirmative emotional contact with nature, with his mother, and with other people in general.

Quantrill differed from thousands of other young rural Missouri men, perhaps most clearly in his contemplativeness and his literateness. But it is impossible to know whether he or any of them would have become killers had the war not occurred. It would be tempting but incorrect to dismiss such boys as natural juvenile delinquents who found a big stage, mounted as they were on the fastest horses they could steal, often dressed in fancy shirts embroidered by their girlfriends, armed with several revolvers and bowie knives. Sometimes they had been the local hell-raisers before the war, but frequently former friends expressed surprise at just which boys had turned to cutting throats. "Little did we think when attending school with [Si] Gordon that he would turn out to be as he has," John Warren wrote his uncle in 1864 of a noted guerrilla captain. Decades after the war, the elderly Sam Clemens from Hannibal, who after a very brief guerrilla outing had fled Missouri for the New Mexico Territory, still found it "incredible" that the "uncommonly sweet and gentle boy" John Meredith had turned into a "remorseless" guerrilla. Clemens then drew a parallel to Robespierre who when young was like Clemens's nice friend, John.[11] It should not have astonished Clemens that young men with a wide variety of prewar personalities fought as guerrillas. Some might well have become criminals in any case, at least while young. The most brutal among them indeed came into their own as guerrillas because their taste for force was now highly functional, as was their undermining of the peacetime virtues. After the war a few of these turned gangster. Others in peaceful times might have turned towards family brutality, for instance, or inward to alcoholism, but most likely they might never have found and acted out the killer within. Most ex-guerrillas did not join the James brothers after the war but went back to the farm, raised corn and children, and attended the Methodist Church (Southern) on Sundays.

The social shift from peace to war and the belief, however ill-formed, in some justifying cause for that war and in some romantic notion of self were necessary if not exclusive preconditions for a fundamental change in behavior and values to fit the new landscape of war. Most began using guerrilla tactics when the Civil War politicized local divisions, and almost all those who survived until the end of the war surrendered and took up the proffered amnesty. These men, whatever they were before the war, whatever they might have become without it, reassembled their personalities as independent young warriors within that war. They shared the relative openness and adaptability of the transitional period of young male adulthood, and they developed outside of a context in which the censorship of elders could have much effect. Indeed, their elders generally encouraged them to do things as guerrillas which they would have attempted to forbid in peacetime. But by and large they put themselves together and collected and refined their shared worldview almost exclusively within the circle of their peers.

Their assertions of grandeur—the transformation into warriors—were *always* interrupted, usually by death, sometimes by flight or capture. I have found almost no records of heroic dying words, but there is instead a rich documentation of the varieties of self-defenses made by captured guerrillas. As Union captors knocked them off their powerful mounts, they returned them to the role of subordinate young men. Suddenly they were subject to the authority of their male elders once more, and their captors were furious with them. As prisoners, all the latent fear, suppressed before their peers during guerrilla days, came pouring out as their bravado withered. One sees in captives' accounts the mirror opposite picture of the guerrillas' views of themselves as bands of heroes.

The typical self-defense of arrested guerrillas was that they had been compelled to become guerrillas against their wills and better judgments. "They took me and my brother," John Kinkead told his captors in the Macon military goal. "I was conscripted by a fellow named West last Fall," Samuel McGowan testified in his own defense. "They carried me around for three or four days and then I got away and went home." At their courts-martial, Henry Griffith and George Caldwell claimed that they had been "impressed," and had intended to leave at the earliest possible occasion.[12]

Many guerrilla captives, like Samuel McGowan, stressed the marginality of their guerrilla participation. At his court-martial, James S. Blacketon would only admit to having piloted a Confederate recruit. Questioned at the Gratiot Street prison in St. Louis, Samuel B. Fizer, who admitted that he had sympathies "both ways," also acknowledged that he had picked up a gun but only once and only "for the purpose of fighting the Jayhawkers" from Kansas who had invaded Saline County, and even then he had remained only on the edge of the action and had participated only very briefly. "I staid out on the edge of the town and was there till the fight was over. I then went into town after the fight and staid a little while and then went home." Edward Johnson of Pike County claimed, "I was present at the time of the killing of a negro. It was Denby Taylor's men. I wasn't with them but only one day. They took me prisoner." James Christerman stated that though armed and mounted and with Perkin's band, "I never done anything while I was with him." Christerman then named three other men as his comrades but denied that the four of them had had a leader. "They wasn't organized. I was no bushwhacker." For Christerman, not doing any significant thieving, burning, or killing and not being in a "proper" band meant he was no *real* bushwhacker. In general, if one's own guerrilla participation had been limited, these boys argued, it should not be held against them to the same degree as if they had been ferocious, genuine guerrilla leaders.[13]

Unlike the bold, brave boys they had proclaimed themselves to be in the bush, many captured guerrillas confessed to having had weak, easily led characters. "I went out . . . for want of sense, I guess," James Goodfellow offered, while twenty-year-old J. A. Wysong pleaded with General

Lewis Merrill, "general for god sake spare my life for I am a boy. . . .
I was persuaded to do what I have done an forsed. I will go in service and
figt for you, and stay with you douring the war. I would been figting for
the Union if it had [not] been for others." These boys were misled: the
wickedness was not in them but in those leading them. Charles White of
Clifton Holtzclaw's band testified at his court-martial that he had converted and was now a Union supporter. "I do now support it—I did not
a short time ago. [I joined Holtzclaw] by taking foolish advice." Now he
had taken good advice and had turned Unionist. Sometimes Union supporters agreed that a prisoner was to be treated as being of weak character.
John C. Estes claimed that he had guided Federal troops to a bushwhacker's camp, as well as the other way around. At Estes's court-martial a
militia captain testified, "His general reputation is that he is just anything,"
while to William F. Davis, a lifelong acquaintance, Estes "was looked on
as a tool used by Hart's band—they hadn't confidence enough in him, it
was thought, to take him into the band, but used him to get information."
In one instance, Jackson Bawyer, a well-known lieutenant of Clifton Holtzclaw, while not denying being an active, committed guerrilla, threw himself on the mercy of the court by reminding them what such terrible circumstances could do to even the best of men: "I only ask that the court
will remember the times in which we live: the fearful extent to which, at
this time, our judgments and actions are controlled by passions and preju-
dices, and that in assessing my penalty, it will take into consideration the
frailities of our nature and the inconstancy of human testimony." Despite
his eloquence—or perhaps that of the script written by his lawyer or clergy-
man—Bawyer was hanged.[14]

Other prisoners claimed that they had been drunk while committing
guerrilla acts and were therefore not responsible for whatever they had
said or done. Charles Watkins knew only that he had been drunk on beer
the night he was arrested, but he was sober the next day and had no idea
of whatever "deviltry" he might have committed. In the hard light of the
morning of September 28, 1864, John Hart and Richard H. L. Stevenson
could not recollect their conduct of the night before. In Hart's words, "I
don't know [what happened], I was very tight." A U.S. detective deposed
that at Dougherty's Tavern on Morgan Street near 4th in St. Louis, Hart
and Stevenson had drunk toasts to Jefferson Davis and General Sterling
Price. After their arrest, the booking sergeant at the Myrtle Street prison
had asked the two whether they were Federal soldiers or rebels, to which
Stevenson replied in the bragging form characteristic of southwestern humor that he was "a Wolf and a Bushwhacker, by God." Stevenson repeated
the same news to the guards in the prison yard who had to be restrained
from hanging him on the spot.[15]

Pleas of forcible conscription, of marginal involvement, of weak character, and of drunkenness all shared the quality of being arguments from

essential unwillingness—" 'they' made me do it—I did not really partici-
pate, not *really.*" Another postarrest guerrilla defense was that one's behavior had been intentional but that it was lawful during war. Some arrested guerrillas claimed to be regular soldiers and demanded to be treated
as military prisoners rather than captured bandits. Others asserted that
they had always acted only in self-defense and out of necessity. Still others
argued that when arrested, they were on their way to surrender: as they
had changed their minds and were in the process of voluntarily reforming
their behavior—they had already left guerrilla illegality and had made
themselves loyal once more.

Reese Gott testified at his court-martial that others had done the murdering; he had only been attached to the guerrilla band temporarily as
a recruiting officer for the regular Confederate army. Stephen R. Smith,
for many months a member of Coleman's band which terrorized Reynolds,
Shannon, and Oregon Counties in southern Missouri, claimed he had always told his victims and everyone else that he was a regular soldier. When
he did kill, he was only obeying the orders given by superior officers, which
was a real soldier's duty. Interestingly enough, few guerrillas made this
argument, perhaps because so few of them expected a bench of Union
officers to believe that as guerrillas they were subject to a regular army
chain of command and because they valued their image as independent,
honorable knights-errant. Charles Tatum argued that he was a Confederate
regular who had deserted, that he had only stolen a horse in order to return
home and surrender. He knew horse stealing was wrong, and he intended
to return the animal. "During my service in the rebel army, I sustained the
character I had learned from my childhood—that I was an honest man.
Robbery is the taking of personal property of and from another forcibly
and against his will and with a felonious intent."[16] Tatum (or his lawyer)
sought to show that he was not a guerrilla because his moral character had
remained straight, just like it had been before the war. He knew that theft
was wrong, and why it was wrong, from his early boyhood moral education. He had only been in the regular army, fighting war lawfully, and had
preserved his character. He had only borrowed a horse to get home and
do the correct thing by surrendering to Union authorities—he had not
stolen it with criminal intent. Tatum sought to distinguish himself as a
regular soldier of honor from lawless guerrillas.

Other prisoners argued that if one had acted purely out of self-defense,
one could not be considered a criminal guerrilla but merely a citizen responding legally out of necessity. Thus, William McDaniels of Nordaway
County in northwest Missouri testified at his court-martial that a band of
Union men had repeatedly threatened that, considering him and several
of his neighbors to be dangerous rebels, they would burn them out and
kill them. McDaniels then "fell in" with "some boys" who also had been
threatened. "We fired only because they were going to destroy us. . . .

I am opposed to Bushwhacking and only took up a gun to defend myself and my property."[17]

Combining arguments in his defense, Charles Wells of Dunklin County in the southeast corner of the state argued that he had not gone into the Confederate army of his own accord, that he had not considered Kitchen's band to be guerrillas, that he personally never plundered or marauded, and that he had wanted out and did not understand the difference between surrendering and being taken captive. He also worked on yet another argument which he later scratched out of his court-martial deposition: "I would rather be taken prisoner believing that the rebels would not then have any chance of a cause for further hurting or molesting me—which I feared they would do if I gave myself up to the Federal authorities."[18] While Wells's fears of revenge from his fellow guerrillas indeed might have been a truthful self-explanation, he seemed to have realized that this was not the right defense with which to exonerate himself before Federal authorities. He wanted to emphasize that he had desired to surrender voluntarily and that his only fault had been in not knowing how. He had been trying to regain his will, reassert his conscience, and return to the fold of the Union.

It may well be that given a truly free choice many guerrillas would have sought to surrender, to make individual peace with the Union. Wishing to end "My Rebellion," Dr. W. H. Callaway, who was hiding in Boone County, wrote to his old friend, Union General Odon Guitar, "to call on you for an armistice of peace, [for] honorable terms" of surrender. Callaway admitted to joining Confederate regulars but not to being a guerrilla. Knowing that his neighbors were "calling me every foul name that could be thought of such as horse thief, traitor, vagabond and d——d rogue and rascal . . . it is true I kept to the bush for my own safety and not as a bushwhacker. I have harmed no man neither in person or property . . . my pill bags have been my only weapons." Callaway asked that this letter "be kept strictly secret," probably fearing guerrilla reprisals if it were known he had written to a Union commander.[19] Callaway claimed to be a regular soldier in spirit and a maligned fugitive, who in any event was a noncombatant doctor—and thus had maintained, he hoped, some immunity from treatment as a guerrilla. He personalized his war and sought to return to neutralism, to wipe his slate clean of slanderous misrepresentations through voluntary surrender. He claimed his conscience and his actions had always been clean; he wished the general to recognize this assertion, through accepting an honorable surrender and to allow Callaway to live on as if there had never been a serious suspicion that he was a guerrilla. He had always been a lawful and morally upright man.

Another response was total denial. "I am just as innocent of being a guerrilla as any babe in the world," Charles White told his court-martial, "and I am innocent of the charges. That is all I have to say." The fourteen-year-old Lafayette Powell told his jailer, "I haven't been bushwhacking nor stealing horses. I have never been a soldier of no kind," while John Brison said simply, "I never Confederated any." Some prisoners claimed they had been caught in a Federal dragnet and had done nothing. Warren Lee testified in his defense that he had been caught in a house near to where guerrillas were fighting, that he had had no connection with them and was just there by coincidence. Similarly, others claimed that they were being held illegally as guilty by association or solely because of their opinions. E. D. Roberts, in jail without charges, assumed he was there because of political arguments he had had with Radicals. Mr. Carson had objected to his voting Democrat in 1864. Roberts had also told an Irishman "who appeared to take a great deal of authority to himself. . . . I thought Americans should rule America." John East denied involvement in the robbery for which he had been charged: "I never stole anything. . . . It was my brother. He took some money from a fellow and I was with him."[20] I do not know if East's brother was under arrest, but John was not about to share willingly in any blame.

Of course, all these defenses were by definition self-serving, meant to lead to freedom or at least to palliate the sentences of captured guerrillas. These arguments were intended to suggest that the guerrillas had never lost their prewar knowledge of justice and good moral behavior even when they acted against them. In their grandly written manifestoes they had posited a kind of counter-law—a contravening, partially thought-through set of moral and legal values. That one should have such values was not in doubt; the rebellion went beyond nihilism when young men proclaimed a reworked set of republican values, based on liberty and justice, against a government and society gone corrupt. Not precisely Confederate soldiers, Missouri guerrillas served as best they could some notion of the Confederate state in the making with a set of rules and forms which they asserted in their areas of control and which they believed would emerge throughout the state when they won their victory. They lacked lawyers and political officers to articulate their values, just as they lacked a regular command structure and general military coordination, but almost instinctively, they asserted a free state in the making as their purpose of battle. They also put themselves forward as the legal authorities and not merely as destroyers.

When captured, this fragile political construct collapsed, and these were isolated young men in the grasp once more of the state. They scrambled to fit back into a society they knew quite well both before and during their rebellion. Most often they then implied that the "not-me"—the warrior—had misbehaved, that the "real-me"—the peaceful man—had been conscripted, forced, misled into behavior known now to have been wrong. These legal defenses were also psychological defenses for the young rebels. Their defenses were in a sense rituals of the reassertion of conscience, reaffirmations of the belief in due subordination to proper authority. It is useful to employ the mytho-psychological language of oedipal rebellion in analyzing this process: displacement and destruction of the father's authority—replacement with the knightly, true young brotherhood—brutal suppression by the fathers—submission once more to the rule of the fathers. The grand romanticism of the spontaneous guerrilla uprising contained enormous emotional and intellectual liberation which these boys expressed in their manifestoes, and the humiliation of their capture and resubmission must have been profound for many of them, despite the obvious attraction of postwar survival. After the war, many of them would justify themselves once again as former members of Robin Hood's band, in part to escape the ramifications of such nakedly dishonorable surrender.

Few guerrillas lived on to fit themselves back into conventional society. Most died in their rebellion, some as a result of reckless behavior that approached suicide. At least, responding to violence by violence, they anticipated death by violence. One cannot know what was on their minds at the moment of death. I have found only one speech at the execution of a guerrilla; he remained unrepentantly defiant to the end. Facing a firing squad at Warrensburg on May 20, 1864, twenty-two-year-old guerrilla band leader Willard Francis Hadly proclaimed, "I went into the war to be a terror to the Feds. No man in this country has done more than I have. I went in to rob and steal without regard to law. I thought the South had her rights trampled upon. I am now sentenced to be shot. But I feel that I have been fully revenged."[21] When in power, Hadly had declared that true law licensed the destruction of an illegitimate authority that was oppressing the noble southern people of Missouri. In service to the higher law he had taken his measure of enemy blood and was willing to forfeit his own.

Union Troops' Conceptions of Self and Others

In the Spring of 1862, S. S. Marrett was marching through Missouri with the Third Illinois Cavalry Regiment. As they passed through what they considered secessionist territory, Marrett joined his fellow soldiers in living off the civilian population. At first he was shocked by such foraging, group behavior so vastly different from peacetime relations. One day "the boys killed a hog which would weigh about 60 pounds and it ate very well. When we first came into Missouri I thought it looked pretty hard to shoot down peoples hogs but I have seen so much of it done that it does not look near so bad as it used to." Such activities "certainly would astonish the folks" back home in Clayton, Illinois, who were still living in peace, but "such is the fate of a country through which an army passes." Marrett did not in fact tie the devastation of Missouri just to fate. His regiment was fighting for the Union and "the supremacy of her Laws," while rebellious Missourians were lawbreakers who deserved to be punished. Although still empathetic toward suffering country folks, he steeled himself for such forms of fighting with a political analysis. Passing armies "have fed away everything," leaving farmers destitute of the means of future production. "I do not see how the people are going to make a crop this season. They have nothing left for seed or to feed their teams on or even for their families to eat and I see no other chance but for them to leave or starve. It is a hard case but the people have brought the trouble on . . . themselves and they must take the responsibility of bearing the expenses as far as they have feed or provisions." Sometimes, amid the "homes . . . made desolate by this accursed rebellion," Marrett wrote, his "thoughts [would] recur to the happy days we have spent at home when our country was enjoying peace and prosperity." The destruction in which he fully participated made him very angry; he hoped that one day "hell [would be] the portion of every southern traitor and northern abolitionist, for I consider them equally to blame for . . . this war." Somewhat revisionist in condemning prewar extremists of both sides for the conflict which most Union soldiers blamed completely on the South, Marrett nevertheless expressed the common sentiment that lawless men were aberrant and deserved punishment. The task of good Union men like himself, who would do the punishing, was to set things back in order and then to go home to live in a redeemed, proper society. Not just the Union and state law but "civilized," normal behavior, as Marrett knew it and as he believed all true Americans knew it, ought to be reinforced. Marrett took time in his letter about the deserved plundering of Missouri to instruct his kid brother, like Polonius, to be a good and ruly boy—"Cass, remember what I have told you before. Mind your mother, mind your teacher when you go to school and learn your book. Tell nothing but the truth, use no bad language and when you get to be a man you will be a man of principle and honor."[22]

S. S. Marrett's responses to the destructiveness of war were not unusual. At first, his own participation in it disturbed him, but he soon grew accustomed to it. He did not wish to become as coarse as his fellow soldiers seemed to have become, but coarsen he did. Yet he dealt with his experiences by, as it were, doubling his character between civilian and soldier portions, similar to that done by guerrillas into what I have called the not-me and the real-me. The soldier plundered, exploited, and destroyed those bad people who had fallen beneath the law and the proper moral code. The soldier also fought to preserve the civilian within himself who, among his other tasks, instructed the young about appropriate conduct. For his long-term task of preserving law and order, the soldier was compelled to use harsh, abnormal means such as foraging off civilians and shooting them. These civilians deserved punishment. Not only were they

Southerners in sympathy, but they aided the vicious guerrillas who were lurking about hidden in their midst. When guerrillas picked at the edges of his regiment, Marrett and his companions had their sense of the dastardly enemy reinforced, and then they could fight against the rebellion in even fiercer ways, dividing ever more clearly the good from the bad with the soldier-self destroying evil in order to return at last to the good civilian life back home.[23]

Many young Union troops resisted coarsening, trying to maintain their prewar civilian sense of self and of others as the appropriate basis for moral analysis. Iowa Private Henry Dysart found everyday army life unacceptably degenerate. Though he believed a soldier had to do his duty, he did not see why that behavior had to include what everyone ought to recognize as sinful acts. Of the doubtless well-named regimental surgeon, he wrote in his diary, "Dr. Slaughter means no harm. The sick are under his care and he knows what is best for them . . . what is best of course he'll do, whilst he cures their wounds and feavers he has a very good opportunity not to improve their morals ('there is no harm in playing cards') by playing for the last two hours in our hospital room with a convalescent lieutenant and other boys who he has invited, 'Diamonds is trumps by G–d.' 'Hell another jack!' sounds *cheerful* in the sick man's ears. Is the gambling table a fit association for the acheing head?" Dysart believed that his elders should set a good moral example, that doctors, for example, had a special social obligation of healing the mind as well as the body and ought not to be promoting sinful ways such as swearing and gambling.

It was difficult for Dysart to become a soldier like the others, to adjust or double his character to fit an army life which was so repellent by ordinary peacetime standards. "Each day I realize more and more the necessity of strong resolution in resisting the many foul temptations which I find to daily increase as the men with whom we are associated give way to immorality. Some who make pretensions, who were well raised and know what is right 'bceause they are in the army' give way and make no resistance to wrong, become offended if the Chaplain makes the least refference to their conduct." Dysart then wrote a colloquy in his diary that a chaplain or perhaps he himself would hold with a soldier who was slipping away from the good life. This was also an internal dialogue between the civilian under duress and the soldier-emergent within Dysart. " 'Is'nt that wrong?' 'Not for a soldier'. 'Are you not breaking the sabbath'? 'There is no sabbath in the army. Were I at home I would not do it.' The result of this instability is that we become so accustomed to a looseness of character, our consciences become so seised, that we do daily what we would be ashamed of at home, indecent expressions in our conversation are unnoticed and become habitual. What is to us unnoticed would seem to a parent or any other one from home rediculous."[24]

That many soldiers shared Dysart's internal moral dialogue was attested to by the religious revivals which took place from time to time in the Civil War armies of both sides. In November 1862, Uriah Eberhart, the Methodist chaplain for the Twentieth Iowa Infantry, wrote his wife from southern Missouri in considerable elation over the effects of the past Sunday's sermon which he had delivered from the text "Let me die the death of the righteous, and my last end be like his." "I felt *right* and we had an uplifting time, many tears were shed—& soon half a dozen men joined the Church." That evening Eberhart preached another *"sharp* sermon," from the third commandment—"on *profane swearing.* I tell you I put it down on them *heavy*—men and officers. I made it out to be the most foolish—ungentlemanly—soul-damning sin that anybody could be guilty of. And from what I can learn, it did more good than any sermon I have preached in the army.—A great many came to me & say they never saw it in that light & will quit it—5 joined that night so you can see we are still going ahead."[25]

Though many soldiers resisted becoming unconscionably harsh, they created what amounted to a cult of toughness to protect themselves emotionally. Ordinary farm boys had become armed soldiers, dealing summarily and as a matter of course with violent men whom they would have found frightening and if possible simply would have avoided before the war. Charles Falker wrote to his wife in Wisconsin from Fort Scott, Kansas, at the end of the war, "It is pretty rough here. There are some Kansas troops here and some of them but little better than bushwhackers. Every few days somebody gets shot or shot at. Almost everyone wears one or two revolvers and where men are acustomed to carrying weapons they soon become accustomed to using them too frequently. It seems a little odd at first to wear a sword and revolvers but I soon got used to it."[26] It was not just that Falker wore the Union uniform and arms; he had become a soldier, calm and comfortable amid what in peaceful Wisconsin still would appear a brutally unreal society.

Union civilians came to accept and even admire tough regiments. Kansas Governor John J. Ingalls visited Jennison's regiment, hardened by their 1861 raids into Missouri, on the eve of their departure for the deep South. "If there was *a band of destroying angels* in one congregation I saw them there. They take no prisoners and are not troubled with red tape sentimentalism in any form."[27] These Kansas cavalrymen frightened Ingalls, but they thrilled him as well—reflecting the fear and admiration created within himself by his own civilian wartime coarsening. He wrote about his feelings in a biblical manner, drawing upon the warrior elements in the same Protestant tradition which had inspired the Reverend Eberhart to his sermons against swearing and bad behavior in general.

During the course of the first few months of army life under guerrilla war conditions, most civilians shifted values dramatically and became, with reservations, quite hard soldiers for the duration of the war. As did the combatants, they too experienced basic training.

Henry Miles Moore, a thirty-seven-year-old lawyer from New York State who lived in Leavenworth, Kansas, wrote in his diary for April 25, 1861, that the old Missouri-Kansas border troubles need not flare up again "if good sense prevails. The people are now friendly and will remain so unless some hot headed scoundrels who want to steal kick up a fuss." His good southern friend in St. Joseph, Missouri, assured him that "the people there are attending to their own business just as we are." On June 6, Moore decried a Kansas raid on Missouri, "We have no more business to inter-fere with Missouri than she has with us." Yet by June 24, Moore ap-plauded Jennison's Jayhawkers as "chastening" the Missourians. On August 31, sharing the panic of his Leavenworth fellow citizens that a guerrilla invasion was imminent, responding in that context to a guerrilla attack on a railroad train near town, Moore wrote of how such outlaws should be punished if captured, "Fiends in human shape who would be guilty of such a cowardly & blatant act should be *burned at the stake,* hanging is too good for them."[28]

During the summer of 1861, Dr. Joseph H. Trego, surgeon with James W. Montgomery's Kansas command, was in his words "disgusted" with his regiment. Most were "villains who joined the force for protection in their plundering operations." The officers encouraged the worst behavior of their men, issuing orders in a legal sounding manner really intended to license wild misbehavior. "After breakfast [at Butler on September 13] there was a general time with the boys collecting together such property from stores as are 'needed by the army,' and in a very short space of time, the stores were all relieved of their valuable contents." The officers com-mandeered the most valuable loot from their own men and also set the standard for brutality. Trego "came to regret [his] connection" with the regiment the day Colonel Jennison shot three prisoners after a drumhead court-martial and dumped their bodies in a single shallow grave. On Feb-ruary 1, 1862, transferred to another Kansas unit, Dr. Trego welcomed the "systematic . . . drill," the first he had ever seen in his army experience, as "much needed," and he favored in general the tighter command of this regiment. Yet by July 1862, Trego shared the resentments of most of his comrades against those officers "who have the controlling influence" in the regiment who used it to protect "the property of *all* the *rich* planters around." These officers "think more of the nobility of the South," than they do "of loyal soldiers going on hard tack & coffee when meat, sugar & vegetables are all around." Once a great opponent of jayhawking, Trego now shared in it with pleasure. One September evening he wrote in his diary, "The boys brushed around and got some chickens, sweet potatoes, and some cooking utensils before guards could be stationed all over the place. We had a very good supper."[29]

A shared resentment of both their own officers and of civilians grew among the ranks. The letters of L. R. Webber, who fought with the First Kansas Cavalry, to the family of a Lawrence Congregational minister demonstrated how a bright and educated good boy adjusted to life in the same brutal regiment to which Dr. Trego had first belonged. At the start of the war, Webber, the subject of derision and of much theft and "borrowing" from the Leavenworth toughs who dominated this regiment, could barely survive emotionally. He wrote that he almost wished he could rather "fall in battle fighting bravely" as a form of honorable discharge than live on in such a mob. "If what is practiced in this regiment is good soldiering then I can never get to be a good soldier. Getting drunk, stealing, shirking duty, rioting, and imposing upon the few who [like me] are steady, is the prevailing discipline(?) in this regiment. It is a perfect hell to me." Wanton destruction was coupled to systematic plunder by the entire regiment. For example, the officers would offer a nominal sum to the men who had stolen horses, in turn reselling them at much higher prices: to Webber the whole lot were "swindlers."

Yet after a year in the regiment, Webber could sympathize with the others, even if he did not join in with them. He came to share the regimental belief in the hostility of all civilians. Thus "to half-starve a man, and then punish him for stealing something to eat is the height of injustice." He even came to accept his comrades' need for drunken brawls. Seeing them straggle onto a Mississippi riverboat, faces bloody and bruised from fights, eyes and speech blurred with drink, Webber could respond to what he still believed to be a human mess, "I suppose though that they drink to drown their misery." Sent down the river, the First Kansas continued their Missouri style in Louisiana. After the Widow Anderson had taunted the troops with the prospect that real southern men would scalp them, one Kansan sent her, gift-wrapped in a box, a pair of ears cut from a rebel corpse. For Webber the "only wickedness" of this act was that those men with a "savage disposition [would] derive malignant satisfaction from the deed itself." The decent and correct Webber no longer worried about the mutilation of enemy bodies or the feelings of enemy women but only about possible demoralization among his comrades, alone in an alien and intrusive world at war.[30]

In search of an elusive enemy, marching through an alien territory, soldiers were always hungry, tired, and often cold. They were generally inadequately provisioned by the Union authorities. To fill their wants, they foraged off the civilian population, just taking whatever they needed, with need defined in a flexible manner.

On December 21, 1861, Dan Holmes from Illinois wrote to his sister about living off the land. "We . . . live quite well, not from what we draw from the commisary, but what we jayhawked. I don't suppose you know the meaning of that word. That means when we are traveling through a secesh country we come to the house of some leading secesh, or of some man in the secesh army. Then we take his horses and property, burn his house, or as we say, clean them out. Well, in the operation we generally get a young hog, not a pig, some turkeys, chickens, and once in a while a crock of honey, then don't we live." Writing nine days later, Dan Holmes was more specific and more defensive about his personal role during jay-hawking foraging. "I went out with four men and *confiscated* a team of horses and a yoke of cattle, which I turned over to the government." Dan had not stolen for his own sake; he had appropriated goods under orders for the Union—an exercise he could define for himself and for his family as being perfectly legal. Furthermore, "Burning houses I did not partici-pate in. It may be necessary, but it is not my style of warfare."[31] Dan knew his regiment did the burning, but it struck him as outside his own prin-ciples and perhaps those of several comrades with whom he discussed the issue. It was as if in his second letter he regretted the pleasure in burning and stealing he had permitted himself to express in his earlier letter. He placed himself within emotional limits more circumscribed than the stretched and threatening behavioral territory he had observed his regiment as a whole to have entered. At least, he would forbid himself to express pleasure about joining in the destruction that was his regiment's task in letters writ-ten home.

When it was just a matter of taking food and fuel, the qualms many soldiers felt about foraging diminished. Indeed, most did not remark on these activities in letters and diaries. In his diary, Iowa Private William Branson justified foraging in a direct fashion. He had breakfasted for the hundredth time on hard tack and coffee—"they have us now reduced to fighting weight." His company was always underfed by the commissary. "The fare we get now is fifty per cent below that which the slaves get here or in any other state. Some of the boys brought in a nice mutton for sup-per this evening. It is against the laws of nature to go hungry in a land of plenty."[32] Branson's belief in the higher law accommodated his hunger. Particularly when one was with an armed military company, it was unnat-ural to go hungry on a long march.

In his war journal, Missouri Private Daniel Leroy tried to square forag-ing, which like Branson he considered natural in times of military want, with his generally high personal standards. He "never chewed or smoked tobaco, do not remember ever being drunk. . . . Never was addicted to visiting places of vice or immorality." However, he was less restrained in seeking culinary pleasures, he admitted, as he was always *"desperately hungry."* Of the spring campaign his company made in 1865, he wrote, "Well this swampy tour was of such a character as many soldiers have tested. Human beings (*or soldiers rather*) will eat almost anything before starvation. Soldiers to be placed on strict guard duty 24 or 48 hours or longer with almost empty haversacks expecting to catch as catch could

. . . and sleepless nights and cold . . . combined with hunger would almost render poor soldiers crazy. Then look out (root hog or die) for searches to be made for food, which was frequently done by plundering houses and visting chicken roosts, etc."[33] Leroy could not quite bring himself to admit that he too was a thief, and he could not quite name the act of stealing. He stilled his regrets by generalizing from personal want to collective behavior based on the natural law of survival. Foraging was such a soldier's law—even if it did not extend to normal peacetime activities, and he like the others was now a soldier.

What was true about filling soldiers' stomachs was true of their need for fuel. Fences provided a ready supply of cut and dried wood for cooking, warmth, and cheer at night. Soldiers burned fences, knowing full well the consequences for farmers. David Garver wrote his sister in the spring of 1862 that the grain was growing in rural Missouri "& the cattle & hogs are destroying it for the army had taken fences for miles around & burnt for wood & wherever they camp they take the fences & destroy whole farms." Combined with the burning of their homes, "it will take some of them 10 or 12 years to catch up again." Well, Garver believed, it served them right: they would now "think what Damd Fools they wer for listening to" Confederate entreaties.[34]

In general the soldiers' explanation for foraging was quite direct: We are cold and hungry, we are passing plentiful farms, the farmers are all probably enemies anyway, we help ourselves. E. T. McLane wrote to his cousin Sam about an army expedition in southern Missouri, "We had all the fruit we wanted and at night when we camped we would burn miles of fence and generally confiscate anything and everything we wanted in the shape of secesh cattle, hogs, sheep, poultry, cabbage, potatoes, honey and molasses for the people are mostly secesh and sometimes we were on half rations."[35] All the countryside was ripe for the plucking. Needing to forage off farmers, it made sense to believe that they were enemies. After all, in a guerrilla war this same countryside provided food and cover for bushwhackers, and apparently innocent farmers were potential guerrillas or their supporters—this was guerrilla territory. Such foraging of course had the counterproductive result of pushing many civilians into guerrilla camps out of an angry desire for retaliation.

Foraging did not always stop with food and fuel, although those were by far the most common goods taken. Some regiments, particularly those from Kansas, conducted what amounted to general jayhawking expeditions, carting off wagon-loads of food, furniture, and clothing, as well as taking livestock for their personal use or sale back home. Sergeant Webster Moses of the Seventh Kansas Cavalry knew all about his regiment's reputation for such jayhawking campaigns, which he denied to his friends back home. "We have been misrepresented by some. Them deserters have told some outrageous stories about us." After more fulminating about deserters, Moses wrote, "Now that we are in Kansas the men are very orderly. Even pigs and chickens can run around camp without being molested. In Missouri it was not so." Moses admitted only to foraging for food and then only in "enemy" country. Camped among good Unionist Kansans, he and his comrades were as clean as hounds' teeth.

Such was the disclaimer in one of Sergeant Moses's letters of March 1862, when his unit was back in camp in Kansas. In another letter written to Nancy Mowry while the Seventh Kansas Cavalry was still in Missouri and probably before he had got wind of the terrible things that were being said about his regiment, Moses had written candidly that his squad had "started out into the country to find some furniture for Capt. Merriman. . . . We took our two waggons and went out into the country about two miles to a secesh house and loaded them with furniture, pork, chickens, etc., then started for camp and got here about 3 o'clock this afternoon. That is the way we jayhawk. We have everything we want."[36]

This was a rare, if matter-of-fact, admission that many Kansas troops were instructed by their officers to strip Missourians of their furniture, livestock, and other moveable goods. Such practices were common; admissions were rare because even soldiers who would justify taking food and fuel as army necessities could rarely bring themselves to declare that furniture was such a basic need. At some point foraging became theft in almost all these soldiers' minds, not that they stopped stealing; they simply kept silent about it. Livestock and portable property showed up on the market in the hometowns of many of the Union troops. For example, Philip Welsheimer wrote to his wife in St. Louis, "You say the people intimate that I am stealing goods and shipping them back to sell. I have sold them too many goods already for my own good. Never mind them, just let them lie." Welsheimer told his wife that the neighbors were just lazy and envious, while he was demonstrating good old American economic initiative. "I guess the poor lousey devils are grieved to think that we are not like them too lazy to do anything and when time gets a little hard have nothing, but go with our sterns out and half starved as they do."[37]

In some outfits, the officers directed the plundering and took most of the resale value after buying the goods off his own men at low prices. L. R. Webber deeply resented this practice of the First Kansas Cavalry. All the "good horses which we took at Lexington as contraband have been taken by the officers at a merely nominal price." Webber would help in jayhawking, but only if "everything [taken] is honestly turned over to the government."[38]

Private Webber was not alone in his sense of outrage when foraging turned into systematic plundering. Many good Union men protested, not only when they were plundered themselves but when their peaceful non-Unionist neighbors were looted, out of fear of retaliation from bushwhackers as well as from a general sense of justice. Union officers from more disciplined regiments believed that such behavior was demoralizing to troops and that it only served to justify guerrillas in their revenge and set the community as a whole against the Union army, which supposedly had been sent into Missouri to protect civilian life and property. Early in 1862, Captain J. D. Thompson of the First Iowa Cavalry wrote from Warrensburg in west central Missouri protesting the widespread and "wanton destruction" done by the Missouri State Militia. He assured his correspondent that he "positively refused to permit his men to engage in [such] nefarious business," as should all proper officers. "The Union men of the town are highly incensed at such outrages, and desired me to lay the matter before the proper authorities. The sufferers [were not] bushwhackers, and were all . . . peaceable citizens, though of Southern or Secession principles. The Union men are fearful, and truly so, that the bushwhackers will retaliate, and between the two lay the whole country in ruins."[39] Whether bushwhackers would have stopped plundering the Unionists near Warrensburg if Union forces had desisted punishing secessionist civilians was doubtful, but such was the hope for peaceful coexistence expressed by people of both sides to this proper Iowa captain, who was willing to protect pro-southern people whom the local Union forces had attacked. In this instance, local tyrants of both sides behaved worse than outsiders.

Thousands of such complaints were made to authorities and passed up to higher military and civil leaders. When coupled to accusations leveled from within some regiments by the men against their officers, the army sometimes attempted to discipline the worst offenders. In some instances, whole regiments were sent out of Missouri. In the case of the Seventh Kansas Cavalry, both Colonel Charles R. Jennison and Lieutenant Colonel Daniel R. Anthony were squeezed out of their commands, and the regiment was removed from Missouri and in the summer of 1862 sent into the Corinth, Mississippi, campaign.[40] Following the summer and fall 1862 expeditions in western Missouri, Union authorities sought to weed out the leading plunderers from other Kansas regiments as well. On January 20, 1862, for example, at Fort Defiance, Kansas, the army courtmartialed many men and officers of the Third and Fifth Kansas Cavalry regiments. Fifteen enlisted men were convicted of stealing horses, mules, buggies, and revolvers. They were fined, had their pay stopped for sixty days, and reduced in rank. In his own defense at his court-martial, Private Micajar Sawyer testified, "I stole the horse because they all said we would get no pay. . . . I thought I must obey my officers whatever they told me to do." Several officers were cashiered, including Captain John D. Stewart, the object of a petition called for his dismissal by sixty soldiers who reported that he had regularly collected and sold confiscated property and that he was frequently drunk on duty. Concerning one incident involving another officer on the night of November 20, 1861, one soldier was asked,

"Did you consider Capt. [Eli] Snider in a proper condition to take charge of the squad of skirmishers that night?" The soldier replied, "I did not. . . . He was so much under the influence of liquor that he made a fool of himself and his squad."[41]

Whatever effect these courts-martial had on these regiments, both un-disciplined pillaging and looting on command continued to be widespread practices in Missouri until the end of the war, as many Union officials made clear in their complaints. On August 18, 1862, Provost Marshal Franklin D. Swap in Jefferson City prepared charges against Captain Joseph Park of the Fourth Cavalry, Missouri State Militia, asserting that when on scout for guerrillas, Park regularly permitted some of his command "to fall behind and pilfer the country" of liquor, horses, saddles, and other property, most of which were shipped off or given to the regimental quartermaster who turned them over "to citizens and soldiers" of Park's choice. On August 31, 1864, Brigadier General J. B. Douglass, com-mander at Mexico wrote to a fellow brigadier in St. Joseph that the Seven-teenth Illinois were "almost worthless . . . when they are out their prin-cipal business is to pillage and plunder the citizens. . . . They robbed soldiers' wives of all their clothing in some instances." Douglass wished to prosecute Lieutenant William J. Laird who "was privy to this indis-criminate robbery, or he was not. In [the first] case, if he failed to keep his men in their proper places the fault is his; in the other, if he did not know the fact, it shows great neglect of his duty." On October 20, 1864, Brigadier General E. C. Pike at Washington complained that his troops were uncontrollable plunderers incompetently officered. "My command is made up largely of Germans, and it has been very hard to restrain them from depredations on people known as Southern sympathizers, from the fact that their countrymen living in the district through which we have passed have been so badly used by the rebel raiders."[42]

Plundering doubtless occurs in all wars, and it can even be generalized into a scorched earth policy as it was in 1864 by William T. Sherman. In Missouri, such pillaging was general, as these attempts to stop it attested. General Pike could do nothing about his German-American troops who had deep communal scores to settle. Such shared resentment was the case for most local militia troops in this guerrilla war. The countryside was filled with hostile forces. The soldiers' comrades had been killed by an enemy who would never come out in the open. Any of these civilians, even the friendliest, could be an enemy agent planning their destruction. This was all the more reason to plunder and burn them, punish them, make them pay, show them who was the ruler.

General foraging and theft both led to and grew from soldiers' con-tempt for the Missouri civilian population. As there were endless guerrilla attacks springing from the host civilian population, the cycle of destruction and counter-destruction deepened until many Union soldiers believed the enemy was everywhere and everyone.

Particularly for soldiers who came from states to the north and the east of Missouri—men who had been inundated with propaganda from the border war with Kansas in the 1850s—Missourians appeared an ignorant and backward lot. "Pukes" abounded. In 1863 Dr. H. P. Strong

A pair of "Butternuts" who "only want to be let alone." Union soldiers from more genteel places, such as Dr. H. P. Strong of Wisconsin, and Robert O. Sweeney, the St. Louis soldier who drew this cartoon, despised the plain folks of southern origin whom they encountered in rural Missouri. Butternuts were so named in honor of their homespun clothes which they dyed with extract of walnut or butternut. Only wanting to be left alone was a common protestation of neutrality made by such people to the Union soldiers they encountered. But the soldiers were convinced that most of this backward lot secretly supported the guerrillas. (*Sketchbook of Robert Sweeney, State Historical Society of Missouri*)

wrote to his wife back in Beloit, Wisconsin, about a typically shabby Missouri country town, "West Plains, like all the *principal* towns in Missouri, consists of a small tavern, a court house and a few poor dwellings." The inhabitants of these down-at-the-heels places were a degraded, inferior people. "The ever-lasting butternut clothes and countenances greet us *here* as everywhere else in the South, pale, cadaverous, senseless looking creatures. I am so tired of seeing them. In all our travels in Missouri I have not seen a single man that I would take for a companion. There may be those who are worthy, but if there are they do not show themselves."[43]

Poverty and illiteracy were the usual explanations northern soldiers gave for the tawdry nature of Missouri towns and their subhuman inhabitants. Such cultural inferiority, they believed, led many Missourians into the political error of joining the secessionist ranks. Estimating that half the population could not sign their own names, one Iowa soldier wrote back to his hometown newspaper late in 1861 from southwestern Missouri, "Schools and schoolhouses are things almost unknown, and the ignorance of the aborigines is, in consequence, extremely great. . . . No wonder that Secession, which is the child of ignorance and wild abandon, has attained such deep root here."[44]

Many Union soldiers from outside the state believed that poverty, ignorance, and secessionism in this backward breed were linked to the institution of slavery. With a typical sense of Yankee cultural superiority, including the faith that energy and not sloth governed the men of the North, Sergeant Webster Moses, who had been born in Maine and raised in Fairbault, Minnesota, commented in his diary about the town of Clinton, Missouri, which his unit razed, "The inhabitants here are most all very ignorant and consequently Secesh. . . . The curse of slavery is visible. Business has been neglected and houses are going to decay. They need a little Yankee enterprise here. Many of the male inhabitants spend their time either in card playing or loafing around the public well."[45]

These degenerate whites were often depicted by northern soldiers as intellectually slower than their slaves. Wisconsin Private Stanley E. Lathrop wrote to his family about the unimaginative diet of those in Bloomfield in southeastern Missouri. "The people live almost exclusively on 'corn dodgers' and 'bacon' or smoked hog. They are as a class rather under the common standard of intelligence, while the slaves seem to be quite intelligent. As one of the boys said the other day—'I was in favor of abolishing slavery before I came here, but now I am more so than ever, when I see that the niggers know more than their masters.' "[46]—not that Lathrop's friend thought well of blacks but that he found fellow whites living under a slave regime to have been rendered ignorant and poor by the effects of the peculiar institution.

Because civilian males who stayed on the land tended to be older and more prosperous than those who joined the army or went to the bush, some Union soldiers made a form of class analysis about the division of labor within the hostile enemy population. Captain Eli Crandall wrote from Brookfield in north central Missouri in 1864 that "the poorer and most ignorant portion of the rebel community have gone into the bush as bushwhackers . . . while the rich, influential ones . . . keep them posted in every move made by our forces." Among these comfortable informants who did not fear the guerrillas were "blood-sucking speculators," taking stolen goods and stock out of the region for sale, often to the Union government itself.[47]

Even Missourians in the Union army appeared a clownish lot to Union soldiers from outside the state—lazy, ignorant, and incapable of fighting the rebellion as might be expected given the general social level of the population. A Wisconsin cavalryman wrote in his diary in 1862 while stationed at Cape Girardeau, "A part of a Co[mpany] of State Militia came in here and camped today. They are a motley looking set and would not harm anyone." For his amusement in January 1862 while stationed near Kansas City, Wisconsin infantryman Private Charles D. Waldo watched local troops drill. "After dinner . . . went down to town to witness a dress parade of the 18th Missouri which came off at 3 P.M. It was a poor excuse for a parade, the officers and men understanding but little in regard to the manual of arms, or even in the bearing of soldiers." Two weeks later Waldo again watched them flounder through a march—"of all the drills I ever witnessed, this beat them all."[48]

Only one soldier I found suggested that the policy of his regiment was to educate and uplift these downtrodden Missourians. Private Stanley Lathrop wrote his parents that when the First Wisconsin Cavalry entered one of these dreadful southern Missouri towns, his colonel, Edward Daniels, would gather the population and give them a long and learned speech "with the brilliancy, clarity and directness for which he is noted." Like a fine, itinerant, revivalist preacher he produced "a great effect upon the people and converted quite a number of secesh. . . . The great reason of there being so many of that class of people in Missouri—and indeed the great reason of the whole rebellion is—*IGNORANCE* . . . very few of them think for themselves, and the demagogues and secession leaders befooled them with talk such as an educated class of people would never believe. The Col. told them this in plain words, and extorted them to *educate their children.*" On July 4, 1862, this emissary of enlightenment spoke to a crowd of thousands, "which if anything surpassed all his previout endeavors." After the speech and a free dinner, "toasts, speeches, and a jolly time," some 1,200 men took the oath of allegiance; this was all in all *"an old-fashioned Fourth."*[49]

As the guerrilla war ground on, very few Union soldiers continued to believe in the restorative powers of education for such civilians who remained both low-down and very dangerous. One miserable cold and rainy

morning in February 1863, Lieutenant Richard J. Mohr of the Tenth
Iowa Infantry wrote his girlfriend from a small outpost near the Mississippi River in southeastern Missouri concerning his anger at all the local
civilians. He had just searched a home where guerrillas had been reported
paying a visit. "Pa, Ma, and Mollie" were "apparently much surprised" by
Mohr's reason for calling and denied all knowledge of guerrillas. He
found no bushwhackers inside and presumed that they had taken "French
leave," but he saw many horse tracks in the yard leading to the road in
front of the house. "I had a strong notion to burn the whole establishment
to the ground" and would have done so but for fear of repercussions from
his commanding general. Back on guard duty that night, two soldiers in
Mohr's platoon had to put out their fires for fear of a guerrilla attack,
"so you may imagine that we had a good time." By 1 A.M., cold and soak-
ing wet from the rain and filled with resentment, the platoon agreed to
send some delegates down to "that secesh house" and demand hot coffee
and corn dodgers as well as butter, cream and sugar, and a dozen chickens
for breakfast. "I do not believe that I ever relished a meal so well in my
life." But the fury at the citizens remained. "The boys are getting desperate, it is with difficulty that they are kept from tearing things to pieces
when we go out where the secesh live." Mohr then recapitulated in his
letter to his girlfriend his genocidal fantasies and the miseries that had
caused them. "If I had my way I would devastate the whole region . . .
and shoot every man I caught running from the flames of the burning
homes. Do you think I am cruel? If you would come down here and . . .
do picket duty by standing for twenty-four hours in a cold rain, with no
fire during the hours that it is dark, sleep on the ground in a tent to wake
up in the morning and find yourself in the water that has gathered during
the night, stand by the bunk of a dear comrade and listen to his dying
groans as his shattered bone pains him for the last time, as we soldiers
have done, and then reflect on the fact that these villians are the cause of
it all, I think that you would feel just as I do now."[50]

This Iowa soldier articulated many of the reasons for the loathing which
most Union soldiers came to feel for Missouri civilians in this guerrilla
war. Life was cold, wet, endlessly boring, and punctuated by moments
of violence when a comrade might well be shot by someone out there in
the dark. Civilians, snug and warm and well-fed, ignorant and accursed,
protected by Union troops, were in return aiding the hidden enemy daily.
Many soldiers wished to exterminate them all. Wishing that, they brutalized
many and killed some.

It was impossible with even the best of intentions to separate civilians
from guerrillas and to kill just the combatants, as the fighters blended
into the general civilian population. Reporting the killing and mutilation
of several of his soldiers, Brigadier General Benjamin Loan wrote his commander in St. Louis that he was taking the "most thorough, constant and

energetic means . . . to suppress these outrages," but that it was impossible to come to grips with the guerrillas while protecting the civilians. "A majority of the inhabitants are intensely disloyal, and bitterly opposed to the government; they harbor, protect, and preserve these outlaws." As his forces were in "an enemy's country," trying to guarantee civil peace amounted to "protecting these enemies in all their rights."[51] In these circumstances, Loan could not suppress the guerrilla war.

Any Missourian might be a guerrilla no matter how peaceful he or she appeared. Writing from Warsaw during the dog days of August 1863, Henry and William Crawford conveyed their impression that on the surface "the people seem to have all gone to sleep and forgot that there was any war." Such indolent appearances were deceiving. "There is one kind of people that is asleep with one eye open and only wait an opportunity to murder loyal people without mercy and these men are the ones that walk up to a federal soldier with outstretched hand and a smile on their face and say they have always stayed at home and never done anything." Such guerrillas were "ten times meaner" than regular Confederate soldiers. Crawford hated such snakes in the grass. "I have talked to nearly every man in this town and find that all but two or three are the stay at home type and don't like the draft because they don't want to take any part in the war. Hell will be full of such men before this war is over."[52]

Many soldiers believed that there must have been an organized conspiracy in this civilian-guerrilla activity. Too many carefully arranged ambushes and other attacks occurred for there not to have been careful spying and tactical planning. Wisconsin cavalry surgeon H. P. Strong commented in 1863, "The guerrillas are just as thick as ever. . . . The inhabitants that are today at home pretending to be either Union men or neutrals are the ones that shoot from the bush and waylay stragglers tomorrow. They are organized and instructed by some head . . . and then they run the thing on their own responsibility."[53] Organized in general but capable of improvised lightning attacks, the guerrillas set the tempo of the war and specified much more precisely than could the Union forces the objects to be attacked.

Union soldiers were aware that the guerrillas had far better sources of information than they did. Good information multiplied the effectiveness of a relatively small number of guerrilla attackers. Wisconsin cavalryman Edmund Newton wrote to his sister from Cape Girardeau in southeastern Missouri in 1862, "This country is infested with marauding bands that murder and plunder all that come in their way . . . all our movements have to be very secret or else the whole country knows whenever any detachment is sent out."[54]

Informed of Union troop movements against them, guerrilla bands would simply split up and melt back into the civilian population or else hide in difficult terrain, in woods or along river bottoms or in swamps. Edmund Newton wrote that near Cape Girardeau "there are some swamps where men can skulk & hide and it is impossible to ride a horse that they have the decided advantage."[55] The guerrillas' ability to vanish enormously frustrated their Union pursuers. Illinois Private Charles C. Curtiss expressed his response to this infuriating guerrilla elusiveness after his return to Jefferson City from a typically inconclusive mission out in hostile Boone County. "The scout returned this evening. They as usual saw nothing of the rebs. The guerrillas . . . always run when you get after them and having the start as they generally do and with their knowledge of the country they almost invariably manage to escape."[56]

If they were operating close to home, which was often the case, guerrillas would cut and run, each to his own domicile. Then which of the smiling, bland chaps you met on their doorstep in the evening had shot up your patrol that afternoon? "They are a pack of cowards. They are like a thief in the night," Illinois Private E. C. Sackett concluded about these dogs who would never stand up and fight like men. "If they are pursued by troops they cut & run for their houses. If you go to their houses to question them & they are good union men & unless you catch them in the very act you dont know who they are & most of them are smart enough not to get catched at all."[57]

Guerrillas used their abilities to scatter and hide in part to diminish the effect of reprisals. Similarly, they nearly always avoided engaging a Union unit of any strength and size, waiting to strike until those moments when they were overwhelmingly strong. Charles E. Beechem's company of the Third Wisconsin Cavalry searched for Quantrill's band in western Missouri in the summer of 1862, offering themselves up for ambush in ravines and woods, "where we expected to be fired upon from the bush by these desperadoes," but Quantrill's band did not choose combat with almost ninety alert, well-mounted and well-armed Union cavalrymen. "Their game is not to fight an equal number even with the advantage of the thick bush to hide themselves in, but they find a person alone or a small squad of men to rob and kill them. We found the body of one man that they had killed . . . about a week [ago, with] two bullet holes in him."[58] There was no fair fight here; the guerrillas did not come into the open, unless to make an easy killing.

Union troops rarely saw guerrillas, and at the same time they had an acute fear that the guerrillas saw them and would choose the moment to attack when they had relaxed their guard. One evening, Henry Dysart recorded in his diary the materialization of an apparition-like stranger among his Iowa company. "A citizen with a blanket over his shoulders was noticed walking among the wagons . . . he soon came up to the fire where he stood a moment with his head dropped hiding his countenance from our view." Asked if he were a Frenchman, he replied he was not and began to walk off. Dysart and a comrade, both unarmed, went after the stranger and asked him who he was. He "whirled around and with an oath drew and cocked a revolver on us" and said he was a "privileged character and went where he pleased." He then "ran into the thicket at full speed [and] when a quarter of a mile off he made two or three Indian like yells as if giving a signal." Knowing that the guerrilla "Coleman and his train burners were in the neighborhood," assuming this to have been a spy, Dysart's company doubled their pickets and waited for an attack which did not come.[59] This weird guerrilla appearance and disappearance, this Indian yell in the middle of the night, greatly discomfited Dysart and his comrades. It was as if a ghost had signaled an imminent invasion; it was as if this elusive guerrilla were other than a mortal man.

Guerrillas depended upon this sort of terror-inducing surprise. They used any possible ruse to give them the edge in a short, sharp fight. It was quite common for them to dress in Union uniforms to fool Union troops as well as civilians. "Many of them are clothed in our uniforms and are often mistaken for our men," Dr. H. P. Strong wrote to his wife. In May 1863, Livingston's guerrilla band in southwestern Missouri rode right into a company of the Eighth Missouri State Militia Cavalry, who, a Union officer reported, "mistook them for our own men, and before discovering them . . . had received a galling fire, and were fighting hand-to-hand."[60] This trick infuriated Union commanders; most of them let their men know it would be a good thing to shoot guerrillas disguised that way on the spot, wearing Union uniforms being deemed sufficient grounds for killing them. Lieutenant Colonel Bazel F. Lazear wrote in 1862, "Col. Boyd has [several] guerrillas under arrest and I hope to God that they will be shot. I hate their getting the clothing worst of all for now we cannot tell them from our own men."[61]

Under such enormous pressures, Union troops rather relished executing captured guerrillas. This was a temporary means of group catharsis in this terrible territory. Stationed in southern Missouri in "mountainous country so favorable to bushwhacking and so hostile at large," Kansas cavalryman Augustus Bondi wrote in his diary that when "Five bushwhackers were . . . captured and executed in front of the Court House, the youngest boys of our company volunteered for the job of execution and burial."[62]

It was a great event when a large guerrilla band was captured. Many Union soldiers would travel great distances just to look at their tormentors behind bars. Dr. Joseph H. Trego traveled forty miles to observe "Taylor and the forty-eight guerrillas taken with him at Montevello a few days since. Some of the party are vicious looking, others appear as harmless as men need be."[63] Expecting to see a set of monsters when he at last laid eyes on a band of guerrillas, Trego was somewhat surprised that many were so ordinary. When captured, these guerrillas were no longer intrinsically fearsome, and Trego could afford to rehumanize them. But lurking in the bush they had been ferocious carnivores.

A free guerrilla was an unseen enemy, skulking, striking, melting away. He was out there; you could make forays into his territory by day, but by night the countryside and its inhabitants were his, while you retreated to your armed camp with your fellow soldiers, waited, and listened. On the night of July 3, 1862, Provost Marshal Thomas C. Fletcher was writing his report to his commander concerning what he considered the salutary effect of the recent execution of the leading southern sympathizer of Washington County. "Since I have been sitting in the block house writing this . . . report I have twice heard the report of fire arms in the woods not over a half mile distant. None of the men belonging to the command here are absent and it is not known by whom the guns were fired." It was as if the landscape itself were animated by destructive forces encircling one's military outpost, making Union soldiers virtual prisoners. Henry Dysart wrote in his diary, "let me live where neighbors are at home. These hills are hosts for hostile pickets, guerrillas haunt these fertile little valleys and make it dangerous to roam."[64]

The Blurring of Combatants

Union soldiers felt surrounded and always under surveillance and potential attack: the frightening "they" out there had become everyone but themselves. Under intense and continuous pressure, they gradually lost most of their ability to discriminate between guerrilla and civilian targets, and they themselves began to adopt guerrilla tactics. They learned that they could not engage the enemy in an open or conclusive battle and realized that to survive they would have to fight a dirty hit-and-run war in the manner of the enemy. They used spies dressed in civilian clothes, destroyed sources of potential aid to the enemy, terrorized civilians, and executed prisoners. Such tactics alienated most civilians, including many erstwhile Unionists, but other civilians joined with Union soldiers in applauding brutal tactics as the only way to beat the guerrillas at their own game. In any event, once a Union unit had been frightened and bloodied by guerrilla bands, it no longer mattered much to them what civilians thought. Soldiers intended to get even for their losses by whatever means necessary. In Missouri-style warfare, the southern guerrillas had determined how the Federal troops would fight.

Right at the start of the war, many Union soldiers concluded intuitively and quickly that they would have to fight fire with fire. On June 30, 1861, stationed on the Mississippi River across from Missouri, Private Henry J.

Marsh wrote in his diary, "One of the picket guard was shot last night over at Bird's Point by some of the sneaking rebels. They seemed determined not to carry on this war as civilized nations do but in Indian fashion. I would like to belong to a guerrilla camp, well mounted and armed over in Missouri. I think such a corps of men could do a great deal in cutting up small parties . . . also annoying the large ones."[65] Marsh sensed the appropriateness of deadly guerrilla tactics to harass, demoralize, and render ineffective organized troops. He knew such methods were effective in part because they departed from all civilized standards, and he understood that his comrades would have to make a similar wartime moral detour in order to respond vigorously to secessionist guerrillas.

If Union troops could turn guerrilla tactics back on the guerrillas, perhaps such treatment, the power of which Union troops felt when used on them, would undermine and finally dissolve the guerrilla will to remain together, which was victory in such a war. On December 1, 1861, Iowa infantryman William Richardson wrote his parents from Sedelia in west central Missouri, "The only way to get the country rid of these sneaking devils who are laying around in the brush and killing men as they pass along the road . . . is to play their own game. Just shoot them down wherever we find them. In so doing we can soon make them sick of their own work."[66] At this early stage of the war, Richardson had hopes that clearly targeted counterattacks would produce quick results, but his "game" included coming to terms with what proved to be a four year cycle of reprisals by both sides.

When not divided into small units stationed in towns and other strategically central points, Union troops would gather in larger numbers, ranging from company to regimental strength (approximately 90 to 1,000 men), and sweep a sector of the countryside, plundering, burning, and shooting what they defined as the enemy, including civilians supporting guerrillas. Private Jeremiah Swart wrote his parents about one such operation of the First Wisconsin Cavalry in May 1862. "This hot sun just uses us up so I can hardly stir. The regiment operates as an independent concern. They go in the regular jayhawker style living on the people as they go along."[67] Since the guerrillas evaporated before the advancing Union troops like the Wisconsin cavalry and re-formed after they had gone, the operation had to be repeated time after time, devastating much of the countryside but never destroying all of the guerrilla's base or most of the guerrillas.

Mirroring guerrilla tactics, Union forces used spies extensively, attempting to infiltrate guerrilla bands and to gain solid information. Frequently, they too would seize hostages to exchange for civilians kidnapped by guerrillas. In a dispatch typical of many, Major J. B. Kaiser, commander of the Union garrison at Licking in the Ozarks, wrote to his district headquarters in May 1863 that seventeen guerrillas under Captain Cook had "arrested and carried away five loyal citizens" and that he had immediately replied by arresting "five of the most prominent Rebel Sympathizers . . . as hostages."[68]

The deadliest sharing of tactics was the general policy both sides had of taking no prisoners. Never quite official Union policy, neither was it the uniform practice of either side. Sometimes both sides took and held prisoners, and sometimes they let captives go after stripping them of arms, money and valuables, mounts, and not infrequently, clothes. But in general and whenever they wished, Union troops shot or hanged their captives, as did their guerrilla foes. Many soldiers alluded to this widespread practice, but few so matter-of-factly as Private Edward Hansen, formerly of the Confederate army, who by 1864 had joined the Union Second Missouri Light Artillery. On July 19, 1864, near Patterson in southeastern Missouri, Hansen noted in his diary, "Up to this day we had done but little skirmishing, and catched several fellows, very mistrusting figures, which we had orders to take with us as prisoners, but no sooner did we find one in arms, we just hung them to the next best tree. . . . We found . . . about a dozen guerrillas, in a big tobacco field . . . and we managed to catch 7 of them. The Cavalry men took charge of them, and the next morning we saw'm all hanging on the trees in the wood." For this Union unit any armed civilian was fit to be hanged as a presumed guerrilla. Yet on September 8, Hansen's unit "overtook some guerrillas in the woods, chased them for awhile, shot three of them, and captured 5 of 'm, which we took into custody, and delivered to a [nearby] military post." Hansen did not indicate why these five guerrillas who had shot back at them were spared. He continued to report that almost all the guerrillas his unit captured were executed immediately, as for example on March 3, 1865: "We hung a guerrilla Captain by the name of Hamilton, alias 'Jim Low.' "[69]

One reason to take a guerrilla prisoner rather than to hang him immediately was to extract information from him, whether by torture or by positive inducement. Knowing this, some guerrillas offered information as a *quid pro quo* for Union protection should they surrender. In 1863 Abiel Leonard wrote from Fayette in central Missouri concerning the two guerrilla sons of professed Unionist Daniel Heard. "Heard had been endeavoring to get his sons out of trouble at their request . . . provided they will not be sent" to military prison. They will "give security for future good conduct. . . . Heard's sons could be made of great use to us, if we could once commit them so that they would not fly the black [flag] upon the first opportunity."[70]

At times, under orders to do so, Union units would dress in civilian clothes and campaign exactly like guerrilla bands, hoping to fool the civilians in the neighborhood into revealing the support system they had established for "real" guerrillas and exposing bushwhacker identities. Warning off other Union units from mistakenly attacking such an undercover band,

Lieutenant W. T. Clarke wrote to a fellow Union garrison commander, "There is a party of soldiers from here in disguise in the neighborhood of Ridgeley, scouting secretly and under orders after the style adopted by the guerrillas. Be careful and not run into them."[71]

Union troops most often became guerrillas, however, not by clever design but out of demoralization. Local militia units in particular were rarely paid, poorly officered, and badly organized—and especially concerned with revenge. In February 1864 in Springfield, Brigadier General John B. Sanborn voiced the constant anxiety he shared with his fellow officers about the danger that his militia units would dissolve altogether into guerrilla bands. "It is impossible to keep up the morale of the troops." In a passive voice, as if from shame or intense frustration, Sanborn described his command's current preoccupation. "Depredations are committed that would not be if the troops . . . had the hope of pay. . . . We are kept in the constant fear that the troops will abandon all organization and go home; and what is worse, their homes having been destroyed by the enemy and their property exhausted in the service, themselves turn into the very bushwhackers and robbers that they have been destroying."[72] Within the service, these troops had adopted tactics of destruction similar to those of the guerrillas. Fighting a fearsome and inconclusive war for which they were underpaid, ill-trained, and badly equipped, their commitment was undermined. The form of war they had learned was guerrilla war; pursuing it, they fought like guerrillas. Only residual loyalty to the Union gave their actions a Unionist coloration. Indeed many militiamen did exactly as Sanborn feared, crossing the thin line dividing Union antiguerrilla soldier and southern guerrilla by putting down the Union flag while staying in armed, roaming bands.

Right from the start of the war, conservative Unionists stated their fears that the local Union troops would behave exactly like guerrillas, thereby driving neutral men into the secessionist camp. On August 5, 1861, D. K. Pitman wrote to the provisional governor from Cottleville that he wanted the Union Home Guards disarmed. "I now feel alarmed, fearing a collision between the encampment and the citizens. They seem to go at will about the village, drinking and insulting with pleasure all that cross their path. . . . Should any violence be committed by the 'home guards' I will not pretend to say where it will end." On August 8, 1861, L. W. Burris wrote from Liberty in west central Missouri that the Union troops were creating secessionists out of neutral citizens. "The shooting of such men as Lightner . . . and the searching of private houses and drawers and trunks where there is no ground for suspicion is causing a great deal of uneasiness in the minds of loyal citizens for they are annoyed in the same manner as the most violent Secessionists in the State."[73]

Avowed conservative Unionists often blamed not only undisciplined enlisted troops for these excesses but Union commanders as well. One citizen complained to the Union commander in St. Louis that Brigadier General Clinton B. Fisk, commander in northwest Missouri, was nothing but a "goose" who sponsored endless killing and plundering on the grounds that everyone who was not an unqualified radical was a rebel or a sympathizer to be "shot or driven from the State. [Fisk] never has had the first case investigated. . . . All men who are opposed to stealing and burning and shooting men down at home, who are just as loyal men as live," had been terrified into silence by these Union marauders. As it happened, at this time Fisk had tried to stop what he called "outrages" committed by his soldiers on furlough. "I should dislike very much to arrest and punish these brave boys, but I shall do so unless the complaints cease."[74] Basically, Fisk supported his soldiers and discounted complaints as coming from sources he suspected to be sympathetic to guerrillas. He wanted to vigorously prosecute the war, believing that to temporize with disloyal citizens would only encourage their treason.

Many citizens and Union troops admired guerrilla-style warfare, believing it to be the only way to suppress the guerrillas in the bush. During the first years of the war, two Iowa soldiers commented separately on their admiration for the swashbuckling Kansas political leader, Jim Lane, U.S. senator and general. One reported to the Keokuk newspaper about the drill of a Kansas regiment, "General Lane stepped about watching the evolutions of the various companies, dressed in long-legged, high-heeled boots, neat dress-coat and sash and glazed cap, lacking only a plume to remind one of a brigand of the old times. It is said that his camp fires are beacon lights to many a slave seeking refuge from his home of bondage." Terrifying as well as dashing, this was just the sort of near-outlaw to have on one's side in such a war. William Richardson, another Iowa soldier, wrote to his parents, "Woe be to the traitors when Jim Lane gets among them. I suppose there are a great many who are opposed to his way of fighting even in Iowa, but it is the only relief." Richardson then told his parents about a recent Iowa soldier convert to Jim Lane's tactical style. "R. J. Jones used to be strong in favor of the South but he, like all of us says he is in favor of taking every thing from them except a hemp rope and that tie around their d——d necks and swing them across the first tree."[75]

For many Union participants, adopting a war of reprisal and extermination—or as they would have defined it, counter-reprisal and counter-extermination—against a foe who had initiated such barbarity was the only potentially effective way of combatting guerrillas. This was the route by which an official army adopted the guerrillas' mode of warfare.

In addition to their uniformed service, Union soldiers often impersonated guerrillas. Sometimes acting the guerrilla was done to entrap secessionist civilians, and thus contained a legitimate quality of spying for the proper authorities. For example, on May 10, 1865, one of R. Helms, Jr.'s "boys passed himself for Captain Porter the noted bushwhacker" and snared Mr. Clifford, a conductor on the Pacific Railroad, who voluntarily offered the so-called guerrillas whiskey, information, and whatever future "assistance lay in his power to render." Three-and-one-half miles north of Clifford's farm at the house of Thomas Alexander, again representing themselves as bushwhackers, the Helms boys obtained a horse given to them voluntarily.[76] Helms made a full official report of this pretend guerrilla episode.

Quite often Union troops would impersonate guerrillas—not on a sanctioned underground scout but completely outside their Union role—for personal gain. Militiaman William Groom of Marshall was caught after holding up a local farmer for $15.20 and shooting a Negro boy in the hand. "He passes or rather attempts to pass (as it appears from the evidence) himself off as 'Bill Darr' a notorious guerrilla who has been doing a great deal of mischief in this part of the country," a Union investigator reported.[77] This incident raised interesting questions about what might have been the difference between impersonating a guerrilla and actually being one, but Groom seemed to have wrapped himself in a guerrilla mantle to appear a more frightening thief while remaining in the Union militia for his own protection, thus trying to have it both ways. Seeking the intimidating coloration of a guerrilla also may have influenced Abner Harrison in the middle of the night of July 7, 1864, near Mexico in east central Missouri when he came roaring up to the house of Edith and J. B. Barker and, in the words of Mrs. Barker, "waked me and my husband and demanded of him his arms, that he was a damned old Union man and that if he did not give his arms to him he would have them anyhow. He said he was a confederate soldier but afterwards said he was a bushwhacker. . . . As soon as he received the gun he rode off swearing and making considerable noise calling to his comrades who I supposed were in the lane. I saw but one man." In fact there were no comrades. Two days later Payton J. Morris, a neighbor of the Barkers, returned the gun, saying that "the man that took the gun was drunk . . . and wished me to forget and forgive it as it was but a joke." If Mrs. Barker would "say nothing about it," Morris promised to bring over the repentant imitation guerrilla, which he did. Abner Harrison then said to Mrs. Barker that he had "only intended" the incident "for a little scare," that he was truly sorry that he had frightened Mr. Barker away from home, and that to make amends he would cut the Barker's oat field. The last laugh was on Harrison whom Mrs. Barker reported to the authorities.[78]

Few stories of guerrilla impersonation ended with such a whimper. Quite often in great exasperation, Union officials reported that groups of soldiers in demoralized and disorganized companies went off marauding on their own. "Robberies are constantly occurring between [Springfield] & Rolla of the mail & of wagons loaded with goods," John S. Phelps wrote to the Union commander in St. Louis in August 1863. "Many are of the opinion that soldiers of Colonel Siegel's regiment & of Colonel Gravelly's regiments State Militia are the perpetrators." Units of both regiments are "represented to be in a state of insubordination. . . . Murders are also perpetrated in Laclade & Pulaski cos., & they are by our soldiers or by scoundrels dressed in our uniforms."[79] One of the extra effects of southern guerrillas dressing in Union uniforms was to render the identity of all men acting like guerrillas while in that dress uncertain, including actual Union troops that did so. The "official" identity of highwaymen and murderers became very unclear, providing cover for all parties who acted outside the law.

At times, a Union spy was given an official order which he would use to legitimize a personal guerrilla-style raid. In June 1864, acting on a detective's commission from the St. Louis provost marshal, Harry Truman, not a Kansan but a native Missourian, swept through Chariton County in central Missouri, acting, in the words of Brigadier General Clinton B. Fisk, the staunch Union commander of the district, as "a disgrace to our Christian civilization." Truman "is plundering the best men in North Missouri, insults and abuses women, travels in the most public thoroughfares in a state of beastly intoxication, with a notorious prostitute in company with him, and is guilty of all the crimes that I, as an officer of the government, am under obligation to put down." Fisk finally arrested Truman and returned a great deal of plunder, but Truman was never convicted of any crimes because after several would-be witnesses were murdered, the remainder would not testify against him.[80]

Given the opportunities as well as the dangers of this guerrilla war and the divided loyalties of those conservative Unionists who made up most of the rural population of Missouri (from which the Union militias were drawn), collusion between them and the guerrillas was common. Frequently, the militia were drafted—or at least compelled to volunteer; they often hated Yankee invaders nearly as much as the secessionists did. They sometimes sought to make a private peace with guerrillas through a less than vigorous prosecution of the antiguerrilla war in exchange for a certain muting of guerrilla violence and theft. These local troops strove for peace in their own neighborhood, believing that they could develop an understanding with local guerrillas to keep the Civil War out of their locale regardless of what was happening elsewhere. Committed Unionists believed that this plausible desire led to collaborationism.

Loyal militia troops frequently came to believe that their own officers had worked secret deals with the enemy, particularly when they could never seem to find any guerrillas. In 1862 John Benjamin wrote to his wife in great frustration that the people were "all rebels" in one part of Shelby County in northeast Missouri, "but you cannot catch them at anything." All the men in Benjamin's regiment suspected their own colonel of collusion. "Our Colonel has pretty nearly extinguished himself—he had such a fancy for showing favors to the secesh that his character for loyalty had become suspect by the majority of loyal folks."[81] Benjamin believed that where there was so much smoke there had to be fire.

Private James D. Meador, who lived near Kansas City, had much fuller evidence of the collusion of Felix J. Burnes, formerly captain of Company G, Seventy-Seventh Regiment, Enrolled Missouri Militia. "Burnes acknowledged to me while he was in command of this Co. and in actual service that he was not afraid of Bushwhackers, that he had met and held conversations with them." Burnes had two brothers in guerrilla bands. Confronted on the street with accusations that he had been seen with guerrillas and that "he shook hands with them and took some to the side of the road and held a conversation with them. . . . Burnes became very much agitated, letting his pipe drop from his mouth and passing urine freely, which caused the bystanders to laugh" and Private Meador to be convinced of Burnes's guilt.[82]

It should not be surprising that in addition to bitter fighting there should also have been widespread Union collusion with guerrillas who were indeed often actual brothers as well as kin and neighbors of long-standing. Large segments of the militia, sometimes whole regiments, collaborated with guerrillas at least some of the time. Loyal officers knew that many of their men were too friendly with the enemy. Major J. M. Bassett, the provost marshal in St. Joseph in 1862, requested four detectives from St. Louis to ferret out the truth about the activities of the soldiers of his district. "The Confederate influence predominates, and a portion of the Militia are inefficient. They never see anything to do or find anyone to arrest."[83] Not only did such militia not find anyone to capture, they never seemed to be able to guard notorious prisoners well enough to prevent their escape. Lieutenant William McIlwrath of Chillicothe in north central Missouri asked his commander for instructions in December 1863. "There is too much sympathy between . . . these militia [and guerrillas] for any reliance to be placed on them." McIlwrath had finally managed to arrest the two men he considered to be bushwhacker ringleaders, "placing them under strict guard—at least such were my orders—both however have escaped."[84]

The membership of guerrilla and militia units intersected in both directions. At times guerrillas would scatter in the autumn and enter Union militia units over the winter when the absence of ground cover made bushwhacking far more dangerous. A Union spy reported in October 1863 that many guerrillas were headed north of the Missouri River: "I also learn that it is their intention to act with the E. M. M. during the coming winter and return again to the brush in the spring."[85]

It infuriated active officers that many militiamen would not fight guerrillas. Inactivity appeared a form of collusion to them, which in a sense it was. In great anger one Union officer in north central Missouri in October 1864 gave a sense of why such militia troops—"cursed coppers," "miserable cowards," he called them—laid low. "They say if they get caught in the service they are sure to be put to death." Rather than fight they were likely to flee, and now "all are remaining in their houses, cooped up for fear a bushwhacker or rebel may find out they are for the Union."[86]

Staying indoors out of the action, like bargaining privately with the guerrilla enemy, was as sensible, if dishonorable, a survival strategy under the circumstances for militiamen as it was for the civilian population from which they came. To minimize destruction, many citizens sought alliances with men of a wide range of loyalties as a form of contingency planning. They wanted friends and protectors in all camps. Thus Provost Marshal O. S. Steele reported, probably accurately, about southeastern Missouri which he believed contained "few loyal men. . . . Rebels is taken in as partners with the best businessmen & merchants and whenever they get in a tight place then the Union man is put forth to accomplish the object."[87] What Lieutenant Steele would not have seen was the Union men putting forth the southern man when they got in a tight spot caused by guerrillas. Such coalitions with all parties made good business sense.

Unconditional Unionists were constantly apprehensive about the loyalty and intentions of their professedly neutralist and their openly pro-southern neighbors. Not only were they afraid of their cooperation with guerrillas; they dreaded a wide-spread secessionist uprising, planned by an organized, secret fifth column. Often this conspiracy was thought to be directed by a secret rebel order, the Knights of the Golden Circle—which many Union men believed was being organized by copperheads and other disloyalists all over the North. But there was also a more diffuse Unionist paranoia, activated by an odd glance or a smirk from a presumed rebel sympathizer. Thus Lieutenant Colonel F. T. Russell, a militia commander, reported on April 3, 1864, from the strong Union garrison town of Columbia about something strange in his pro-southern neighbors' collective mood. "Sympathizers look and act bolder, and have increased confidence. It is so marked as to be talked of by Union men as obvious in all the county, and excites serious fears." Russell was certain the enemies were concocting some devilish scheme, though exactly what it was he did not know. This something, big and imminent but as yet hidden, had nearly panicked good Unionists in the region. "To my mind it is clear that there is some mischief coming, although I cannot make it out. They are counting on an invasion or an insurrection. So very marked is the change that it is founded on something generally known to them and in which they confide."[88]

In northwest Missouri, Unionist fears of widespread collusion and conspiracy were focused on the activities of the local militia. The Paw Paw militia consisted of formerly disloyal men, including ex-Confederate soldiers, who Union authorities had believed would protect their own homes against all marauders, whether Kansans or guerrillas. The derisive name applied to them by Unionists came from a bush which grew along Missouri river bottoms, the preferred hiding grounds for bushwhackers. In the summer of 1864, it was clear to Brigadier General Clinton B. Fisk, beleaguered Union commander in northwest Missouri, that the Paw Paws in his region were nearly interchangeable with the guerrillas, who shared the countryside and operated in concert with them against loyal Union troops and citizens. "Many of the Paw Paws have themselves gone into the brush. No bushwhackers . . . have as yet harmed a Paw Paw. They do not harm each other in the least, and I very much fear the understanding is they will not. Union men are plundered and murdered, and refugees from the two counties are asking for protection that I cannot give from the means at my command." A citizen of Parkville put the matter more succinctly, "Paw Paws will never find the bushwhackers. Secesh are laughing in their sleeves."[89]

Not only did the Paw Paws collude with guerrillas, not only might they one day rise in mutiny, they also terrorized loyal Unionists. Many petitioned the authorities for the disbanding of the Paw Paws, among them fifty-four men of Mound City, who wrote General Rosecrans on February 27, 1864, asking him to "deliver us from the hands" of these enemies of the Union. Nearly all the Paw Paws were southern sympathizers. "They threaten that the day of Union men is past and that others will fall at their hands." Already they had shot two Union men. Their leader, Colonel Scott, had made a speech calling loyal men "the meanest men in the country. . . . Often they have spent months in a Southern army or in the bush shooting Union men. Are they to be looked upon as our friends and armed?"[90] Many Union men shared the sentiments of young Wiley Walker, who swore in an affidavit on March 2, 1864, "I think if these Paw Paws are left to guard the Union men of Platte County much longer, there will not be many Union men left to guard pretty soon. It seems to be their principal business to hang, jayhawk, rob and plunder Union men there."[91]

Conspiracies did happen. In July 1864 in northwest Missouri, approximately 1,500 Paw Paws rose up and openly joined the Confederate rebellion. On July 7 at Parksville, and on July 10 at Platte City, where they raised the Stars and Bars, several companies joined the command of Confederate Colonel John C. Calhoun Thornton. A "great mass of citizens have thrown off the mask," General Fisk stated. The militia company commander at Platte City reported that "some of the men in all the companies would have fought had it not have been that they knew the others would join the bushwhackers." Instead, clearly having planned to revolt, this garrison of 130 permitted a band of bushwhackers to ride into town and then emerged from their blockhouse "in a few minutes . . . in full-dress rebel uniform."[92] Seeing this success, many other young men in northwest Missouri rode in to join Thornton. This conspiracy was probably meant to clear the ground for the arrival of Confederate General Sterling Price, who invaded the state that summer, expecting to trigger a general uprising of what he presumed to be the hidden secessionist majority in Missouri. By the time Price arrived at the Missouri River, Thornton's recruits had long since scattered, and Price gathered relatively few men, most of whom deserted him when his army fled the state in September after a crushing series of defeats near Kansas City. There was no general uprising.

The guerrilla war of a thousand nasty incidents continued unabated, still aided by many civilians and militiamen who had not chosen openly to join the Confederate army. There was no more southern hope for the sudden emergence of a Missouri Confederate army in full-dress uniform; that possibility, which would have led to a different sort of warfare, had never been likely, though it had given guerrillas and their backers an enhanced sense of potential political purpose in their fighting. Still the guerrillas carried on in full brutality, as did the Union troops searching for them, with a majority of the population caught between the two forces.

With the use of spies, the taking of hostages, the shooting of prisoners, and the impersonation of each other, guerrillas and counter-guerrillas blurred together in their tactics and in their identities. They had shared values before the war, and in tandem they entered new emotional and ideological as well as behavioral thickets.

Blood Sport

As well as being horrifying, it must be said that guerrilla war held intense pleasure for many of the combatants on both sides. Among the positive prewar values which were reworked in the guerrilla war were a sense of play and a search for honor and personal glory. One must remember that the active soldiers on both sides were very young men, almost all under twenty-five and probably 80 percent under twenty-one. Particularly in loosely organized war such as this where discipline was weak, there was no clear line between playing at war and being at war. When there was little immediate danger, these young men would horse around, joke, drink, and have a much better time than they would have had back home on the farm under their fathers' thumbs.

Before the war, the chief form of recreation for many of these boys was hunting, and hunters they remained with the human enemy as the newly licensed quarry. With recently acquired military abilities, these bands of young men sought glory—an ennobled manliness—through the greatest of games—war.

Often, their tongues loosened by drink, these young men would brag about what mighty hunters they had become. In a sense they were merely carrying on the great southwestern tradition of braggadocio, each screaming out that he was the toughest man in creation, ready to lick a hundred men and a thousand alligators, and that if anyone wanted to see a *real* man, here he was. In peacetime, such declarations frequently had been an invitation to a fight, and this carried over into war, though now in a more political framework and often with graver, longer-term consequences. On October 10, 1863, a very drunken Hendon Hall called out to one Wicks in Wornell's Saloon in Springfield, "keep away from me you son of a bitch or I'll blow the top of your head off," and when Wicks made no reply, Hall moved menacingly toward him along the bar, shouting, "I am a son of a bitch *on wheels*," drew his pistol and fired. Happily both men were too drunk to hit one another. In this instance both the roosters were Union men, and no permanent harm was done. In other cases, self-proclaimed mighty guerrillas would ride while drunk into Union-garrisoned towns and declare their prowess, only to be thrown into prison and court-martialed if not shot on the spot. Prison was the fate of Marion D. Erwin, who rode into Randolph City in north central Missouri late in 1864 "swinging his hat and saying [to Union soldiers] if we wished to see a living bush-whacker to take a look at him." Also in late 1864 near St. Louis, Oscar Davis started drinking toasts to Jeff Davis in Francis Backleiter's saloon. Told to shut his mouth, he continued shouting, "I will hurrah as much as I please. I came . . . to get six horses . . . I belong to Bob Highly's gang. . . . If I am interrupted I will burn down the whole town, and if I can't do it alone, I can soon get up my company."[93]

Foraging, the chief means of terrorizing civilians, could also be a source of much pleasure, a kind of neo-hunting. Nothing was so immediately satisfying as a good hot meal, especially one with a big helping of meat, whether game or livestock. Finding and helping themselves to meat on the hoof could be great fun, and many letters and diary entries were devoted to fond and humorous recollections of this type of chase. On Christmas Eve 1861, Wisconsin infantryman Henry Twining was standing guard duty on a railroad bridge during a snow and hail storm. "I had to stand it all the time and I got pretty cold before morning," he wrote to his girl friend back home. "'We had some fun in the night. There were some cattle in the woods and one came up to one of the sentinills and he said 'Halt, Halt' but it did not stop so he blared away and shot Miss Cow so we had some beef." Dave Garver, another Union soldier standing rail-road guard late in 1861, wrote to his sister about the "singular accidents happens here sometimes. Like this. We was out hunting yesterday when one of our guns went off and struck a fat pig right behind the ear and killed him." Another time four of Garver's company were pitching horse-shoes "and there was a fat pig around when one of the quoites struck him right on the head and knocked him down, so we cut his throat to keep him from dieing." The boys hunted down plenty of cows, sheep, chickens, pigs, and vegetables to keep themselves supplied. "We ain't agoing to starve in the land of the seceshers."[94]

The peacetime pleasure most nearly akin to fighting guerrillas was wild game hunting. Hunting was a great pastime, a diet enricher for country boys, and the reason most of these young men had learned to handle firearms. The stealthy tracking, the wild chase, the moment of triumphant killing and the number and size of the animals killed appealed to men on the hunt. In 1858 in the same letter in which he bragged of his manly prowess with the Indian girls, William C. Quantrill wrote from Kansas Territory to his best friend in Canal Dover, Ohio, about his passion for hunting. "Last week I helped to kill a deer & since I have been here I have killed myself 2 antelope & one dear & about 25 wild turkeys & geese & before you see me in Ohio I will have killed buffalo."[95]

During the guerrilla war, many letters written to friends back home, as well as diaries and military reports, were studded with similar hunting imagery, enemy soldiers replacing animals as the quarry. In 1864 militia Captain E. J. Crandall wrote his district commander that he would give Carroll and Chariton Counties "a good raking over, and may get tempted over the [Missouri] River if I see game." In 1863 Colonel Chester Harding reported with either genuine boredom or an assumed nonchalance, "Nothing more exciting than the everyday business of hunting and in some cases exterminating bushwhackers has happened lately."[96] Guerrillas were beasts to be hunted down like other animals. The language of the hunt gave Colonel Harding an appropriate metaphorical dissociation from the dehumanized object for slaughter—his business was vermin eradication.

In pursuit of the enemy, army units would get their collective blood up, like hounds after the stag. At the end of the war, Lieutenant David Freeman begged his district commander to send him on one more guerrilla hunt, this time after Jim Anderson. "My boys fight like veterans, making fun of the enemy all the time. . . . My men say they can track the bushmen like a dog will a deer. They are anxious to get the job of catching Jim and gang. I wish you would give me the job. I will follow him day and night till I get him."[97]

In the human hunt, these young men could prove their individual and collective manly nobility. Thus Major H. Hilliard reported to his commander in August 1864 that his men had killed two of Si Gordon's gang after a running "wolf hunt." Si Gordon himself "escaped very narrowly. . . . The chase was most exciting. . . . Our men behaved nobly." Also during the summer of 1864, Colonel John F. Phillips reported on the blood initiation rite of a young soldier in his command. Private Barnes chased one guerrilla for half an hour, "holding his fire until he drew up on his game. . . . Barnes is a mere boy and quite small, but is as bold and dashing a trooper as ever looked an enemy in the face."[98] Barnes had been blooded; he had made a man of himself by getting his game, killing his man.

One Kansas cavalryman, George Titcomb, obsessed with the hunt, wrote in his diary about becoming the game. On April 16, 1863, his company had swept a ravine "only to find that the birds had flown," except for the two guerrillas they did kill. On May 6, they "scoured the timber all day through" for guerrillas and saw none, while two days later they "had a lively time all day chasing bushwhackers. Chased the notorious Capt. Marchbanks and several of his gang but they were all smarter than we for they got away." The game was often clever and elusive, and therefore worthy prey for the hunters. On May 20, Titcomb's unit "went over to Grand River and hunted that timber all day but saw no guerrillas." But on September 29, the situation was reversed when four guerrillas chased down Titcomb and his companion Tom who gave up the chase "and allowed them to ride up and take him prisoner which he certainly must have known was sure death." Titcomb dashed off on his horse, the guerrillas after him. At one point during the chase, "one of them says to the other run around him Jim and head him." His horse shot out from under him, Titcomb took off on foot and hid in a wooded ravine. After hiding four days and hiking five nights without food or water, Titcomb walked back into his company's camp, where he was immediately promoted to sergeant. When he wrote the story up in his diary on October 20, he referred to it as "my adventure." Titcomb expressed a sense of personal immortality in his account—after all he had survived being the hunted animal in the wilderness. The language of hunting defined his role as hunted as it had of hunter. From either vantage point, the guerrilla conflict was a kind of blood sport, which reduced and eased war's moral dimension. It was as if this were only a game, an absurd, fatal game.[99]

Not all soldiers on the hunt could accept unequivocally the moral conclusion that war was only a capital game. In his diary, Illinois cavalry Lieutenant Sardius Smith described much as others I have quoted one evening's exciting chase. "We had quite a hunt last night. Having heard that a notorious Secesh by the name of Jackson was in the neighborhood . . . we started after dark to his house. Having taken our sabres off our belts and taking only our pistols," his company surrounded and crept up to the house. "I sprang upon the fence leveling my revolver at a dog in the way. The guide said don't shoot. I stopped when the dog took to his heels secesh style and was seen no more." Smith then demanded to search the house, only to find that the guerrillas had fled just like dogs. At this point in his recollection, Smith broke the narrative line in his diary and made an analysis of what had changed inside him during the war. "We are getting quite hardened to this kind of thing and I can go into a house with a pistol in my hand, with a smile on my face, speak politely to the ladies, ask where their men are in order that I may shoot them or take them prisoner with as much grace as though I was making a call for friendship sake."[100]

Where Lieutenant Smith took one giant step back and looked with some dread at the case-hardened human hunter he had become, more soldiers appeared just to have enjoyed the game. They were reaching for glory, for the noble expression of their manliness, and the guerrilla war had become their stage, a great game, far more intense and vivid than ordinary life. Although no records of such guerrilla sentiments remain, judging from their behavior, I am certain that they had the same attitude toward blood sport.

An armed unit rode carefully through rough country, galloped up to a guerrilla lair, chased after the fleeing guerrillas through a natural obstacle course, the men as a whole operating like a well-oiled machine, but each soldier exercising his individual initiative. Such was the archetypal guerrilla hunt depicted in 1862 by an Iowa cavalryman for the readers of the Keokuk *Weekly Gate City*. "Nothing but hills and hollows. . . . Now we march by file through by-paths and old roads, now we lie down on our horses to dodge limbs, and now we go at bull speed to surround some rebel's house that abruptly comes in view. Perhaps some men run from the house when they see us in time. Then comes the fun and excitement— Every man is his own commander, and each strives to get ahead. 'You go this way, you go that way.' And away we go, leap fence. . . . 'Halt, Halt! or I'll shoot you!' someone commands, and if they don't halt, he is shot. This hunting rebels is as interesting as deer hunting."[101]

Whether consciously or not, this war correspondent wrote the story of the ideal guerrilla hunt in a mythic manner, distilling the essence of the chase and the glory of the hunter from the course of a successful guerrilla-killing expedition. This was not a natural description of the frustrations and defeats of what was in fact the typical search for guerrillas. The great Keokuk guerrilla hunt was mostly a fantasy of omnipotence of the spokesman for this Iowa brotherhood of hunters. It served to solidify the band and to help them deal with the hostile world as the setting for the chase after manly glory. In this instance, the depiction of the hunt was also meant to strengthen solidarity with the good folks back home, who would remember and reward their powerful young men gone off to war for them, would sing their praises in their absence, would honor their dead, and would treat them as heroes on their return.

Official reports and war correspondence to hometown newspapers in the North concerning the great game of the guerrilla hunt frequently were written in a high-flown literary language, somewhere between the style of the immensely popular Walter Scott and that of the dime novel. Another Iowa cavalryman depicted the chase by three hundred men of his regiment after sixty guerrillas of Colonel Parker's command. "The Secesh dashed into the bush as usual. . . . It was only our best mounted men who were able to keep up with our chivalric but nomadic foes. The chase was quite an exciting one, stirring even the current of my phlegmatic nature. The path through the brush was strewn with [equipment] abandoned by the Southern bloods to facilitate their hegira." Finally the Union boys closed on the enemy. Many ran off, "while not a few of them en-sconced themselves beneath logs, sought retirement from this troublous world in tree-tops and tangled underbrush, or courted modest obscurity by sinking quietly into some friendly gutter nearby." Ten were killed, fif-teen captured.[102] I do not believe this writer intended his report to be humorous. Rather, he wanted to depict the momentous, epic hunting scene for his readers, in language which would elicit their awe and admiration.

The writers of such grand reports were not insincere—this was the way they had learned to apply their prewar educations to the task of making public explanations of their role as soldiers in the guerrilla war. They be-lieved that they ought to be brave and noble manly men: they expected this of themselves and believed that others back home wanted them to be such soldiers. Reports to superior officers, who were the most significant figures of social authority as long as they were in the army, often were written in the same proud style. At the start of the war, Confederate Briga-dier General M. Jeff Thompson wrote to his commander of a raid on a German settlement which had been intended to gather horses and wagons. "The temptation to have a brush before leaving was too great, and they charged into the town of Hamburg, scattering the Dutch in all directions. My men fired on them as they ran through the fields, although unarmed, and killed 1, mortally wounding 5 . . . others, and brought away 13 pris-oners and 25 horses."[103] It was somewhat bizarre that Thompson would brag about shooting unarmed men on his hunt, but he justified this by say-ing that they were Federal militia, and his men had done fine by being so quick to fire. And after all, they were only Dutchmen. His troops had demonstrated a commendable eagerness for combat: they were strong men.

In 1864 in southwest Missouri, Union Captain John Kelso was thrilled by the fine hunting and shooting of his manly company. One June evening his men raided some guerrillas at a dancing party, killing four. "We arrived too late to dance any ourselves, but we made Lieutenant McGee and his men dance. . . . The keen cracks of rifles and revolvers soon rang out on both sides of me, accompanied by the hearty yells of my brave boys." After the battle, the captain rewarded trophies to his knights. "I presented the horses of the dead bushwhackers to the brave lads who had killed them." They expressed themselves "highly pleased with their 'fun.' " Kelso concluded that he was "proud to command such men."[104]

There was a great deal of denial of everyday boredom, hunger, filth, cold, and brutality contained in such high-flown renditions of guerrilla warfare. Such language helped to distance the fighter from his ugly sur-roundings and could be a form of self-reassurance that he was a noble fellow after all, despite his base forms of behavior. It was important to reassert personal honor in a setting where so much dishonor was present—the soldier should be rendered more honorable, the war a struggle for per-sonal and group nobility.

The central metaphor of war as the great hunt could be stretched to include war by stealth. In this version of the chase, the hunter used all his wiles to sneak up on the game and snare it. In June 1863 in the Ozarks, a guerrilla named Crow "was lurking about and took [a Wisconsin soldier] prisoner." That night, the Wisconsin soldier played possum, "being apparantly sound asleep until he was confident his captor was really so when he crawled up to the rebel and got [his] gun and blowed his head nearly all to pieces." After returning to camp, Wisconsin told his story and to prove his word rode back with several of the other men and showed them the corpse. Over on the other side of the Ozarks in rebel territory in Arkansas during the summer of 1862, Henry Crawford and five of the boys who believed that the "excitement of the bushwhacking there suited [us] finely . . . concluded we would give the bushwhackers a parting farewell" before returning to the North. They headed south, impersonating guerrillas, and fooled the people completely. They went after a noted guerrilla named Hall and "as good luck would have it" found him at home. They learned the composition and whereabouts of many guerrilla units, "and while he was in the midst of his glory atelling us what he had done to the feds, we put a few bullet holes through his head and went on."[105] The heroism in both these stories was in the soldiers' great risktaking, based on stealth. Such victories, under circumstances which justified sneak tactics, demonstrated courage, as did more open tactics in situations approaching the ideal, fair, face-to-face fight. It was fine to report such stories about oneself. Many situations could be explained by guerrilla fighters in such a manner, ennobling as the higher cunning what might appear to others as dirty tactics.

There were few opportunities for courageous and manly engagement with an enemy who was almost always unseen, who rarely came out to fight in the serried ranks of storybook wars. In such a nasty war where few prisoners were taken, it was unusual to look the enemy in the face, to discover in him the manly foe truly worthy of your honorable battle. Still, if you did capture your enemy, you would execute him and want him to die nobly, and if you were captured, you would be shot and would want to die an honorable death. That was the fit end of the great hunt.

Union Major Wilson died a good death at the hands of Reeves's guerrilla band in southeastern Missouri in the fall of 1864. Two southern men on their way back north to their homes stopped off at Mr. Alexander's house in Greenville and reported Major Wilson's honorable death. At the execution Reeves had said to Wilson, " 'Major, you are a brave man—but you never showed my men quarter, neither will I give you quarter.' At the execution Major Wilson himself commanded; 'ready, aim, —fire!' Those two men," Alexander wrote, "though his enemies, praised his bravery." In a similar manner, the guerrilla John B. Wilcox died with honor in Jefferson City on August 12, 1864, as Charles Curtiss recorded in his diary. The streets were crowded that afternoon "by persons anx-ious to obtain a glance of the victim." Curtiss went early to the execu-tion ground and stationed himself where he "had a good view of his face. He was composed and bore it nobly [though] he protested his inno-cence to the last and many believed him to be an innocent man." So bravely did he die, Curtiss concluded, that Wilcox always must have been a man of honor, even if he had been misguided in his opinions. Whether or not he was guilty of bushwhacking, he was finally a victim of the war. He played out his death finely, lending final honor to himself, to the oc-casion, and to his captors. The "notorious" guerrilla Benton Gann of La-fayette County in west central Missouri died a more defiant but no less brave death in 1864. He and his two comrades claimed they had killed nine Union soldiers and were prepared to die themselves. Union cavalry Captain J. H. Little wrote to his colonel, "They refused to give any useful information; said their trial had been fair and that they were not afraid to die, which boast they made good. They calmly walked to the grave, looked contemptuously on the detail assembled, said they were ready, quietly folded their arms, kneeled down, and met death with a dauntless-ness worthy of a better cause."[106]

Like the stag dying nobly at the climax of the hunt, these three men died in what was to them and to their executioners a redeeming manner. They completed their warrior task, cooperating with their final mythic assignment. Such reports were all the more important for being so rare— most guerrillas and counter-guerrillas died painfully of sickness or wounds, dragged into the bush by their comrades to die or dropped from the saddle by an unexpected pistol shot. A noble death should by rights have com-pleted the great game. Such was the ideal moral structure desperately clung to by young men trapped in the guerrilla war morass.

Parallel to the image of the noble death ran the desire to turn war into a personal, open, face-to-face fight, a duel, so different from the war that was under way. Civilians and subterfuge ought to be left aside, and the combatants should engage in a conclusive fair fight. "If you and I would let [civilians] alone," the guerrilla Charles P. Taylor wrote to Union Captain Kemper near Kansas City in 1864, "we could fight one another, and we will be fighting men who have put themselves out for that pur-pose." Taylor then proposed that he and Kemper enter the ring like two barons within their circle of men. "If you will fight me alone I will return the compliment." Concluding a note in which he had threatened reprisal if Colonel S. N. Boyd executed his men taken prisoner, guerrilla chieftain William Coleman wrote, "you talk about fighting. I will fight you with an equal number of men in any part of the country."[107]

Proposing a duel had a bookish, nostalgic quality about it. This was the way such a messy war ought to have gone, ideally speaking. If it had, the life and death of the warrior would have been noble. As it transpired, the guerrilla war was, most combatants agreed, mainly opposite to open and conclusive fighting, tarnishing the honor of all the parties involved. After one typical skirmish in which guerrillas struck and fled, cavalry Major George S. Avery wrote to his wife, "I detest such fighting. I wish they would stand their ground and fight like men." Iowa Private Henry Dysart wrote in his diary for April 12, 1862, "Guerrillas still infest the county who shoot down neighbors as game, who prowl about at dead of night and rob and steal, unprincipled men who will not even be so honorable as to fight in the open field." There was no honor, no bravery involved in fighting such a war with such an enemy. For Dysart, the hunt was a rat hunt done at night from hiding. All the community was the actual victim. "They know they have been and will be defeated in their project so they take this mode of revenge. It is no uncommon thing for the peaceable citizen to be shot from the plow or while about his daily business, on mere suspicion. Certainly civil war is the bloodiest of wars. . . . In Missouri especially have the ties of friendship and everything else that makes home and a community happy been torn asunder. Alienation reigns in place of peace."[108]

Blood Revenge

Reclaiming honor from the damages of guerrilla war devolved into seeking revenge—an eye for an eye, two houses burned for one house, five lives for one life. Vengeance became an everyday matter-of-fact. In flat language, George Wolz of Newton City in southwestern Missouri wrote his brother in 1863, "The bushwhackers burn a house and then we burn two houses."[109] The apparent acceptance of revenge as a quotidian reality masked a deep rage which fighters on both sides harbored: their houses had been plundered and burned, their women and parents insulted, they had been driven into never ending combat, their closest military comrades wounded, tortured, killed, mutilated, their very manhood invaded. They would get even. They would destroy the destroyers and wash their hands in the blood of the enemy. Then justice would be theirs.

Southern guerrillas believed they had been driven from the peace of their homes and neighborhoods by the alien Yankee invader. Many Southerners who had fled far into the South to find protection behind Confederate lines, ached to return, preferably with a regular army, in order to reclaim what would be to them the freedom of their state. But if necessary, they would return as avenging guerrillas. Late in 1862, Edwin H. Harris wrote to his wife in Paris, Texas, from Johnson County, Arkansas, "I do not wish to again enter Missouri until an army goes, strong enough to sustain itself, unless I go as a guerrilla and seek vengeance—aye, and seek it too upon the heads of those who have plundered us and driven from their homes the thousands who are now pining to return to their beloved homes." According to Harris only a regular army could reconquer the soil, but a guerrilla band could exact vengeance for the physical and emotional deprivations caused by the Yankees. Samuel W. Richie wrote from Horse Head, Arkansas, in 1862, greatly discouraged about the defeatism he believed most Missouri secessionists were expressing, "When we start in Missouri I think we will pass over only *conquered soil*. And when we do get there, *vengeance* will be our motto."[110] Richie intended to get even with all Union collaborationists as well as with overtly Union men and troops.

Missouri Union troops, like guerrillas, sought vengeance with the greatest lust when they were stationed close to their prewar homes. In conjunction with local citizens, often over shared whiskey, they worked up their rage and then went out to attack those old neighbors against whom they felt aggrieved. Their officers, who often encouraged them, were unable to stop revenge seekers even when they wished to do so. In 1863 two officers in central Missouri wrote to higher authorities about the destruction caused by troops they could not restrain. Brigadier General E. B. Brown wrote, "Prompted by feelings of revenge in the soldiers, and by the counselings of the citizens, who do not fail to use whisky if necessary to make soldiers more reckless, the most heartless murders have been committed." Brown's troops had murdered relatives of Union men killed in the Cole Creek massacre of 1861. Brown wrote in the passive voice, perhaps in part out of his own frustration at being unable to stop such attacks, perhaps in part to shirk responsibility—the passion for vengeance lay in his men, outside his control. He also understood and shared the passion. Lieutenant Colonel T. A. Switzler admitted that among his troops in Warsaw "there is no discipline whatever exercized over the soldiers here, which, added to the indiscriminate sale of liquor renders the soldiers fiends rather than soldiers." In their bitter resentment, they menaced even the "best citizens" and terrorized anyone they construed to be the enemy."[111]

If most officers at least tried to limit undisciplined vengeance seeking (and many did not), they vigorously sought retribution within official channels. If a man were known to be a guerrilla, he was to be shot on the spot: as one brigadier general put it in an official communique to a subordinate in charge of part of his district, "these rebels are not to be captured under any circumstances, but to be killed when found." If in spite of this widely agreed-upon policy—the same one practiced by the guerrillas—bushwhackers were captured or if captives were proven to be guerrillas, they were to be executed quickly. On April 16, 1864, Brigadier General Clinton B. Fisk ordered a lieutenant colonel, "Try the bushwhacker by drumhead court-martial tonight, and let every soldier in Macon shoot him if he is guilty, as he doubtless is." Kansas Seventh Cavalry Sergeant Webster Moses wrote in his diary for October 20, 1864, that his unit had marched until 2 A.M. to reach Lexington in west central Missouri, "capturing a few Rebs in blue uniform who are next morning hung and shot both at the same time."[112]

These Union soldiers wished not merely to kill guerrillas but to tear them apart. One bullet or a firing squad would have been sufficient to cause death, but the acts of both hanging and shooting the captured guerrilla or of having every soldier in Macon shoot the guerrilla were overkill, expressing a need for destruction beyond killing. Every man was to share in a vengeance deeper than death. In this way revenge would be diffused and shared by the whole band of soldiers and solidarity in blood would be strengthened. It was the same for guerrilla bands.

Soldiers and civilians elsewhere in both the Union and the Confederacy were aware of the special ferocity of this war of mutual vengeance in Missouri. For example, in August 1864 Charley Buford of Scott, Kentucky, in a letter to his wife responded to news of nearby Federal prisoners being shot in retaliation for Confederate prisoners shot by the Union army in revenge for Confederate guerrilla raids, "It seems that all the horrors of the strife in Missouri are to be reproduced here. What it will end in God only knows."[113] Throughout the border states, cycles of vengeance became nearly as endemic as in Missouri.

Revenge included shared exaltation in looking upon the bloody body of the fallen enemy. It was pleasurable to see the corpse of your formerly dreaded foe. When the noted guerrilla Bloody Bill Anderson was shot, a photographer took several shots of his body, dressed in a handsome embroidered shirt, his bearded head propped up, pistols in both hands, one across his breast. When Alfred Bolan, the terror of southeastern Missouri who boasted of killing forty Union men, was shot in 1863 by a Union spy who struck him repeatedly over the head with a broken plowshare, Bolan's body was brought to Forseyth and placed on display. "I went to see the murdered murderer," Iowa infantryman Timothy Phillips wrote in his diary. "His hair was all matted with blood and clotted over his face, rendering him an object of disgust and horror. Yet there were hundreds of men who gloated over him, many who were acquainted with him and had many reasons to rejoice at his death. There had perished a monster, a man of blood, of every crime, who had no mercy for others and had died a death of violence, and today hundreds gaze upon his unnatural carcass and exult that his prowess is at an end."[114] In peacetime a body would be washed and dressed neatly and put in a position of peaceful repose. But this man was left as he was killed, looking like an ogre. The whole community of men who had feared him and suffered at his hand could now come and rejoice at how bloodily and painfully he had been laid low. Viewing his mangled body, an evidence of his lost power, they could regain some strength.

Revenge extended to the disfigurement of living men and the mutilation

Bill Anderson in death. This photo was taken as a souvenir on the day of Anderson's death at the hands of Union troops. Anderson was armed with two "Navy" revolvers, the guerrilla's favorite Colt, and dressed in a "guerrilla shirt," lovingly embroidered by his mother or his sister or his girlfriend. (*State Historical Society of Missouri*)

of corpses. Early in the war the physician in Jennison's jayhawking regiment wrote in his diary, "Another act was committed this morning which caused many to regret their connection with this regiment. It was the cropping of a man's ear—a secessionist—by Jennison." It seems most likely that this foe was disfigured but then released. Such was not the fate of Gustavas Trout of St. Charles County just north of St. Louis in September 1864. Suspecting Trout of armed robbery, four militiamen seized him at a public auction. There in the presence of the crowd over the course of several hours, they hanged him by the neck several times and beat him with clubs, breaking his arms and then dragging him two miles out of town, shot him in the head and left him dead on the road.[115]

Often Union troops found the mutiliated bodies of dead comrades left in the road. In the course of one week in January 1863, Colonel William R. Penick, cavalry commander in Independence, reported finding the mutilated bodies of five of his men killed in as many separate incidents. "They were all wounded, and killed afterwards in the most horrible manner fiends could devise. All were shot in the head, and several of their faces are terribly cut to pieces with boot heels. Powder was exploded in one man's ear, and both ears cut off close to the head. Whether this inhuman act was committed while he was alive or not, I have no means of knowing." In June 1862 in Warrensburg in west central Missouri, Major Emory S. Foster found, following a night-time skirmish, two of his soldiers "stripped of their clothing and horribly mutilated, one of them with more than a dozen revolver-balls in his body and his head frightfully broken and mangled." On September 29, 1864, at Centralia, Bill Anderson's gang stopped a train and executed twenty-four unarmed soldiers riding on it; subsequently they slaughtered 124 militiamen who broke and fled under attack. Of the twenty-four executed at trackside, Lieutenant Colonel Daniel M. Draper reported, "Most of them were beaten over the head, seventeen of them were scalped, and one had his privates cut off and placed in his mouth. Every man was shot in the head. One man had his nose cut off."[116]

Fighters took human scalps and body parts—ears, noses, scalps, teeth, facial skin, fingers—to keep or to give away as trophies. Sometimes men made rings, charms, and necklaces from the bones and teeth gathered off old battlefields. On September 14, 1864, Major Austin King's command killed five of Bill Anderson's men, "some of their bridles being decked with human scalps." The *Missouri Statesman* reported on August 5 concerning Bill Anderson's men that "from the forehead of Daniels a round portion of skin had been cut about the size of a Mexican dollar, and from that of Nichols a longer piece was taken, extending from the forehead to the region of the left temple." On July 24, Archie Clement, reputed to be the "executioner" in Anderson's gang, attached a note to the remains of a Union soldier which read, "You come to hunt bushwhackers. Now you ar skelpt. Clenyent skept you."[117]

Such accounts of the mutilation of corpses were common. As the Union army kept the records, one reads only of guerrilla behavior of this sort, but there is every reason to believe that Union soldiers retaliated in kind, just as they shared in every other guerrilla terror tactic. Killing was insufficient; one had to complete the dehumanization, "de-face" the enemy, reduce him to mere flesh and bones, obliterate his beauty and the container of his soul. Some groups of fighters wished to push on to some final place of total destruction, some land where "we" in all our force are all and "they" are made nothing at all. Glenn Grey, the social philosopher of combat, writes that there can be on such occasions a kind of aesthetic of destruction which can hold its own beauties: if Manichaeanism was the most powerful subterranean American heresy, which I believe it was, this sort of act may have been a sacrifice, a reaching out toward the other all-powerful One. Drenched in the endless terrors of a guerrilla war, combatants sought release in the annihilation of the face of the Other.[118]

Rituals of mutilation also served to tighten the knot of brotherhood among the inner circle of fighters. These were not acts done in isolation but social and human acts of destruction. It was as if the soldiers were declaring—We are of the all-powerful men as they are of the nothing at all. . . . We will debase the foe as we are exalted, outside and above their lowliness. . . . Through their consumption shall our brotherly love burn in pure flames. . . . We shall live forever. At the core of guerrilla war, blood revenge was a religious rite, a reaching by blood brothers for the mythic land of the nihilist dream.

The male body was the target of these warriors. Everything was done to obliterate the maleness of the enemy fighter. Conversely, there was a concomitant, rigorously observed ban on raping, killing, or mutilating white women. Defending the honor of *their* women and of *all* women was the cardinal principle of maleness toward womanhood, shared by all fighters on both sides. Protection of women was the central means—reigning above hunting and dueling and other rituals ennobling manliness—to keep alive for the killer and the mutilator a sense that he was still sound and honorable morally, that he still served absolutely a high and abstract moral principle—the ideal of home with pure womanhood standing on a pedestal in the center. As the fighters destroyed and debased the maleness of other men, their need to enshrine women increased. The goddess of redemptive love also had to be worshipped when one served the god of the dark forces.

Christ too could be served by his avenging angels. Sergeant Sherman Bodwell was one of these, a deeply religious Connecticut Congregationalist who in 1856 had gone to join the antislavery settlers at Topeka, Kansas.

As sergeant in the Eleventh Kansas Cavalry in 1862 and 1863, he rode with his regiment on punitive expeditions into Jackson County, that secessionist stronghold around Independence. In his diary one reads of Bodwell's service to the people of God and his righteous destruction of the people of the Devil. On July 13, 1863, Bodwell's unit heard that the Widow Holly had warned guerrillas of the coming of the Kansans. "That amiable lady had gone to Hamilton on a sympathizing expedition. We put fire to her house. . . . She probably knew better how to sympathize on her return and having no home to keep will be able to devote more time to carrying the news." Down the road, Bodwell's platoon found "strong indications of [guerrillas] sojurning" at the Alderman house. "Alderman taken to one side to *examine* as to bushwhackers whereabouts, he attempted to escape, and was killed by R. Heard. Capt. Harry tells his wife of the death. She showing no feeling but a little more anger, and the children none at all." A subhuman race showed no such genuine emotion as would be expected from real humans. Bodwell saw enemy civilians that way rather than as ordinary humans numbed by extreme shock when just told of the execution of their husband and father. The day before these two incidents, the cavalry brought in two citizens who, knowing that a guerrilla band had intended to ambush the Kansans, had failed to report the news to Union authorities. To Bodwell these were typical "Missouri union men, of the kind they raise in this delightful locality." Having no absolute proof of their complicity, having heard their protestations of loyalty, the captain let them go. "Boys thought they were dismissed, hunted one of them out, and had the rope around his neck when Capt. stopped them."

Bodwell felt nothing but contempt and destructive rage toward civilians whom he suspected of supporting guerrillas. On behalf of good Union people of all races and national origins, he acted with great sympathy. And he always wished to act in a lawful, correct manner. On August 24, 1863, his platoon burned some suspected secesh houses but not on a direct command from the captain. "The burning has been, I think, against orders," Bodwell worried in his diary, "& so distasteful to me." Bodwell opposed wanton destruction—he wanted it to be purposeful and licensed.

When he could aid good Union people in this bad secesh country, Bodwell was at his happiest. On August 2, three Union families which had been made homeless by guerrillas appealed to Bodwell's unit for help. The guerrillas had burned them out in the middle of the night, "not giving the women and children time to dress even. Arrangements made today to outfit them at the expense of the secesh about." This was justice, weaving together aid to the good and punishment to the bad.

For Bodwell, justice was to be applied to all good Union people, regardless of race. He ran a Sunday school in the summer of 1862 in Jackson County, taking his sabbath break from guerrilla hunting to teach the alphabet and the Bible to little black children. "Am so sorry we are liable to be ordered away from here. We have the best of opportunities for doing good Christian work among the colored population here." On July 4, Bodwell's regiment attended a fine dinner, the week's work "of the kindly colored friends of Independence . . . a better table, with more variety or abundance of substantials that I have ever seen on any such occasion. . . . The colored people seemed very intelligent, and glad to be able to do us such a kindness." Bodwell was one of the few Civil War Union soldiers to be a racial liberal, albeit in a paternalist manner, and the moral of the banquet preparation pleased him. "It will I think have a good effect upon our few 'negro haters' who by the way, were not slow to enjoy it."

As well as admiring and supporting loyal blacks, Bodwell, again unlike almost all his fellow Union soldiers, honored German-Americans who fought the good fight. On August 21, he responded in his diary to the news of the death of his old comrade Charley Schmidt, killed in the Lawrence massacre. He had been "a German and without exception the finest soldier I ever knew." Charley, who had been in the Prussian army and had participated in the revolution of 1848, had been "obliged to fly the country." Coming to America because of the principles of liberty, it was little wonder that he had come to Kansas to join in the free state ranks in 1856. His only fault was his antagonistic attitude toward Christianity. "O! that he had been a friend of God. His main argument was that the Ministers of Christ at home sided with the despot against the people." Bodwell worried about his friend's soul, but he deeply admired him as a fellow principled man and could not really believe that he had died unredeemed.

Bodwell fought as a Christian soldier for liberty, the Union, noble Germans, struggling blacks, and all good Union people everywhere. To serve these honorable causes he had to hunt down and destroy the last monstrous guerrilla. On October 4, 1863, his unit happened onto a guerrilla camp deep in the woods, where they saw a dead man swinging from a tree with a rope around his neck. On his back was pinned a paper which read, "This man was hung last evening, in revenge for the death of Ab Haller. He says that his name is Thomas and that he belongs to the Kansas 7th." In his diary, Bodwell responded to what was to him the fetid animalism of this hidden enemy camp. "There seems to be something of the deathlike brooding over these camps. Always hidden where hardly more than a horse track points the way, in heavy timber and creek bottoms, offal lying about, cooking utensils, cast off clothing . . . the very air seems thick with the clime with which so lately they seethed."

The beast must die. Bodwell expressed the rage engendered by seeing such scenes in his depiction of hunting down and exterminating bushwhackers. On September 26, Bodwell's unit chased down a small guerrilla gang—shooting their horses, dismounting, and "then a foot race. . . . The race lasted for about ¾ of a mile, the boys firing after them as they ran, Lt. R[eese] finally bringing down the last. I came up, just as the Lt. finished him with a shot through the head. Took supper and moved on." On October 1, Bodwell's unit surprised two bushwhackers, one of whom dismounted and ran into the brush. The major "brought him down" with a pistol shot. After the wounded prisoner was searched, Lieutenant Reese asked the major, "are you through with him & Major nodded assent." As the others mounted and rode off, Bodwell stood by while the lieutenant "aimed and fired, a revolver ball striking just back of the eye & he was with his judge with all his imperfections on his head." Bodwell later regretted that he had not looked on the countenance of the enemy at the moment of his execution. "Lt. stood between us so I did not see his face. Lt. says he intentionally raised his hand to protect himself and an ashy paleness overspread his face, as when a cloud passes over the sun." Bodwell wanted to see this inner death, the flight of a damned soul to Hell. Presumably an upward flight would have been indicated by a glowing radiance in the place of ashy paleness and a welcoming hand rather than a self-protective one warding off a hellish fate.

In his last diary entry on the day he was mustered out of the army, September 20, 1865, Bodwell thanked the Holy Spirit for never deserting him during the war. He had faltered, but the Spirit had never failed him. "So ends my service, in all three and a half years filled with tokens of loving kindness of Him who granted me the privilege of standing in my lot . . . on every march and in every engagement. [For] the loving, comforting, strengthening of the Holy Spirit, even when I have been most unfaithful and forgetful of my Christian obligation, I can never, I feel, be grateful enough."[119]

More devotedly and consciously Christian than most of his brother killers, Sergeant Bodwell also made the polarities of Manichean worship more explicit than did most of them. His was a holy hunt; his prey, damned souls; the blood revenge he sought was the blood of the lamb. Was he any more or less brutalized than any of the others? Like them, he reworked everyday, peacetime language and experiences in ways to service fighting within the terrible confines of a guerrilla war. These revised attitudes were not those of reborn monsters, nor of natural frontier savages, but of ordinary, overwhelmed young men. They restructured the fragments of their desires, their fears, and their educations—doubtless feeling as intense a love for the sanctified few within their circle as they did hatred for the alien, contemptible many who populated the frightening land all around them. They were the primal horde.

CHAPTER 5

WOMEN AS VICTIMS
AND PARTICIPANTS

Participation

The furious moral dislocation of guerrilla war was visited on women as well as on men. Disintegration, demoralization, and perverse adaptation engulfed women's behavior and self-conceptions as it assaulted the family and undermined male-female and female-female—as it had male-male—relationships. Like male civilians in a guerrilla war theater, women were both victims and actors. They were compelled to participate, which they did with varying degrees of enthusiasm, fear, and rage. Women were also attacked by men who behaved towards them as never before. Male attitudes and actions towards women were both undermined and exaggerated by the catastrophe of guerrilla war. This war also pulled away most of the peacetime footings for sexual relationships, setting men and women adrift. Wartime insecurities destroyed homes and families, driving many into panic. Yet the slightest glimmer of hope reinvigorating the peacetime ideals of romantic love and home and family kept both women and their fighter compatriots alive emotionally.

Women as well as men carried romantic preconceptions into war. War meant sacrifice, but this was a noble means to achieve victory—peace with honor. Women would be brave and supportive of their warrior sons and lovers. They would remain true and loving, patient yet eager to welcome home their conquering heroes.

At the end of the evening of December 29, 1861, Adelia Allen sat by her fireside in Princeton, Illinois, writing to her "dear friend" Dan Holmes, who had gone soldiering through rural Missouri. She recalled their having sat together late one evening by such a fire drinking wine. She reminded Dan of dinner parties other evenings with their chums, when "fine sentiment—polished wit—keen sarcasm—and charming originality—" flew around the table. In a similar schoolgirl-pretentious tone she also exhorted him to fight the noble war: "strike till the last armed foe expires . . . we do hope you will succeed in crushing this unholy rebellion. I am glad you see it your duty to stiffen the sinews and summon up the blood."[1] Dan was killed by guerrillas in 1862.

This was a conventional war letter to a soldier in the field from a young woman back home. Recalling happy times, just tinged with erotic nostalgia, also promised a future worth fighting to preserve. Such domestic anticipation was explicitly linked to the higher morality of the war. Adelia was preparing Dan and herself for his possible sacrifice, which was all the more reason to intensify general war aims in such personal, emotional ways. For Dan and Adelia, death could have value, and this meant that life could have more meaning as well.

In some cases, women were more ideologically committed than their male friends and kin whom they pushed into war. Lizzie Brannock wrote to her brother from the village of Chapel Hill concerning her southern principles and behavior. For her, the Republicans were abolitionist rebels who had captured and destroyed the "dear old government with all its rights and priviledges," most especially the right of freedom of thought. "I think every man is entitled to his honest opinion and no one has a right to interrupt or disturb him for his sentiment." The Union had turned barbarian, burning and plundering her county to impose an alien antislavery ideology upon it. Lizzie wrote that she had come to these secessionist conclusions five months prior to her husband, and that only on August 15, 1862, had he "voluntarily" gone South to join J. O. Shelby's cavalry regiment rather than submit to an oath and enlist in the local Union militia. He had become "an honest Christian soldier from principle and conscience battling for what we think the right." Lizzie Brannock was clearly in the political lead and not merely by five months. "Mr. Brannock would be willing to live on as a loyal citizen if he could, but I am not willing he should take an oath that he desires the north to triumph over the south, [an oath] which would be against conscience and it would be guilty before God and man." Political correctness, conscience, and Christianity were all activating appeals made by his wife to Mr. Brannock, who had preferred to stay home and take it easy. His wife defined the cause in which he had to fight.[2]

I am not arguing that most women were so eager to send their male kin into war nor that many men were so much more reluctant than their women relatives to go off and fight, but rather that there was a constellation of values—traditional liberty, Christian conscience, defense of the domestic realm—which were generally held ideals leading many women to conclude that this war was just and necessary. There is no reason to believe that women were intrinsically more pacifistic than men in defense of this configuration of values and feelings, even if later generations of suffragists, often citing the Civil War, argued that such was the case in nature and society. War as a traditional defense of cherished institutions and intimate relationships was as necessary to women as to men, and these women did not see themselves as victims but as participants.

Other women, even among those who preferred one side to the other, believed that the war was not worth fighting and that their male relatives would be well off out of it. An inelegant, if common, expression of this form of antiwar sentiment, one far more widespread in the North than copperheadism, was written by Lucy Thurman of Pine Oak to her cousin Larkin Adamsay. "Do come home if you can get out of old Abe's clutches, for I think you have served the old ape long enough. We are getting along first rate since the negro stealers are all gone to Dixie to whip the southern boys. I tell you they can't do it for they have not the pluck to whip a swarm of gnats."[3] Antiwar northerners as well as Southerners commonly enough referred to Old Abe as "old ape" and as leader of the "black Republicans" and to the North as an effeminate society during most of the war. Doubtless, there were as many such reluctant Union participants as there were those committed to the higher cause.

In a civil war of such great dislocations and carnage, in the daily grind of a region experiencing guerrilla war, ideological and moral commitments were put under just as severe a strain for women as for men. Women were left behind on farms when their husbands joined armies or went into the bush. They tried to remain loyal to their beliefs, but they also had to survive at any cost, had to come to terms with wildly contradictory pressures. Women had somewhat more leeway than men in being able to "get away" with the expression of overt opinion, as soldiers on both sides were generally horrified about the implications of making war on women; yet women too were severly injured by guerrilla war. In this sense they were compelled to be full participants in the war and to use all the cunning they could muster to the great goal of survival.

The court-martial of Mrs. Mary Jackson and her two daughters, Bettie and Sue, charged with feeding and informing William Jackman's notorious guerrilla band in the summer of 1863 in Saline County, exemplifies both active commitments and defensive survival lying strategies among women. A domestic slave woman reported the Jacksons to First Lieutenant W. D. Blair of the Fourth Cavalry, Missouri State Militia. He then rode out to the Jackson farm alone to confront the Jackson women, whose husbands were absent fighting for the South. Bettie defiantly told Lieutenant Blair that she had "ordered the black woman away and said no one should stay about her that would inform on her friends. . . . Bill Jackman and his gang had that day been fed by her sisters and she did not care who knew it." Bettie was proud of her strength of personal loyalty. She told off the lieutenant because he ought to have understood that personal loyalty as a fundamental value transcended mere political choices. Her sister Sue added that if the Union soldiers "had not taken their arms she could fight for [the guerrillas] too because the Lieutenant had insulted her." Sue shared in that sense of the necessary defense of honor that her male peers in the bush believed was the fundamental justification for their form of warfare. These teenage girls had not learned to dissemble their angry opinions in front of the enemy and shared the desire for violent glory in combat with their brothers and boyfriends.

At the court-martial itself, Mrs. Mary Jackson made the usual defense: she had tried to send William Jackman away and was coerced into feeding his band. The previously fiery Bettie deposed at her trial that no one had witnessed the supposed conversation reported by Lieutenant Blair and that besides, "with reference to uttering disloyal sentiments, her being a lady and unaccustomed to being held responsible for anything she might say, she really did not know what was loyal or disloyal." Some adult likely put these words into Bettie's deposition, but whoever composed the words, retreat into helpless, apolitical womanhood was a useful defense strategy in a culture politically dominated by men. Lieutenant Blair had seen the aggressive, undefensive Bettie when she had lashed out at him. The court saw the properly submissive good girl. This was one young woman's replication of the experience of the defiant guerrilla in the bush who became the supplicating guerrilla captive.[4]

Even women older and cooler than the Jackson girls were placed in a terrible bind if their male kin were off fighting for one side or the other, and they were then visited by either guerrilla or Union troops—a common set of circumstances. In general, they would attempt to placate whoever visited, to minimize their losses, to attempt to build up some protection for themselves. As this was a fluid war, such goodwill from one group of fighters would not be readily transferrable to the next group or the next.

In Jackson County in 1863, a Mrs. Garrison extracted a letter signed by Union Lieutenant J. C. Lindsay: "To officers and soldiers, USA. This is to certify that Mrs. Garrison has treated my command with the utmost kindness cooking for my men and ministering to the wants of my wounded. She is entitled to the respect and protection of all good soldiers."[5] Most likely the purpose of this letter was to show to other Union soldiers in the single Missouri county most overrun by guerrillas that summer. One cannot know from the remaining evidence if Garrison had obtained a similar letter from a guerrilla chieftain whose men she might also have fed and nursed.

Almost all the power in daily confrontations was held by armed men who could respond to women's arguments or ignore them as they willed. This would be true especially for soldiers who came from far away, particularly if they were just passing through. Coming from an area, or being stationed there, might lead to some constraints on behavior toward women not characteristic of fleeting contacts. For example, Private George Spratt from Fond du Lac, Wisconsin, wrote his "Friend Mary" about calling for dinner when his regiment was marching past Sedelia. The three women alone in the house said that their husbands, against their wills, had been "conscripted into the rebel army," that they themselves were "neutral," that they were "sorry that their husbands were not fighting for a better cause," that they had always respected "the free soldiers of the North but could never side with the aristocracy of the South." None of this appeal carefully crafted for his presumed sentiments worked on Private Spratt. "Having heard all I wanted I came to the conclusion that they were disloyal and stepping back from the door I confiscated a large chicken by drawing my revolver from my belt and sending a leaden messenger after him."[6] Spratt's pleasure in his power and his redirected violence are clear in his letter. The careful arguments of these women might have worked before or after this instance, but they were not the deciding factor in the outcome of this exchange.

Guerrilla war broke ordinary civility between men and women, separated women from their male kin, and strained the relationships within neighborhoods and families and between women. An example of these pressures undermining normal kinship ties can be found in the interrogation of Mary Vaughan, her daughter-in-law Nancy Jane Vaughan, and her daughter Susan, which took place in the Gratiot Street prison in St. Louis in the spring of 1865.

Mary was the mother of Dan Vaughan, a well-known member of Quantrill's gang, as well as being kin to many other guerrillas and regular Confederate soldiers. She testified that in 1861 guerrillas "frequented my house and I had to feed them. I left home to get rid of them." She had lived in Kansas and Illinois from 1862 to 1864, and when Price's army made its raid in the summer of 1864, she fed and supplied those troops only because they had coerced her. "I never willingly furnished the rebels anything last year except my own sons and son in law who belonged to Price's army, whom I willingly fed when at my house. . . . I have tried hard to act as a loyal woman." Clearly frightened and confused in prison, Mary Vaughan also testified against her son, that he had come in civilian clothes rather than in uniform with Price's regulars. Civilian clothes were the mark of the guerrilla, and Vaughan here added to a case against her son Dan (who was probably known to the local Union forces as a guerrilla anyway). Mary Vaughan also knew that less guilt would attach to feeding regular soldiers of the enemy side. She also claimed a certain immunity by relating that it was her own flesh and blood she was aiding willingly rather than guerrillas unknown to her, whom she fed only when forced to do so. Yet at the same time she turned on her son, claiming that she had "reported my son and two others" to Union authorities, and testified against her daughter-in-law, who had just died in prison, that she had often seen guerrillas eating at her home. Vaughan sought to free herself by attaching guilt to others in her family, who, however, were not in immediate danger of Union retribution.

In her turn, before her death Nancy Jane Vaughan named nine young men who had taken to the bush, as well as the Widow Henry and Suzzie Rule, both neighbor women who were "bad rebels." Susan Vaughan testified that she had talked only on one fleeting occasion with her brother Dan since he had taken to bushwhacking and that he had remained on his horse outside the yard. In that sense she had not taken him into the house and made "real" contact with him. No near neighbors she knew of willingly helped bushwhackers, Susan testified, but one time when both bushwhackers and Union troops were present at Nancy's house, "the bushwhackers rode around the house and then left. The soldiers did not fire upon them or pursue them."[7] Susan was implying that if armed Union troops coexisted peacefully through some deal with guerrillas, no special blame should attach to unarmed women who sought to survive by giving out essentially harmless meals.

Mary turned on at least the memory of her daughter-in-law and in a manner on her son; Nancy turned on her neighbors; Susan provided the context of a deep and extreme uncertainty in which unarmed women could never know who was fighting whom or what the battle meant. All these women pursued survival strategies which would make them appear loyal, even at the expense of their own kin. Yet in testifying against her own son, Mary gave away no secrets about him; certainly she did not betray him at a time when he could be seized immediately. In testifying against Nancy, both Susan and Mary knew she had died in any event. Blaming subjects beyond harm was a useful means for these prisoners to attempt to deflect the wrath of their Union interrogators. It is difficult to understand the intent or the actual harm in the testimony against neighbors.

Prewar values were dislocated with bits and pieces remaining from which these women attempted to construct sensible self-defenses, without much success. Mary Vaughan made a partial defense of her normal values when it came to having fed her own son willingly—such need for mothering, she seemed to argue, overcame her desire to be a loyal Unionist. Even here she stressed that when she fed him, Dan was attached to Price's regular command and that thus he was not a criminal guerrilla, though elsewhere in her testimony she acknowledged that she knew him to be a free-lance bushwhacker. What had become of Mary Vaughan's peacetime ordering of the values by which she had lived? The roles of mother, mother-in-law, neighbor, good citizen—all she had known clearly—had gone ajumble.

Fighters and Women

Just as traditional women's roles and values were deeply compromised by guerrilla war, so too were male attitudes and behavior toward women. Both Union soldiers and pro-Confederate guerrillas struggled to focus their rage on men and leave women on their elevated plane. Yet the force of war divided their attitudes and behavior as women clearly participated in the war and thus were dangerous to them. In an evangelical society where civil behavior to all women and submission to the "Empire of the Mother" was so deeply ingrained, Union soldiers tried to differentiate their responses to men from those to women in a host civilian population in which both genders were often openly hostile and frequently mortal threats. Any person might act as an enemy, whatever his or her professions. Some women loyal to the enemy were painfully rude, but as Union soldiers knew, others could be friendly to their faces while acting as spies and suppliers for the lurking guerrillas. A wish to strike back at those women who were active participants on the enemy side contradicted a powerful desire to remain gentlemen to the ladies, who after all were disarmed and defenseless, even when professing sympathy for the enemy. Good-natured or at least silent toleration alternated with coarseness and brutality in Union soldiers' behavior toward enemy women.

Union soldiers, knowing how ladies ought to respond to them, responded positively to what they deemed appropriate behavior. Private Hiram Crandall from Iowa recorded in his diary that he took kindly to the visits the ladies of Glasgow, Missouri, made to his regiment's camp, where they witnessed dress parades and tended to the sick, bringing "many luxuries" to them. Crandall was very proud when "A lady said in my hearing 'I have heard that the Iowa troops are gentlemen and from the conduct of the 5th I believe that statement warranted.' " Crandall was offended when secessionist women did not behave similarly. While waiting for a ferry during a march, "a number of the boys amused themselves by talking to a number of secesh ladies. One of these *ladies* was very bloodthirsty and said she hoped that we would all get killed, for which expression of good will I thanked her as kindly as I knew how and politely as I could."[8] Even though this woman was no lady, judging by her behavior, Crandall reined in his anger and responded as he would were she a lady. He demonstrated to her, to his comrades, and to himself in his diary, that he believed in a general ideal of ladies even when provoked by a specific woman who did not measure up to proper norms.

Another Iowa private, one less genteel than Hiram Crandall, wrote home about his responses to the "rampant secesher" women of Boonville. "They said the Iowa boys had conducted themselves more like gentlemen than any other troops that had been there. The women were the spunkiest

I ever seen and when a squad of us would visit a house we would have to take a few broadsides but our orders were to do things as civil as possible and we had to stand it as best we could but I felt several times like if I could see them strangled."[9] Dan Smith was proud to be thought an Iowa gentleman; he stayed cool when provoked, more from obedience to orders concerning civility than from the more internalized decorum expressed by Hiram Crandall. In a backhanded way he admired that "spunkiness" of pro-southern women which had offended Crandall, but unlike Crandall, he also permitted himself to express homicidal fantasies toward them. His notions of women were less idealized and his feelings toward them less controlled than those of the other Iowa soldier. It is also significant that his reveries were self-censored: Smith's desire to kill were expressed in the passive voice—he could not permit himself to come right out and say that he would like to strangle these bad women with his own hands.

Under extreme provocation, many Union soldiers expressed their anger in the manner of one cavalry captain who wrote his commander, "General, if Mrs. Byrne was a man, and guilty of the crimes that she is, he would not live here twenty-four hours."[10] Sometimes this formulation would be expressed directly to a woman. In the hot days of August 1861, one officer wrote a friend: "Our reception in St. Louis was extremely cool. When our soldiers were almost fainting and some dropping in the streets, and all were pleading for water, one young lady declined to give a cup to one of our boys remarking that he was not the right kind of soldier to suit her. Another lady said to one of our Captains that she would not give bread or water to our 'beer swilling, nigger loving, cowardly dogs to save their lives.' I replied, 'you are a woman: if you were a man, we would have an answer in our guns.' "[11] For that captain, the violation of the principle of ladylike behavior lay in the refusal to bring water to thirsty men as much as in the insults. Still, although enormously frustrated in his anger, he would remain the gentleman and would not use force against even such an evil woman.

Such restraint was often violated, but never totally, and it was asserted frequently and explicitly enough to lead to the conclusion that restraint toward women had real meaning in conduct as well as in principle. Of course, pro-southern women were deeply resented by Union troops for the terrible things they would say, as well as for getting away with saying them—Union soldiers sensed that what they considered to be their own most noble sentiments of forbearance and helpfulness to ladies were being manipulated by enemy women. Indeed these women seemed even to prosper, when good Union folks and the soldiers themselves were suffering real deprivations. Private Charles E. Calkins, in a shaky semi-literate hand, wrote to his mother back in Illinois from Otterville, Missouri, in 1862, "Secesh ladies visit town a great deal more than they did previous to the departure of our army and every day they can be seen flaunting along the streets, dressed in their costly silks and furs."[12] Such resentment was often a prelude to looting but not to rape or murder.

Provoked as they wei all the evidence indicates that Union soldiers and guerrillas did not shoot, violate, or beat women who aided the enemy, restraints not upheld in many other guerrilla wars. At the most, women were tormented, arrested, or sent into exile. To give a vivid example, in February 1864 three of Captain James A. Ewing's cavalrymen were killed by guerrillas hiding in the house of a southern woman sympathizer. Ewing wrote his colonel, "The wife of one of the scoundrels told my men when they first rode up that there was no one in the house, which I suppose caused them to be more careless than they would have been. I have ordered her to leave the country; if it was not for the name of the thing I would shoot her sure, for she murdered those men." Ewing would not have hesitated in executing the woman's husband had he caught him, but even under these circumstances where to Ewing she was a murderer, shooting this woman was morally impermissible.[13]

Truly total war would have meant the erasure of all lines between civilian and soldier and the treatment of men and women. Many public figures as well as soldiers immersed in the fighting knew that this was so and could at least contemplate absolute war. At the onset of the war a prominent St. Louis politician recognized what a guerrilla war might become. "There will be trouble in Missouri until the Secesh are *subjugated* and made to know that they are not only powerless, but that any desperate attempts to make trouble here will bring upon them *certain* destruction and this [certainty] of their condition must not be confined to Soldiers and fighting men, but must extend to non-combatant men *and women*."[14] As the guerrilla war deepened, it became clear that only with women supporters could it be continued. But how could soldiers know which women were involved and how could they keep from making mistakes, thus committing the terrible crime of harming guiltless women? By using women as their final screen, guerrillas had created a situation in which Union troops would have to war on women to destroy guerrillas. Union soldiers could never bring themselves to make this final moral adjustment—one more reason they could not win such a war.

I have already described the notorious General Orders #11, by which Union troops depopulated and burned much of west central Missouri in 1863 and the way popular opinion recoiled against what was perceived as an impermissible war on innocent civilians. Unlike war against an alien race far away, this was a civil war among people who at some levels perceived themselves to be much alike. This sense of similarity, a blurring of noncombatants, revolved around a belief in the sanctity of womankind. Furthermore, many staunch Unionists believed that making war on women would justify secessionists in their guerrilla warfare, as they themselves would defend "their own women" at any cost were they attacked. Defending women and home were shared values which often contradicted political commitments, placing a limit on the level of violence which could be applied in good conscience.

On the everyday level, such conscientiousness made many soldiers remorseful when they pillaged homes and frightened women or when they reported about other soldiers committing such excesses. Most often in such descriptions, *other* soldiers were doing the dirty work, and the reporting soldier was merely observing. Only a few soldiers bragged about their brutality to women.

One way for Union soldiers to distance themselves from the hardships they were causing women was to blame it all on the German-American troops in their army. That they were more violent to women than other Union troops is doubtful, but sharing the anti-German bigotry of their pro-southern counterparts, native-born American Union troops believed them to be so and blamed them for activities in which they themselves frequently participated. Thus General E. A. Carr reported to headquarters about behavior on the Missouri-Arkansas border, "Men of mine who were with the Germans today in foraging report great excesses on their part, going into the private apartments of ladies and opening trunks and drawers, and ransacking everything and taking away what they wanted. If these excesses are permitted we cannot wonder at guerrilla warfare."[15] The invasion of women's private spaces by foreigners, even if they were military comrades, was the sort of lethal act which Anglo-Saxon Unionist Missourians would recognize as sufficient cause to justify even the horrible guerrillas in their illegal war. This recognition made it useful to blame Germans in self-exoneration, but it also highlighted the complex political dilemma in which even the most committed Unionist was placed when fighting a guerrilla war.

If enemy women were welcoming rather than rude, their political opinions could be overlooked. They would usually be able to buy some protection by appropriately acknowledging the power and manliness of Union soldiers. Iowa infantryman Timothy Phillips wrote of one of the ladies of Lebanon, Missouri, "I got my supper in town of a secessionist ladie's house. She was rebel to the backbone but very kind (and very good looking.)"[16]

Probably working quite consciously on the compunctions of ordinary men, welcoming hostesses portrayed themselves as dependent women to be protected. It bothered most soldiers to see women abused, especially when those women behaved as did the nice women back home. Wisconsin infantryman Dwight Stevens wrote to his wife concerning foraging off defenseless women in northern Arkansas. "Although I used to think it right to take all that belonged [to already impoverished rebels,] when I came to see it, it looks hard. I have known men, Union men, to go into houses where there were nothing more but women and children and take everything they could find consisting of a few potatoes, a little butter, a few chickens, this seemed to be their whole living. Our teams drive into the fields and load on their corn, fodder and all and drive off again without a word and the owner stands and looks in silence. This is well enough, but to strip a woman of all she has don't look right." The defenselessness of the women, their benumbed silence when being plundered, and their poverty and potential starvation made them seem pitiable victims to Stevens. He continued his letter to his wife with what he knew was most likely a fantasy about returning home on furlough for Christmas and then concluded, "Kiss the little boys for Papa. I should like to seen them . . . and for yourself accept the warmest affections of your husband." Stevens drew a lesson in this letter of the contrast between his paternal love for his family and his sense of dread about what, but for the grace of God or fortune, would become of fatherless women and children—so much like his own family—in war.[17]

If women behaved "nicely" and if soldiers only needed a meal or a drink of water, Union troops could convince themselves that they were correctly defending women and children. S. S. Marrett, an Illinois private, expressed this conventional formula concerning the ladies of Batesville, Arkansas, whose husbands were off in the rebel army. "The ladies are as friendly as if their husbands were not our enemies. We do not make war on the women and children. It is the men with arms in their hands upon whom we make war and the women are entitled to protection even if they are the wives and daughters of rebels."[18]

However, when S. S. Marrett's company needed forage, he could revise his code. He wrote about taking supplies by the wagonload, "it looks very hard to take their property when the men are gone and the women left to take care of themselves but we must have corn for our horses and hams and there is no use to get down in the mouth about it even if the women do cry about it. It is God's truth that we have taken corn from places where the women would beg with tears in their eyes for enough corn to keep their children from starving. . . . Northern soldiers that has the true principles of a gentleman will not punish a woman and children just because she happens to have a rebel for a husband but as far as the men are concerned it is no matter if they had to starve till the corn grows again."[19] Marrett's ambivalence was clear. How would he propose to starve only the men when the whole family was looted? He was confused, on the one hand wanting to protect women, on the other trying not to get "down in the mouth" about causing them pain and privation. It is significant that he was bothered enough to write his wife about this everyday military brutality, and it is important to stress as well that Marrett and many others like him probably would not have acted alone as they did in uniformed concert. Although he did not reconceptualize enemy women as beasts, with a disturbed conscience he acted in ways he would never have imagined in peacetime.

Under the pressures of guerrilla war, ambivalence could exact a high psychological cost, and so there were expeditious reasons for hardening one's attitudes toward enemy women. Interestingly, more articulate soldiers who had clear ideological positions were better able to divide "good" women from "bad" in their minds and to attack the bad. This was especially true of two committed Christian New England abolitionists who had settled in Kansas in the 1850s, L. R. Webber and Sherman Bodwell.

Webber, it will be recalled, wrote to the wife of an esteemed older friend back in Kansas concerning his regiment's brush with the Widow Anderson in Louisiana. She had taunted the Union troops that "real southern men would scalp them, that she would not believe union soldiers were anything but cowards and braggards unless she should see scalps they had taken." Later, one Union man sent her, gift-wrapped, a pair of ears cropped from a dead rebel. Webber wrote, "a great deal of horror has been pretended against the deed as compromising the civilization of the whole Union army. Yet under the circumstances I don't think it so horrible an affair, I suppose the man who did it didn't think of it as an example, and only wished to plague widow Anderson. The only wickedness of such a deed, per se, arises on the ground that the man has such a savage disposition to derive malignant satisfaction from the deed itself."[20] Webber, who earlier in the war had been upset by the drinking and swearing of his comrades and who in this passage worried about risks to their souls, did not concern himself at all with the feelings of the enemy Widow Anderson, who in his opinion got what she asked for.

Sergeant Sherman Bodwell, as I discussed earlier, taught Sunday school to little black children during the war, eulogized a fallen German comrade, and in general was a concerned liberal, unlike most of his fellow soldiers, whom he consciously tried to reform on racial matters. When three Union families in western Missouri were burned out by guerrillas, Sergeant Bodwell had his company take the time to "outfit them again for housekeeping at the expense of some of the secesh about," and then burned the secessionists' houses, "not giving the women and children time to dress even." Bodwell was good at hating enemy women. He believed the Widow Holly had warned nearby guerrillas of their coming. His company burned down her house in her absence. With heavy sarcasm, Bodwell wrote, "Having no home to keep [she] will be able to devote more time to carrying the news." Punishing such enemies, women included, was a duty based on higher values and should not upset the righteous soldier. The morning after Bodwell watched his captain execute a captured guerrilla with a bullet in the back of the head, he "was startled by the cries of the sister of the dead man, as she found his body lying where the bullet left it. Took breakfast as we did supper."[21] If momentarily startled, Bodwell carried on as if this woman's distress came from a subhuman unworthy of his sympathy.

Most Union soldiers ranged in their responses to women from confused empathy to cold indifference. In behavior there was still a belief in a code of decency to women who were by definition innocent—a widely shared value, judging by these letters and diaries written when the soldiers were under great wartime stress. Limits were placed on actions, thoughts, and feelings, even in guerrilla war. Most soldiers did not give themselves over to assaulting women directly, though they often did things to them they regarded as terrible. They floundered between sympathy and brutality. It did not take perfect monsters to behave monstrously, and even monsters had to wish that they were behaving according to notions of decency, especially where women were concerned.

Defined by the Union forces as criminals, cut off from the Confederacy for which they were fighting, roaming in unformed bands, living off the citizenry by a combination of pleading and force, guerrillas had an even more desperate need than Union soldiers to believe that they were gentlemen to the ladies. This need was functional, as guerrillas depended upon women allies for supplies and information, but it was also a psychological necessity—a reinforcement of their belief that they were defenders of the local virtues against alien invaders. At the center of their notion of community was family with inviolate women in the very middle. Elevation of women in times of social catastrophe was also a means of keeping alive positive views of morality and self-esteem to counter that endemic destructiveness the guerrillas knew they must employ.

One October Sunday in 1863, four men, pistols in hand, burst into the house of Lucy Jane McManus of Andrew County. They said they had come to search for arms. I "told them to search ahead" (she later reported to the local justice of the peace). "They asked her if she was a widow woman. She said she was not but was alone. They said if that be the case they would not interrupt anything but would like to get some supper." While dining, they told her that they were looking for her husband Richard and that when they found him, "they would soon put him under the sod."[22] They treated the wife of this man they hunted with what they considered all due respect. They were showing McManus and themselves that they distinguished between guilty men and innocent women. She should understand they meant her no personal harm, as they were good men compelled to' ruthless action by military necessity. They sought to deny that they were directly intimidating a woman by breaking into her house, pistols in hand, and threatening to kill her husband by behaving like gentlemen when they learned that she was alone and undefended by a man, and of course no threat to them.

Such a combination of gentility and brute force lies behind the legends of outlaws who would leave thousand dollar bills under their plates after being served by just such defenseless women. Missouri guerrillas certainly believed in the noble outlaw—the better to convince themselves that though called lawbreakers, they were indeed serving nature's law. Sam Hildebrand, who bragged of killing over 100 Union men single-handedly in the Ozarks during the war, wrote of his chivalry toward one German woman (he was indicating to his presumably xenophobic readers that if he was nice to a German woman, he was better than other guerrillas). Seizing her husband, her horse, and her mule, Hildebrand refused to take her side-saddle. "I told her I could not rob a lady; to keep the saddle and that I was sorry from my heart to be compelled to give her uneasiness or trouble; the war had no mercy; and that through it all I hoped she would be protected from harm." He subsequently took the husband about a mile down the road and hanged him. Then he returned the man's pocket money, horse, and mule to the poor widow.[23] What is especially striking about this story is that Hildebrand later published it, clearly to put himself in a good light. Killing this man had been acceptable because it was war and not the soldier which had been merciless, something he demonstrated by being gallant to the new widow he had just made.

Part of the perversity of armed chivalry was the God-like power it gave the warrior over the fate of women. In their moments of armed dominance, which was precisely what their mode of warfare was meant to create, guerrillas had the power to do what they alone willed, including murder; thus, withholding destruction could also give them an enormous sense of power. This led to random killing which was part of the terror they administered: no woman could predict whom guerrillas might choose to kill and whom to let go. This was particularly true of the male relatives of Union women, who were considered fair game for slaughter, whether a mile down the road or directly in front of their women kin. During the slaughter of Quantrill's raid on Lawrence, Kansas, Sophia Bissell wrote shortly afterwards that her son Henry was spared by two guerrillas. Her daughter Arabella "was pleading all the time with him to spare her only brother, running from him to the leader and back again in *agony*. The leader relented and spoke to the man. He let go his hold and Henry ran for the corn. . . . They tipped their hats and bid me good morning."[24] Few men were spared on such a whimsical response to a supplicating and one would guess attractive young woman. Such an incident no doubt heightened the self-image of the gentleman outlaw for these two guerrillas; it was a demonstration of their total if momentary power over Arabella, even more than over Henry, who in this battle would have had no effective means to plead for himself.

Primary in the code of these guerrillas was the injunction against harming women and children. Guerrillas were the protectors not the despoilers of home and family, and honoring this code was a daily demonstration of their ideals. In his open letter to Union General Egbert B. Brown in 1864, the notorious Bill Anderson made the demand for the release from prison of his women sympathizers the demonstration of his social respectability and power. "I do not like the idea of warring with women and children, but if you do not release all the women you have captured in LaFayette County, I will hold the Union Ladies in the county as hostages for them. I will tie them in the brush and starve them. . . . I will have to resort to abusing your ladies if you do not quit imprisoning ours."[25] Defending "their" women was the chief function of masculinity. Honor demanded vengeance if they were injured. Indeed the massacre at Lawrence was justified at the time and after the war by Quantrill's men in large part because several of the guerrillas' sisters, including two of Bill Anderson's, had died when a rickety prison had collapsed on them in Kansas City.[26] In response, guerrillas sought to kill only the male perpetrators of such deeds, and always spared the women and children on the other side. Thus they were morally superior to Union soldiers; they were the true upholders and enforcers of the natural law enjoining honorable conduct toward women.

Many on the Union side attested to the guerrilla maintenance of this code. An Illinois journalist wrote during the worst summer of guerrilla violence around Independence, "In this country the old notion that men are the protectors of women has exploded, the tables are turned, men are now the weaker vessels, and women the protectors. A man dare not travel alone five miles from Kansas City, but with his wife he feels comparatively secure. Bushwhackers have not yet raised a hand against a woman, they sometimes burn a house over her head but are careful not to injure her person."[27] In fact the world had not been turned upside down. Male efforts to dominate other men had become a lethal game. Customary deference to women had become twisted, making them pawns to be kept upright while the knights and rooks knocked over each other. All the while, the warriors could proclaim that the slaughter of men was done in service to their righteous worship of women.

Strikingly, there are only infrequent reports of rape of white women, and all of those second hand. To give an example, N. F. Carter had heard that "Ned Ellis was shot at [one recent] night; his wife and Mrs. Stevens were raped by the Militia and everything they had taken from them."[28] It is hard to analyze this report and the absence of others. It is possible that rape did occur with some frequency and was such a badge of shame as to go undisclosed. But if that is the case, rape was the only violation to remain unmentioned, as everything else was told to the authorities and broadcast as propaganda against the enemy. It is possible as well that rape was infrequent.

If rape was unusual, extreme brutality toward women was common, including what one might call near rape or symbolic rape, often combined with looting and the killing of men. Sometimes men insulted women sexually. For example, Union Captain John M. Richardson destroyed two whiskey stills near Springfield because they were places of rendezvous for plundering secession bands: "bad men would get drunk there, and go to the Union men's houses and expose their naked persons to Union women."[29] A southern sympathizer reported several cases of harassment of pro-southern women in his neighborhood. "They forced Mrs. Trigg to play for them while they danced . . . one of the men remarked to Mrs. Thos. Shields (who is quite a fine looking young woman) that he liked her looks and would come back that night and stay with her. At Col. Bellis's they . . . abused his wife shamefully, felt of her person, and used insulting language."[30] These might be considered very nasty pranks, less likely to have occurred during peacetime, though there was some political discrimination and hence intent concerning which women were chosen to be violated.

More often attacks on women took place in the context of looting and sometimes of killing of civilian men. For example, M. G. Singleton, a wealthy farmer who lived near Centralia under oath and bond after having served in the secessionist state militia at the start of the war, reported the attack of twenty Union militiamen who came calling for dinner. His wife, who had her two nieces as company, refused to serve the men. The militia commander flew into a rage and demanded to be fed. The troops then commenced ransacking the house, "all the time using the most profane and vulgar language" in order to offend the women. "One fellow danced with the heels of his boots on the carpet in my wife's chamber till he cut it through. They had thrown their overcoats and a gun on her bed, which she quietly removed—placing the coats on a chair and set the gun up by the side of the bed—when one of them threw them on again and called on the rest to pile on their guns—and then jumped on the bed and rolled over it—took the pillows threw them down on the floor, sat and then stamped them under his feet." After they had dined, two armed Negroes who accompanied them ate "the family dinner" and then took a pan of bread dough and threw it on the kitchen floor.[31]

Mrs. Singleton enraged the troopers, who doubtless would have looted the house of a known southern sympathizer in any event, by correcting the soldier's etiquettte, first refusing them dinner, then taking their coats and guns off her bed. They further violated her domestic space by encouraging Negroes to eat off the family china (albeit after they had eaten, thus preserving their Caucasian superiority while violating hers) and to desecrate her kitchen. In front of her, they also assaulted her bedroom, her most private space, piling guns on her bed and tearing apart her bedclothes. The soldiers attacked the setting of Mrs. Singleton's femaleness, yet they did not actually rape her or her nieces. Symbolic rape such as this was frequent. The impulse to rape, which was certainly present, was projected onto this woman's most intimate objects in place of her body.

There was also an additional element here of bad boys acting out against a nagging, smothering mother. Mrs. Singleton put their coats and guns in the proper place; they heaped them on the improper place as part of the destruction of her bed and her rules. Some of these young men may have been vandals during peacetime, but here they could be rule breakers openly and defiantly. Uniformed, empowered, they were not forced to run off after breaking a window but could stay on, encouraging one another in competitive destructiveness until they reached some mutually understood implicit limit, one which would vary from instance to instance and group to group. They pushed at the limits of a code they did not violate entirely.

On the night of May 6, 1865, Mrs. Mary Hall was awakened by a group of guerrillas. They demanded she light a candle and then took it and set light to her children's clothes, shoving them under the bed where the three children were sleeping. "I caught the clothes they were burning and threw them in the fire place. One of them says God damn you let them; if you don't I will burn up the house. I answered they will burn just as well where they are and will give more light." They then went to the bed of her eighteen-year-old son and demanded his pistol. He said he had traded it for a watch and added, "its hanging by the glass though some of you have it—as I do not see it. One of the guerrillas said God damn him. Shoot him. I thought they would shoot him and knocked up the pistol several times, injuring my shoulder by so doing," Hall reported. "They finally succeeded in shooting him in the head killing him instantly. I was screaming and entreating them all the time to spare his life. After they had killed him one of them says shut your God Damn mouth or I will blow a hole through your head. . . . All this time my niece, 16 years of age was lying in bed. One of the guerrillas stood by the bedside and as she made an effort to rise ordered her to lie still saying one woman was enough at a time. After they had killed my son and plundered the house one of the guerrillas ordered me out of the house and shut the door. The door had scarcely closed before I heard my niece scream and say Lord Aunt Mary run here to me. I started and as I reached the door my niece who had succeeded in effecting her escape from the men came rushing out. I says let the poor girl alone you have done enough. . . . I do not think they effected their designs on the girl." Since they had destroyed all her son's clothing, Hall had to buy a suit in which to bury him.[32]

Mary Hall could not protect her son from slaughter, but she could aid in preventing her niece's rape. The assault went up to the edge of rape and murder of women. Breaking into a house in the middle of the night, destroying and burning property out of pure malevolence, killing a man right in front of his mother simply because he was grown and probably sympathetic to the other side, and threatening women in the grossest manner were all characteristic guerrilla invasions of the realm of women. This passion for destruction, which had little to do with military necessity, stopping just short of rape and murder of women, lay on the dark side of the code of protecting women.

In some cases such twisted vestiges of gentility broke down. In one very exceptional incident, recorded in the diaries of two different Union soldiers who were both horrified by the event, Union men shot a woman to death. Once again, the event which triggered the rage was the refusal of the woman to serve men supper. Captain Clark and Private Rice of the Kansas Fifth Infantry Regiment were stationed with the Union army in Springfield in the spring of 1862. One May evening they had demanded supper of a widow and her daughter, members of a family in which both sons had been shot to death in the front yard earlier in the war by southern guerrillas. Clark and Rice behaved so abusively that evening that neighbors had intervened. After this traumatic night the widow begged for protection from the local Missouri Union regiment. The colonel sent two privates, one of whom was engaged to the daughter. A few days later, Clark and Rice, both drunk, returned to this home, and while still mounted on their horses in the front yard, screamed their demands for supper. As Private Sardius Smith told the story in his diary, "the widow said supper was over and she did not feel like getting any more. They then dismounted, drew their revolvers and swore they would see about that. The guard ordered them to halt three times and told them that he was placed there to guard the house and if they advanced he would fire, but they cursed him and said they did not fear all the guards in the world. They came on with cocked pistols until they reached the porch when the guard fired, shooting the Capt. through the breast. Rice then fired and shot the young lady through the head when the other guard shot him through the shoulder. Thus all three shots took effect."

Sardius Smith and Henry Dysart (the other diarist who told this story) rendered it as a temperance tale. In Dysart's words, Clark was "a fine intelligent looking man who has come to a bad end from intoxication the consequence of which not only he but the innocent girl had to suffer."[33] Drink destroyed a good man and an innocent woman; drink subverted the moral code. To demand a meal by force violated the western rural norm whereby friendly and respectable strangers were fed supper by the women of the house, as an act of generosity and a response to politeness not as submission to male power. Clark and Rice took a refusal to serve them not as a response to their prior coarseness and their drunken and brutal behavior but as an insult to their honor from alien women who broke the rules of good treatment to visiting strangers. They would be served, they would show these women how to behave, or they would punish them for their rudeness.

Some inviolable positive value—the protection of women—was necessary psychologically to guerrilla war fighters. The attacks on women I have described were indeed assaults on those traditional values, but there was usually some mitigation of violence. It seems that these warriors did *not* make fundamental distinctions between the images of the angel and the whore. "Bad," abusive, or duplicitous women, departed from the general code of nice ladies, but they were rarely re-conceptualized as completely debased. The fighters were eager to maintain ideals of honor in their relations with women.

This moral framework applied to white women only: black women and

Indian women were below the pale for fighters on both sides. Indeed one might argue that all white women were treated with respect in part because other non-white women were available to be trampled. One can find evidence of behavior toward blacks and Indians which was never accorded whites. Racism, tied to the license to destroy, was the deadliest combination. However, the liberation of blacks during the war which led to white resentment also tended to mitigate brutal treatment of black women.

Raping and beating black women, sometimes beating them to death, were intrinsic parts of slavery, an institution which gave superhuman powers to the owners. Good owners avoided random and excessive brutality and decried the viciousness of harsh masters. Yet few good masters refrained from whipping, and many used their enormous power over slave women to coerce them sexually with varying degrees of explicitness. White men were not punished for raping black women.

There were many allusions to the rape and abuse of black women during the war, particularly those "contraband" who followed the army. There are few direct reports, however, of actual rape. One concrete example came in the court-martial of guerrilla James Johnson of Platte County. Frances Kean testified that Johnson, John Nichols, and another bushwhacker seized her eighteen-year-old slave girl. Kean reported what the girl had told her. "They rode on a piece and said to her, 'God damn you we will punish you.' . . . Nichols then got off his horse and said now boys ride and she told me they all done with her what they wanted to—she said they violated her person."[34]

In March 1864, a slave owner named Tapley of Pike County recaptured his escaping slave woman. As she would not tell him where she had hidden her three children, she was, an unsigned letter to the Chicago Tribune later reported, "stripped and beaten on the bare back with a band saw until large blisters formed, and then the wretch sawed them open, under which treatment the poor woman died." Mrs. J. R. Roberts, secretary of the Freedman's Relief Society of Quincy, Illinois, clipped this newspaper story and sent it in a letter to the provost marshal of Missouri. The story went on to say that Missouri slaveholders in general were enraged with Lincoln's proclamation freeing the wives and children of black soldiers: this woman was running off to join her soldier husband when her owner caught her.[35] I do not know what became of Tapley, but James Johnson was sentenced to death, in part for his crime against a black woman.

The Civil War led many whites to re-work at least in part their attitudes towards blacks, including black women. Physical punishment of blacks, formerly a disciplinary norm, and murder of them were in the process of becoming crimes in the eyes of whites. This was in large part due to the reliability of black information given Union troops concerning secessionist activities and later in the war to the appearance of black regiments fighting for the Union. White Union soldiers had some sense of camaraderie with black soldiers; therefore, they came to understand that black soldiers sought to protect their women kin in the same way they wished to shelter their own.

In February 1863, the First Iowa Cavalry was foraging on the farm of a noted northern Arkansas rebel. They asked a slave woman if there was a gun hidden away. "She denied knowing anything about it but being threatened she owned that it would be death to her if she told anything," Private Timothy Phillips recorded in his diary. "Our boys promised to rescue her and take her along with them," Phillips wrote. Perhaps this was the *quid pro quo* the woman was bargaining for all along, perhaps she wished vengeance against her owner, perhaps she was terribly frightened. In any event, the Iowa troops found the gun where she had said they would, and she was placed on a horse in the baggage train. Later, the owner caught up with the column and offered twenty dollars in gold to anyone who would return his slave. She was returned and the twenty dollars paid. "The whole thing was got up so quick that few in the train knew anything about it," Phillips wrote in his diary that evening. Lieutenant Edward A. Dunham, the head of Phillips's squad, was blamed and forced to turn the money over to the colonel. Phillips concluded, "There is considerable excitement in the regiment about this matter and if the boys had it in their power they would make short work of Lieut. Dunham."[36]

The most obvious conclusion one might draw is that Lieutenant Dunham was glad to turn over a "nigger wench" for twenty dollars. Phillips's moral was more complex. The exchange took place so quickly he did not respond at the time, he wrote later, perhaps in expiation for what he realized—between the act and the pen—had been a terrible betrayal by omission of his own. Unlike his lieutenant, he believed that breaking an official word given a black woman was criminal. Also, he reasoned, other slaves hearing of this incident might be less forthcoming in the future. It was just plain wrong to him. The analogy to Judas in the payment of gold for a life would not have been lost on Phillips and his comrades. This was a practical lesson in abolitionism for them.

For many Kansas regiments, freeing slaves was central to their agenda, less out of racial sympathy than because of their desire for revenge against their long-time enemies, the Missouri slaveholders. Surgeon Joseph H. Trego reported that two captains had resigned their commissions in his Fifth Kansas Cavalry Regiment when Colonel Powell Clayton ordered the return of a group of fugitive slaves. "This case was particularly agrivating because the fugitives were wenches and one of them was whipped severely when her master got her home." Although Trego used racist language and shared the obsession for punishing Pukes, he empathized with the female victims of his enemies and sought to free and protect them.[37]

General James A. Pile, who was organizing black regiments at Benton Barracks in St. Louis in 1864, sought assurance from the commander of the military district concerning protection for the wives and children of his new troops. He was particularly concerned about Richard Glover, whose wife and six children were being cruelly treated by George Caldwell, the master from whom Glover had escaped. Caldwell had beaten Glover's wife with a buggy whip," and this when she is *Pregnant* and nearing *confinement*," in order to procure her consent to be taken to Kentucky. And, Pile added, "This is not an isolated case, but only a sample." He protested against "this *Infamy* in the name of *God—Justice—and Humanity* . . . against these Sable patriots and true heroes."[38] Pile wished to recruit more willing troops, and he understood that success would be in part contingent on real aid to their families. Because he sought out black men, he had all the more reason to be sympathetic toward the stories of the beatings of their wives. In a similar fashion, many Union troops and their civilian allies learned something of the humanity of these captives of their enemies.

Captain Louis F. Green of a Kansas black regiment wrote to the former master of "Ed Payton colored boy," who had just joined his company, telling the master that he had better send on Payton's wife and children. *"I have promised him that he shall have them and he shall."* Failure to comply would mean "your *life* or property. When that black man Ed Payton enlisted here yesterday, he purchased his wife and children from you and from now on he is fighting for the government, and is entitled to the privileges it now gives—*freedom to all.*"[39]

If paternalistic and condescending to their charges, white officers in black regiments were attuned to their recruits' pleas for their families. Most whites maintained their traditional racist views or were indifferent to blacks. In many parts of Missouri guerrillas turned on free blacks at the end of the war. Timothy Phillips reported seeing many black bodies floating in a river in Arkansas at the end of the war, and lynching first came into style in Missouri in the spring of 1865. During and after the war black women were violated far more frequently than whites. These letters, diaries, and reports document all the mayhem but also the glimmerings of recognition of blacks as humans, which in the context of that culture included respect for black women.

The most horrendous example counter to the general nonviolation of white women in Missouri and counter to the partially limited behavior of Missouri fighters toward black women was the Sand Creek massacre of the Cheyenne Indians, committed by the First Colorado Cavalry on November 19, 1864. This slaughter of about 500 Cheyenne, mainly women and children, took place west of Missouri, but similar Union troops did it. In fact, the Second Colorado Cavalry had been brought into the Kansas-Missouri border counties that year to replace Kansas troops, in hopes, to an extent realized, that they would prove more disciplined and less likely to plunder and murder civilians than the Kansans. Lieutenant James D. Cannon reported on Sand Creek:

> In going over the battle-ground next day I did not see a body of man, woman, or child but was scalped, and in many instances their bodies were mutilated in the most horrible manner—men, women, and children's privates cut out, etc. I heard one man say that he had cut a woman's private parts out, and had them for exhibition on a stick. I heard another say that he had cut the fingers off of an Indian to get the rings on the hand. According to the best of my knowledge and belief, these atrocities that were committed were with the knowledge of J. M. Chivington, and I do not know of him taking any measures to prevent them. I heard of one instance of a child a few months' old being thrown in the feed-box of a wagon, and after being carried some distance left on the ground to perish. I also heard of numberless instances in which men had cut out the private parts of females and stretched them over the saddle bows, and wore them over their hats while riding in the ranks. All these matters were a subject of general conversation, and could not help being known by Col. J. M. Chivington.[40]

These troops believed their behavior was licensed by their colonel, their society, and their consciences. Prior sanctioning prepared them for acting against Indian women and children without an insuperable sense of moral violation. At least Leiutenant Cannon and two others did not agree and were so shocked that they reported their colleagues to higher authorities. In response, Chivington half denied and half justified what he had encouraged. He was reported to have justified killing Indian children with the remark, "nits make lice." Even when Lawrence, Kansas, had been for that one morning in 1863 completely subject to their control, guerrillas did not extend their massacre to white women and children. This is but one more example of the well-proven thesis that to almost all American settlers Indians were a subspecies to be exterminated. If Sand Creek was in some respects the ultimate contemptuous expression by men at war, the ban on raping, killing, and mutilating white women in Missouri suggests a pulling back from that expression, an attempt to put a boundary on behavior. This suggests that some dualism—some ambivalence—was maintained and thus that nihilism did not become the synthesis of all belief and action.[41]

Family, Home, and Womanhood Undermined

Ambivalence toward convention, which in any event had been largely undermined by cultural chaos, led women as well as men into contexts where they were compelled to at least consider dangerously new conceptions of self and of others. The ability to function within traditional roles and values was weakened, altered, and at times reversed during the guerrilla war. Under great stress and novel opportunity, women sometimes impersonated men (and occasionally men impersonated women), and in general, sexual mores became more fluid as the boundaries between male and female roles weakened. If men and women struggled to retain many of their received notions of proper roles and behavior, they also entered situations where the old values were challenged by dramatically disorienting experiences which could not be explained in ordinary terms.

During such a war, where a guerrilla could be defined at a minimum as a mounted, armed troublemaker, there were openings for at least a few adventurous women to join in. There are a few first hand reports of women bushwhackers. In June 1864, Major Jeremiah Hackett reported the arrest of Mrs. Gibson and her daughter, caught while tearing down telegraph wires. Iowa Private Henry Dysart wrote in his diary in April 1862, "A few days since a party, several of whom were women, plundered the hospital at Ketesville robbing the wounded of their arms, clothing, money and the women taking the lead, the latter whose presence in the hospitals should rather be to cheer the wounded than to terrify and rob them are now here prisoners with several of the men." Dysart was struck by the symbolism of women who should be nurturing wounded men in the hospital, instead attacking them like "inhuman savages," as he called all guerrillas.[42] It was bad enough that men behaved this way, but nearly inconceivable that women should do so.

Each time a man would comment on women warriors, he would remark, as had Dysart, on the departure from those conventional womanly roles he expected and valued. Lieutenant Sardius Smith wrote in his diary, "The gentler sex are anything but gentle and I am told that some of them have went so far as to dress in mens clothes and go to a union mans house and demand his property." Unlike Dysart, Smith had not actually seen such women who disguised themselves as men and behaved like the worst bushwhackers, but he reported a popular rumor which indicated male soldiers' fears that women were no longer unarmed and gentle. Wanting to maintain a monopoly on violence, soldiers like Smith especially feared armed women. Even if a woman picked up the gun in defense of home and family and even if she were on the right side of the conflict, this actively aggressive version of women was troubling to many soldiers. Smith wrote, "If [southern guerrilla women] are warlike, union women are about equally so, and the old lady with whom I supped once stood between her husband and a Secesh with a loaded gun who was trying to shoot her husband and actually kept him out." For Smith, it should have been the husband defending the wife. Although he rather admired the ferociousnes of this Union woman, who after all was on his side and who still served him a nice supper when she was not being Judith of the Holofernes, Smith did not expect or like to see a woman acting as soldier of the hearth. Smith also reported with wonder about the organization of two militia companies in southern Missouri, "I have seen at an early hour they began to assemble in squads women as well as men and the place was soon full of men and women of all ages and descriptions."[43]

Such changes disturbed women as well as men. It was important for them to attempt to maintain "normal" sex roles. Women dressing and acting like men upset other women; this possibility contained complex and threatening implications for women too when they defined gender. Take for example a story told by Private James H. Guthrie of the First Iowa Infantry as his regiment was traveling south on board a Mississippi River steamboat. "We have a boy on board with very long hair and the most feminine appearance I ever saw. It was an easy job to make the women on board believe it was a woman in soldier's clothes. It created quite a sensation and lots of fun. One of the women got so high that in distributing pocket handkerchiefs she gave all but our supposed woman one and would not even speak to her. I slipped the boy one and posted him where he played the joke finely. The women went to the Doctor to get him [to] make an examination and if a woman to put her overboard. One of the women said 'look at the shape of her ankles, legs and hipps which proves her to be a female.' "[44] Guthrie did not seem anything but amused about an effeminate soldier, and the soldier himself enjoyed confusing women about his sexual identity, but the women were furious about the possibility of a woman impersonating a male soldier. They wanted to discover and maintain the "truth," to retain clear gender distinctions.

War also meant that men had contact with women a long way from the security and limitations of home, and that these women met armed strangers from what often might have seemed an alien planet. Distances were most keenly felt when northern soldiers from more modern and tidy locales encountered poor, backcountry Missouri farm women. Such soldiers were often shocked by what to them were female emblems of cultural backwardness. These appeared to be less than ladies, proof that Missouri was a foreign and inferior culture where proper values hardly existed. If not rendered as completely laughable, such women could be objects toward whom Northerners allowed themselves to express that more general cultural contempt for "Pukes" they felt. Sardius Smith wrote of those women he observed one day drilling in militia companies that they "are generally an ignorant set dressed in old fashioned costumes of divers colors and appearing awkward and bashful in presence of so many Strangers."[45] Though Smith proudly reported that his regiment carefully refrained from openly ridiculing such female yokels, who had the virtue of being pro-Union hicks, others were not so kind.

St. Louis cartoonist Robert Ormsby Sweeney depicted two neatly uniformed Union soldiers questioning a pregnant and barefoot young woman who had two other naked children in tow. " 'Well old lady are you a Union Woman?' 'No Sir I ain't!' 'Are you a secesh?' 'No Sir! I'm not that neither!'

Road Scene in Southwest Missouri. St. Louis cartoonist, Robert O. Sweeney, portrayed a confrontation of two Yankee soldiers with a poor southern white, "Butternut" woman. (*Sketchbook of Robert Sweeney, State Historical Society of Missouri*)

'Then what in the hell are you? I'd like to know!' 'Well, I'd have you'ns know I'm Baptist!' "[46] Innocent of grammar and of any worldly knowledge, breeding like rabbits, and dirt poor were common preconceptions northern soldiers had of rural southern women, often confirmed on contact. It should be added that if Sweeney had reported an actual conversation, he overlooked the possibility that this woman had evaded the question by manipulating the preconceptions the two Yankees had of her.

Colonel of artillery John Van Densen Dubois, a West Point man, wrote to his father in Hudson, New York, commenting on one woman's reaction to his unit's artillery caisson, which carried a spare wheel in the back. "The ignorance of these people is perfectly tremendous. . . . An old woman came out to look at the battery. 'Well now,' said she, 'I'm an old woman and thought I had seen enemost everything. My old grandmother used to say that some things was as unnecessary as five wheels to a wagon but I never expected to see a five wheel wagon. I don't want to bother you stranger but will you tell an old woman what that fifth wheel is meant for?" Dubois concluded, "They had never seen a soldier, a cannon, anything in fact."[47]

As well as ignorant and uncivilized, such women were frequently believed to be unclean, a notion always applied by those who believe themselves to be culturally superior. In the best of circumstances, it was difficult for rural women to keep their homes and clothes clean, and this was made harder by the absence of men to help out and the other dislocations caused by war. However, for northern soldiers such dirtiness was an indication of cultural slovenliness. Charles W. Falker wrote to his "darling wife" in Wisconsin from camp near Warrensburg in 1865, "I have not seen a barn on the road not one church and but one or two school houses. The women are the homeliest dirtiest specimens of the feminine gender I ever saw. I cant conceive how a white man could be induced to live with one. Niggers are quite plenty."[48] The lack of schools and churches and the proximity of dirty white women to blacks, whom he described as livestock rather than humans, formed a package to be rejected totally by this agent of northern civilization.

Some soldiers who carried the same preconceptions about southern rural women into the war learned to look beyond first appearances and gained at least some sense of their humanity and essential ladylikeness. When he saw women performing traditional male tasks in southern Missouri in 1864, Ohio-born Corporal Seth Kelly placed this unsexing in a wartime context. "Saw two women each with a yoke of oxen plowing a field by the roadside," he wrote in his diary. "War and the Rebellion has taken away the male population." Most people had fled the guerrilla devasted countryside and had crowded into garrison towns. In Berryville, Arkansas, Kelly observed, "The women are better looking and more tidy than I expected to see them." His preconception was that they should be homely slatterns, but they seemed quite all right on a closer look. In fact if a bit strange, they could even be appropriate sex objects. Thus Kelly wrote of a particularly successful foraging expedition in northern Arkansas, "Several pretty women, secesh, bewitching. Good circumstances, no men. Got plenty of corn, also honey. Ladies chew tobacco—it's a fact—I saw it. Widow Carter."[49] This unpromising country could be land of feasts, honey, and the Widow Carter after all. She might chew tobacco—imagine that—but she sure was a lot of fun.

Unlike Corporal Kelly, many Union troops came from milieus similar to rural Missouri and found nothing unusual about the women they met. They could be attracted by all these unescorted, unprotected, lively ladies without reservation. K. Veatch wrote to his nephew in Iowa about the 1863 winter holidays in Chariton County in northern Missouri, "Madison I think that if you will come down here I will show you some girls that will dance you down and they are good looking to and dont no anything about work . . . the young folks never stoped the whole week. You come down here it is a fast place."[50] It is impossible to know if by a fast place Veatch meant that the girls made themselves available sexually or that they were just friendly in a "proper" manner. Veatch probably just observed and invited down his young nephew upon whom he projected his desire for participation in a pretty good time.

In Missouri as elsewhere, army camps were filled with camp followers who offered pleasures less innocent than dancing. The familial dislocations particularly true in a guerrilla war, added to the ready cash and plunder in soldiers' hands, doubtless multiplied the number of prostitutes. Such women made themselves available in exchange for money and some security and carried on with elements of women's work, albeit in an untraditional context. A semiliterate Illinois infantryman of German descent described such women at the big Union base, Benton Barracks, in St. Louis. "There is a lot of women that have some friends in camp and they furnish them with whiskey. They pedle fruit and do washing. They with a pass are alowed to go in and out but they was caught last night. They searcht two or three of them and got about 40 bottles of the clear stuff. They had secreted them under there dress strung on there hoop skirts, they marched them to the gard house."[51]

Sometimes prostitutes would march with an army column, and some of these women would attempt to maintain respectability, often portraying themselves as widows in need, which doubtless many were. Surgeon Joseph H. Trego recorded in his diary his contemptuous response to one heavily veiled, self-proclaimed widow, "Capt Miller has a woman with him . . . represented as a widow returning to her friends in Missouri, her husband having been killed when they were making their exodus from Dixie. . . . She has proven to be the commonest kind of 'Army Woman' . . . she is called Capt Miller's 'masked battery.' "[52]

Often treated as objects of derision, at other times at least some soldiers analyzed the wartime pressure on women and felt sympathy for army whores. Kansas cavalry Sergeant W. W. Moses wrote in his diary about the fall of sixteen-year-old Mary French, "a very respectable young girl," who had been seduced "by promises of marriage (although indirectly promised)" by Lieutenant William Henry. "For about a month [he] slept with her every night while William Sheldon slept with her mother." Her father, a Union soldier, when on leave took Mary back home to St. Louis and left his wife behind, "a public whore," but Mary returned "to see her intended husband Lieut. Henry. Alas she is unaware that disgrace and disappointment are in store. She fondly hopes some day to be his wife. She does not know that Henry has a family at home. She will soon be added to the no. of prostitutes that throng our cities and towns and hang around the camps of our soldiers." Moses blamed the lieutenant, though he evidently failed to do anything to warn Mary of her danger. He seemed to wish to let the drama take its course. To Moses, she was the victim of a scoundrel, but she had fallen. Moses then drew a conclusion about his own threatened probity. "Alas how has this war corrupted the morals, destroyed the health and blighted the fond hopes and joys of our land. Virtue is indeed scarce. A wonder few have passed through the army without yielding to the tempter. God help me to still live right and shield me from all sin."[53] Moses should never be party to debasing virtuous women, lest he himself fall from grace.

If one's own female kin were involved in sexual debasement, the shame would be heightened. An Iowa cavalryman in Springfield reported A. J. Kinetz's suicide. "Cause—family difficulties at home and conduct of Sister here. It is a Sad Sad tale. He shot himself through the head dying instantly."[54] More suffering of this sort must have taken place silently by soldiers who believed that the virtue of their women relatives was an extension of their own honor. And thousands of women were subjected to stress which forced them into choices involving their sense of honor and implicating their male kin.

Sometimes soldiers like Private Kinetz could not cope with such tension; others dealt with problems of sexual etiquette and honor with humor. This was one means of defusing those intensified temptations and threats offered by war. Colonel Bazel F. Lazear of Callaway County, for example, wrote long letters to his wife, both funny and nasty, which illustrate some of the ways he managed his strong erotic love for his wife and his interest in those women war pushed toward his lap. He both threatened and reassured his wife with his letters, which gave a clear notion of peacetime sexual norms under wartime pressure, particularly for such a handsome colonel who cut a grand figure as his regiment marched into town after town.

When at an inactive post, pining for his wife, Lazear repeatedly begged her to come, disregarding any danger she might undergo on the voyage and asking her to leave behind her household duties. "I am very tired and lonesome here. I have so little to do. You being with me last winter has spoiled me." Two weeks later, moved to a livelier town, Lazear wrote to his wife, "When I wrote you last I was very anxious for you to come and see me but you need not come now for I had dinner yesterday with a dozen of the prettiest girls in the town and that aint all . . . there is a nice young widow here . . . who I expect will steal your old man so you need not come." Lazear let his wife know that he could have the choice of the seraglio of ladies left manless by war. Nor were these the only potential bedmates. "I now have two very pretty rebel girls on my hands as prisoners and what the devil to do with I dont know, as I dont like to put them in the guard house. I expect I will have to take them into my room and let them sleep with me."

One should note the defensive passivity of that last barb—Colonel Lazear would have to let the saucy rebel girls do what they wanted with him, so how could he be to blame? Also, in a vein of humor probably central to their relationship, he wrote his wife frequently and always unfurtively about his erotic fantasies. Yet there was a significant element of threat and abuse involved as well. Whatever jostling had occurred during ordinary times in this household was clearly highlighted by the peculiarities of this extraordinary set of circumstances. We do not have Mrs. Lazear's replies, so we cannot know whether she just absorbed such banter or dished it back to him. She was not so annoyed as to destroy the letters either during the war or later. In any event, after the war Lazear went back home to Auxvasse (where he was a mere postal clerk and dutiful husband) as he had promised he would in his usual manner in a letter written from Jefferson City in 1864, "I have been trying to find me a nice widow here but I can't come across one yet and I reckon I will have to come home to that old black snaggle tooth again don't you think so too but we will make this all right when I come."[55]

The women who dined with Colonel Lazear would not in peacetime have entertained roaming military officers without their husbands present. Other women frequently made negative comments about such loose socializing. Even this much role reorientation opened doors to incorrectly altered behavior. Clearly, however, sexual relations with men were more diverse than in peacetime.

In other respects as well, women acted in ways which cut against ordinary expectations. This included treatment women accorded one another. A brutal, almost Dickensian example concerned Mrs. William J. Dixon, wife of the keeper of the St. Charles Street prison for women in St. Louis. Prisoner Mary Pitman testified to a Union board of enquiry concerning the prison, about the terrible food, lack of heat, sale of "dainties" sent to prisoners, burning of letters of protest to the Union command, and continual demands for bribes made by Mrs. Dixon. Poor women without the means to bribe were especially mistreated. Dixon forced Mrs. Carney, who was pregnant, to sew for the Dixon family, to sleep in filthy rags, and to be segregated as supposedly "lousy." On one occasion, Dixon demanded prisoner White's new comforter in exchange for an old one, which White refused, saying "it was too dirty for a white person or a negro to sleep under." Dixon then threw the old comforter in her face. White said, "if you throw those into my face again I will knock you down," to which Dixon replied, jerking the new comforter away, "[you] had better try it—[you are] a lousy, dirty hussy and ought not to have anything to sleep on." Dixon then locked White in her room on half rations and without toilet facilities, so "she had to do the best she could." Dixon only allowed her to clean herself and her room when the Union colonel who employed the Dixons came for one of his inspections. Dixon also arranged evenings alone in the parlor for one prisoner, Miss Warren, and Captain Keyser, a defense lawyer. One evening, Pitman "saw her lying in his arms. The Captain had his arms around her and his hands in her bosom. Then I saw him get up and turn the light lower down and [I] went upstairs."[56] Despite all of the evils which were normal for life in this prison, Pitman maintained a sense of outrage and appealed to authorities believing that women should not so abuse one another and that some greater justice still could be served. Dixon's behavior was not acceptable to Pitman, who herself may have felt compromised as a trustee running favors for Dixon. The moral erosions war caused women were not all brought about by men using women but included damage they did to one another.

Guerrilla war undermined the peaceful settings in which good—that is to say conventional—conduct could be maintained. When conditions grew even worse, widespread guerrilla warfare uprooted women and children from their homes and sent them fleeing for security. The chaotic lives of Union troops and bushwhackers torn from their homes, roaming from firefight to firefight, was matched by wandering, fatherless, destitute families. Frequently family members lost contact with one another for many years and lost the sense of a safe and stable family home to which to return. Timothy Phillips, the Iowa infantryman, who noted in the refugee camp in Forseyth, "We have now here some two dozen women and not less than a hundred children—more or less—varying in age from two weeks to 15 years," went on to tell what was to him a touching tale of the reunion of a wandering soldier with his war-displaced wife. "One soldier belonging to the 1st Ark (Union) having business in our camp found his wife here which he had not seen for twelve months. The meeting was a joyful one and was brought about by singular circumstances. His wife fleeing from starvation seeking protection from us."[57] Phillips told of many other refugees but not about any other reunions.

Many women and children had the better fortune of being able to return to safe havens with family in other states, though they too had the anxiety of not knowing what was happening back home. Mollie McRoberts returned to her parents' home in Circleville, Ohio. Yet she found little peace of mind since her husband, A. J., remained back on their Missouri farm. She wrote to him at one point that she had just received his first letter in two weeks and "that when I don't get a letter it makes me almost sick. I was so troubled last night that I could not sleep." She told him to simply abandon their farm, "for I feel sure you will be killed and dear, your life is far more precious than all the wealth on earth. I would much rather go out and wash by the day than have you expose yourself the way you have been doing." She was willing to lose the family assets and to do the most demeaning labor if that would reunite her family. Survival outweighed conventional respectability. He should get away from those guerrilla "bloodhounds." "I know we won't starve. We have a kind father in heaven who is willing to help those who help themselves." McRoberts was not exaggerating her husband's danger. In one letter he wrote her, "I have been at home at work all last week but I take care not to sleep in the house at nights. I expect to get pretty well through my crop this week and then I will have more time to watch the rebs. The rumor is circulating among the rebels that I was killed last Friday week as I left Marshall on that day, and they have not saw or heard of me since. I have been careful not to contradict the report." Such a letter could have only made his wife more frantic. Although she had gone to Ohio voluntarily, McRoberts was an exile from her home and her husband. "I know it will not be any better as long as the war lasts and for many years afterward."[58]

If Mollie McRoberts was a Union exile gone North, Mrs. Edwin H. Harris of St. Clair was a secessionist exile gone South to Paris, Texas. She hated Texas with its bleakness and sandstorms and was filled with anxiety and homesickness. "So many rumors" of events in Missouri circulating among the exiled Missourians filled her with a "constant dread. . . . I sometimes feel that I cannot stand so much uneasiness and think I will start to Missouri to see if I can find you," she wrote her husband Edwin. She heard from him about Union troops ransacking their house, "I was indeed sorry to hear of our dear home being so much torn up. Oh how I long for the time to come we can again be together and live in peace in our dear old home." At one point Edwin wrote his wife to scotch rumors of his having turned Unionist. "That Devil's dam, Aunt Polly Fewell, is at the bottom of all the damned villainy here, and I suppose she would like to cover up the short-comings of her own foul brood by bringing odium upon others. . . . Say to one and all that when I cease being a Southern man to all intents and purposes there will not be many left."[59]

Aunt Polly Fewell doubtless had spread malicious gossip before the war, but now she could be answered only with difficulty. Hundreds of miles away from home, Mrs. Harris could only gnash her teeth in the face of rumors and bad news, some of which might well prove to be true. Her war in exile was lived in a necessarily passive and lonely fearfulness.

Although Mrs. Harris went voluntarily, her exile was nonetheless painful for her. Banishment was a common punishment meted out by Union authorities to known women supporters of guerrillas. Sarah M. Scott of Sarcoxie appealed her banishment and that of 150 other married women in southwestern Missouri to General John B. Sanborn. "I say with a clear conscience, I have done nothing against the Federal Government." This appeal enraged Sanborn, as Scott neither bothered to apologize for her actions or those of her fellow southern supporters nor to express sympathy for victimized Union families. He replied to Scott, "How strange it is that the simple fact of women and children being compelled to seek a new place of residence . . . strikes your mind in horror, while the spectacle of honest, peaceable men laboring in the fields for the support of their wives and little children shot down like dogs by men whom these families you refer to are harboring and feeding, does not even call for a sympathizing word or even a remark."[60] Sanborn felt altogether justified in his action; he would not waste his sympathy on an unsympathetic enemy woman—a stance he himself almost certainly would have found callous outside the context of the antiguerrilla operations he was leading. Hundreds of women were banished officially, and thousands more burned out and threatened out. They often lost all their property, gaining in return only perpetual fear.

Women who remained at home in Missouri while their husbands went off to war were anxious for their own homes and safety. Both during and after the war, the old home would no longer be home in the sense of a safe retreat, and a replacement might be unavailable. A fully documented case of such homelessness is the correspondence of Phineas M. Savery and his wife, Amanda. Phineas was an officer with a regular Missouri regiment fighting in Texas and Mississippi, who wrote long, loving letters to his wife back in Smithville throughout the war, despite the fact that he did not receive a letter from her in four years nor meet his youngest son and namesake until after the war.

Phineas was the southern gentleman pining for his "Queen of the fairies among the gay and happy throng." While others danced with the lovely southern ladies of Springfield early in 1862, he did not because of his fidelity to Amanda. He contented himself instead, he wrote Amanda, with whist and "social chats" with "accomplished and educated women" to whom he showed her miniature. Two years later, much further away in Mississippi, Phineas told Amanda that other Missouri women had "voluntarily exiled themselves from home and the luxeries they have been accustomed to enjoy for the privilege of being with or near their husband & father," but Amanda did not take the hint and leave her extended family in Missouri to join him.

After the war, Amanda's letters finally began to reach Phineas in Memphis. They contained lists of woes. Many of her Clay County neighbors had been banished, some had been killed, some had moved to Idaho, Kansas, and Oregon. All had been looted. Son Charlie had become an unmanageable truant; she had moved three times to caretake the homes of fleeing pro-southern neighbors; she had lost her looks: "You would hardly recognize me. I had all my upper teeth extracted." She had, nun-like, given up all pleasures for him during the war, even more thoroughly than he had renounced gaiety. "I could not think of attending parties and places of amusement as you are so much doing. I often looked at the Southern Widows as they are termed by the Feds and wondered how they could enjoy their Selves and their husbands in so much danger. They were walking and buggy riding all over the country and showing the Fs marked attention." The Feds did call on her for supper frequently, and if she was not at home, they "would break the doors open and help their Selves. Last fall they took my bed clothes. It was nothing to have the house searched and get a cursing from the officers." Furthermore, though officially over, she warned him that the "civil war is still in force" and that southern soldiers were being shot "as fast as they [were] coming home." He should not come even as far as St. Joseph. Phineas agreed. "I shall not return to Missouri—I shall never live there again—I wish to dwell in the sunny south where my friends reside and where my wife & little ones will meet with a cordial welcome." In Memphis, Phineas found that "southern soldiers are as brothers & Masons more than brothers." His fellow southern Masons fed, clothed, and sheltered him. They loaned him money to set up a house and a bookstore in Baldwyn, Mississippi, "A beautiful & romantic [town] which with a little improvement might be made an Eden, a Paradise on earth."[61]

Perhaps because of the completeness of his separation from Amanda and because of his need for unwarlike fantasies, Phineas had kept alive his dreams of her and of some magical place they should seek together. She reported far more realistically on her situation. She was loathe to leave Missouri and her family, but one presumes she did join Phineas in Mississippi as the correspondence ended at the point of planning her voyage. His sunny new South was not hers; she had become embittered by the war's poverty and terror; he had turned his back on Missouri and insisted that she should as well. Such alienation from one another and loss of the sense of home was part of that psychological as well as physical exile guerrilla war visited on thousands of families. At the center of battered families, generally less actively engaged in the fighting, displaced women paid the larger emotional price.

Knocked so far off traditional moorings, in so many ways and with such frequency, women had a desperate need to cling to their sense of self. Chaos intensified the need for order and for the notion of love on which that order was, they dearly wished to believe, based. One might wonder that they did not all capitulate to disorder through psychological numbing or cynicism, and indeed many women went down those paths to silent depression. Awareness that they were in danger of permanent alteration made even more urgent the need of frightened women to believe in loving ties, in the potential reassertion of the circle of the family and home with women at the hub. Pounded by guerrilla war, men had parallel needs, and they too insisted on the centrality of love as a means to link the memory of past warmth to hopes for the future in order to combat the traumatizing present.

One expression of this internal struggle to maintain the ideal of womanly love was the conscious attempt to remain poised and forbearing when attacked rather than to return blow for blow, to remain soft rather than turning hard. The staunch St. Louis Unionist, Minerva Blow, was deeply wounded by the secessionist sentiment which separated her from many of her kin and friends early in 1861. She was a Republican and, she wrote her daughter Susie, "This party you know does not embrace many of our circle of acquaintance. Consequently we are compelled to listen to many absurd and provoking things said by them—I have tried to feel kind & act the part of a Christian *lady* though at times I have had my feelings very much hurt."[62]

Many women instructed their daughters and younger sisters to rein in their anger and maintain womanly equipoise as the only proper response to provocation. Even if other girls misbehaved in accordance with popular pressures, a lady should rise above the tumult. Mary Hall wrote to her sister, Venetia Colcord Page, who had been imprisoned in Kansas City along with the sisters of Bill Anderson as an active guerrilla supporter, "Don't say one word before any. That will only make your case worse. Let others do as they please. Remember you are a lady and act accordingly. The guards say they like you & Miss Parish. They say very hard things of the others. The officers told me this."[63] Hall argued that ladylike deportment was functional in this situation, but she also insisted that it was correct in principle. A true lady would rise above a guerrilla war, as above all adversity.

In this theater of war, such sentiment often was insufficient to overcome adversity, and many women felt compelled to accept overwhelming circumstances in Christian resignation. Such a spirit was in its way contrary to utter defeat, as at least the woman involved could feel she had not given in to violent feelings and actions. The impoverished and elderly Widow Bethiah Pyatt McKown one day intercepted a letter addressed to her daughter-in-law. She wrote her eldest son, John, of the ensuing events. The letter to her daughter-in-law read, "My dear Mrs. McKown *where are you, do tell me where I can find you,* write directions and enclose in the envelope herein enclosed. . . . I want to see you, I am all O.K., let me know soon as I have a message from a friend of yours." Bethiah McKown already hated her daughter-in-law, and with this letter she tried to force her son James to choose between them. Curiously, she did not assume this letter to be a sexual assignation and instead believed rumors that her daughter-in-law was a paid double-agent. "I say she is a weathercock, Union with Union people and Secesh when she is with secessionists and in that way her slanderous heart will be gratified." Despite his mother's pressures, James stuck by his wife. His brother Will told James he would never speak to him again until he divorced his wife. "It grieves me to the heart to see such a *Cainlike* disposition among my *sons,*" Bethiah wrote her eldest son John, "oh if you could all meet in the bond of brotherly love and friendship what a joy it would be to my widowed heart, yet I fear it will not be, and I must bear it, how sad it is that, *woman,* who should be the comfort, should be the bane of man's existence."[64]

Bethiah McKown had added to the ambiguities of war, setting son against son and one son against her by attacking his wife. She wished to resolve this conflict with a counter-assertion of both brotherly and motherly love, and yet she knew familial disintegration had gone too far to be healed so simply. Her daughter-in-law became something of a scapegoat for her; she was the villain who was the bane of her son's existence. Yet there was something oddly more universal in Bethiah's resignation—women in general were blamed as Eve leading Adam to sin, and her sons were Cain and Abel. In the face of original sin, which she apparently believed inhabited the hearts of her sons as well as her more actively evil daughter-in-law, Bethiah had to bear the pain. Opening her daughter-in-law's mail, setting that woman against her husband by bearing tales, encouraging her other sons to ostracize both James and his wife, and in the end pushing the fallen woman and her husband into opposition to her, did she have sufficient insight to see that she too was a sinner in her way? The turmoil in her family, which reflected the destructive passions of war, made all the more compelling Bethiah's need to believe in the love of a God who would save those poor women who took on the world's burdens. This was a desperate appeal to a belief in the redemption holy love alone offered women.

Belief in women's love, often related to the love God gave and to the higher purposes of the war, offered many male combatants solace and hope in the face of the destructiveness they saw all around them, a destructiveness which invaded their innermost sense of self. After depicting a terrible beating of a secessionist prisoner, a wounded Ray County militiaman, Charles E. Calkins, wrote his mother, "There are several ministers in the place who come to see me every day and do all in their power to make me comfortable and they really help me along a great deal. There is a lady in the place from Iowa, and she is cooking soup and delicacies for the sick. This is Sunday and we are to have preaching in the Hospital this afternoon."[65] Other soldiers resented such do-gooder preachers and women who clearly reassured this private that the domestic values he had learned from his mother remained real.

Illinois Private John A. Higgins linked his love for an adoring wife to his religious faith in a manner which allowed him to almost float above the brutal struggle against bushwhackers. "Nancy, God Bless you sweet soul, I feel like I wanted to see you now as bad as ever I did in my life. . . . I suppose you are in continual dread about my welfare and life. I have always felt and feel that my life is to be prolonged beyound the duration of the ignominious war now going on in our unhappy country. My sphere of action is above that of war. The Infinite Mind in his boundless mercy and wisdom hath placed within my soul nobler and purer conceptions than that of war can give in all its ramifications and developments." As so many Union sermons proclaimed, Higgins believed that both worldly love and God's love demonstrated that through a higher intelligence "truth and justice will prevail . . . and both are on the side of the Loyal sons of the Constitution."[66]

One might conclude in the modern vernacular that Higgins's testimony was evidence of psychological doubling, narcissism, and grandiose delusions and that the asserted realm of the higher spirit was an unreal place, belief in which allowed him to deny reality and responsibility, as was the case for Bethiah McKown as well. One might also conclude that such beliefs allowed the faithful a means to maintain psychological health precisely through dividing belief in some greater, final justice from the human mess surrounding and invading war participants, demarcating the transitory from the permanent. What could be called denial viewed one way was affirmation looked at differently.[67] A softer sense of self could be rescued from a harsher one if the complete reality of the harder self could be denied. This was the most important survival lie.

Few soldiers were so religious in the explicit and consistent and somewhat mystical sense that Higgins was. Yet many held a vague belief in the civil religion of Unionism and a diffuse evangelical conviction that they had half absorbed on Sundays and at revivals, that there was a God who would judge in the spirit of justice but also of love. Even more often in letters written from the field, fighters expressed love and affection for their mothers and wives and sisters, clearly gaining release by so doing, in contrast with the brutal life they were living.

Second Lieutenant Henry J. Traber of the Thirty-Third Wisconsin Infantry Regiment wrote his sister Margaret just after disembarking from a Missouri River steamer in St. Louis concerning the survival of his deeply threatened sense of humanity. During his voyage the boat had stopped and the troops had been drawn up to witness the execution of a guerrilla who just had been convicted by drumhead court-martial. Though he agreed with this Union policy in dealing with guerrillas and though he felt that he could "wade as deep as anyone . . . in the heat of the battle," shooting that guerrilla "in cold blood" was beyond his moral capacity to justify. Yet he seemed to know that he would indeed obey a direct command to execute such a prisoner. After describing what he had so painfully observed and dreaded being ordered to do himself, Henry burst out in grateful memory to this sister, "Whose home was my home when I had no other. Who during that winter tried all in their power to make me happy and let me go back further, who when I was a little wee one taught me to read and tried to learn a little brother to be a good boy, was not it Sister Magie, may God bless you for it sister mine."[68] Feeling isolated in his unpopular beliefs, his life-affirming desires under relentless attack, Henry was swept with a sentimental memory of an older sister who had always protected him when he had needed shelter. His letter seemed to suggest that he had been left an orphan and that it was his sister who had given him a sensibility of nurturance which he could call upon even at a climatic moment in guerrilla war—the shooting of an unarmed prisoner. His gratitude to his sister was evidence of his knowledge of the sustenance her love offered.

Often of course, the memory was of a loving wife. Writing by lantern light at 11 P.M. when all his tentmates were asleep, George Avery told his wife, "It is now that I can talk to my Lizzie with emotions of pleasure; but much sweeter would be the interview could I but sit by your side with your fair form reclining upon my bosom."[69] To write this was to enter a kind of trance where writing was conversation and "talk" triggered a palpable feeling of physical presence, both as memory and as promise. In the quiet of night, George Avery could find an escape by reffirming his ties with his wife.

To be close to sleep and entering a borderland where you were dreaming of your wife was to be close to her bed and the comforts of shared physical affection. Many soldiers must have sought that peaceful memory in order to fall asleep, in a manner similar to George Avery and Private Charles W. Falker who wrote their wives at just that moment. Charles wrote Sarah, "It is now ten o'clock and I suppose you are tucked away snugly in your bed and are probably asleep. May be you are awake and thinking about me. I know you think of me often and I certainly do of you." Charles then rehearsed the positive parts of their relationship. "I have been thinking over how we got acquainted and our courtship and marriage and the first time and the last time I kissed you. My dear girl how fresh every little circumstance connected with you seems. I do not believe I ever realized how much I loved you and how dear you were to me until I had to leave you. . . . When I get back I mean to hold you in my lap a whole week without letting you get up." Two weeks later Charles wrote Sarah that he had been dreaming the most realistic dream that she was lying in his arms. When awake and "when I am off duty," he wrote, he constantly thought of her and of their daughter. Duty that week had included visiting a town called Morrisville which was deserted of all life except one cat. The town had been inhabited by bushwhackers who had been driven out by Union troops. In one bullet-riddled house, "the stairs were covered with blood and we could see where the blood had spurted on the walls and the marks of bloody hands on the door and window casings." In contrast, Charles recalled the conversations he and Sarah had had just before he left for the war. "Don't you recall pet that night I came up and took you in my lap and you told me you would like to sit in my lap and lay your head on my bosom but you were afraid to. Oh Sarah how bad I felt then and how many bitter recollections it has given me to think I had made my darling little wife afraid to lay her head on my shoulder." Their alienation should change after the war. "When I come home I want you to kiss me twenty five times regularly besides extras. . . . I know and feel Sarah that we were not as affectionate towards each other as we should have been and I think I was to blame." Having assumed guilt for her fear of him and for their emotional distance when they were together, Charles then voiced his resentment for her coldness. "Some mornings I have gone down to the office feeling cross and blue and downhearted when I would have given everything if you had only kissed me before I started." But finally they had been able to communicate their longings before Charles had left, and they would take up from there when he returned after the war. "I feel so happy that we parted loving each other and understanding each other as we ought to, and I know my pet you feel happy too." This hopeful emotional innerscape contrasted with the ruined guerrilla landscape through which he was marching. "In Missouri they build a large brick chimney at each end of the house on the outside and we could often see half a dozen of these chimneys standing alone and bare against the sky on the prairie."[70]

The lifeless remains of family homes stood in tribute to men's capacity for destruction. In a metaphorical juxtaposition, Charles seemed to suggest that his marriage with Sarah had been going that way through the effects of his anger toward Sarah and her coldness to him. He recalled the memory of marital love with a real urgency, threatened as he was. What he was now seeing of the brute refined his desire for possible affection, for not missing out on the expression of love. Men and women may have inhabited separate spheres, especially in war, but without any loving intersection of those realms, the male sphere lost its most fundamental creative functions, as some soldiers grasped.[71] Even shreds of loving memory for men behaving unlovingly were crucial when the world of normal expectation had come undone. For women too such desire made survival possible. It reminded them of times of comfort, security, and even joy, of times when life consisted of more than just grimly holding on. Love was often distant from an everyday wartime life that was filled with brutality and lying and running, but that one had loved meant one might love again, and this possibility sustained people even as they terrorized and betrayed other people. Perhaps guerrilla war had so altered values that the capacity for love was a mechanism by which the wicked could think well enough of themselves to carry on destroying without feeling empty. But more generally, even destroyers sought to be human, and loving humans also could be destroyers.

CHAPTER 6

AFTER THE WAR

Postwar Violence and Reconstruction

In Virginia on April 9, 1865, rejecting advice to scatter his troops to the hills and fight on as guerrillas, Lee surrendered his army to Grant. In any event, the majority of his army had already deserted and gone home, a pattern true in the other southern commands, including the trans-Mississippi army of General Edmund Kirby Smith, the last Confederate commander to surrender on May 26, 1865. Disorganized guerrilla forces in Missouri and elsewhere stayed in the saddle well into the summer, fearing that their surrender would not be accepted. Frequently their fears were justified, as many were executed by Union forces or by enraged civilians who now knew for certain which was the winning side they ought to join. The guerrilla war sputtered out, nastily and inconclusively.

"Some have concluded to stay and tough it out and tough enough it will be—for all we hear great talk of peace but the bushwhackers are plenty in here." Such was the fear Sarah P. Harlan expressed in a letter to her brother, written on April 12, 1865. Harlan was a young milliner who lived in the hamlet of Haynesville in the guerrilla war-ravaged west central portion of Missouri. She was, she wrote her brother, "very lonesome" living alone in the Harlan family home. Her parents and brothers and sisters had fled to other parts of the state. Most of the few remaining neighbors were leaving as well. "Dr. Scrugs has gone to Atchison [Kansas], Charles Smith had gone to Illinois. . . . Newton Deny has gone to Illinois and many others have gone too numerous to mention." Although some guerrillas had surrendered, others were still skulking about planning to strike, and several Union soldiers had been murdered in the vicinity. "The evening after the soldiers were in here Will Logan gathered up a company of men and started out after them. They came on to eight of them near Carneys and killed two." All in all, although the war was ending out East, matters did not look promising in Missouri.

On April 19, hearing the "sad" news of Lincoln's assassination, Harlan feared that hopes for "peace [which] was so near at hand" now would be dashed. "I fear that we will have worse. . . . We do not hear much about the BW [Bushwhackers] now but I believe that they are still in the country waiting for the leaves." When their cover bloomed, Harlan was afraid they would go on yet another summer's rampage. On May 2, she wrote her brother about sporadic guerrilla murders and the reorganization of the local Union militia. She also reported going to hear the new "(Northern) Methodist Preacher" who had just moved to town and organized a church. "Several of the members of other churches have joined." This was a way Haynesville Methodists, previously members of the now politically compromised Southern Methodist church, joined the victorious local Unionists' congregation. Despite her southern origins, Sarah Harlan was joining the Union.

Although she had grown up with boys who had become infamous guerrillas and was no radical, by the spring of 1865 Harlan was unqualified in her desire for the destruction of the guerrillas. Hearing that Ol Sheppard and his gang, the terrors of Clinton County, had surrendered, Harlan was both relieved that they had capitulated and angry that they had not been killed. Everyone told her peace was at hand. "I suppose we will" have it, as the guerrillas had surrendered, Harlan wrote. "Yet it looks very strange to me that such robbers and murderers can be turned loose to do as they please after causing so much trouble but maybe it is all right but I cannot see it." Harlan carried a desire for revenge against the guerrillas into her postwar social views.

There was no culminating victory, no clear defeat, no catharsis for Harlan and her neighbors. The terrible grudges of neighbor against neighbor created in the guerrilla conflict remained unresolved at the end of the war. No one apologized. No one forgave. Violence remained widespread in 1865 and 1866 as men reopened barely closed wounds. On the afternoon of June 16, 1866, Harlan wrote to her sister, Loft Easton got drunk and accused the former guerrilla captain, Jim Green, of being in the company that had burned out Easton's father during the war. Green denied the charge "and tried to reason the case with him . . . not to get in a fuss." But after a while the two men met up in the grocery again and recommenced quarreling. Pistol in hand, Green backed out of the store. Easton shouted at him to halt, which Green did, telling Easton not to approach, but Easton came on. A grocery clerk knocked Green's gun out of his hand, and at that moment Easton shot, unintentionally killing the clerk rather than Green. Easton kept firing while Green dove for his pistol. Green got up and shot Easton, knocking him over, and then walked up to him and killed him with two more shots to the head. Harlan concluded, "I believe that everybody that seen it justifies Jim." Green gave himself up to the sheriff and was freed on $100 bond awaiting trial. One of Easton's brothers then let it be known all over town that "he intends to kill Jim if he follows him to the end of the world. I fear it is not done with yet," Harlan concluded. "I fear it will do for an excuse for someone to go to the bush." In Harlan's opinion, for these young men the recourse to guerrilla warfare as the means to resolve old disputes was still close at hand.[1]

Most of the minority of guerrillas who had survived that long had surrendered in May and June 1865. On May 12 in St. Louis, Major General Grenville M. Dodge had set the terms of surrender Union officers were to offer to guerrillas. "Any of these bands . . . that propose to lay down their arms can do so, and the military authorities will take no further action in the case." On May 19, Dodge had further instructed that "no quarter is given against any civil action . . . for any crimes," and in fact, many were arrested by local sheriffs immediately after they had surrendered and had taken the oath of loyalty to the Union. Most guerrillas who were not arrested immediately on civil charges simply surrendered and went home, an officially unretributive conclusion to their actions, which infuriated their Unionist neighbors.[2]

At about the same time, many secessionists who had gone south into exile returned to Missouri. On October 10, Maddie Perkins of Fayette wrote to Benjamin Cocke, an old neighbor who was one of the large number of Missourians who had fled to Texas during the war. "Do you expect to make Texas your future home, or will you return to Missouri? Almost everyone is coming back and it is more like old times."[3] These civilians were not officially punished by the Union military or civil authorities: they just came back.

The road home was treacherous. Everywhere in the state well-armed guerrillas and militiamen turned into highwaymen, robbing returning soldiers and civilians from both sides. The folks back home anxiously warned prospective returning family members of the continuing dangers. For example, William Crawford told his son, a discharged Union soldier mustered out with a fat pay packet, to take the railroad home. "Thare ought to be as maney of you as could be together and arm yourselves well if you hante sole your own sixteen shooter. . . . The citticens knowes whem your times is out and they [tell] the Bushwhakers." Even the trains were not safe as "thare is another class of robbers that will . . . follow the railroad and pick the pokets of the soldiers."[4]

In addition to the dangers highwaymen posed to all travelers, returning Confederate soldiers had armed Union patrols to fear as well. On August 7, 1865, Mrs. Benton Stout, writing from the family farm in Lafayette County in west central Missouri, warned her returning husband that she simply did not know if it was safe for southern veterans to return. "There are a company of Federals scouting through the country every few days. Sometimes they get very much excited if they hear of bushwhackers," and they did not always distinguish discharged regular Confederate soldiers now in civilian dress from guerrillas. Even if Benton Stout made it home, his wife did not know if it would be safe for him to stay, so angry and vengeful were the now dominant local Unionists. His wife was eager to see him—"I do want to *see you so much*"—yet she did not want to confuse her desires with her analysis of his prospective safety back home. "Al says you can come to see us on a visit. Then you can tell whether it will do to stay or not."[5] Both the road home and home itself were unsafe.

The rapid postwar demobilization of the Union army, which included the abandonment of almost all of the hundreds of small garrisons in Missouri towns, threw many Unionists into panic and flight. They feared that the guerrillas "out there" would resume their destructive ways once Union military protection was withdrawn. In many locales such fears were not misplaced: though some guerrillas surrendered, others did not, and among those that gave up, part-time night riding often continued.

Union soldiers were aware of the unresolved mess they were leaving behind. Kansas cavalry Sergeant Webster Moses wrote his wife on May 7, 1865, from south central Missouri that the Centerville garrison would be evacuated within a month as all large scale rebel forces had surrendered. Moses recognized that guerrillas were still a major threat but insisted that the Union army was not the means to flush them out. "The country is overrun now with robbers but the citizens will have to organize and introduce 'lynch law.' Soldiers are of little use in hunting them. They live principally in caves in the hills and mountains and make their excursions mostly in the night times. They go in bands of five or six and have plenty of friends through the country." Moses recognized that only the Union garrison had kept the guerrillas at bay. "All the inhabitants and all who are so unfortunate as to have the ill will of the robbers are leaving here for Ill[inois]. When we leave this place there will be no one left here. All are leaving." Moses was callous toward these Missourians, even the loyal Unionists among them, believing them all to be low-life types who merited their misfortune. "The inhabitants here are of the lowest class of 'poor whites' and very ignorant. Sometimes we hear of a school in the town."[6] These were not real humans who deserved continued support. They were victims—losers—who by definition ought to be left to their own degradation.

In several places after the war, loyal Unionists petitioned state and army officials for new garrisons which would permit them to resettle in areas still dominated by the guerrillas. For example, in July 1865 thirty-five citizens, mostly ex-militiamen, of McDonald County in the southwest corner of the state petitioned Governor Thomas C. Fletcher for a new army post. They had all fled to the garrison town of Newtonia in the next county north. "Why our County has been left unguarded to be plundered and destroyed while this has been protected by their garrisons is not our purpose to enquire," but as things stood, they could not risk reclaiming their farms until they "should not be longer overrun by bands of lawless marauders."[7] The disappearing Union army, coupled with continuing bad news from home, kept these Union men and thousands like them near the edge of panic during the summer after the official war had ended.

These fears, triggered by rumors of guerrilla plotting and sporadic outbursts of violence, continued throughout 1865 and 1866. On March 15, 1866, the mayor and city council of Lawrence, Kansas, wrote to General Dodge, now stationed at Ft. Leavenworth, Kansas, where he was leading the war against the Plains Indians, requesting a garrison of three companies of cavalry. Kansas "agents" had reported to them that a large band of Missouri guerrillas was forming, "determined to plunder the town" as Quantrill's band had in 1863 and to release old guerrilla companions then on trial for their roles in the earlier massacre. "The terrible history of August 1863, demonstrates with what ease they can move undiscovered through the country even when occupied by troops." The citizens of Lawrence deeply feared "a probable recurrence of the horrors" of 1863; these fears already had served "to paralyze our business & destroy the peace of the community." Dodge did not brush off this hysterical petition from the Lawrence city fathers but sent a company of infantry to serve as a nucleus for armed resistance should the need arise. His own spies told him that "about 1,000 men, most all old Bushwhackers," in fact had been meeting in Missouri. Fearing arrests, unfair trials, and harassment in general, they were planning a westward trek. Dodge feared that they would go to the Great Plains where they would link up with the Kiowa and Comanche Indians in the war against Dodge's army. Thus was Dodge's fear added to those of the citizens of Lawrence, a town which, Dodge agreed, the former guerrillas might sack—to free their old comrades and to plunder, or just for old time's sake—on their route west to resume the Civil War in a strange new alliance.[8] Such rumors were fanciful but plausible; people conditioned by the long guerrilla war believed them. In itself, this uncontrollable public fear, a full year after the end of the war, demonstrated some of the special scars the Missouri guerrilla version of civil war had left among civilians. As there had been no geographic or role clarity during the war, with outbursts potentially coming from any quarter at any time, so there was still no temporal certainty—violent men could visit destruction whenever they wanted, even now after peace supposedly had broken out.

Widespread defeatism was the postwar southern concomitant to Unionist fears of guerrilla uprisings. Many ex-Confederates and southern sympathizers believed themselves so oppressed and hated that they lost their nerve. In September 1866, Charles S. Bryan wrote to his brother William back in Raleigh, North Carolina, that he could not return to his farm in southwest Missouri, "so unsettled were the conditions of affairs." In general, "Southern people & their friends" were too poor "to extend much pecuniary relief to each other. . . . Wherever their property could be found, it was generally confiscated by military satraps, if it was not of a perishable or destructible character." Stripped of their property, southern sympathizers had no means of redress as all the political and police power was now in vengeful Unionist hands, so many southern men felt. William S. Miller was so discouraged that he petitioned a former Union colonel for aid, "notwithstanding the estrangement which has existed between us" over Miller's having chosen the southern side during the war. Miller begged for money to leave the state, being bankrupt, daily threatened, "taunted, jeered and insulted [by the] Mobocracy," without "resort to the civil law," and without the means to make a living.[9] Many ex-southern men believed they could not offer much aid to each other: having gone outside the law of the winning side, they were banished from participating in the community. In their defeat, some, like William Miller, went on bended knee to former enemies. Some left the state, while still others held on silently or defiantly.

After the war, the balance of power clearly shifted in the Unionist direction. Although ex-southern men continued to resist the domination of the victors, on the whole, public opinion and power was seized by the best organized portion of the population, the most radical of the Unionists. They elected local officials or browbeat and threatened existing ones into acquiesence, whenever necessary resorting to terror tactics and mob action in order to dominate the countryside which so recently had been in guerrilla hands. Not merely did they want control, they wished to punish their wartime enemies, both to redress what to them were old injustices and to suppress what they believed to be the naturally evil southern predisposition to violent rebellion.

At the end of the official war, some Federal authorities observed what they considered to be genuine contrition among some of the Missouri prosouthern population. On July 1, 1865, Captain C. E. Rogers, the provost marshal in Warrensburg, wrote to St. Louis headquarters that the "state of society has undergone a great change." During the month of June there had not "been a shot fired by a Rebel in arms," and returning southern exiles as well as local sympathizers had all taken the loyalty oath "and seem thoroughly subdued and willing to accept peace on any terms our government may dictate." Rogers also observed that local Unionists were not prepared to accept southern surrender, forgive their enemies, and resume civil relations. "I am sorry to say there are some professing loyalty who do not seem as well disposed" as many former southern men. For them, the government had been too lenient, and they were "inclined to take the punishment of those men into their own hands," in which task elements of the Union army aided them. For Captain Rogers this was a matter of "only a few evil disposed persons who seek to cover their evil deeds with a great protestation to loyalty and hatred of anything that has ever been evil."[10]

Vengeance rather than forgiveness characterized postwar social relations. Filled with unassuaged anger, provoked by rumors of renewed

guerrilla war, old Union men needed to strike back. After they realized
that all would not be forgiven, that they would not be welcomed back into
society, southern men either left or fought back. The ensuing revenge and
counter-revenge took place on an individual level and collectively, through
both legal and extra-legal channels.

Once the civil courts began to function again late in 1865, many Unionists immediately filed suit against their former guerrilla neighbors. As the
courts were in Unionist hands, many ex-southern men doubted the possibility of evenhanded justice. Few disputes could be solved with civil settlements, as cash was scarce and most valuable property had long since been
burned or stolen. In 1865 poverty gave former guerrilla Richard Huston of
Polk County in southwest Missouri perverse satisfaction. Noting that "the
loyal men in [Polk] County are bringing all kinds of suites against the
Reble soldiers," and that he and several others had been sued for $6,000
for false imprisonment and stealing by John Ross and Mr. Hill, Huston
concluded, "I dont think they will make any thing out of it. I am certain
that they will make nothing out of me for I am broke as flatt as hell."[11]
Huston was still living in the relative safety of Boone County north of the
Missouri River. Had he gone back to his farm, he might well have found
that Messrs. Ross and Hill would have found other ways to settle up
with him.

Diaries, letters, and military reports were filled with stories of old neighbors returning home to get even with each other, man to man. For example, in October 1866 in Chariton County, a former southern sympathizer
noted the fight between two longtime enemies: "Old Dave came down here
last week & told Jube West he came down to straighten the damn Rebels.
Jube immediately knocked him down twice & beat him vere severly in the
face. Dave left immediately on [the] stage. Everyone was glad & said it
was the best thing ever happened here."[12] Old Dave did not try a civil suit.
Neither did he join with any organized Unionist group to seek revenge. He
was still fighting a traditional personal battle, and Jube West had had the
better punch.

Most Unionists maintained their wartime civilian and military connections and banded together when necessary to get even with the more disorganized former southern men. On February 21, 1866, William E. Hill
reported a typical postwar incident of collective Unionist vengeance in
Chariton County in central Missouri. "About 10 Dutch," had shot up Pugh
Price and Jim Ling, nearly killing them. "The sheriff was there at the time
but as they were all *radicals* it was all right," because Price and Ling were
southern men. For Hill, this scrape was just one more demonstration that
vengeful Union men were riding high, fully supported by the legal system.
"Alas what enormous taxes we have to pay and no protection, shot down
like hogs if a radical wills it. Hope our land will advance in a few years so
it can be sold & we find some other home."[13]

Postwar Unionist groups played both sides of the law to grasp for dominance. If the sheriff and judge of a county were clearly on their side, they would use that road. Where there were blockages along that route, radical Unionists would intimidate officials or bypass them in direct action. During 1865 and 1866, para-military Unionist bands organized in several sections of the state to gain power and exact vengeance.

In Daviess, Livingston, and Caldwell Counties in north central Missouri during the summer of 1866, the Unionist band chieftain was Daniel Proctor, a radical state legislator. Local conservatives, who identified themselves as loyal law-and-order men of all parties, appealed to the St. Louis military command for protection from Proctor's men, whom they blamed for four recent murders. To protest the political killings, the conservatives had called a meeting, which Proctor and sixty of his men had packed. Proctor had denounced the law-and-order resolution "cursed them as hellish" and vowed to "break up with a fight" any subsequent meeting in opposition to him. Four of the law-and-order men fled to a neighboring town, where they petitioned the Union army for protection, being certain that Radical Governor Thomas Fletcher would back Proctor, who had seized all effective power in the region.[14]

Throughout southwestern Missouri in the summer of 1866, strong-arm Union bands organized, with such names as Vigilance Committee, Regulators, Avengers, Advance Guard of Freedom, Union Leagues. According to James F. Hardin, a lawyer from Newton County, these well-led "mobs" had killed and burned out many men they had deemed disloyal and had overthrown the civic governments and circuit courts in several counties. In Springfield, for example, they had compelled the recorder of deeds, the marshal, and the police to resign, and they had stormed a grand jury session, telling the jurors precisely what actions they planned to take, regardless of the law. Such a mob called on lawyer Hardin at 2 A.M., one night, forcing him to flee to St. Louis because he had brought a civil suit on behalf of a nineteen-year-old boy who had been assaulted by a mob in Newton County. Hardin and others had notified Governor Fletcher of these "outrages," who replied "that when the sheriff called upon him he would act." Anyone with any sense would have told Fletcher, Hardin was certain, that the Newton County sheriff "did not want the mob interfered with." Therefore Hardin appealed to the Union military to station troops in the leading towns of southwest Missouri.[15]

Ironically, most often former southern men appealed to the national military for protection. For them, the Federal army was the last remaining force potentially countervailing radical tyrants who controlled state and local government. The readiness of Unionists to resort to force to maintain power in 1865 and 1866 was in large part a response they had learned during the guerrilla war. This was not communal vigilantism—actions taken against men the whole community would have defined as deviants worthy of punishment. Rather, this violence was undertaken by only one faction, the dominant Unionist vanguard, against all other factions they deemed politically suspect. The techniques of intimidation and lynch law were not unrelated to prewar communal justice, but grew more directly from methods learned in the war itself.

The legal system was one of the sources of civil authority Unionists sought to dominate, when necessary through para-military means. Another was the church—or more precisely, local religious structures. In each town and hamlet, the preacher was the commonly agreed-upon moral and spiritual shepherd. What he preached as the right path held great influence over his communicants. The largest Missouri sects were the southern branches of the Methodists and the Baptists, many of whom had preached equivocal or pro-southern sermons during the war. Both during and after the war, silencing preachers who were to them seditious traitors and seizing their churches were important ends of committed Unionists. They used all the usual means of intimidation, including speedy recourse to violence.

Southern preachers certainly felt themselves to be under the gun. In his two volume memoirs published in 1870, William F. Leftwich discussed the "martyrdom" of sixty-six pro-southern preachers who were driven from their pulpits or shot during the war for preaching what they believed to be the Christian Gospel. After the war, the "persecutions" redoubled, causing one southern farmer to comment in a letter to his brother in North Carolina in August 1866 about the past five years worth of "the curses of mosis. . . . Their had been a greate deel of murdering done in this state this summer. A great many ministers of the gospil have been shot at their churches whilst ministirring the gospil by the Radicals." In his autobiography, Joseph King wrote that during the war he had been forced from his pulpit in Jackson County after preaching in favor of authority when visiting Federal troops had demanded that he preach for President Lincoln's leadership. King had fled South. Following the war, "After my return home, I found it impossible to preach in peace as my life was constantly being threatened and the people were afraid to come together."[16] Clearly, King's experience was typical of that of many preachers who had leaned to the South during the war.

In some cases, Unionists murdered pro-southern ministers who insisted on preaching the Gospel as they understood it. Such was the fate in August 1866 of Reverend Hadlee, a preacher in Webster County in south central Missouri. According to the Springfield sheriff sent by Governor Fletcher to investigate the case, Hadlee had been an unrepentant "bitter Rebel." He had fled south in 1861, when the Federal army had approached and had returned home and resumed preaching at the end of the war "in violation of the constitutional oath which he had refused to take." One August Sunday in 1866 with "some of his followers," Hadlee returned to preach in his old church despite the protests of "a company of loyal men" in the congregation to whom he was so "obnoxious" because of his "rebellious acts [that] that they did not want him to preach to or teach them." Refused entry to the church, Hadlee pulled down an American flag flying there and then with his followers started down the road toward his own land where he intended to preach. Someone then rode alongside of him and shot him dead. No one was willing to identify the killer—the loyal men for reasons of group protection, the southern men out of fear.[17] Where they were able, Unionists insisted on dominating by any means necessary the dispensation of the good Word. Most ex-southern men were so demoralized, disorganized, and discredited that they gave in. Weary of guerrilla war, the majority of the population was willing to accede to Radical rule, voting in the Radicals as the party to attempt postwar reconstruction.

The 1866 electoral campaign marked the climax of postwar violence in much of Missouri, particularly in the west central part of the state. Although the Radicals won a sweeping victory based primarily on widespread assent to their rule, they used coercion to guarantee their victory over their conservative foes. They considered conservative Unionists—the old softs— to be near-traitors, trying to recapture through the ballot box what they had lost in their alliance with the men of the bush. During the war, unconditional Unionists believed that all who were not for them were traitors: for the Radicals in 1866, a vote against them was a disloyal act. For their part, the conservative Unionists believed that the Radicals were a rabble who threatened law and order and stole elections for selfish ends through violence and cynical appeals to loyalty. As did Radicals, they often appealed to Union authorities for protection and sometimes took up the gun.

The focus for electoral violence was the registration procedure. Radical Governor Fletcher appointed strong Unionists as registrars and gave them wide discretionary powers to disfranchise those whom they considered to be disloyal men. If the county officials were Radicals in heavily conservative counties, they often were unable to protect the registration officer. On November 7, 1866, in Clay County, the sheriff, the clerk of the court, the former militia captain, and the supervisor of registration pleaded with the Union commander at Ft. Leavenworth for a company of troops. "We deem the lives of Union men in great danger. . . . Several of the most respectable citizens have been ordered to leave and many others have been publicly insulted and their lives threatened. An armed mob consisting of the most dangerous men in the county numbering more than a hundred men resisted the Sheriff . . . while attempting to arrest a man for breach of the peace." On October 9, the registrar, circuit court judge, and twenty-five other loyal citizens of Saline County petitioned the radical governor for 100 troops to meet a similar crisis, linking it to the earlier guerrilla slaughters. "The fact of the bold defiant threatening course of Woodson Thornton's band & other Bushwhackers who maltreat Registration Officers at different precincts recently impel good men to look after the peace of our county." On August 6, the registrar of Lafayette County, C. W. Howard, petitioned the governor for troops in response to a resolution passed by a public meeting of "the rebels and their sympathizers that they will resist the Registry law with armed force . . . that on Election day there should be more blood spilled . . . than had been done during the war." These threats had terrified local Union men, for "having passed through such horrible times, they are now naturally timid." In one breath, Howard claimed that he had not been traumatized by the guerrilla war—"I for myself do not much fear these threats"—but in the next added, "I am a poor man, my death would leave my family destitute. . . . I would like an assurance from your Excellency that the State will take care of my wife and children if I should be killed or crippled in the attempt to fulfill my duty towards my country."[18]

On election day, November 8, an armed band of about 100 conservatives, whom the radical sheriff characterized as bushwhackers, rode into Lexington, shot hundreds of rounds in the air, and surrounded the voting stations, forcing the election of their slate. The radical sheriff and other self-proclaimed "loyal men" complained to the governor about this misrule by the "Bushwhacking and thieving debris of the rebel army." In response the governor dispatched a company of state militia under the command of Major Bacon Montgomery. It was then the turn of the local conservatives to complain, directly to the Union army command in Ft. Leavenworth, about the brutal behavior of the radical militia who kept the radical county officers in office, overturning the election. The army sent out Major James R. Kelly to investigate, and he reported what he saw as a radical reign of terror. Within two days of arriving in Lexington, he observed a barroom brawl which resulted in a bullet wound to a passerby, one murder, three armed robberies committed by soldiers in the street, and a stagecoach robbery near town. Kelly concluded that the militia were "the most condemned set of ruffians I ever saw, [while] it is strange but true, that nearly all the Conservative men of this place . . . are apparently gentlemen, and men of good standing and wealth." Kelly did not analyze the mob action of election day but concluded that duly elected conservative officers were "powerless to act . . . in the presence of such desperate men." The crisis deepened. The newly elected conservative officers were either arrested or sent fleeing. J. A. Berry, the local newspaper publisher, was arrested for criticizing the militia. Major Montgomery destroyed his press and threatened him with hanging as a "God-damned traitor, rebel liar . . . and Son of a Bitch," thereby extracting a retraction of the offensive story. On December 21, believing the conservatives' stories, Major General W. S. Hancock dispatched three infantry companies to Lexington, dispersed the militia, arrested Montgomery, and allowed the conservatives to take office.[19]

It would be impossible to sort out the merits of the cases of the aggrieved parties in such a confused and violent scenario. Perhaps the most significant aspect was that conservatives called on national authority to overturn a state militia which was in Radical hands. Five years earlier, many conservatives had joined the Confederate side precisely because national troops had "invaded" their society. In this ironic manner, national sovereignty was much more widely accepted by Missourians in 1865 than in 1861.

Although postwar violence ebbed slowly and left behind endemic bitterness, it did decrease with the passage of time. Violence became more scattered as men and women put a lid on their seething rage. There was no dramatic resolution to the conflict, but as the reconciliationists had always believed possible, communities were rebuilt with cooperation as well as wariness. The key contributing factor to this reconstruction in rural and small-town Missouri was the statewide postwar economic and demographic boom. War-induced depopulation meant that cheap farmland, often sold by county governments for back taxes, was available to land-hungry Easterners. In most localities, whole populations moved in, not only to take up the land of departed Missourians but also to settle in previously untilled portions of the countryside and to fill and create jobs in St. Louis and other towns. Governed by a relatively efficient and progressive Radical administration in Jefferson City, new people and new wealth assuaged old wounds.[20]

Missouri's population increased and changed dramatically during the five years after the war. Settlement grew over 45 percent between the 1860 and 1870 censuses, from 1,182,012 to 1,721,295. This growth moved Missouri from the eighth to the fifth most populous state in the Union. When one considers the widespread depopulation of the war-ravaged countryside, which I would estimate as a loss of at least 300,000 by 1865, the population may nearly have doubled between 1865 and 1870. St. Louis grew rapidly during the decade, from 190,524 to 310,864, making it the fourth largest city in the nation. Kansas City became the state's second city, growing from 4,418 to 32,260. Fueled by the same industrial and transportation revolution, the countryside grew at exactly the same pace as St. Louis. Indeed many rural counties doubled in population during the late 1860s, particularly those in northern Missouri along the newly completed Hannibal & St. Joseph Railroad.

The composition of the population emphatically altered between 1860 and 1870. The black population actually dropped from 118,503 to 118,071, or from 9.8 percent to 6.8 percent of the total population. This decline continued a trend dating from 1830, when the number of blacks peaked at 17.8 percent of the population—117,995 of these blacks were born in Missouri, which meant that almost no blacks entered the state from outside during the late 1860s and that sizable numbers left.

After the war, Missouri's population became more native-born as well as whiter. The number of foreign-born residents increased by 61,726 be-

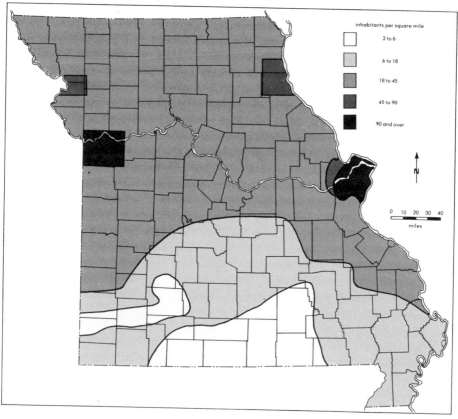

Population density in Missouri, 1870

tween 1860 and 1870, of whom 5,131 were from Germany and 30,677 from the British Isles, primarily Irish, but their percentage decreased from 15 to 13 percent of the population. In St. Louis, the number of foreign-born people increased by 16,163, but this was only 13 percent of the population increase for the 1860s. Foreign-born residents composed 36 percent of the St. Louis population in 1870 as opposed to 60 percent a decade earlier.

The largest portion of the increased Missouri population was children born in the state, approximately 75 percent of whom came from southern stock. This figure was 398,760 by 1870, or 61 percent of the total increase. However, the most dramatic population shift was in the origins of the non-Missourian, white, American-born population. Only 5 percent of this increase in the 1860s, 9,727 people, came from the South, defined as the former Confederate states and Kentucky, with decreases in the numbers of Carolinians, Tennesseeans, and Virginians. Ninety-five percent of new

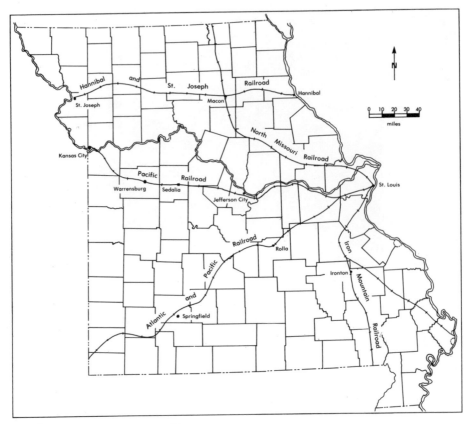

Railroads in Missouri, 1870

American in-migrants (184,000 out of 193,728) came from the Union states, Kentucky excepted. Seventy-eight percent of all in-migrants came from Illinois, Ohio, Indiana, New York, and Pennsylvania—43 percent of those from Illinois and Ohio alone. Stated another way, where in 1860 Southerners composed 62 percent of the non-Missouri-born, native, white population, by 1870 this southern-born in-migrant population had decreased to 44.3 percent and the northern-born percentage had increased from 38 to 55.7 percent. New settlement was northern, and it was concentrated in the most rapidly growing rural and urban areas, making growth a north-ern-tinted phenomenon.

This new population was concentrated in the cities and along the newly completed railroad lines. The first track in Missouri had been laid in 1854, with 810 miles completed by the start of the Civil War. Then new con-struction halted and much trackage and many bridges were destroyed by guerrillas. In the five years after the war, 730 new miles were completed

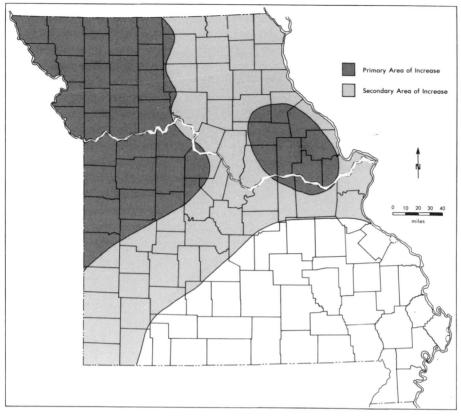

Land development in Missouri, 1860–70 (The darker areas indicate the regions of most rapid agricultural development. The white areas remained the least developed.)

(four routes crossed the state, linking the western and southern Missouri countryside to St. Louis and thence to the northeastern states), while trade down the Mississippi River to New Orleans continued to decline sharply.

Agriculture became more market-oriented in the late 1860s, both in terms of products sold and goods produced. Far more farmers were tied to St. Louis and the national market economy by the railroads. Investment in farm machinery nearly doubled. Most striking were the collapse of cotton and hemp production and the decline of tobacco planting. These declines reoriented farming along the Missouri River, where about 70 percent of the slaves had been concentrated in 1860 growing those three crops. The tobacco crop of 1870 was 12,320,483 pounds, down from 25,086,198 in 1860, and cotton production dropped from 41,188 bales to

1,246. Hemp collapsed as a commodity: 19,267 tons were harvested in 1860 and only 2,816 tons in 1870. Hemp never recovered for technological reasons—jute bagging and iron bale ties replaced hemp products in the 1870s. These old, slave-produced crops were replaced by an increase in less labor-intensive corn and hog farming as well as by rises in other livestock and grain production. The agricultural strengths of the old, Missouri River slaveholder elite disappeared along with slavery.

Concurrent with the decline in the former slave-based sectors of the rural economy and the orientation of the more mechanized general farmers to the northern market economy was a five-fold increase in industrial production in the late 1860s. In terms of the value of product, Missouri, which had ranked fifteenth in the United States in 1860, was by 1870 the fifth largest industrial state. St. Louis was the third largest industrial city in terms of number of plants and value of product, behind New York City and Philadelphia (see Table 6.1). In addition, St. Louis was the trade entrepôt between the Missouri countryside and eastern and foreign markets, selling goods to the farmers, buying, processing, and shipping their products.[21]

It is impossible to judge whether the Civil War retarded or accelerated this rapid economic development. St. Louis manufacturing was applied to military production during the war and may have grown. However, internal trade declined markedly during the war with the partial destruction of the means and security of transportation and the devastation and depopulation of much of the countryside by the guerrillas. After the war, relatively cheap land, new railroads, the industrial and population boom in

Table 6.1. Manufacturing in Missouri and St. Louis

	Manufacturing in Missouri		
	1850	1860	1870
Establishments	2,923	3,157	11,871
Workers	(not known)	19,681	65,354
Capital Investment	$8,576,607	$20,034,220	$80,257,244
Value of Product	$24,324,418	$41,782,731	$206,213,429

	Manufacturing in St. Louis	
	1860	1870
Establishments	1,126	4,579
Workers	11,737	40,856
Capital Investment	$12,733,948	$60,357,001
Value of Product	$27,610,070	$158,761,013

Sources: U.S. Bureau of the Census, 1850, 1860, 1870.

St. Louis, active encouragement of immigration, and a state government committed to rapid economic development fueled a boom which may well have been all the larger for the prior destruction and subsequent rebuilding caused by the guerrilla war.[22]

What seems clear is that the rapid reorientation of all the major sectors of the Missouri economy and population, which began in the 1850s, grew at a much increased pace in the late 1860s. The forces represented politically by Frank Blair and the other members of the St. Louis industrial and banking elite increasingly linked that city to the farmers and merchants in the countryside and dominated the growing elements of economy. Meanwhile the old slaveholding, southern-sympathizing elite lost much of its previous power in the ten years after the war. The invasion of Missouri had been deeper and more sustained than the physical visitation of Yankee troops. An assault on a traditional way of life, already well underway before the war, was solidified by the outcome of the conflict and increased exponentially afterwards. Traditional southern men had not been wrong in expressing fears of being overwhelmed, even if their political and military resistance to the invasion had been too narrow in focus. It remained for them to reorient their politcial, economic, and social views sufficiently to create a more conservative version of the new order, something they accomplished through the revival of the Democratic party by the late 1870s. More traditional practices and values persisted, but in the context of the new economic and social order. Despite this conservative retrenchment, the northern victory and the economic and social meanings of that triumph were clear in Missouri.[23] However, on the symbolic front, the southern cause was less clearly the loser. Images of the noble guerrilla rather than the triumphant Yankee came to dominate postwar reconstruction, surviving even into the twentieth century.

The Legend of the Noble Guerrilla

Like all former Confederates, the Missourian ex-guerrillas and their allies expended much energy after the war in justifying their wartime activities to others and to themselves. They created a subspecies of the argument that theirs was the noblest of lost causes. They had been men of honor defending womankind, home, and neighborhood against the barbarous invader. They had only responded to attacks. In dozens of books and poems, and when they gathered together in reunions, they portrayed their nobility, and this version of their guerrilla careers was incorporated as well in popular ballads sung in thousands of farmhouses all over the South and West. Over the course of the last thirty-five years of the nineteenth century, this legendary figure merged with the image of the famous postwar Missouri outlaws, nearly all of whom in fact had been guerrillas, particularly Jesse James. This legendary reconstruction exists to our day, broadcast to the world in scores of Westerns.

Defeat was ennobling—the hero had fought and risked his all for a cause of more than mundane significance. After all, his loss proved that self-gain had not been the end; he had sacrificed for principle. In this way after the war, many ex-Confederates reasserted their code of personal and southern honor, justifying the many deeds which might in a less romantic light have looked like the products of malice and brutality.

Missourians who had gone south to join the regular Confederate army took special satisfaction in the belief that they had risked everything for the South so far away from their homes. They believed that they obviously had fought a disinterested war. In a poem written on the back of his photograph, taken in June 1864 while he was a prisoner of war at Fort Delaware, Confederate Brigadier General M. Jeff Thompson took deep satisfaction in the honor he had borne for his forebears. He was of Revolutionary War "stock," and so he had been honor-bound to join the southern rebellion.

> My Father's Father was a *Rebel,*
> And Mother's Father was a *rebel* too,
> So when the South called out her soldiers,
> Pray what else would you've had me do?
> But buckle on my Father's sabre,
> And seize at once his trusty gun,
> And strike a blow for Southern freedom,
> Like old Virginia's faithful son?

Victory was not the main point—honor was. Serving the South, M. Jeff Thompson had been true to his lineage and to the highest traditions of American liberty.[24]

In equally romantic verse, "A Missourian" wrote "The Missourian's Feelings Before the Surrender at Shreveport, La." "A Missourian" believed all had been sacrificed at the altar of a concept of liberty which now was dashed forever.

> Yield to the Yankee: Oh that thought
> Thrills madly through my wildered brain.
> Give up the cause for which we fought
> And humbly be base slaves again.

Unlike M. Jeff Thompson, this veteran feared that men like him had failed their fathers in their inability to win a victory for southern liberty.

> Thank God my father does not live
> To witness his son's return
> I would cause his proud old heart to grieve
> His aged cheeks with shame to burn.

"A Missourian" almost regretted that he had not been martyred, but at least he felt certain that he forever would be eager to give his life for southern liberty.

> Dear land of sunshine and of flowers
> We yet would die for Thee
> If this last bloody act of ours
> Could make the people free.

Knowing he still was prepared to die meant he had not lost his honor in defeat but had proved it in his battle for the true cause.[25]

All of the many ex-guerrillas who wrote memoirs turned hungrily to the same postwar reconstruction of their honor to justify themselves. The public codification of the guerrilla as noble hero which they embraced was primarily the creation of one man, John N. Edwards, in his 1877 book, *Noted Guerrillas*. A Missourian, professional journalist, and former Confederate cavalryman with J. O. Shelby, Edwards constructed a set of symbols concerning the wartime guerrillas that had a great impact on all subsequent writers. He created a cast of heroic men who became intrinsic parts of the late nineteenth-century creation of the western hero in the popular press.

Edwards presented his guerrilla types, consciously and luridly, as mythic figures. Fletch Taylor, for example, "was a low massive Hercules, who, when he had had one arm shot off, made the other all the more powerful. Built like a quarter-horse, knowing nature well, seeing equally in darkness and light, rapacious for exercise, having an anatomy like a steam engine, impervious to fatigue like a Cossack, and to hunger like an Apache, he always hunted a fight and always fought for a funeral."

Edwards painted all his guerrillas this heroically. The centerpiece of his book was his ultimate hero, William C. Quantrill. In *Noted Guerrillas,* all the other guerrillas radiated out from him and the virtues he embodied. "He was a living, breathing, aggressive, all-powerful reality . . . laying ambuscades by lonesome roadsides, catching marching columns by the throat, breaking in upon the flanks and tearing a suddenly surpassed rear to pieces, vigilent, merciless, a terror by day and a superhuman if not a supernatural thing when there was upon the earth blackness and darkness." Quantrill was a super-hero, a great hunter, an animalistic force of the night, a thrilling, frightening, avenging force. Whatever the historical Quantrill might have been was irrelevant: Edwards was creating a fearsomely attractive guerrilla chief.

If Quantrill was Edwards's ultimate hero, so were all the guerrillas heroes. Edwards created an imaginary biography of the ideal guerrilla type for his readers. By breeding, this hero had been a gentle farm boy stirred to action only by repeated, unprovoked outrages made by the Yankee in-

vader on him and his family. "Reared among the bashful and timid sur-
roundings of agricultural life, he knew nothing of the tiger that was in him
until death had been dashed against his eyes in numberless and brutal ways,
and until the blood of his own kith and kin had been sprinkled plentifully
upon things that his hands touched, and things that entered his daily existence." This naturally passive and peaceful young man had turned tiger
only in response to wrongs done him; he was always defending, never ini-
tiating aggression. With his mother insulted, his sister imprisoned, his house
burned, and his brother and neighbor shot down, only then he exploded
into violent reprisal as should any true American man of honor, only then
"He lifted the black flag in self-defense and fought as became a free man
and a hero."

If the enemy had imposed a war without limit, the guerrilla had responded with even greater ferocity than his dastardly foe had exhibited,
because it was he who had fought on the side of honor. Edwards did not
claim that these had been civilized soldiers, but rather that they had been
avenging angels of destruction. "Every other passion became subsidiary to
that of revenge. They sought personal encounters that their own handiwork
might become unmistakably manifest." This had been a proud assertion of
lex talionis, as honorable manliness had dictated. Edwards's ideal guerrilla
indeed had become an "untamable and unmerciful creature." When captured Union soldiers "begged for mercy upon their knees, the guerrillas
heeded the prayer as a wolf might the bleating of a lamb." Yet the guerrilla
had had a softer side which had proved him to be human after all. Often
he had distributed mercy. "Something, no matter what—some memory of
other days, some wayward look, some passing fancy, some gentle mood
. . . made him merciful when he meant to be a murderer."

Edwards asserted that had all Confederate soldiers turned guerrilla, the
South would have won the war. It was the guerrilla hero who had understood the true meaning of war. To prove this point, Edwards fabricated a
story about a visit by Quantrill during the winter of 1862–63 to Richmond,
where he had told President Davis and the secretary of war that the guerrillas' path was the only way to destroy the enemy. "I would cover the
armies of the Confederacy all over with blood," he had Quantrill declare.
"I would invade. I would reward audacity. I would exterminate. . . . I
would win the independence of my people or I would find their graves."
The genteel, timid, unheroic southern leadership had rejected the word of
this brave young man. Pusillanimous leaders lost a war real men like
Quantrill could have won for them.

Although Edwards justified unbridled revenge, his depictions of battles
were rather bloodless; they had an unnatural and abstract quality. The
enemy did not consist of live persons but potential notches on guerrilla
guns. Thus in a typical engagement portrayed by Edwards, "Todd fought
as he always did—cool, smiling, deadly. Taylor with his five loads emptied

five saddles. Jarrett, hemmed in on a flank by three troopers, all of whom were shooting at him at the same time, killed them. . . . Gregg, his grave face fixed as it was always fixed in absolute repose, added three to his already long list." Edwards depicted violence in the tradition of the dime novel—killings were marks of the hero's prowess against a foe emptied of all humanity. The reader would not feel empathy for the cardboard enemy and could admire his heroes for their powers of offensive self-defense without guilt. By relating the guerrillas to the stock romantic dragon-slaying hero of popular literature, Edwards bled both the hero and the foe of their human, emotional qualities, thereby whitewashing guerrilla war.[26]

Edwards, the semi-official postwar guerrilla apologist and publicist, helped create the notion in popular culture that Quantrill had been the only important guerrilla leader of a unified, epic struggle. Gone was the war of ten thousand nasty incidents, which I have attempted to depict in this book, to be replaced by a narrative of the romantic outlaw. This figure held appeal for many reasons. One purpose it served was to strip away the horror of the memory of guerrilla war for ex-guerrillas and their sympathizers. Edwards replaced realism with supernaturalism. And his book had a great impact on the guerrillas themselves, helping them justify their activities after the fact. Many ex-guerrillas, hoping to cash in on their notoriety, wrote autobiographies decades after the war, most adopting Edwards's explanations, many plagiarizing whole chunks of *Noted Guerrillas*.

Even the military officers in Washington who selected documents during the 1870s and 1880s for the *Official Records* of the rebellion, the extensive official documentation of the war, were influenced by Edwards and other guerrilla apologists in their selection of materials on the guerrilla war in Missouri, focusing on Quantrill and his gang far out of proportion to their wartime importance in the state as a whole. Most modern historians also have been influenced by Edwards's stories far more than they are aware, not in the least because of dependence upon the slanted *Official Records*. Almost all of this literature, even the best-intentioned, has focused on Quantrill and west central Missouri, on the issue of whether he or the Kansas jayhawkers were to blame for the worst conduct. Though most have not glorified Quantrill and his men, they have placed them in the center of their stories, unconsciously following Edwards even while knowing that he was not a historian at all but a fantasist. It was the narrative power of Edwards, who employed traditional mythic forms, which captured the popular mode of presentation of the guerrillas' histories after the war.

One should not exaggerate Edwards's independent influence. His lively fabrications were not original at all; he drew on and amplified the tradition of folk legends of the hero which, in the late nineteenth-century was in the process of being put to new uses concerning the "Wild West."[27] His focus on guerrilla honor and love of liberty pleased the ex-guerrillas because that was always their most cherished view of themselves. In the only guerrilla diary I have found which may have been written during the war, William W. Welsh dealt with his guerrilla activities solely as defensive vengeance, usually in response to comrades killed. When many of the families of the guerrillas were banished in 1863, Welsh wrote, "evry body nose how our blud boiled then." He and his comrades evidently held long conversations concerning wrongs done the innocent as a form of moral preparation for subsequent actions. After Lawrence, "we fell back to sny hills and had a nother rest, but talk a grate deal about what been dun, but we had no regret on that score, that we had dun, only wishied we had dun more. We was not made to wore with wimmin and children."[28]

"Retributive justice" for wrongs done his family and his honor was for Sam Hildebrand the moral of his guerrilla career in south central Missouri, according to the autobiography he dictated in 1870. As Hildebrand told his story, in the fall of 1861 the local Union vigilance committee became "a machine of oppression, a shield for cowards and the headquarters of tyranny." They burned down his house—with his little brother Henry inside— and barn, drove his mother from the county, killed his "kind and inoffensive" brother Frank and his uncle John Roan, and left Hildebrand himself for dead in a gully, shot in the head. Only then did Hildebrand respond. "I declared war. I determined to fight it out with them, and by the assistence of my faithful gun 'kill-devil,' to destroy as many of my blood-thirsty enemies as I possibly could. To submit to further wrong from their hands would be an insult to the Being who gave me the power of resistance." After the war, believing that he had acted justly and purely in self-defense, Hildebrand boasted of his powers, claiming that he had killed over 100 men without compunction. "I make no apology to mankind for my acts of retaliation; I make no whining appeal to the world for sympathy. I sought revenge and I found it." Hildebrand's favorite tactic had been to go alone or with three to five others up into his home region from Confederate Arkansas, to lay in wait in the woods by the edge of a field of a Union farmer, shooting him as he came out to work, then cutting another notch in "Kill-Devil." He had taken special pleasure in killing local Germans, his worst enemies; for example, noting of the fate of two German captives, "we hung them and went on our way rejoicing."

Despite his avowed blood-thirstiness, Hildebrand held himself accountable to a moral code. His war had been primarily one of personal vengeance to redeem honor. He also claimed he had held a major's commission from Confederate Brigadier General M. Jeff Thompson, who had told him, "go where you please, take what men you can pick up, fight on your own hook, and report to me every six months." In this fashion, he claimed to have been a legitimate Confederate. More important to Hildebrand as evidence of his submission to a moral code was his self-imposed limitation on fighting. After all, no external authority had prevented him from becoming a savage: he had been an independent rule-observer. "I never made war on women and children, neither did I ever burn a house." He had observed limits the Union soldiers had transgressed. "Did I ever punish a man for feeding a federal? Did I ever shoot a man for not reporting to me the fact of having seen a federal pass along the road? If that was really my mode of proceeding, I would deserve the stigma cast upon my name." After the war Hildebrand had surrendered and had returned, like Cincinnatus, to farming in northern Arkansas, coming back to Missouri only in 1869 when a price was put on his head. He then went into hiding where, being illiterate, he dictated his autobiography, claiming amidst the bragging about his efficiency as a wartime killer that he was now willing to live and let live.[29]

Clearly, the two journalists who compiled this autobiography helped Hildebrand construct his defense. Like John N. Edwards, they were working out of a popular literary tradition of the noble outlaw, or Rob Roy, as they referred to Hildebrand in the subtitle of the book. Doubtless, Hildebrand believed the guerrilla code that he or his editors articulated five years after the war. The code had served many as a psychological screen during the war, blocking out the conflict's brutality with webs of proclaimed social justification. After the war, the code became even more meaningful, providing a mold for the recasting of memories, so that the harsh parts of past experience were downplayed and the noble intentions highlighted. Using a legendary heroic literary form could accelerate this process of cultural and self-expurgation.

In their memoirs, ex-guerrillas cleansed their histories in this manner. They insisted that they had always acted exclusively in self-defense, that they had avenged personal wrongs personally. They were real men, who had responded to attacks and had come to the aid of the weak and the downtrodden. They had never reshaped their personalities. They had remained consistent men of honor, always acting within the normative confines of their traditional culture.

For the ex-guerrillas, it was the invading Union which had caused them to act brutally. Living in peace, they had been attacked. Responding to attack, they had been outlawed. After the Union had stigmatized them, they had had no choice but to act as social renegades. All the ex-guerrillas would have agreed with their comrade William Gregg's autobiographical chronology that at the onset of their resistance, guerrilla bands had been "vying with each other who should be the most magnanimous toward prisoners" until General Halleck had declared on March 13, 1862, that guerrillas were outlaws not to be taken prisoner. According to Gregg, only then, when the Union had left them no choice, did guerrillas begin to kill their Union prisoners. "When a man is not permitted to live under the laws that govern other men," Captain Kit Dalton, another ex-guerrilla, wrote decades later, "he must live by whatever means he can." The Union was the party in the war that had, as it were, raised the black flag for the guerrillas and had made them keep it flying throughout the war. John McCorkle wrote in 1915, "We tried to fight like soldiers but were declared outlaws, hunted under a black flag and murdered like beasts."[30]

Even the destruction of Lawrence, including the slaughter of at least 150 unarmed civilian men and boys, had been but a response to Union proscription and attack. In William Gregg's memoirs, Lawrence and all of Kansas actually had become by 1863 one vast armed camp, filled with men who had been attacking Missouri for years. "The town was full of soldiers, but the sudden and unexpected appearance of Quantrill and his men completely paralyzed them. . . . At the time of the Lawrence raid, the entire male populace of Kansas were soldiers, minute men, organized and equipped by the government. I tell these facts to show the world that Quantrill and his men only killed soldiers in Kansas." In this reworking of memory, all Kansas men had been Unionist attackers to be destroyed; attacking them had been defensive, even when they had been fifty miles west of the Missouri line and unarmed. There had been many would-be Unionist exterminationists who used the same argument in a war which always had tended to genocide. For the ex-bushwhackers like Gregg, because the guerrillas had been targeted for destruction, whatever they had done to enemy males, civilian or soldier, had been merely responses to the end the Union had intended for them. "I want it remembered that [we] had long since been outlawed by all federal troops, and when captured by them, all hope vanished; if not shot on the spot [we] were taken to some station where [our] execution was made a kind of circus for the edification of the troops."[31]

Almost no ex-guerrillas generalized politically beyond this personal reconstruction of a Union leviathan relentlessly attacking. One who did generalize was Sam Hildebrand (or his editors) when he asked, "what is a regular army but a conglomerate mass of Bushwhackers?"[32] This was the question John N. Edwards put in the legendary Quantrill's mouth during his fantasy visit to Richmond. In fact a philosophy of total war, such as William T. Sherman promulgated in 1864, would have been the most general and strongest defense the guerrillas could have made. Therefore it is significant that so few made the argument. These men were limited to the intellectual discourse to which they had access. Within their purview there was sufficient justification in the argument of collective self-defense.

For the ex-guerrillas, the most telling aspect of their postwar self-defense was the immediacy of the grievances that they had suffered. Most often the ex-guerrillas wrote of the Union killing of their immediate family members. For Sam Hildebrand, it was the death of his brother by Union vigilantes that set him to bushwhacking—for William Gregg, "I at once went to work in a systematic way to get revenge for the wrongs heaped upon me and my brother." Many ex-guerrillas retailed a story Quantrill evidently created for their benefit during the war (though here they might have been reproducing yet another Edwards fantasy) that when Quantrill had lived in Kansas before the war, Jim Lane's men had killed his brother and that this had been the cause of his later guerrilla captaincy. All the evidence suggests Quantrill had no brother. Most ex-guerrillas asserted that the deciding event for the Lawrence raid and the cause of its special fury had been the collapse of the Kansas City jail on August 11, 1863, which had killed four and wounded seven of the women kin of the guerrillas. The guerrillas believed the Union had purposefully collapsed the jail. This Union escalation of the war, turning it on women, had screamed out for vengeance. Fifty-two years later, that Union deed still infuriated John McCorkle. "We could stand no more. Imagine, if you can, my feelings. A loved sister foully murdered and the widow of a dead brother seriously hurt by a set of men to whom the name of assassins, murderers and cutthroats [would be kind]. People abuse us, but my God, did we not have enough to make us desperate and thirst for revenge."[33] In retrospect, all these men felt that they had been honor-bound to pick up the gun in revenge for wrongs done their families. Theirs had been a face-to-face war against the Union which had attacked them in the most immediate, concrete sense.

Ex-guerrillas believed that they had banded together to seek cooperative revenge for each man's personal wrongs. During the war they shared their past and on-going grievances like brothers, so that harm to one had been dealt with as harm to all. In the florid words of Jim Cummins, "Mad through the repeated insults which had been heaped upon their unoffending fathers, mothers, wives and sisters by these [Union soldiers], and who had shown them no mercy, now they need not expect any nor did they receive any mercy. They went into the fearful charge like furies, with the thought of their loved ones whom these men had repeatedly insulted and made to suffer."[34]

The Union had slaughtered the true brotherhood. If, for example, guerrillas had mutilated Union bodies, ex-guerrillas could mitigate that horror by insisting that the Union had initiated the practice and had been even more extreme in carrying it on than had been the guerrillas. William Gregg wrote concerning what he believed to have been the fate of one of the guerrilla raiders in Lawrence who had been shot off his horse. Union men had dragged him through the streets by a rope tied behind a horse, "till the body was nude and terribly mutilated, then hanged the body and further mutilated it, by cutting it with knives, shooting and throwing rocks, clubs, etc." Gregg claimed his band had never done "anything that mean."[35]

Cooperative personal vengeance as principle had been extended beyond that taken for actual guerrilla families to include revenge for harm done all sympathetic women, children, and old men, who were always characterized in ex-guerrilla recollections as harmless, weak, and innocent. William Gregg claimed that one day he had been standing by while Union men burned Mrs. Crawford's house. When two of the Union men had "snatched a lace cap from [her] head and threw it into the flames of the burning building," Gregg had disregarded all danger, whipped out his pistols, and killed both men. Defense of womankind was Gregg's retrospective justification for having acted as a killer. This was a typically personal category for explaining revenge, extended to include all women, all of whom, to Gregg, had resembled his mother.[36]

The next step beyond the belief that they had defended their personal honor, loved ones, and all good, defenseless people was for ex-guerrillas to wrap themselves in Robin Hood's mantle. They had been reared on that noble outlaw legend. As Captain Kit Dalton described the guerrilla assumption of this mythic title, "My little band not only fought for our country, but we foraged among the enemy and the fruits of our labor went to gladden the hearts of starving women and children, whose husbands and fathers were at the front or lying . . . in crowded ditches on some deserted battlefield."[37] However much aid they may have rendered to the poor and weak during the war, after the conflict it was very useful to argue that they had assumed the role of Robin Hood. They had been the men to respond to nature's laws when the people had been outlawed by tyrants. They had served the good through their innate moral sensibility, through service to the guerrilla code. Called bad by the state, they had been good in deed and in inner quality. They had not become amoral or immoral but rather truly moral, so that they need not have later regrets or guilt.

In 1898 Missouri ex-guerrillas who had ridden with Quantrill in what was by then one of the most legendary Civil War units, organized a veterans' group to celebrate their combat experiences. Some Kansans objected, but the men held annual meetings like those of other Civil War veterans until 1930. At the start of each summer's festivities the "boys" would gather "inside the corral," where they would converse privately about old times, and then they would parade on horseback, join public picnics, listen to Democratic politicians, and have their group photograph taken with one of the boys holding a portrait of Quantrill. At the 1901 meeting, Frank James proposed that a monument be erected "to the noble women who stood by them in the dark days of the war." In the haze of memory, these guerrillas had become just another group of prosperous-looking, aging farmers and small town merchants who had once been boys at war.[38]

In their reminiscences of the Civil War, many Missouri ex-southern women affirmed the moral picture painted by the former guerrillas. The Union had been heinous, the guerrillas the defenders of family and traditional liberty. In her memoirs entitled, "Can Forgive, But Never Forget," Mrs. William H. Gregg recalled that as a girl she had "never known a sorrow" until the day Federal soldiers had come to her home and had forced her family slaves to go to Kansas. Her father was imprisoned several times during the war, once for feeding families made refugees by

Reunion of Quantrill's Raiders. This photograph was taken in Independence in the early 1900s. Just as did regular army units, these noted guerrillas, legends in their own times, gathered to talk over old battles. Democratic politicians were quite eager to court their favor, though some Union veterans in Kansas reportedly objected to their effrontery in meeting as if they had been regular soldiers. (*B. A. George Collection, State Historical Society of Missouri*)

General Orders #11. "O, the misery! Old men, women and children plodding the dusty roads barefooted, with nothing to eat save what was furnished by friendly citizens." Mrs. N. M. Harris described the horrible Jennison as an Alaric, Attila, or Herod, far worse than Quantrill. She reported stories about the terror visited by the Kansas blackguards on defenseless little girls like herself. "A little girl, who was sleeping with her mother, was awakened by the unusual noise [of Union raiders] and began to cry, and one of the men went to her and, holding a saber against her face, told her if she uttered another sound he would cut her head off." This had not been an isolated incident. "The outlaws then turned their attention to the [older] girls, using insulting terms, searched their persons for valuables, all the while singing ribald songs or telling obscene jokes

Reunion of Quantrill's Raiders. In appearance these were typical aging farmers and small-town merchants. Nothing would indicate that they disbelieved their own legend. (*B. A. George Collection, State Historical Society of Missouri*)

[and then] took by force three of the girls into the yard and marched them back and forth in the moonlight, making most vicious threats and insinuations."[39]

The implication of the stories told by both these women was clear: Union troops had broken the fundamental moral code by abusing and symbolically raping little girls—the guerrillas had been justified in whatever they did in response to such bad men. Mrs. R. T. Bass also wrote in her recollections about the bad Union soldiers of her childhood memory. These were men who had "set fire to the houses that sheltered helpless women and children" who had had no "male protector" to defend them. In contrast, the avenging hero Quantrill had "looked as little like a bloodthirsty bandit he is usually described as it is possible to imagine. Instead of this, he was a modest, quiet, good-looking man . . . gentle of manner and courteous as well, true as steel to his friends if implacable to his foes." One Saturday night, Quantrill and his men had come calling for supper. "Laying their side arms upon the piano they . . . enjoyed . . . a boiled ham which our good Presbyterian mother had prepared for the

Sunday dinner." These had been fine young men defending good Christian southern folks against the devilish Yankee.[40]

The legend of the noble guerrilla, defending honor, family, and home against a brutal invader—as depicted by Edwards, the ex-guerrillas, and their female supporters—became the standard southern explanation for the horrors of Missouri. In the quasi-official *Confederate Military History,* published in 1899 for nostalgic southern readers, Missouri guerrillas were depicted as having fought "strictly a war of retaliation. . . . The guerrillas simply paid back the insults and wrongs to which they and their families and their friends were subjected." The Union soldiers had been the ones who had created the no-prisoners policy. "The guerrillas had accepted the black flag when it was forced on them and fought under it, but it was not of their seeking, nor did they inaugurate that kind of warfare."[41] In this manner, the public image of the guerrilla was cleansed. After all, he too was a man of southern honor, always the Christian gentleman even when pushed to the extreme. He was recreated in the image of the virtuous fighter for the lost cause, as a slight variant of the regular Confederate military leadership—that leadership which in fact had refused to adopt guerrilla methods of combat during the war and had rejected the guerrillas themselves for their indiscipline and brutality.

Popular folklore seconded this self-exculpating, ex-guerrilla legend. In camp songs and ballads which might have originated during the war but which certainly grew through the late nineteenth century, rural Missourians depicted guerrillas as romantic heroes, serving the southern cause and bolstering defenseless civilians. In one "literary" rendition of a Civil War camp song, "The Call of Quantrell," the guerrillas were rescuing, avenging angel-warriors, defeating the Union commander of west central Missouri and his militia troops.

> When old Penick is weary and the chase given o'er
> We'll come as a thunderbolt comes from the cloud;
> We'll pass through their midst and bathe in their gore,
> We'll smite the oppressor and humble the proud.
> Few shall escape us and few shall be spared,
> For keen is our sabre, in vengeance 'tis bared;
> For none are so strong, so mighty in fight,
> As the warrior who battles for our Southern right.

On a less elevated plane, the guerrilla was depicted as a daring and powerful roving young man, wonderfully attractive to the girls. Thus "The Roving Gambler," was adapted to fit the "Guerrilla Boy" of Missouri. The boy sings, "I am a roving gambler/ I rove from town to town,/ And whenever I spy a pretty little girl/ So willingly I get down." The girl replies, "I'll bundle up my clothing/ with my true love by my side,/ And I'll rove this wide world over/ And be a guerrilla's bride. . . . With his pockets lined with silver,/ A Navy in each hand,/ A long life and full success/ To the roving guerrilla man!"

In an Ozark variant of this song, the enchanted girl compares the romantic qualities of the guerrilla to the soiled, impoverished life of ordinary men: "I do not like the blacksmith/ That works in all the coal,/ I had rather have the guerrilla man/ That carries a purse of gold." And "I do not like a farmer/ That works in all that dirt,/ I had rather have the guerrilla man/ That wears a ruffled shirt." As for the roving guerrilla, who sat down with joy by every pretty little girl, there were material rewards for him as well. "Every pocket-book I find/ With joy I slide her down." Having each other's "purses" was an enormous material as well as sexual pleasure for the pretty little girl and her dashing swain.

In another ballad, William C. Quantrill was treated both as the avenging hero of Lawrence and as Robin Hood.

> Come all you bold robbers and open your ears
> Of Quantrell the lion heart you quickly shall hear.
> With his band of bold riders in double quick time,
> He came to lay Lawrence low, over the line . . .
>
> Oh, Quantrell's a fighter, a bold-hearted boy,
> A brave man or woman he'd never annoy.
> He'd take from the wealthy and give to the poor
> For brave men there's never a bolt to his door.[42]

Folkloric categories based on almost ageless models of the noble outlaw provided explanatory categories into which the guerrilla experience could be sorted. Whatever might have happened in actuality was beside the point for people seeking to arrange history to fill their needs. The demands of ex-sympathizers paralleled and reinforced those of the ex-guerrillas and their defenders. In the instance of the image of the Missouri ex-guerrilla, the collective folk portrait of guerrillas as social bandits meshed with the presentation of Jesse James as Robin Hood. James and all his gang in fact had been Missouri guerrillas, and in ballads and polemics their later outlaw careers were portrayed as an extension of their wartime activities. James was the most famous American noble outlaw, and by extension, what justified him served in addition as an *ex post facto* justification for all the guerrillas. The popular creation of the noble guerrilla overlapped the creation of the legendary Jesse James.

Many Missouri ex-Southerners linked Jesse James to the guerrillas in an effort to ennoble them all. In *Noted Guerrillas,* written in 1877, four years before Jesse's assassination, John N. Edwards, the great publicist of the noble guerrillas, presented the James-Younger gang as honorable men who were compelled to continue as postwar bandits by the same forces of oppression which had first compelled them to become guerrillas during the war. "Wanton war" made them outlaws. "They were hunted, and they were human. They replied to proscription by defiance, ambushment by ambushment, musket shot by pistol shot," night attack by counter-attack, charge by counter-charge, "and so they will do, desperately and with splendid heroism, until the end." The end for Jesse James came on April 3, 1881, when one of his gang, Robert Ford, shot an unarmed Jesse in the back to collect the $10,000 reward offered by Governor Thomas Crittenden.

In his obituary for the fallen outlaw, Edwards depicted James as a paragon of honor who had had always to fight against the false law to serve an honor higher than his society had allowed him. To Edwards, Jesse's life had contained a mythic profundity. "We call him outlaw, but Fate made him so. When the war came he was just turned fifteen. The border was all aflame with steel and fire and ambuscade and slaughter. He flung himself into a band which had a black flag for a banner and devils for riders. What he did he did, and it was fearful. But it was war." After the war the hero had been forced into permanent social exile in his own land. "When the war closed, Jesse James had no home. Proscribed, hunted, shot, driven away from among his people, a price put on his head—what else could he do?" Again, James had been fate's servant. His life and his inevitable death had a mythic clarity. "He had to live. It was his country. The graves of his kindred were there. He refused to be banished from his birthright, and when he was hunted he turned savagely about and hunted his hunters." Edwards was on Jesse James's side. "Would to God he were alive today to make a righteous butchery of a few more of them."[43] The oppressed people cried out for direct vengeance which only the bold hero Jesse James had supplied.

According to William Settle, an astute student of the history and legend of the postwar bandits, the Jameses always had had widespread popular support in postwar Missouri, in large part because of their wartime record. One editorial writer commented in 1882, when Frank James voluntarily surrendered, holding a position Settle believes was widespread: "Was it wrong for the Confederates of the State—when the war had closed—to look with some degree of gratitude upon the man whose vigilance saved hundreds of rebel homes and thousands of rebel lives from unmilitary desecration? . . . There should be no mistake about this feeling toward the outlaws. The gratitude and remembrance were for Frank James the Confederate—not for Frank James the bandit."[44] This editorial writer was more of a law-and-order man than John Edwards. He could not believe in even the noblest of bank robbers. But neither could he dismiss Frank James as a common criminal; his guerrilla past gave him a moral stature that outweighed the nastiness of his postwar holdup techniques. Large numbers of Missouri ex-Southerners, who agreed with Edwards, blurred the wartime and postwar activities of the Jameses, holding in their minds a composite image of the heroic then-guerrilla, now-bandit.

Indeed, so popular were these ex-guerrilla outlaws that on March 20, 1877, the lower house of the Missouri state legislature nearly passed an amnesty resolution on their behalf. The first section of the bill demonstrated the diffusion of the heroic legend right up the social and political ladder of Missouri society. "Whereas, under the outlawry pronounced against" the James and Younger brothers and others, "who gallantly periled their lives and their all in defense of their principles, they are of necessity made desperate, driven as they are from the fields of honest industry, from their friends, their families, their honor and their country, they can know no law but the law of self-preservation; can . . . feel no allegiance to a government which forces them, to the very acts it professes to deprecate" and puts a bounty on their heads, inviting in "foreign mercenaries," the Pinkertons, to kill them. This bill gained fifty-eight "ayes" and thirty-nine "nays," failing by only six votes to get the required two-thirds majority on a concurrent resolution.[45]

Although there is no evidence that they ever rescued a poor widow or starving child, the James-Younger gang was fully aware of their social reputation, through which they sought to justify their actions in the eyes of "their" public. In 1903 Cole Younger explained that the gang had selected the Northfield, Minnesota, bank to rob in 1876—the holdup which had resulted in the death or jailing of most of the gang—by claiming that General Benjamin Butler had had large sums of money invested in it. "Beast" Butler was hated all over the South because of his reputedly brutal military suzerainty over New Orleans during the Civil War. Younger wrapped himself in the flag of the lost cause in order to argue that the bank robbery had had historical and political purpose—it was not the mere loot. Even during their bank robbing careers, the Jameses frequently had written to the newspapers to gain public favor. After sticking up the Kansas City fairgrounds in 1872, one of them, probably Jesse, signing himself "Jack Shepherd, Dick Turpin, Claud Duval," noted European outlaws all, wrote the Kansas City *Times,* declaring, "we rob the rich and give it to the poor."[46] The James gang wanted admission into the brotherhood of noble outlaws.

Jesse James became the central American Robin Hood figure in folklore. The most widely told Jesse James story, one broadcast all over the rural South and Midwest, concerns his response to a poor old widow just about to be evicted from her country shack. With great modesty, Jesse hands her the rent money and rides on down the highway, where he waits in the shadows for the landlord. James then holds up the landlord, taking back the cash from the old woman's mortgage payment.[47] In his role as benefactor, in his gentleman-avenger character, in his trickster quality, and in his death by treachery, the legendary Jesse James became a classic folk hero.[48]

To an extent Jesse James, the American Robin Hood, was also a social bandit. In his elegant essay on the subject, Richard White stresses that gangs like the Jameses' avoided robbing local inhabitants, indeed paying them very generously in hard cash for supplies, while they robbed the railroads and the banks. "They preyed upon institutions that many farmers believed were preying on them," White concludes. In addition, the outlaws gained support because ordinary people believed that law enforcement agents were corrupt and incompetent. But most tellingly, the Jameses were honored, White argues, because they were "strong men who could protect and avenge themselves." It was the personal nature of their struggle which had such great popular appeal—the independent outlaw gang overcoming the oppressive forces of an alien and intrusive society.[49]

I would stress that it was not the actual bandit but the *emblematic* nature of the guerrilla-outlaw figure that gave him such force in popular culture. In this symbolic context, he was both a gritty social bandit and an anarchic superhuman figure—striking out against the very social forces which had ground down the southern cause during the war and had continued to wear down American farmers and small-town residents after the war. He was soft. His heart was with the little people, to whom he reputedly gave money and kindness so generously. He was hard. He destroyed and exploited the exploiters. As had Robin Hood, he reveled in blood revenge, which also gave deep pleasure to those honoring his legend. Such an attractive figure, not the real but the mythic one around whom facts were selected and arranged, was socially necessary. The figure was also a useful justificatory mask for the guerrilla-outlaw to wear. It was his postwar survival lie. If he looked at himself in the mirror through this mask, he could see a hero rather than a terrorist, a murderer, a robber, an arsonist, a mutilator of other men's bodies. Journalists, pulp fiction writers, and Hollywood filmmakers, selling dreams to that huge audience which continues to enjoy the presence of the noble outlaw, have had every reason to perpetuate the legend rather than to realistically portray selfish bank robbers and cold-blooded bushwhackers.

Conclusion

Violent reprisals and counter-reprisals, which had been the very stuff of the guerrilla war, continued for a period after the war. As prosperity returned, the numbers of such incidents decreased. Nor should one overstate the disruption of everyday life caused by the famous postwar outlaws. Most ex-guerrillas went back to the plow, their families, and the Methodist or Baptist Church. Although probably most of them retrospectively conceived of themselves as having been noble outlaws during the war, there was every reason for them to make peace with their neighbors and with God as well.

In his memoirs, after repeating the heroic image of self and family, defending guerrillas, and telling his war stories in a matter-of-fact, covertly prideful way, the ex-guerrilla John McCorkle concluded, "My record since the war is known to my neighbors and friends and, while, in my declining years, these scenes come up to me as horrible dreams, I feel thankful that my life had been spared this long and hope that my enemies will forgive me for any wrongs of mine, as I know my Maker has."[50] This may have been a hollow formula McCorkle repeated because he knew it was what he ought to say to his evangelical neighbors and readers, but even if he thought of himself as a wronged noble outlaw, he may well *also* have been contrite for the excesses he knew in full conscience he had committed. If he meant what he wrote, he believed that he had redeemed himself socially by behaving after the war according to high standards of peacetime decency to all his neighbors—of whatever wartime stance. He believed that he had redeemed his soul by baring it before his forgiving God. A belief in the process of Christian redemption was a second, even more comforting self-exculpation to put beside that of the noble and wronged guerrilla.

It may well have been that what McCorkle believed and how he said he had sought to act after the war were characteristic of most ex-guerrillas and their Unionist foes. Mutual forgiveness was an indispensible element of the voluntaristic, self-governing society of nineteenth-century America, as well as of evangelical religion which stressed human freedom. In peacetime, the softs characterized social relations more than the hards did.

I have not been able to discuss the number and depth of the scars the guerrilla war left in the long term and the daily outbursts, both inward and outward, which resulted from the wounds inflicted during the war. That is the subject for another book. Civilians and fighters, men, women, and children had all been swept into a maelstrom beyond their worst fears. They had not performed with grace under pressure, as indeed few ever do. Neither, however, had they simply collapsed into monstrosity. The war undermined their social security and eroded their ability to remain within the moral structure in which they believed. Re-made wartime culture pushed and pulled them apart, enraged them, and benumbed them, and they had to patch together a daily morality as best they could. They doubled their characters; men and women cheated, lied, and acted duplicitously in order to survive. They bore false witness and attacked others with great ferocity in the name of the defense of honor, liberty, family, and home. They identified the enemy men as the Devil to be destroyed, not because they fell in love with evil so much as because they believed in the reality of an evil which they projected onto their enemies and then found in them. Therefore, destruction was necessary service to Christ militant, but with the other half of themselves, people on both sides believed that they were serving the sweet Jesus of love and maternal memory.

Missourians were not savages but good, ordinary, American evangelical yeomen in a society that was rapidly drawing them into a marketplace relationship with the rest of the world. They were both repelled and attracted by the new order, but they had no choice in the matter. The invasion was well under way. They might join or resist, but they would be swept up. War interrupted long-term change and pulverized their expectations, their very senses of self and of all others. Deeply frightened, they urgently sought to tell their stories. Because of this need and the dislocations which led to letter writing, because the local provost marshals took down every word of their depositions, and because after the war many relatives saved the remains of what they knew to have been the most extraordinary historical and personal event of American history, the historian has a window through which to view their lives, their thoughts, their beliefs, and their personalities, all tattered by guerrilla war. In their emotional nakedness and in the self-serving clothes they put on, one can see what they wanted to be at the same time seeing what they feared they actually might be.

Brigadier General John B. Sanborn from Minnesota had been a brigade commander with Ulysses S. Grant in Tennessee prior to being assigned the southwestern district of Missouri in October 1863. In a speech given in his home town of St. Paul in 1886, Sanborn tried to make some moral sense out of the guerrilla war he had fought. He noted that the five counties of his jurisdiction had had an average of 5,000 to 8,000 people each in 1860, but that by the end of 1864, the population had been reduced to about 300 per county. He described the mode of guerrilla warfare in this portion of Missouri which had led to those results. "During one week a Confederate force would pass through the country for a hundred miles or more and burn the houses and destroy the property of every loyal man, and before my arrival the Federal forces would soon go over the same section of country and destroy the houses and property of all the disloyal." Although he had stopped such violent Federal countersweeps after assuming command, on January 1, 1865, Sanborn accelerated the pace of depopulation by banishing 150 families, mainly headed by women, from his district. Twenty years later, Sanborn admitted that no policy had worked, that every effort had poured fuel on the fire, and that both sides had been culpable.

Sanborn did *not* take the easy explanatory route by asserting that Missourians had been savages predisposed to mayhem. Instead he insisted that there was something in the hearts of these good and typical American Christian farmers which had exploded when basic social and moral ties had distintegrated under the stress of the guerrilla war. "If there is anything of value to a future age to be learned" from the guerrilla war in Missouri, he wrote, "it is that there exists in the breasts of the people of educated and christian communities wild and ferocious passions, which in a day of peace are dormant and slumbering, but which may be aroused and kindled by . . . war and injustice, and become more cruel and destructive than any that live in the breasts of savage and barbarous nations." Sanborn believed that civilized men had fought tooth and claw when the "element of justice implanted in [their] bosoms" was violated. The central event had been "the putting to death of innocent men for the offense of another man," even when "authorized by . . . government." Both sides had practiced this form of capital punishment, which had pushed them further into an endless cycle of retaliation. "Human nature itself" had risen up "in open opposition to such an exercise of tyranny," which had led directly to the "introduction of the reign of chaos." Leaders had failed utterly; the principle of authority had collapsed because men had forgotten the injunction of King David that "He that ruleth over men must be just, ruling in the fear of God."[51]

In a civil war, with neighbor attacking neighbor, justice was impossible. In Missouri, restraint and forbearance had not been the guiding qualities. As Sanborn also could have quoted from the Scriptures, Missourians followed the angry voice of Christ proclaiming to his disciples, "I came not to send peace, but a sword."[52]

NOTES

All places of reference are in Missouri unless otherwise noted. Some of the capitalization and punctuation has been altered; original spelling is maintained. Frequent citations have been identified by the following abbreviations:

Beinecke   Beinecke Library, Yale University
CHS   Chicago Historical Society
Duke   Manuscript Department, William R. Perkins Library, Duke University, Durham
Huntington   The Huntington Library, San Marino, California
Ill.SHL   Illinois State Historical Library, Springfield
Iowa SHS   Iowa State Historical Society, Iowa City
JC   Joint Collection, University of Missouri, Western Historical Manuscript Collection—Columbia, State Historical Society of Missouri Manuscripts
JCHS   Jackson County Historical Society, Independence, Missouri
KSHS   Kansas State Historical Society, Topeka
LC   Library of Congress, Washington, D.C.
LSU   Department of Archives and Manuscripts, Louisiana State University
MHR   *Missouri Historical Review*
MHS—St.L.   Missouri Historical Society, St. Louis
NA   National Archives, Washington, D.C.
UNC   Southern Historical Collection, University of North Carolina Library, Chapel Hill
OR   *The War of the Rebellion: A Compilation of the Official Records of the Union and the Confederate Army,* 130 vols. (Washington, D.C., 1880–1902), Series 1. Series 2, 3, and 4 identified as such in notes.
Wis.SHS   Wisconsin State Historical Society, Madison

PREFACE

1. For surveys of guerrilla warfare, see Walter Laqueur, *Guerrilla: A Historical and Critical Study* (Boston: Little, Brown, 1976), and Laqueur (ed.),

The Guerrilla Reader: A Historical Anthology (Philadelphia: Temple University Press, 1977).

2. Among the best studies of guerrilla war during the American Civil War are Philip Shaw Paludan's study of an East Tennessee massacre, *Victims: A True Story of the Civil War* (Knoxville: University of Tennessee Press, 1981), and two analyses of guerrilla activities in North Carolina: Paul Escott, *Many Excellent People: Power and Privilege in North Carolina, 1850–1900* (Chapel Hill: University of North Carolina Press, 1985), 59–84; and William T. Auman, "Neighbor against Neighbor: The Inner Civil War in the Randolph County Area of Confederate North Carolina," *North Carolina Historical Review*, LVIII (October 1981): 327–63.

3. Richard Beringer, Herman Hattaway, Archer Jones, and William N. Still, Jr., *Why the South Lost the Civil War* (Athens: University of Georgia Press, 1986), 342.

4. Of the many fine works concerning men in combat, I am especially indebted to John Keegan, *The Face of Battle* (New York: Viking Press, 1976); J. Glenn Gray, *The Warriors: Reflections on Men in Battle* (New York: Harcourt, Brace, 1959); and two recent studies of combat soldiers in the Civil War: Gerald F. Linderman, *Embattled Courage: The Experience of Combat in the American Civil War* (New York: The Free Press, 1987); and Reid Mitchell, "The Creation of Confederate Loyalties," in Robert Abzug and Stephen Maizlish (eds.), *Race and Slavery in America* (Lexington: University of Kentucky Press, 1986), 93–108.

INTRODUCTION

1. Entry for November 17, 1864, Pauline H. Stratton Diary, JC.

CHAPTER 1. BEFORE THE WAR

1. Historians frequently have been tempted to deal with capitalist transformation as just such a *volte-face,* sometimes with contempt for "traditional" cultures and sometimes with nostalgia for the "old order" and antipathy for the new. David Thelan, in his fine study of Missouri culture, tends, in my opinion, to overemphasize and romanticize the extent of traditionalist resistance to the emerging marketplace. On the other hand, he alerts us to an awareness that the marketplace did not simply overwhelm family farmers, but that they interacted with it, using it for their ends as well as being used. See Thelan, *Paths of Resistance: Tradition and Dignity in Industrializing Missouri* (New York: Oxford University Press, 1986).

2. Steven Hahn and Jonathan Prude (eds.), *The Countryside in the Age of Capitalist Transformation: Essays in the Social History of Rural America* (Chapel Hill: University of North Carolina Press, 1985), 14. For the framework presented here I am indebted to Hahn's analysis, here and elsewhere, to the excellent essay by John Schlotterbeck, "The 'Social Economy of an Upper South Community': Orange and Greene Counties, Virginia,

1815–1860," in Orville Vernon Burton and Robert C. McMath, Jr. (eds.), *Class, Conflict and Consensus: Antebellum Southern Community Studies* (Westport, Conn.: Greenwood Press, 1982), 3–28; to Hans Medick, "The Proto-Industrial Family Economy: The Structural Function of Household and Family During the Transition from Peasant Society to Industrial Capitalism," *Social History,* III (1976): 291–315; and to Arthur C. Menius III, "James Bennitt: Portrait of an Antebellum Yeoman," *North Carolina Historical Review,* LVIII (October 1981): 305–26, a splendid case study.

3. This picture of roughly egalitarian landowners on top with landless drifters beneath is drawn quite clearly in John Mack Faragher, *Sugar Creek: Life on the Illinois Prairie* (New Haven: Yale University Press, 1986). On rural democracy also see Merle Curti et al., *The Making of an American Community: A Case Study of Democracy in a Frontier County* (Stanford: Stanford University Press, 1959).

4.

Presidential Election of 1860

Candidate	Votes (no.)	Votes (%)
Stephen A. Douglas	58,801	35.5
John Bell	58,372	35.2
John C. Breckenridge	31,317	18.9
Abraham Lincoln	17,028	10.2

5. The most comprehensive political, social, and economic analysis of Missouri in the period leading up to the Civil War is Walter H. Ryle, *Missouri: Union or Secession* (Nashville: George Peabody College for Teachers, 1931). A useful brief analysis, in a volume which includes an excellent bibliography, is William E. Parrish, *A History of Missouri. Volume III, 1860–1875* (Columbia: University of Missouri Press, 1971). Also see Parrish, *Turbulent Partnership: Missouri and the Union, 1861–1865* (Columbia: University of Missouri Press, 1963); Arthur R. Kirkpatrick, "Missouri on the Eve of the Civil War," *MHR,* LV (January 1961): 99–108; and Robert E. Shalhope, "Eugene Genovese, the Missouri Elite, and Civil War Historiography," *Bulletin of the Missouri Historical Society,* XXVI (July 1970): 271–82.

6. Ryle, 3.

7. *Eighth Census of the United States.* Volume III. *Population* (Washington, Government Printing Office, 1863), 301.

8. See James F. Hopkins, *A History of the Hemp Industry in Kentucky* (Lexington: University of Kentucky Press, 1951); Miles W. Eaton, "The Development and Later Decline of the Hemp Industry in Missouri," *MHR,* XLIII (July 1949): 346–67.

9. *Eighth Census of the United States,* Volume II, *Agriculture,* 234. Slavery in Missouri is analyzed in Robert W. Duffner, "Slavery in Missouri River Counties, 1810–1865" (Ph.D. dissertation, University of Missouri-Columbia, 1974); Harrison A. Trexler, *Slavery in Missouri, 1804–1865* (Baltimore: Johns Hopkins University Press, 1914); Philip V. Scarpino, "Slavery

in Callaway County Missouri: 1845–1855," *MHR*, LXXI (October 1976, April 1977): 22–58, 266–83; George R. Lee, "Slavery and Emancipation in Lewis County, Missouri," *MHR*, LXV (April 1971): 294–317; and James William McGettigan, Jr., "Boone County Slaves: Sales, Estate Divisions and Families, 1820–1865," *MHR*, LXXII (January, April 1978): 176–97, 271–95.

10. *Eighth Census*, Volume III, xxix; cxxiv, 288–98; Volume IV, *Statistics*, 614.

11. Parrish, *A History of Missouri*, 207–21.

12. *Eighth Census*, Volume 4, 614.

13. *Eighth Census, Volume I, Manufactures*, 310–12. Suggestive for St. Louis development is Steven J. Ross, *Workers on the Edge: Work, Leisure and Politics in Industrializing Cincinnati, 1788–1890* (New York: Columbia University Press, 1985).

14. Ryle, 208–9.

15. For an analysis of later nineteenth-century southern hill-country whites see Steven Hahn, *The Roots of Southern Populism: Yeoman Farmers and the Transformation of the Georgia Upcountry, 1850–1890* (New York: Oxford University Press, 1983).

16. In addition to the sources listed in note 5, see William E. Smith, *The Francis Preston Blair Family in Politics*, 2 vols. (New York: Da Capo, 1933), II: 19–52; and Elbert B. Smith, *Francis Preston Blair* (New York: Free Press, 1980).

17. For an analysis of Republican ideology in the 1850s see Eric Foner *Free Soil, Free Labor, Free Men: The Ideology of the Republican Party Before the Civil War* (New York: Oxford University Press, 1970); and Michael Fellman, "Theodore Parker and the Abolitionist Role in the 1850s," *Journal of American History*, LXI (December 1974): 666–84. On eastern writers' cultural attacks on southwestern rural types see Fellman, "Alligator Men and Card Sharpers: Deadly Southwestern Humor," *Huntington Library Quarterly*, XLIX (1986): 307–23.

18. The following analysis is adapted from Michael Fellman, "Rehearsal for the Civil War: Antislavery and Proslavery at the Fighting Point in Kansas, 1854–1856," in Lewis Perry and Michael Fellman (eds.), *Antislavery Reconsidered: New Perspectives on the Abolitionists* (Baton Rouge: Louisiana State University Press, 1979), 287–307.

19. Julia Louisa Lovejoy to the Concord (N.H.) *Independent Democrat*, March 13, April 13, and May 22, 1855, in "Julia Louisa Lovejoy, Letters from Kansas," *Kansas Historical Quarterly*, XI (February 1942): 31–34, 37. Also see Michael Fellman, "Julia Louisa Lovejoy Goes West," *Western Humanities Review*, XXXII (Summer 1977): 227–42.

20. The best account of events in Kansas, set in the context of national politics, remains Allan Nevins, *Ordeal of the Union: A House Dividing, 1852–1857* (New York: Charles Scribner's Sons, 1947); *The Emergence of Lincoln: Douglas, Buchanan and Party Chaos, 1857–1859* (New York: Charles Scribner's Sons, 1950). Alice Nichols, *Bleeding Kansas* (New York: Oxford University Press, 1954), is a useful, if uncritical, recapitulation of contemporary accounts of the events in Kansas. James A Rawley, *Race and*

Politics: "Bleeding Kansas" and the Coming of the Civil War (Philadelphia: J. B. Lippincott, 1969), concentrates on national politics. James C. Malin, *John Brown and the Legend of Fifty-Six*, 2 vols., Rev. ed (New York: Haskell House, 1971), provides a mine of information. Don W. Wilson, *Governor Charles Robinson of Kansas* (Lawrence: University of Kansas Press, 1975), is a useful biography of a central antislavery leader. The New England Aid Company has been perhaps overemphasized. Two solid accounts are Samuel A. Johnson, *The Battle Cry of Freedom: The New England Aid Company in the Kansas Crusade* (Lawrence: University of Kansas Press, 1954); and Ralph V. Harlow, "The Rise and Fall of the Kansas Aid Movement," *American Historical Review*, XLI (1935): 1–25. Paul W. Gates, *Fifty Million Acres: Conflicts Over Kansas Land Policy, 1854–1890* (Ithaca: Cornell University Press, 1964), is an elegant and brilliant study. Two essays concentrate on Kansas journalism as unnecessary, irrational, but effective propaganda: Bernard A. Weisberger, "The Newspaper Reporter and the Kansas Imbroglio," *Mississippi Valley Historical Review*, XXXVI (March 1950): 633–56; David Potter, *The Impending Crisis, 1848–1861* (New York: Harper and Row, 1976), 199–224. Malin, *John Brown,* II: 515, uses the 1855 voter census to suggest that only 6.4% of the settlers at that point were New Englanders; 1.6% from the lower South; 19.6% northern border states; 7.7% southern border states; and 47.6% from Missouri. In 1860, the figures were 16% from New England and the northern tier of states; 13.5% from the lower South; 35.3% from northern border states; 13.5% from southern border states; 10.6% from Missouri; and 11.8% foreign-born. Of course, a mountain Tennessean may have been antislavery back home, and a southern Indianan of Virginia origins proslavery, but the northern and western and non-Missourian slant of the population shift from 1855 to 1860 is unmistakable.

21. The first printed mentions of Missourians as Pukes came in the 1830s, but the origin of this term, like Wisconsin Badgers or Michigan Wolverines, is obscure. Perhaps the malarial bottomlands of the first Missouri settlements induced this symptom. Antislavery writers quickly adopted the name as it suited their martial needs.

22. *New York Christian Enquirer,* July 6, 1854. Unless otherwise noted, copies of all non-Kansas journalism quoted can be found in the Webb Scrapbooks, KSHS. A broad and representative sampling of newspaper opinion is in Malin, *John Brown,* I: 31–245. The similarities of "Gooks" to "Pukes" are more than verbal. For an analysis of "Gooks" which illuminates the study of "Pukes" as well, see Robert Jay Lifton, *Home from the War: Vietnam Veterans, Neither Victims nor Executioners* (New York: Simon and Schuster, 1973), 189–216.

23. William Phillips, *The Conquest of Kansas by Missouri and Her Allies* (Boston: Phillips, Sampson and Company, 1856), 29.

24. Lovejoy to the Concord (N.H.) *Independent Democrat,* September 5, 1856, in "Letters of Julia Louisa Lovejoy, 1856–64," *Kansas Historical Quarterly,* XV (May 1947): 131.

25. Charles B. Lines to the New Haven (Conn.) *Daily Palladium,* May 30,

1856, in Alberta Pantle (ed.), "The Connecticut Kansas Colony: Letters of Charles B. Lines to the New Haven *Daily Palladium," Kansas Historical Quarterly,* XXII (Summer 1956): 144.

26. See especially the Lawrence *Herald of Freedom,* February 16, December 20, 1856.
27. Chicago *Tribune,* April 20, 1857.
28. Entry for September 9, 1856, Journal of Richard J. Hinton, KSHS. In a similar vein, see New York *Tribune,* March 21, 1856.
29. In his "Crime Against Kansas" speech of May 21, 1856, Charles Summer vilified Senator Andrew P. Butler of South Carolina, among other things, for his verbal incontinence, with innuendo of a wider loss of self-control by slaveholders. Cf. David H. Donald, *Charles Sumner and the Coming of the Civil War* (New York: Alfred A. Knopf, 1960), 286.
30. Lovejoy to the Concord (N.H.) *Independent Democrat,* September 19, 1856, in "Letters of Julia Louisa Lovejoy, 1856–64," 134.
31. Boston *Liberator,* January 4, 1856; Milford (Mass.) *Practical Christian,* January 26, 1856. These passages are quoted and Stearns analyzed in a somewhat different manner in Lewis C. Perry, *Radical Abolitionism: Anarchy and the Government of God in Antislavery Thought* (Ithaca: Cornell University Press, 1973), 240–46.
32. Phillips, *Conquest of Kansas,* 64–65. The reporter for the New York *Herald,* who was not antislavery, came to similar conclusions: George Douglas Brewerton, *The War in Kansas* (Cincinnati: H. W. Derby, 1856), 381–84.
33. Charles B. Lines to the New Haven (Conn.) *Daily Palladium,* July 31, 1856, in Lines "The Connecticut Kansas Colony," 171.
34. Lines, 171.
35. Charles B. Lines to *Daily Palladium,* May 23, 1856, in Lines "The Connecticut Kansas Colony," 141; Julia Louisa Lovejoy to the Concord (N.H.) *Independent Democrat,* August 1, 1855, in "Letters from Kansas," 43.
36. Lawrence, *Herald of Freedom,* April 12, 1856.
37. Dover (N.H.) *Morning Star,* November 24, 1854.
38. Worcester (Mass.) *Daily Spy,* May 22, 1854.
39. Entry for September 3, 1856, Journal of Richard J. Hinton.
40. For example, see the letter of Amos A. Lawrence to Mrs. Charles Barber, January 8, 1856, in the Amos A. Lawrence Letterbook, New England Aid Company Papers, KSHS.
41. Phillips, *Conquest of Kansas,* 327.
42. Lawrence *Herald of Freedom,* December 27, 1856. On July 10, 1856, Gerrit Smith told a Buffalo convention called to aid Kansas that they should be "looking to bayonets, not to ballots," that "if all manhood has not departed from us" plentiful arms had to be shipped forthwith to Kansas. Quoted in Harlow, "The Rise and Fall of the Kansas Aid Movement," 15. It was Thomas Wentworth Higginson who preached in Lawrence in October 1856, taking as his text "Be ye not afraid of them," the same text which, Higginson said, John Martin had preached to the patriots after the battle of Bunker Hill. New York *Tribune,* October 7, 1856. Higginson's and Martin's text was Jeremiah 10.5.

43. For accounts of the proslavery position in Kansas see James C. Malin, "The Proslavery Background of the Kansas Struggle," *Mississippi Valley Historical Review*, X (December 1923); 285–305; William E. Parrish, *David Rice Atchison of Missouri: Border Politician* (Columbia: University of Missouri Press, 1961); Elmer L. Craik, "Southern Interest in Territorial Kansas, 1854–1858," in *Collections* of the Kansas State Historical Society, XV (1919–22): 334–450; Walter L. Fleming, "The Buford Expedition to Kansas," *American Historical Review*, VI (October 1900): 34–48.

44. Leavenworth *Weekly Herald*, December 1, 1855, May 24, 1856. The ideal of southern patriarchy is developed in Bertram Wyatt-Brown, "The Ideal Typology and Ante-Bellum Southern History: A Testing of a New Approach," *Societas*, V (Winter 1975): 1–29.

45. Leavenworth *Weekly Herald*, August 30, September 13, 1856.

46. Leavenworth *Weekly Herald*, March 29, 1856.

47. Leavenworth, *Weekly Herald*, March 29, 1856, March 30, 1855.

48. Leavenworth *Weekly Herald*, July 19, 1856; William Walker to David R. Atchison, July 11, 1854, in Atchison Papers, JC.

49. Springfield (Ill.) *Register*, reprinted in Leavenworth *Weekly Herald*, July 5, 1856. At other times, employing the reverse side of the nativist coin, proslavery forces sought immigrant, especially Irish, support on the grounds that Anglo-Saxon Yankees were the real oppressors of the Celts, in northern cities as well as in the motherland. See the Atchison *Squatter Sovereign*, August 28, September 18, 1855.

50. Leavenworth *Weekly Herald*, August 30, 1856. The development of the slaveholding, libertarian American revolutionary is the theme of Edmund S. Morgan, *American Slavery, American Freedom: The Ordeal of Virginia* (New York: W. W. Norton, 1975).

51. Atchison *Squatter Sovereign*, May 27, 1856.

52. Leavenworth *Weekly Herald*, September 20, 1856; Lawrence *Herald of Freedom*, May 10, 1856, June 16, 1855.

53. Topeka *Tribune*, August 25, 1856.

54. New York *Tribune*, October 23, 1856.

55. Atchison *Squatter Sovereign*, May 8, 1856; Lawrence *Herald of Freedom*, February 2, 1856.

56. Entries for September 30, 1855, February 19–20, June 20–21, July 4, August 9, September 3, 1856, Dairy of Samuel J. Reader, KSHS.

57. Charles B. Lines to the New Haven *Daily Palladium*, May 2, June 13, 16, 17, 1856, in Lines, "The Connecticut Kansas Colony, " 35, 151, 155, 160.

CHAPTER 2. TERROR AND A SENSE OF JUSTICE

1. Statement of Mrs. Nancy C. Leavitt, Court-Martial of Thomas J. Thorp, Pilot Knob, April 14, 1864, Case NN 1815, Record Group 153, NA. Thorp was sentenced to be hanged, a decision confirmed by Abraham Lincoln, who usually was lenient.

2. Testimony of Francis Tabor and Edmund Shaw, Court-Martial of James

Hamilton, Macon, January 30, 1865, Case OO 303, Record Group 153, NA. Hamilton was hanged on March 3. Pulling off toenails concerned an incident in Cooper County in central Missouri, related by Assistant Adjutant General O. D. Greene, St. Louis, to General Alfred Pleasonton, September 3, 1864, *OR,* XLI (3): 47; see also the *Missouri Statesman* for May 6, 1864, discussing incidents in Newton County in southwest Missouri, where bullet molds were the torture implements.

3. Mary Savage to her Mother and Sister, Lawrence, October 10, 1863, Mary Savage Papers, KSHS. The most careful of the many accounts of the Lawrence raid is in Richard J. Brownlee. *Gray Ghosts of the Confederacy,* (Baton Rouge: Louisiana State University Press, 1958), 110–127.

4. Sophia L. Bissell to Henry Asbury, Lawrence, September 8, 1863, Henry Asbury Collection, CHS.

5. Testimony of Ellen Brookshire, Rolla, February 24, 1864, Citizen File 2636, Record Group 393, NA.

6. Deposition of Pauline Ellison, Rushville, October 16, 1863, Provost Marshal Charges of Disloyalty File 2792, Record Group 393, NA.

7. This note, written June 14, 1864, was passed on to First Lieutenant W. T. Clarke of St. Joseph, who sent on a copy to his commander, Brigadier General Clinton B. Fisk. In response, Clark put out the word that ten rebels would be killed for each Union man. *OR,* XXXIV (4): 420–21.

8. Court-Martial of John W. Carty, Pilot Knob, October 28, 1863, Case LL 1238; Court-Martial of Lafayette Carty, Pilot Knob, October 28, 1863, Case LL 1301, Record Group 153, NA.

9. Court-Martial of Aaron S. Alderman, St. Joseph, November 3, 1864, Case NN 3356, Record Group 153, NA. Of course, Jacob Chuck might have been using his power as a courtroom witness to take revenge on these boys who were perhaps not the trigger men in his father's killing but who clearly were ineffective in whatever protests they may have made at the moment of the shooting.

10. P. A. Hardeman to her husband, Columbia, October 17, 1862, Dr. Glen O. Hardeman Collection, JC.

11. S. P. Harlan to her mother and father, Haynesville, November 1, 1864, Bond-Fentriss Family Papers, UNC.

12. Frances Bryan to William Bryan, St. Louis, October 16, 1863, William Shepard Bryan Papers, UNC; G. M. Barker to A. H. Garland, Drew County Arkansas, January 26, 1864, *OR,* XXXIV (2): 990.

13. Deposition of Elizabeth Hawkins, Washington County, November 26, 1864, Letters Received File 2593, Record Group 393, NA.

14. Deposition of Mrs. Elizabeth Vernon, Lebanon, November 26, 1863, Provost Marshal Statements of Property Stolen File 2798, Record Group 393, NA.

15. Deposition of Mary E. Austin, Livingston County, October 20, 1863, Letters Received File 2593, Record Group 393, NA.

16. Daniel Smith to his family, Boonville, September 17, 1861, Daniel R. Smith Papers, Ill.SHL.

17. Statement of James L. Chandler, 37th Enrolled Missouri Militia, *United States vs. William H. Banks,* Troy, October 26, 1864, Two or More Name

File 2635, Record Group 393, NA. Banks, a paroled Confederate prisoner of war, later admitted only to knowing some of the guerrillas. I do not know what became of him.

18. J. L. Morgan to W. H. Morgan, St. Louis, July 26, 1864, James Lorenzo Morgan Papers, UNC; Thomas A. Peters to Dr. John F. Snyder, Bolivar, June 8, 1863, John F. Snyder Papers, Ill.SHL.

19. Daniel Grant to General Odon Guitar, At Home [near Bottsville], February 28, 1864, Odon Guitar Papers, JC. There is no reply from Guitar in the collection.

20. Report of the Headquarters Board of Officers, Kansas City, September 6, 1864, Thomas Ewing Family Papers, LC. In this case, General Thomas Ewing, the district commander, months later finally released Crenshaw, who was by then ill and going blind, as well as being destitute and home-less, on condition that he keep his treatment a secret. He had never been charged with a crime. The board of officers hearing the case one year after the events ordered full payment to Crenshaw for his livestock and other losses in compensation for what they called a conspiracy to rob and murder by Ewing and all the others on down through his regiment. Ewing was reassigned but not because of this case.

21. Assistant Provost Marshal Charles D. Ludwig to Lieutenant A. J. Har-ding, Fulton, September 2, 1864, OR, XLI (3): 35; Conrad C. Ziegler to Governor H. R. Gamble, St. Louis, [April 1863], Provost Marshal Letters Received File 2786, Record Group 393, NA.

22. Margaret J. Hayes to her mother, Westport, November 12, 1861, Novem-ber 24, 1862, Margaret J. Hayes Letters, JCHS. There is an excellent analysis of jayhawking in Stephen Z. Starr, *Jennison's Jayhawkers: A Civil War Cavalry Regiment and Its Commander* (Baton Rouge: Louisiana State University Press, 1973).

23. Entry for February 14, 1862, in Margaret Mendenhall Frazier and James W. Goodrich (eds.), " 'Life Is Uncertain . . .' Willard Hall Men-denhall's 1862 Civil War Diary," *Missouri Historical Review,* LXXVII (July 1984): 444; E. A. Christie to Dear Pa, near Platte City, February 24, 1863. E. A. Christie Letter, JC.

24. Daniel De Witt, List of Loses at Federal Hands, 1861–63, JCHS.

25. Daniel R. Anthony to Aaron McLean, December 3, 1861, in Edgar Langs-dorff and R. W. Richmond (eds.), "Letters of Daniel R. Anthony," *Kansas Historical Quarterly,* XXIV (Spring, Summer, Autumn, Winter 1958): 6–30, 198–226, 351–70, 458–75, at p. 356.

26. Analyses of justice as the root of small town and rural community in the American West include Don Harrison Doyle, *The Social Order of a Fron-tier Community: Jacksonville, Illinois, 1825–70* (Urbana: University of Illinois Press, 1978); John P. Reid, *Law for the Elephant* (San Marino: Huntington Library, 1982); Merle Curti et al., *The Making of an Ameri-can Community* (Stanford: Stanford University Press, 1959).

27. Deposition of Mrs. Susan Hornbeck, Jefferson City, July 25, 1863, Two or More Name File 2635, Record Group 393, NA.

28. Testimony of Jesse Chrisman, Court-Martial of William F. Galloway, Rolla, May 4, 1864, Case NN 2192, Record Group 153, NA. Galloway had

been captured at Vicksburg and paroled. He was sentenced to five years in prison for horse theft, though he successfully defended himself against charges that he was a guerrilla. It is significant that Galloway tried to make Chrisman trade in a "fair" manner, a code both men shared in general if not in this instance. Chrisman forced Galloway to use overt, illegal coercion, the appearance of which Galloway attempted to avoid, whether for future legal reasons or to keep his conscience clear is unknowable. Other neighborly direct action against thieves was not so successful. For example, on October 31, 1864, six Missouri Unionists, some of whom were in the militia, went to Oskaloosa, Kansas, to retrieve stolen goods and horses. The local sheriff had them in his possession and was willing to return them. A mob formed, seized and beat the six Missourians, and took back the returned property, driving the six bleeding men out of town: George D. Tolle et al. to Major H. H. Heath, n.p., November 2, 1864, Two or More Name Citizen File 2637, Record Group 393, N.A.

29. Entry for June 18, 1861, Diary of Henry J. Marsh, Wis.SHS.
30. Abiel Leonard to his Wife, Marshall, March 7, 1862, Abiel Leonard Collection, JC. This consensus broke down and in 1864, after a great deal of dispute and killing, Marshall was sacked and burned in Price's raid.
31. Testimony of John A. Bean, Court-Martial of Henry A. Griffith, St. Joseph, September 7, 1864, Case LL 2638, Record Group 153, NA. Griffith argued in his defense that he had been forced to go with the guerrillas and that subsequently he only followed orders. Griffith's mother and a neighbor scheduled to testify for him did not appear at the trial. Griffith was hanged on September 23. Testimony of F. W. Gresham, Edmund Kean, John Beard, and William Sharp, Court-Martial of John Nichols, Jefferson City, June, 1863, Case MM 746, Record Group 153, NA. Abraham Lincoln approved Nichols's death sentence on September 10.
32. Thomas _____ to his Wife, near Boonville, November 14, 1862, Civil War Letter, 1862, JC.
33. John Barnes to Colonel N. Cole, St. Louis, March 8, 1864, Provost Marshal Letters Received File 2786, Record Group 393, NA.
34. [Report of Gustavas St. Gem], Headquarters of the 8th Sub-District of the St. Louis District—Office of the Assistant Provost Marshal, St. Genevieve, December 1, 1864, Provost Marshal Letters Received File 2786, Record Group 393, NA.
35. C. C. Ziegler, Application for Protection, St. Louis [circa April 1, 1863], Provost Marshal Letters Received File 2786, Record Group 393, NA.
36. Austin A. King to Major General John M. Schofield, St. Louis, May 30, 1863, John M. Schofield Papers, LC.
37. John A. Higgins to Nancy, Warsaw, October 19, 1861, John A. Higgins Papers, Ill.SHL.
38. G. O. Yeiser to Brigadier General J. M. Schofield, Mexico, July 19, 1862, Letters Received File 367, Record Group 393, NA. One cannot know if Yeiser's prewar religious faith had been so Calvinistic.
39. Petition of 88 residents of Boone County to Major General Samuel R. Curtis, February 23, 1863, Letters Received File 367, Record Group 393, NA.

40. A. J. McRoberts to Molie, Saline County, July 5, 1863, A. J. McRoberts Papers, JC.

41. *The United States vs. C. Percy Rawlings,* St. Louis, July 3, 1863, Provost Marshal Charges of Disloyalty File 2792, Record Group 393, NA. I do not know Rawlings's fate.

42. R. J. Anderson to Brigadier General Clinton B. Fisk, Williamstown, June 6, 1864, *OR,* XXXIV (4): 249. I do not know if Fisk followed through. In his letter, Anderson wrote that he would gladly testify before a military tribunal should Fisk pursue the case.

43. Case of Mrs. Margery J. Callahan and Miss Lulu Kinkead, Provost Marshal Charges of Disloyalty File 2792, Record Group 393, NA.

44. *United States vs. Abel Crawford,* Mexico, February 25, 1863, Two or More Name Citizen File 2637, Record Group 393, NA.

45. Deposition of William Powell, July 28, 1864, Two or More Name Citizen File 2637, Record Group 393, NA; N. T. Allison to Captain J. L. Ferguson, Warrensburg, July 24, 1864, Provost Marshal Letters Received File 2786, Record Group 393, NA.

46. Thirty Citizens of Knox, Scotland, and Clark Counties to Colonel B. G. Farrar, n.d., Letters Received File 367, Record Group 393, NA; Twenty-Four Citizens of Boone County to J. Dorr, January 10, 1863, Two or More Name Citizen File 2637, Record Group 393, NA.

47. Abraham Allen to Brigadier General Clinton B. Fisk, Crab Orchard, May 25, 1864, *OR,* XXXIV (4): 37.

48. Deposition of Richard W. Alexander, Greenville, August 14, 1864, Provost Marshal Charges of Disloyalty File 2792, Record Group 393, NA.

49. Court-Martial of Silas Best, Macon, February 1, 1865, Case OO 303, Record Group 152, NA.

50. George W. Carter to James O. Broadhead, Snow Hill, July 23, 1863, James O. Broadhead Papers, MHS—St.L.

51. Barton Bates to Edward Bates, St. Louis, July 7, 1861, Edward Bates Papers, MHS—St.L.; James O. Broadhead to Edward Bates, St. Louis, July 24, 1864, James O. Broadhead Papers, MHS—St.L.

52. Joseph H. Trego to his wife, Motevelo, October 28, 1861, in Edward Langsdorf (ed.), "The Letters of Joseph H. Trego, 1857–1864, Linn County Pioneer," *Kansas Historical Quarterly,* XIX (May, August, November, 1951): 113–32, 287–309, 384–400, at pp. 297–98; Lizzie Renick to Molie McRoberts, Waverly, August 14, 1862, A. J. McRoberts Papers, JC; John Johnston to his Brother and Sister, Kansas City, April 9, 1863, Jarbec-Johnston Correspondence, JCHS.

53. J. R. French to Major General William S. Rosecrans, Pisgah, September 14, 1864, *OR,* XLI (3): 191; P. Harlan to her Sister, Haynesville, March 15, 1865, Bond-Fentriss Family Papers, UNC.

54. George Gresham to Judge Gale, Lexington, July 24, 1864, Provost Marshal Letters Received File 2786, Record Group 393, NA; George S. Avery to his Wife, Iron Mountain, February 24, 1863, George S. Avery Letters, CHS.

55. George S. Park to Major General William S. Rosecrans, Parksville, March 28, 1864, *OR,* XXXIV (2): 759–60.

56. James D. Head, J. B. Thompson, and W. R. Samuel to Major General William S. Rosecrans, Huntsville, July 18, 1864, *OR,* XLI (2): 235.

57. Deposition of Robert L. Pollard, *United States vs. Josephus Woodcock,* Andrew County, November 3, 1863, Two or More Name Citizen File 2637, Record Group 393, N.A. On vigilantism, the best analyses are contained in H. Jon Rosenbaum and Peter C. Sederberg (eds.), *Vigilante Politics* (Philadelphia: University of Pennsylvania Press, 1974), and in the excellent works of Richard Maxwell Brown, most succinctly in *Strain of Violence: Historical Studies of American Violence and Vigilantism* (New York: Oxford University Press, 1975), 93–179. Rosenbaum and Sederberg define vigilantism as "acts or threats of coercion in violation of the formal boundaries of an established sociopolitical order which, however, are intended by the violators to defend that order from some form of subversion" (p. 4). In language which more nearly captures the spirit of the institution, Brown defines it as a "conservative mob gathered to carry out a violent sanctification of the deeply cherished values of life and property" (p. 97).

58. Deposition of Leo B. Manning, Chillicothe, November 8, 1863, Odon Guitar Papers, JC.

59. W. L. Bone to Professor Mims, Independence, December 22, 1863, W. L. Bone Letters, JCHS.

60. Charles Sheppard to Henry, Springfield, October 17, 1864, Sheppard Family Papers, JC.

61. Lieutenant Colonel T. A. Switzler to Brigadier General E. B. Brown, Warsaw, August 11, 1863, *OR,* XXII (2): 446.

62. Charles Monroe Chase to the Editor of the (Sycamore, Illinois) *True Republican and Sentinel,* St. Joseph, August 7, 1863, reprinted in Lela Barnes (ed.), "An Editor Looks at Early-Day Kansas: The Letters of Charles Monroe Chase," *Kansas Historical Quarterly,* XXVI (Summer 1960): 113–51, at pp. 115–16.

63. Brigadier General Richard C. Vaughan to General S. R. Curtis, Headquarters, 5th Military District, February 11, 1863, Letters Received File 367, Record Group 393, NA.

64. Brigadier General Benjamin Loan developed this analysis in a series of letters written in 1862 from his district headquarters in Jefferson City to General Samuel R. Curtis, his commander in St. Louis, November 14, 16, 19, 1862, *OR,* XIII: 791–92, 798–99, 806–07. On the warehouse fire at Brunswick see Captain E. J. Crandall to Brigadier General Clinton B. Fisk, Brookfield, November 23, 1864, *OR,* XLI (4): 658.

65. W. W. Moses to Miss Mary Mowry, Humbolt, Kansas, February 13, 1862, Webster W. Moses Collection, KSHS.

66. W. A. Brannock to his Son, Pleasant Hill, February 26, 1865, W. A. Brannock Family Letters, JCHS.

67. J. W. Woods to Aunt Zelia, Newton County, May 2, June 2, 1864, Woods-Holman Family Papers, JC; John _____ to Doctor J. F. Snyder, Bolivar, June 16, 1863, John F. Snyder Papers, Ill.SHL; Samuel Ayres to L. Langdon, Koueka, Kansas, June 1, 1863, Samuel Ayres Papers, KSHS.

68. The best single historical analysis of psychological numbing is Robert Jay

Lifton, *Death in Life: Survivors of Hiroshima* (New York: Basic Books, 1982).

69. S. W. Richey to E. E. Harris, Paris, Texas, July 25, 1863, Bland Collection, JCHS.
70. H. L. Brolaski to Brigadier General Davidson, Kinswick, May 18, 1863, Two or More Name Citizen File 2637, Record Group 393, NA.
71. Emma Tizer to the Provost Marshal, Arrow Rock, September 24, 1863, Provost Marshal Letters Received File 2786, Record Group 393, NA. Tizer made her plea in a language suggesting that it was basically personal and not political. In her supplication she demonstrated belief in some higher, just authority in the provost marshal's personage, "Oh if he dont soon get out he will die and then I dont know what will become of me and my baby—My dear good sir will you please look into his case and give him a fair and just trial. He cant be hurt for he has never done enething toward aiding in this rebellion."
72. Thomas E. Birch to Dr. J. P. Vaughan, [Howard County], October 3, 1863, Abiel Leonard Collection, JC.
73. L. H. Rogers to General Odon Guitar, n.p., October 8, 1862, Odon Guitar Papers, JC.
74. Thomas J. Babcock to General William S. Rosecrans, Mt. Pleasant, September 5, 1864, Provost Marshal Letters Received File 2786, Record Group 393, NA.
75. G. O. Yeiser to Brigadier General J. M. Schofield, Mexico, July 19, 1862, Letters Received File 367, NA. See Frank L. Klement, *Dark Lanterns: Secret Political Societies, Conspiracies and Treason Trials in the Civil War* (Baton Rouge: Louisiana State University Press 1984). For a general analysis of nineteenth-century conspiracy theories see David Brion Davis, *The Slave Power Conspiracy and the Paranoid Style* (Baton Rouge: Louisiana State University Press, 1969); Richard S. Hofstadter, *The Paranoid Style in American Politics* (New York: Knopf, 1965).
76. Brigadier General Clinton B. Fisk to Colonel John V. DuBois, St. Joseph, November 12, 1864, *OR*, XLI (4): 548.
77. "A Friend" to the Provost Marshal, St. Louis, May 26, 1863, Provost Marshal Letters Received File 2786, Record Group 393, NA.
78. Lieutenant Colonel T. A. Switzler to Brigadier General E. B. Brown, Warsaw, August 11, 1863, *OR*, XXII (2): 446.
79. Deposition of F. F. Sheppard, Independence, May 3, 1862, Two or More Name Citizen File 2637, Record Group 393, NA.
80. Brigadier General E. B. Brown to Major Oliver D. Greene, Jefferson City, November 4, 1863, *OR*, XXII (2): 694.
81. Entry for January 26, 1864, David R. Braden Diary, KSHS.
82. Private Sanford Bullock to General [Odon Guitar], Fayette, September 9, 1863, Odon Guitar Papers, JC.
83. J. H. Ellis to Colonel _____, Chillicothe, February 24, 1863, Odon Guitar Papers, JC. Much of the material in this section first appeared in my article "Emancipation in Missouri," in *MHR*, LXXXIII (October, 1988), and is reprinted with the permission of the State Historical Society of Missouri.
84. See Abraham Lincoln to John C. Frémont, September 2, 11, 1861, in

Roy P. Basler (ed.), *The Collected Works of Abraham Lincoln* (New Brunswick: Rutgers University Press, 1953), IV: 506–7, 517–18; and Andrew Rolle, *He Must Blaze a Nation: The Controversial John Charles Frémont* (forthcoming), chap. 15.

85. Dan Holmes to his Parents, Kansas City, November 15, 1861, Daniel B. Holmes Correspondence, CHS; Benjamin Quarles, *The Negro in the Civil War* (Boston: Little, Brown, 1953), 20. Daniel Holmes did not approve of such independent abolitionism by army units, if it was not official Union military policy. "I don't fight under any other banner than the Stars and Stripes; if Col. Jennison pursues a course the government will not sanction I don't fight with him."

86. A. J. McRoberts to Molie, Saline County, April 19, 1863, A. J. McRoberts Papers, JC; Lieutenant Colonel A. Krekel to General John M. Schofield, St. Charles, March 10, 1862, *OR,* VIII, 333.

87. Ephram J. Wilson to General Odon Guitar, near Palmyra, July 27, 1863, Odon Guitar Papers, JC.

88. Stanley E. Lathrop to his Parents, Wittsburg, Arkansas, July 18, 1862, Stanley E. Lathrop Correspondence, Wis. SHS.

89. Charles E. Cunningham to Governor H. R. Gamble, Sedelia, August 13, 1862, Missouri Militia Papers, Duke.

90. James L. Morgan to James M. Nash, Glasgow, July 30, 1863, James Lorenzo Morgan Papers, UNC.

91. Margaret J. Hayes to her Mother, Westport, November 12, 1861, Margaret J. Hayes Papers, JCHS.

92. J. B. Henderson to J. O. Broadhead, Louisiana, October 23, 1862, James O. Broadhead Papers, MHS—St.L., R. C. Vaughan to J. O. Broadhead, Lexington, May 8, 1863, in Broadhead Papers. White male sexual fears of black men are a central theme in Joel Kovel, *White Racism: A Psychohistory* (New York: Vintage, 1970).

93. "In the matter of John Lemmel," Osage County, January 28, 1864, Provost Marshal Letters Received File 2786, Record Group 393, NA. Subsequent events became complicated. The Osage County constable had John Lemmel, a white colleague of Jim, arrested for shooting at Reynolds. The provost marshal arrested Reynolds in return, claiming that his sons, supporters, and the constables were a pack of copperheads and returned rebels. The military disallowed a civil trial of Reynolds in part because they were sure Lemmel would be shot if he turned up to testify. It is not clear from the record if Reynolds was eventually tried by a military tribunal.

94. Included in the letter of A. H. Lancaster to the Provost Marshal at Hannibal, New London, March 16, 1865, Letters Received File 2593, Record Group 393, NA.

95. S. F. Aglar to General William S. Rosecrans, St. Louis, November 17, 1864, Letters Received File 2593, Record Group 393, NA.

96. Deposition of Paris Bass, Calloway County, Two or More Name Citizen File 2637, Record Group 393, NA.

97. Court-Martial of Fanny Houx, Warrensburg, July 19, 1864, Case NN 2733, Record Group 153, NA. After the 1861 engagement at Boonville where the pro-southern state militia was routed, one Union soldier reported the

death of the richest Confederate leader: "Five negroes brought the news of the intended attack and were inside the entrenchment during the engagement. Among them was a slave of Col. Brown's. Whilst fighting he took hold of a gun and shot his master who fell and soon after expired. The darky is tickled almost to death." Dan Smith to his Parents, Boonville, September 17, 1861, Daniel R. Smith Papers, Ill.SHL.

98. P. Welsheimer to his Family, Mexico, July 21, 1861, Philip Welsheimer Papers, Ill.SHL.

99. Stanley Lathrop to his Family, Wittsburg, Arkansas, July 18, 1862, Stanley E. Lathrop Correspondence, Wis.SHS. Similarly, General Samuel R. Curtis wrote to his brother from northern Arkansas earlier in 1862, "The poor ignorant people of this country are to be pitied. The monstrous lies that have been told of us have frightened everybody to death, and the men have run away leaving their wives and little ones poorly provided and subject to the demands of my hungry troops many of whom have been four days without bread. Even the sick were unprovided for and I am obliged not only to improvise a system of supplies for my men but also for the families and the sick of the enemy." Samuel R. Curtis to Henry B. Curtis, Camp Halleck, Arkansas, February 25, 1862, Samuel R. Curtis Manuscripts, Huntington.

100. Calvin _____ to his Brother, Independence [1861], J. C. Iserman Letters, JCHS.

101. [N.A.], to her Aunt Linda, July 31, 1863, Phineas M. Savery Papers, Duke; Mary Bedford to A. M. Bedford, n.p., July 1, 1863, Bedford Family Papers, JC.

102. Thomas H. Hess to the Provost Marshal, Green Hill, April 6, 1864, Provost Marshal Letters Received File 2786, Record Group 393, NA.

103. P. J. Bond to Dr. J. F. Snyder, Columbia, May 10, 1863, John F. Snyder Papers, Ill.SHL.

104. J. L. Morgan to his Brother, New York, October 27, 1864, James Lorenzo Morgan Papers, UNC.

105. Sarah McDonald to her Children, St. Louis, January 18, 1865, Charles B. France Papers, JC.

106. P. Welsheimer to his Family, Salt Creek, July 16, 1861, Philip Welsheimer Papers, Ill.SHL.

107. H. C. Crawford to W. H. Crawford, Springfield, June 13, 1862, H. C. and W. H. Crawford Letters, JC.

108. John A. Martin to his Sister, Westport, December 31, 1861, Josephine B. Martin Papers, KSHS. Samuel Ayres, also from Kansas, commented in a parallel manner about West Point, "a few months since a thriving border town doing quite a lively business but now O how *desolate*. But one family I think is living in the town. The remaining buildings are now standing empty with their door and windows open or broken in except those which are occupied by soldiers and their horses. Such are the blighting, *destructive* effects of war." Samuel Ayres to L. Langdon, Humbolt, Kansas, February 17, 1862, Samuel Ayres Collection, KSHS. Henry Dysart wrote about the appearance of Springfield after the departure of the Confederate army which greeted the Union soldiers as they entered the town. "The

houses have all been desecrated by [southern] soldiers and furniture destroyed. The filth in every house makes it appear more like a slaughter pen than a dwelling." Entry for February 17, 1862, Henry Dysart Diary, Iowa SHS. The desecration of the home was the desecration of the domestic temple for Dysart and many of his comrades. Destruction and dirt marked everything, put where cleanliness ought to demarcate the living zone of the proper family.

109. J. Freeman to W. A. Brannock, Pleasant Hill, May 30, 1864, W. A. Brannock Family Letters, JCHS; "Miles" to the Editor of the *Iowa City Republican,* Salem, January 3, 1863, Iowa SHS.

110. W. A. Wilson to Jeanette [Wilson], Marshall, December 11, 1864, Abiel Leonard Collection, JC.

111. A. Comingo to James O. Broadhead, Lexington, August 30, 1863, James O. Broadhead Papers, MHS—St.L; Comingo and R. C. Vaughan to Hamilton R. Gamble, Lexington, October 30, 1863, Hamilton R. Gamble Papers, MHS—St.L.

112. Brigadier General John McNeil to Major General Grenville M. Dodge, Warrensburg, March 15, 1865, *OR,* XLVIII (1): 1183.

113. Entries for February 22 through June 4, 1863, Forseyth, Huntsville and Rolla, Diary of Timothy Phillips, Wis.SHS.

114. Entry for July 30, 1863, Civil War Journal of Francis Springer, Ill.SHL. Springer began his reflections by stating that, "In the midst of continual violence and alarm, we soon learn to be comparatively indifferent. Such is the deadening effect of a state of war. Its dangers and cruelties gradually cease to make a strong impression in minds daily rendered more callous by its spirit of bravado and revenge and [amid] destruction of property and life." Springer was referring to a desensitizing he feared was occurring within him as well as in and between others. What he then wrote demonstrated his continued compassion. But he could not absorb directly all the misery from the refugees and was hard on himself in his high expectations that he should be able always to do so. Seemingly dispassionate observations such as he wrote were a means to maintain enough inner composure to carry on fighting war while remaining responsive to the emotions and needs of others.

CHAPTER 3. OFFICIAL ATTITUDES

1. General-in-Chief H. W. Halleck to Dr. Francis Lieber, Washington, August 6, 1862, and Lieber's reply, "Guerrilla Parties Considered with Reference to the Laws & Usages of War," *OR,* Series 3, II: 301–9. In addition to legal treatises, Lieber's chief historical sources, which focused on Napoleon and the Spanish guerrillas of the Carlist wars, were W. F. P. Napier, *History of the War in the Peninsula* . . . , 6 vols. (London: Thomas & Wliliam Boone, 1834–60), especially Vol. IV, Book XVII, chap. 2, 23–44, and François Guizot, *Memoirs* . . . , 6 vols. (London: R. Bentley, 1861), IV:

92–116. Halleck's brief analysis of guerrilla war appeared in *International Law, or Rules Regulating the Intercourse of States in Peace and War* (San Francisco: H. H. Bancroft, 1861), 386–88. On Mosby and the other Partisan Rangers in western Virginia see two books by Virgil Carrington Jones, *Gray Ghosts and Rebel Raiders* (New York: Henry Holt, 1956) and *Ranger Mosby* (Chapel Hill: University of North Carolina Press, 1944), and Charles W. Russell (ed.), *The Memoirs of Colonel John F. Mosby* (Boston: Little, Brown, 1917). The most complete analysis of martial law is Charles Fairman, *The Law of Martial Rule,* 2d ed. (Chicago: Callaghan, 1943).

2. War Department, General Orders #100, Washington, April 24, 1863, *OR,* Series 3, III: 148–64.

3. Abraham Lincoln to General John M. Schofield, Washington, May 27, 1863, in Roy P. Basler (ed.), *The Collected Works of Abraham Lincoln,* 8 vols. (New Brunswick: Rutgers University Press, 1953), VI: 234.

4. Lincoln to Charles D. Drake and others, Washington, October 5, 1863, in Basler, VI: 500.

5. Lincoln to Thomas C. Fletcher, Washington, February 20, 1865, in Basler, VIII: 308.

6. Fletcher to Lincoln, Jefferson City, February 27, 1865, in Basler, VIII: 319–20, n.1.

7. Edward Bates to H. R. Gamble, Washington, July 24, 1862, Edward Bates Collection, MHS—St.L.

8. Report of R. B. Marcy, Inspector-General, United States Army to O. D. Green, St. Louis, March 29, 1864, *OR,* XXXIV (2): 776.

9. General Orders #2, St. Louis, March 13, 1862, *OR,* VIII: 611–12. Richard S. Brownlee, in his *Gray Ghosts of the Confederacy* (Baton Rouge: Louisiana State University Press, 1958), 65, focuses on this order as the cause of mutual extermination, with guerrillas responding in kind to a policy originated by Halleck. It seems more likely to me that Halleck's orders merely recognized and licensed for Union troops practices that men on both sides already had instituted in the field. Of course, after they received news of the orders, guerrillas would have had all the more reason neither to be taken prisoner nor to take prisoners.

10. Major General H. W. Hallack to General George B. McClellan, St. Louis, December 6, 1861; Halleck to Hon. Thomas Ewing, St. Louis, January 1, 1862, *OR,* VIII: 409, 476.

11. General Orders #46, St. Louis, February 22, 1862, *OR,* VIII: 563–64.

12. General Orders #30, St. Louis, April 22, 1863, *OR,* XXII (2): 239.

13. Hamilton R. Gamble to Abraham Lincoln, Jefferson City, August 26, 1861, Hamilton R. Gamble Papers, MHS—St.L. Also see Wilbert H. Rosin, "Hamilton Rowan Gamble, Missouri's Wartime Governor," Ph.D dissertation, University of Missouri, 1960; John F. Phillips, "Hamilton Gamble and the Provisional Government of Missouri," *MHR,* V (October 1910): 1–14; Marguerite Potter, "Hamilton R. Gamble, Missouri's Wartime Governor," *MHR,* XXXV (October 1940): 25–71.

14. Hamilton R. Gamble, "Message to Fifth Session of the State Convention,"

June 15, 1863 in Buel Leopard and Floyd C. Shoemaker (eds.), *The Messages and Proclamations of the Governors of the State of Missouri* (Columbia: State Historical Society of Missouri, 1922), III: 459–60.

15. Brigadier General J. M. Schofield to Hon. E. M. Stanton, St. Louis, May 16, 1862, *OR*, XIII: 386.

16. Biennial Message of Willard Preble Hall, in *Messages and Proclamations*, IV: 9–10. For a clear analysis of the emphasis on human freedom in frontier Christianity see Sidney E. Ahlstrom, *A Religious History of the American People* (New Haven: Yale University Press, 1972), 429–54. One should always emphasize, I believe, that this same Protestant religion continued to contain more Calvinist elements. On the furious civil expressions of the Calvinist streak in American Protestantism projected onto Indians, the best study is Richard Slotkin, *Regeneration Through Violence: The Mythology of the American Frontier, 1600–1860* (Middletown: Wesleyan University Press, 1973).

17. Barton Bates to Edward Bates, Chevrieux, St. Charles County, September 8, 1861, Edward Bates Collection, MHS—St.L.

18. Brigadier General Thomas Ewing, Jr., to Commanding Officer, St. Louis, June 7, 1864, *OR*, XXXIV (4): 260–61.

19. Major General S. R. Curtis to Hon. Benjamin Loan, St. Joseph, July 19, 1864, *OR*, XLI (2): 275.

20. Brigadier General John M. Schofield to Brigadier General B. M. Prentiss, St. Louis, January 11, 1862, *OR*, VIII: 494; Schofield to Brigadier General Odon Guitar, St. Louis, September 14, 1863, in Register of Courts-Martial File 2751, Record Group 393, NA; Brigadier General Benjamin Loan to Schofield, St. Joseph, May 31, 1862, Missouri State Militia Letters Received File 2909, Record Group 393, NA.

21. These standard forms were adopted in General Orders #30, St. Louis, April 22, 1863, *OR*, XXII (2): 243.

22. Brigadier General John Pope to Brigadier General Stephen A. Hurlbut, St. Louis, August 17, 1861, *OR*, Series 2, I: 211–12; General Orders #24, St. Louis, December 12, 1861, *OR*, VIII: 431–32; General Orders #3, St. Louis, June 23, 1862, *OR*, XIII: 446–47.

23. Lincoln to Major General Samuel R. Curtis, Washington, January 5, 1863, in Basler, VI: 36–38; Curtis to Lincoln, January 15, 1863, *OR*, XXII (2): 42–43; E. M. Stanton to Curtis, Washington, January 20, 1864, *OR*, XXII (2): 64. Also see Brownlee, *Gray Ghosts*, 165–69, and the thorough discussion by W. Wayne Smith, "An Experiment in Counterinsurgency: The Assessment of Confederate Sympathizers in Missouri," *Journal of Southern History*, XXXV (August 1969): 361–80.

24. General Orders #11, Kansas City, August 25, 1863, *OR*, XXII (2): 473. Of the many analyses of General Orders #11, the fullest are Ann Davis Niepman, "General Orders No. 11 and Border Warfare During the Civil War," *MHR*, LXVI (January 1972): 185–210, and Charles R. Mink, "General Orders No. 11: The Forced Evacuation of Civilians During the Civil War," *Military Affairs*, XXXIV (December 1970): 132–36.

25. Major General John M. Schofield to Governor Thomas Carney, August 27, 1863, Thomas C. Stevens Papers, KSHS; Report of General John M. Scho-

field to Colonel E. D. Townsend, St. Louis, September 14, 1863, *OR*, XXII (1): 572–75; General-in-Chief H. W. Halleck, General Report for 1863, Washington, November 25, 1863, *OR*, XXII (1): 11.

26. General Orders #30, Adjutant and Inspector General's Office, Richmond, April 28, 1862, *OR*, Series 4, I: 1094–95, 1098.

27. Henry T. Clark to Hon. G. W. Randolph, Raleigh, July 13, 31, 1862, *OR*, Series 4, II: 4–5, 31.

28. Secretary of War James A. Seddon, Annual Report, Richmond, November 26, 1863, *OR*, Series 4, II: 1003.

29. Brigadier General Thomas L. Rosser to General Robert E. Lee, Headquarters Valley District, January 11, 1864, *OR*, XXXIII: 1081.

30. General Robert E. Lee to General S. Cooper, Headquarters, Army of Northern Virginia, April 1, 1864, *OR*, XXXIII: 1252; Act of Congress, April 21, 1864, *OR*, Series 4, III: 194.

31. Here I am trying to explain some of the reasons why the Confederate leadership refused to adopt guerrilla warfare wholesale, which might well have won them the war according to Richard E. Beringer et al., *Why the South Lost the Civil War* (Athens: University of Georgia Press, 1986).

32. Thomas C. Reynolds to Jefferson Davis, Abbeville, South Carolina, August 17, 1862, Eldridge Collection, Huntington; Thomas A. Harris to George W. Randolph, Richmond, June 10, 1862, *OR*, XIII: 833–35.

33. Colonel C. Franklin to President Jefferson Davis, Camp Bragg, Arkansas, November 6, 1863, *OR*, XXII (2): 1058–60. Marmaduke was as well-born and nicely bred a landed gentleman as Missouri could offer. Franklin probable thought Marmaduke had fallen from grace by bad behavior.

34. Richmond *Daily Dispatch*, September 1, 1863, quoted in Mink, "General Orders No. 11," 135.

35. General Report of Major General Thomas C. Hindman, Richmond, June 29, 1862, *OR*, XIII: 29–51, especially at p. 45.

36. General Orders #17, Headquarters Trans-Mississippi District, Little Rock, Arkansas, June 17, 1862, *OR*, XIII: 835.

37. Thomas C. Hindman to Colonel W. P. Johnson, Ft. Smith, Arkansas, November 28, 1862, Waldo Porter Johnson Letters, JC.

38. General Orders #187, Headquarters District of Texas, New Mexico, and Arizona; Houston, Texas, October 19, 1863, *OR*, XXVI (2): 339–40; Major General Sterling Price to Governor Thomas C. Reynolds, Camp Bragg, November 2, 1863, *OR*, LIII: 907–8; Major Maclean to Col. William C. Quantrill, Camp Bragg, November 2, 1863, in *OR*, LIII: 907–8. Quantrill had reported his exploits to Price on October 13, *OR*, XXII (1): 700–701.

39. Brigadier General Henry E. McCulloch to Captain Edmund P. Turner, Bonham, Texas, October 22, November 1, 1863, *OR*, XXVI (2): 348, 379.

40. Lieutenant General E. Kirby Smith to Lieutenant General T. H. Holmes, Shreveport, Louisiana, June 4, 1863, *OR*, XXII (2): 856; Smith to H. E. McCulloch, Shreveport, November 2, 1863, *OR*, XXVI (2): 382–83. On November 19, after Quantrill's visit, Smith, clearly having accepted Quantrill's analysis of the soldiers involved, wrote to McCulloch suggesting the employment of Quantrill to entrap deserters, *OR*, XXII (2): 1072–73.

41. Brigadier General H. E. McCulloch to Major General J. B. Magruder, Bonham, February 3, 1864, *OR,* XXXIV (2): 942; McCulloch to Brigadier General H. P. Bee, Bonham, February 9, 1864, *OR,* XXXIV (2): 957–58; McCulloch to Captain E. P. Turner, Bonham, April 6, 1864, *OR,* XXXIV (3): 742.
42. Governor Thomas C. Reynolds to Brigadier General Joseph O. Shelby, Arkadelphia, Arkansas, September 19, 1863; Reynolds to Major E. C. Cabell, Marshall, Texas, January 5, 1864; Reynolds to Colonel D. C. Hunter, Marshall, January 16, 1864, all in the Thomas C. Reynolds Papers, LC.
43. Court-Martial of John Thrailkill, St. Louis, January 23, 1864, Case NN 1233, Record Group 153, NA. When Thrailkill told this story in court he was not contradicted. He must have been believed, for the court sentenced him to imprisonment for the duration of the war.
44. Statement of Mike Kelly, Rolla, September 7, 1864, Letters Received File 367, Record Group 393, NA.
45. John H. Winston and John C. C. Thornton to Major General Price, n.p., November 22, 1863; Price to Winston and Thornton, Camp Bragg, January 3, 1864, Eldridge Collection, Huntington.
46. Governor Thomas C. Reynolds to General Sterling Price, Marshall, July 18, 1864, *OR,* XLI (2): 1011–12.
47. Sterling Price to Thomas C. Reynolds, Camden, Arkansas, July 22, 1864, *OR,* XLI (2): 1020; Brigadier General J. O. Shelby to Lieutenant Colonel J. F. Belton, White River, Arkansas, August 9, 1864, *OR,* XLI (1): 192.
48. Lieutenant General E. Kirby Smith to Major General Sterling Price, Shreveport, August 4, 1864, *OR,* XLI (2): 1040.
49. The 1864 Confederate army revival is discussed in Robert T. Handy, *A Christian America: Protestant Hopes and Historical Realities,* 2d ed. (New York: Oxford University Press, 1984), 237 n.39, and in James W. Silver, *Confederate Morale and Church Propaganda* (Tuscaloosa: Confederate Publishing, 1957), 38–39. The fullest accounts of American revitalization movements concern those among American Indians. See, for example, David H. Miller, *Ghost Dance* (New York: Duell, Sloan & Pearce, 1959); Robert M. Utley, *The Last Days of the Sioux Nation* (New Haven: Yale University Press, 1963); and most notably, Anthony F. C. Wallace, *The Death and Rebirth of the Seneca* (New York: Knopf, 1970), 239–337. Also see Wallace's excellent theoretical essay, "Revitalization Movements: Some Theoretical Consideration for Their Comparative Study," *American Anthropologist,* LVIII (1956): 264–81.
50. The best depictions of Price's raid are in Stephen B. Oates, *Confederate Cavalry West of the River,* (Austin: University of Texas Press, 1961), 113–54; Brownlee, *Gray Ghosts,* 206–27; Jay Monaghan, *Civil War on the Western Border, 1854–1865* (Boston: Little, Brown, 1955), 307–45; Albert Castel, *General Sterling Price and the Civil War in the West* (Baton Rouge: Louisiana State University Press, 1968), 196–255; and Robert E. Shalhope, *Sterling Price: Portrait of a Southerner* (Columbia: University of Missouri Press, 1971), 256–80. Beringer et al., in *Why The South Lost the Civil*

War, 183, argue that the Confederates misunderstood the tactical nature of raids, looking at the necessary retreats at the end of raids as defeats. This was another example of the handicaps of honor with which the southern gentry willingly hobbled itself.

51. Thomas C. Reynolds to Sterling Price, near Boonville, October 10, 1864, Thomas C. Reynolds Papers, MHS—St.L.

52. Special Orders, Boonville, October 11, 1864, *OR*, XLI (4): 354; Brownlee, *Gray Ghosts*, 224.

53. Major General William S. Rosecrans to Major General Sterling Price, Lexington, October 22, 1864, *OR*, XLI (4): 1011.

54. John S. Price to Dear Old Friend, Boonville, November 21, 1864, John F. Snyder Papers, Ill.SHL. On Centralia the best brief account is in Brownlee, *Gray Ghosts*, 216–20.

55. Major General Sterling Price to Brigadier General W. R. Boggs, Washington, Arkansas, December 28, 1864, *OR*, XLI (1): 632. The proceedings of Price's court-martial, which convened in Shreveport on March 8, 1865, are in *OR*, XLI: 701–29.

56. Secretary of War, *Missouri Troops in Service During the Civil War* (Washington: Government Printing Office, 1902).

57. Colonel J. H. Shankling to Brigadier General Clinton B. Fisk, Chillicothe, August 6, 1864, *OR*, XLI (2): 587; Provost Marshal William R. Strachan to the *New York Times*, Palmyra, December 10, 1862, reprinted in *OR*, XXII (1): 861–66.

58. Samuel N. Wood to Colonel S. N. Boyd, Houston, March 29, 1862, Samuel N. Wood Papers, KSHS; Major General Samuel R. Curtis to Colonel Woodson, Ft. Leavenworth, Kansas, January 27, 1864, *OR*, XXXIV (2): 169.

59. Major Henry Neill to Colonel James McFerran, Clinton, April 1, 1864, *OR*, XXXIV (3): 10. In 1862, General McClellan had fought an intentionally limited war, attempting to achieve reconciliation rather than conquest.

60. By 1864, General William T. Sherman implemented total war on a grand scale in a manner much like the hards in Missouri of 1862, who had argued that those back East did not understand the true nature of civil war. In this sense, the argument over means in Missouri was an early, microcosmic version of the debate between war Democrats and radical Republicans in the North as a whole. In both instances the call to radicalism increased during the war. Lincoln accepted much of the hard line in practice, although he emphasized his retained desires for a later reconciliation.

61. Captain E. J. Crandall to General Clinton B. Fisk, Brookfield, June 4, 1864; G. A. Holloway to Crandall, St. Joseph, June 4, 1864, *OR*, XXXIV (4): 225–26.

62. Captain W. E. Prince to Major Robert T. Van Horn, Ft. Leavenworth, August 14, 1861, Robert T. Van Horn Papers, JC.

63. General Orders #5, issued by Major George M. Houston, Macon City, August 20, 1862, *OR*, XIII: 588.

64. Record of Orren A. Curtis, KSHS.

65. Brigadier General Benjamin Loan to Lieutenant Colonel C. W. Marsh, St. Joseph, May 25, 1862, Missouri State Militia Letters Received File 2909, Record Group 393, NA.

66. Brigadier General E. B. Brown to Colonel John C. Tracy, Springfield, July 14, 1862, OR, XIII: 471.

67. Benjamin Loan to Hamilton R. Gamble, Jefferson City, October 13, 1862, Hamilton R. Gamble Papers, MHS—St.L.

68. Colonel J. T. K. Hayward to Brigadier General Clinton B. Fisk, Brookfield, August 1, 1864, OR, XLI (2): 508.

69. Exchange between Colonel J. B. Rogers, Cape Girardeau, and Brigadier General Clinton B. Fisk, St. Louis, February 6, 1864, OR, XXXIV (2): 253–54.

70. Brigadier General Clinton B. Fisk to Major Samuel A. Garth, Macon, January 10, 1865, OR, XLVIII (1): 485.

71. Captain R. M. Box to Colonel John F. Phillips, Warrensburg, January 25, 1865; Phillips to Major General Grenville M. Dodge, Warrensburg, February 8; Dodge to Assistant Adjutant General W. A. Nichols, St. Louis, February 19, 1865, all in OR, XLVIII (1): 643–45.

72. Captain John D. Meredith to Assistant Adjutant General J. H. Waite, Glasgow, March 24, 1865; Brigadier General Clinton B. Fisk to Major General Grenville M. Dodge, Macon, March 31, both in OR, XLVIII (1): 132–35.

73. Special Orders #47, Jefferson City, April 21, 1862, OR, Series 2, III: 468; General Orders #18, St. Louis, May 29, 1862, OR, Series 2, III: 607–8.

74. Major General Samuel R. Curtis to S. E. Brown, Esq., Wyandotte, Kansas, October 15, 1864, OR, XLI (3): 899–900.

75. Major General Samuel R. Curtis to Captain J. C. Kelton, Batesville, May 19, 1862, OR, XIII: 392; Colonel James H. Ford to O. D. Greene, Independence, July 26, 1864, Two or More Name File 2635, Record Group 393, NA; George Wolz to his Parents, Springfield, August 11, 1862, Civil War Letter, JC.

76. Lieutenant Colonel Bazel F. Lazear to Captain Dyer, Jackson, February 14, 1863, OR, XXII (1): 224–25.

77. William C. Long to his Children, Butler, December 23, 1863, William C. Long Papers, JC; Captain Thomas Thomas to Captain J. Lovell, Houston, Missouri, January 11, 1864, OR, XXXIV (2): 57.

78. Major F. W. Reeder to Lieutenant Colonel Bazel F. Lazear, Jackson, February 7, 1863, OR, XXII (1): 226.

79. First Lieutenant John W. Boyd to Captain Richard Murphy, Houston, November, 1863; Boyd to Captain J. Lovell, Houston, November 23, 1863, OR, XXII (1): 746–49.

80. Captain W. T. Leeper to Brigadier General Clinton B. Fisk, Patterson, March 5, 1864, OR, XXXIV (2): 506; Lieutenant Colonel Bazel F. Lazear to Captain Steger, Marshall, August 10, 1864, OR, XLI (1): 220; District of Central Missouri General Orders #57, Jefferson City, September 17, 1863, contained in the records of the Court-Martial of Francis Norvell, Case MM 1258, Record Group 153, NA.

81. Colonel W. R. Penick to Major General Samuel R. Curtis, Independence, March 23, 1863, OR, XXII (1): 244.

82. Bazel F. Lazear to his Wife, n.p., August 11, 1864, Bazel F. Lazear Collection, JC; Colonel James McFerran to Brigadier General Thomas A. Ewing, Jr., Lexington, August 10, 1863, *OR*, XXII (1): 547.

83. District of Southwest Missouri, General Orders #1, Springfield, January 1, 1865, copy in the Dennis H. Connoway Papers, JC.

84. "Letter from the 22nd Regiment to the *Iowa City Republican*," Houston, January 14, 1863, Iowa SHS.

85. Major James A. Price to General Thomas A. Davies, Ft. Leavenworth, August 1, 1864, James A. Price Letters, JC.

86. Brigadier General Benjamin Loan to Major General Samuel R. Curtis, In the Field near Kansas City, February 26, 1862, Letters Received File 367, Record Group 393, NA.

87. Captain Eli J. Crandall to Brigadier General Clinton B. Fisk, Brookfield, June 20, 1864, *OR*, XXXIV (1): 1030.

88. First Lieutenant A. H. Engle to Major Frank J. White, St. Louis, April 7, 1862, Missouri State Militia Letters Received File 2909, Record Group 393, NA. Lieutenant Engle had been sent to St. James by Major White to investigate this incident.

89. Brigadier General E. B. Brown to Major General John M. Schofield, Warrensburg, September 29, 1863, Letters Received File 2593, Record Group 393, NA; Lieutenant William McIlwrath to Colonel J. H. Shanklin, Chillicothe, August 11, 1864, *OR*, XLI (2): 668–70.

90. Brigadier General J. B. Douglass to Brigadier General John B. Gray, Mexico, November 2, 1864, Missouri Militia Papers, Duke; Also see Lieutenant Isaac Gannett to Major R. A. De Bolt, Hannibal, March 14, 1865, Letters Received File 367, Record Group 393, NA. Major De Bolt, who was provost marshal for the central district of Missouri in 1865, the man in charge of investigating the lawlessness of the Fiftieth Regiment, Enrolled Missouri Militia, was none other than the Judge De Bolt who had led the jayhawkers terrorizing Grundy County in the summer of 1864. De Bolt, officer of the law, was a sometimes outlaw. One of the chief characteristics of this guerrilla war was its fluidity.

CHAPTER 4. BROTHER KILLERS

1. Court-Martial of Marion D. Erwin, alias Robert St. Clair, Macon, February 14, 1865, Case OO 303, Record Group 153, NA. Erwin was hanged on March 17.

2. Joseph C. Hart to his parents, July 13, 1863—a letter found on Hart's body and reprinted in the Liberty *Tribune,* July 24, 1863.

3. Joseph C. Hart to Captain W. G. Garth, June 27, 1863—a letter found on Hart's body and printed in the Liberty *Tribune,* July 31, 1863; Fletcher P. Taylor to Colonel Kemper, printed in the Liberty *Tribune,* July 8, 1864; William Coleman to S. N. Wood, April 3, 1862, Samuel N. Wood Papers, KSHS; Clifton D. Holtzclaw to Captain Stanley [Chariton County], July 29, 1864, *OR*, XLI (2): 894–95; W. Anderson to the editors of the two papers in Lexington, to the citizens and the community at large, General

Brown, and Colonel McFerran and his petty hirelings, such as Captain Burris, the friend of Anderson, July 7, 1864, *OR,* XLI (2): 75–77.

4. S. Cockerill to Major General Samuel R. Curtis, Camp Morgan, Jackson County, February 7, 1863, *OR,* XXII (2): 102.

5. Holtzclaw to Stanley, *OR,* XLI (2): 894–95; Hart to Garth, Liberty *Tribune,* July 31, 1863; Liberty *Tribune,* July 8, 1864.

6. Taylor to Kemper, Liberty *Tribune,* July 8, 1864.

7. Wedington to Colonel Clark, near Harrisonville, October 20, 1863, *OR,* XXII (II): 675.

8. W. Anderson to the editors, *OR,* XLI (2): 77.

9. Letters of William C. Quantrill to W. W. Scott and to his Mother, Ft. Wayne, Indiana, February 5, 1855; Stanton, Kansas Territory, July 9, 1857, January 22, 1858, January 26, February 8, March 25, 1860, William C. Quantrill Collection, Spencer Library, University of Kansas, reprinted in W. E. Connelley, *Quantrill and the Border Wars* (1910; reprint, New York: Pageant Book Co., 1956), 50–101.

10. J. Glenn Gray, *The Warriors: Reflections on Men in Battle* (New York: Harper & Row, 1970), 64.

11. John Warren to James A. Price, Washingtonville, June 30, 1864, James A. Price Letters, JC; Charles Neider (ed.), *The Autobiography of Mark Twain* (New York: Harper & Row, 1959), 78–79. I am indebted to Joshua Fellman for the reference to Twain.

12. Testimony of John Kinkaid and Samuel McGowan, "Proceedings of the Investigation of the Military Prison at Macon by Brigadier General Clinton B. Fisk," April 2, 1865, Two or More Name File 2635, Record Group 393, NA; Courts-Martial of George Caldwell, New Madrid, December 19, 1863, Case MM 1302, and of Henry A. Griffith, St. Joseph, September 7, 1864, Case LL 2638, Record Group 153, NA.

13. Court-Martial of James S. Blacketon, St. Louis, December 28, 1863, Case NN 1252, Record Group 153, NA; Statement of Samuel B. Fizer, Gratiot Street prison, St. Louis, April 24, 1863, Letters Received File 367, Record Group 393, NA; Testimony of Edward Johnson and James Christerman, "Proceedings of the Investigation . . . at Macon."

14. Testimony of James Goodfellow, "Proceedings of the Investigation . . . at Macon"; J. A. Wysong to General Merrill, Missouri *Statesman,* October 10, 1862; Court-Martial of Charles White, St. Louis, December 21, 1864, Case NN 3245; Court-Martial of John Estes, St. Louis, August 23, 1864, Case NN 2672; Court-Martial of Jackson Bawyer, St. Louis, September 8, 1864, Case NN 2737, Record Group 153, NA. The foolish Estes was also charged with raping Melinda Poage but satisfied the court that he had not forced her and that she was a bad girl to whom he had paid $1.00 to $1.50 for her favors four of five times.

15. Statement of Charles Watkins, "Proceedings of the Investigation . . . at Macon"; Proceedings against Stevenson and Hart, Provost Marshal Charges of Disloyalty File 2792, Record Group 393, NA.

16. Court-Martial of Reese Gott, Springfield, August 10, 1864, Case LL 2674; Court-Martial of Stephen R. Smith, St. Louis, July 15, 1864, Case NN

2125; Court-Martial of Charles Tatum, Springfield, July 26, 1864, Case LL 2616, Record Group 153, NA.

17. Court-Martial of William McDaniels, St. Joseph, May 19, 1863, Case MM 671, Record Group 153, NA. Mistake corrected in the original.

18. Court-Martial of Charles Wells, New Madrid, December 17, 1863, Case NN 1237, Record Group 153, NA.

19. W. H. Callaway to General Odon Guitar, Boone City, October 17, 1862, Odon Guitar Papers, JC. There is no record of a reply from Guitar.

20. Court-Martial of Charles White, St. Louis, December 21, 1864, Case NN 3245, Record Group 153, NA; Testimony of Lafayette Powell, John Brison, E. D. Roberts, John East, "Investigation of the Proceedings . . . at Macon"; Court-Martial of Warren Lee, St. Louis, July 4, 1864, Case LL 2213, Record Group 153, NA.

21. Statement of Willard Francis Hadly, Warrensburg, as reported in the Missouri *Statesman,* May 20, 1864.

22. Letters of S. S. Marrett to his "Companion," Lebanon, February 2, 1862; Keytesville, March 27 and March 29, 1862, S. S. Marrett Papers, Duke.

23. "Doubling," a term which is more precise than the more commonly used term "character splitting" is employed effectively in Robert Jay Lifton, *The Nazi Doctors: Medical Killing and the Psychology of Genocide* (New York: Basic Books, 1987).

24. Entries for February 2, 1862, St. Louis; April 19, 1862, Cassville, Henry Dysert Diary, Iowa SHS.

25. Uriah Eberhart to Lovicy, Ozark, November 11, 1862, Uriah Eberhart Letters, Wis.SHS. On revivalism among Civil War soldiers see Drew Gilpin Faust, "Christian Soldiers: The Meaning of Revivalism in the Southern Army," *Journal of Southern History,* LIII (February 1987): 63–90; James H. Moorhead, *American Apocalypse: Yankee Protestants and the Civil War* (New Haven: Yale University Press, 1978); William W. Bennett, *A Narrative of the Great Revivals Which Prevailed in the Southern Armies* (Philadelphia: Claxton, Demsen & Haffelfinger, 1877).

26. Charles W. Falker to his Wife, Ft. Scott, Kansas, May 2, 1865, Charles W. Falker Letters, Wis.SHS.

27. John J. Ingalls to his Brother, Atchison, Kansas, January 2, 1862, John J. Ingalls Collection, KSHS.

28. Entries for April 25, June 6, August 31, 1861, Henry M. Moore Diary, Beinecke.

29. Entries for June 27, 29, September 13, 18, 1861; February 1, July 19, September 1, 1862, Dr. Joseph H. Trego Diary, KSHS.

30. Letters of L. R. Webber to the John Stillman Brown Family, Lexington, January 11, 1862; Kansas City, February 1, 1862; Collierville, Tennessee, January 8, 1863; Memphis, January 16, 1863; Lake Providence, Louisiana, May 29, 1863, John Stillman Brown Family Papers, KSHS.

31. Dan Holmes to his family, Cass County, December 21, 30, 1861, Daniel B. Holmes Correspondence, CHS.

32. Entry for August 10, 1861, William W. Branson Diary, JC.

33. Entry for January 11, April 25, 1865, Daniel Burdette Leroy Diary, JC.

34. Dave Garver to his Sister, Casseyville [Cassville], April 15, 1862, David Garver Letters, UNC.

35. E. T. McLane to Cousin Sam, Springfield, April 1, 1863, Lucian B. Case Letters, CHS.

36. Webster W. Moses to Friends, Humbolt, Allen County, Kansas, March 14, 1862; Moses to Nancy Mowry, n.d., n.p., Webster W. Moses Collection, KSHS.

37. Philip Welsheimer to his Wife and Children, Riley County, April 5, 1862, Philip Welsheimer Papers, Ill.SHL.

38. L. R. Webber to John Stillman Brown, Joplin, February 1, 1862, John Stillman Brown Family Papers, KSHS.

39. Captain J. D. Thompson to Major Torrence, Warrensburg, March 30, 1862, *OR,* VIII: 356–58.

40. Stephen Z. Starr, *Jennison's Jayhawkers* (Baton Rouge: Louisiana State University Press, 1973), 119–90. The regiment carried on its foraging style in the deep South as it had in Missouri.

41. Notes from the General Court-Martial, Camp Defiance, Kansas, January 20, 1862, H. Miles Moore Papers, KSHS. Lieutenant Moore was the judge advocate at this post.

42. Charges against Captain Joseph Park, Jefferson City, August 16, 1863, in the Franklin D. Swap Papers, MHS—St.L; Brigadier General J. B. Douglass to Brigadier General Clinton B. Fisk, Mexico, August 31, 1864, *OR,* XLI (2): 963; Brigadier General E. C. Pike to Brigadier General Thomas Ewing, Washington, October 20, 1964, *OR,* XLI (4): 133.

43. H. P. Strong to his wife Sarah, Crowell's Farm, January 29, 1863, Dr. H. P. Strong Letters, Wis.SHS.

44. "Chasseur" to the (Council Bluffs, Iowa) *Weekly Nonpareil,* December 14, 1861, Iowa SHS. From reading hundreds of depositions, I would estimate that 20% of Missourians could not sign their own names, but that in certain remote rural districts, as many as 40 per cent could not sign their own names.

45. Entry for June 5, 1861, Clinton, Diary of Webster W. Moses, Webster W. Moses Collection, KSHS.

46. Stanley E. Lathrop to his Family, Bloomfield, May 9, 1862, Stanley E. Lathrop Correspondence, Wis.SHS. On northern beliefs in the degenerative effects of slavery see Eric Foner, *Free Soil, Free Labor, Free Men: The Ideology of the Republican Party Before the Civil War* (New York: Oxford University Press, 1970); Michael Fellman, "Theodore Parker and the Abolitionist Role in the 1850s," *Journal of American History,* LXI (December 1974): 666–84.

47. Captain Eli J. Crandall to Brigadier General Clinton B. Fisk, Brookfield, November 26, 1864, *OR,* XLI (1): 921–24.

48. Entry for October 3, 1862, Cape Girardeau, Diary of Coleman C. Chubb, Wis.SHS; Entries for January 18, 30, 1862, Weston, Diary of Charles D. Waldo, Wis. SHS.

49. Stanley E. Lathrop to his Family, Wittsburg, Arkansas, July 18, 1862, Stanley E. Lathrop Correspondence, Wis.SHS. Lathrop sent on a collection

of excerpts from his diary which he had entered on June 29 and July 4, near Cape Girardeau, Missouri.

50. Lieutenant Richard J. Mohr to Friend Mattie, Bird's Point, February 13, 1862, Richard J. Mohr Letters, Huntington.

51. Brigadier General Benjamin Loan to Major General Samuel R. Curtis, Jefferson City, January 27, 1863, *OR*, XXII (2): 80.

52. Henry C. and William Crawford to their Friends, Warsaw, August 19, 1863, H. C. and W. H. Crawford Letters, JC.

53. Dr. H. P. Strong to his Wife, West Plains, January 31, 1863, Dr. H. P. Strong Letters, Wis.SHS.

54. Edmund D. Newton to his Sisters, Cape Girardeau, May 12, 1862, Edmund D. Newton Papers, Wis.SHS.

55. Newton, May 12, 1862.

56. Entry for August 24, 1864, Jefferson City, Diary of Charles C. Curtiss, CHS.

57. E. C. Sackett to his Family, St. Joseph, December 27, 1861, Edwin C. Sackett Papers, Ill.SHL.

58. Charles E. Beecham to his Mother, Ft. Leavenworth, July 15, 1862, Charles E. Beecham Letters, Wis.SHS.

59. Entry for June 10, 1862, near Rolla, Henry Dysart Diary, Iowa SHS. Other lone strangers were more lethal. In the spring of 1862, one soldier wrote back from northern Arkansas about a foraging party drawn from his regiment which had left one man on guard outside a house they then had ransacked. "A 'native' rode up with a shotgun, and began talking to the sentinel, but watching an opportunity, shot the sentinel, and rode off again as fast as he could" and escaped. Ed to Friends at Home, Randolph County, Arkansas, April 26, 1862, Abby E. Stafford Papers, Duke.

60. H. P. Strong to his Wife, West Plains, January 31, 1863, Dr. H. P. Strong Papers, Wis.SHS; Major Edward B. Eno to Colonel William F. Cloud, Greenfield, May 29, 1863, *OR*, XXII (1): 330.

61. Letter of Lieutenant Colonel Bazel F. Lazear to _____, n.p., n.d., Bazel F. Lazear Papers, JC.

62. Entry for June 17, 1862, Eminence, Diary of Augustus Bondi, KSHS.

63. Entry for April 27, 1862, n.p., Diary of Dr. Joseph H. Trego, KSHS.

64. Thomas C. Fletcher to Lieutenant Colonel Bernard G. Farrar, Block House, Deck Bridge, Washington County, July 3, 1862, Letters Received File 367, Record Group 393, NA; Entry for April 21, 1862, Cassville, Henry Dysart Diary, Iowa SHS.

65. Entry for June 30, 1861, n.p., Diary of Henry J. Marsh, Wis.SHS.

66. William A. Richardson to his Parents, Sedelia, December 1, 1861, in George S. and William A. Richardson Letters, Iowa SHS.

67. Jeremiah D. Swart to his Parents, Cape Girardeau, May 26, 1862, Jeremiah D. Swart Letters, Wis.SHS.

68. Major J. B. Kaiser to Captain T. Lovell, Licking, May 2, 1863, Letters Received File 367, Record Group 393, NA.

69. Entries for July 19, September 6, 1864, March 3, 1865, Diary of Edward Theodor Hansen, LSU.

70. Abiel Leonard to Lieutenant Adam, Fayette, July 8, 1863, Abiel Leonard Collection, JC.

71. First Lieutenant W. T. Clarke to Major John M. Clark, St. Joseph, June 13, 1864, *OR*, XXXIV (4): 349.

72. Brigadier General John B. Sanborn to Honorable S. H. Boyd, Springfield, February 27, 1864, *OR*, XXXIV (2): 439.

73. D. K. Pitman to Hamilton R. Gamble, Cottleville, August 5, 1861; L. W. Burris to Gamble, Liberty, August 8, 1861, Hamilton R. Gamble Papers, MHS—St.L.

74. W. G. Guthers to General William S. Rosecrans, DeKalb, August 3, 1864, *OR*, XLI (2): 893–94; Brigadier General Clinton B. Fisk to Lieutenant Colonel Elias Parrott, St. Joseph, June 24, 1864, *OR* XXXIV (4): 540.

75. (Anon.) to the Keokuk *Weekly Gate City*, Warsaw, November 16, 1861, in "1st, 2nd & 3rd Iowa Cavalry in the Civil War Collection"; William A. Richardson to his Parents, Tipton, February 1, 1862, George and William A. Richardson Letters, both in Iowa SHS.

76. Statement of R. Helms, Jr., May 10, 1865, Transcript of Record for May, 1865, Assistant Provost Marshal, District of Central Missouri, Letters Received File 367, Record Group 393, NA.

77. Lieutenant William McIlwrath to Brigadier General Odon Guitar, Marshall, n.d., Odon Guitar Papers, JC.

78. Deposition of Edith Barker, Mexico, July 15, 1864, Two or More Name Citizen File 2637, Record Group 393, NA.

79. John S. Phelps to General John M. Schofield, Springfield, August 27, 1863, John M. Schofield Papers, LC.

80. Brigadier General Clinton B. Fisk to Colonel O. D. Greene, St. Joseph, June 8, 15, 1864; Hon. William A. Hall to Major General William S. Rosecrans, Huntsville, June 12, 1864; Fisk to Hon. William A. Hall, St. Joseph, June 14, 1864; Lieutenant W. T. Clarke to Colonel W. E. Moberly, St. Joseph, June 17, 1864; Fisk to Major General William S. Rosecrans, December 9, 1864, in *OR*, XXXIV (4): 270, 324, 376, 397, 437; XLI (4): 815.

81. John F. Benjamin to his Wife, Shelbyville, August 25, 1862, John F. Benjamin Letters, Wis.SHS.

82. Deposition of James D. Meador, Kansas City, November 30, 1864, Letters Received File 367, Record Group 393, NA.

83. Major J. M. Bassett to Colonel F. A. Dick, St. Joseph, December 26, 1862, Provost Marshal Letters Received File 2786, Record Group 393, NA.

84. Lieutenant William McIlwrath to Brigadier General Odon Guitar, Chillicothe, December 7, 1863, Odon Guitar Papers, JC.

85. Major Joseph H. McGee to General E. Brown, Lexington, October 27, 1863, Letters Received File 367, Record Group 393, NA.

86. Captain Eli J. Crandall to Captain G. A. Holloway, Brookfield, October 4, 1864, *OR*, XLI (3): 620–21.

87. Lieutenant O. S. Steele to Colonel _____, New Madrid, April 22, 1864, Provost Marshal Letters Received File 2786, Record Group 393, NA.

88. Lieutenant Colonel F. T. Russell to General William S. Rosecrans, Colum-

bia, April 3, 1864, *OR*, XXXIV (3): 30. It is significant that Russell reported such a vague rumor. He clearly shared the widespread fears these rumors had induced.

89. Brigadier General Clinton B. Fisk to Major General William S. Rosecrans, St. Joseph, June 19, 1864; George S. Park to General Samuel R. Curtis, Parkville, June 20, 1864, both in *OR*, XXXIV (4): 457, 477. The best available discussion of the Paw Paws is Howard V. Canan, "The Missouri Paw Paw Militia of 1863–64," *MHR*, LXII (July 1968): 431–48.

90. Petition of 54 Citizens of Mound City, February 27, 1864, Letters Received File 367, Record Group 393, NA.

91. Affidavit of Wiley Walker, Platte City, March 2, 1864, Two or more Name File 2635, Record Group 393, NA.

92. Brigadier General Clinton B. Fisk to General William S. Rosecrans, Glasgow, July 12, 1864; Captain R. D. Johnston to Fisk, July 20, 1864, both in *OR*, XLI (2): 158, 296–97.

93. Testimony of O. S. Fahnstock, Sgt. of Hopkins Battery, Springfield, October 10, 1863, Two or More Name Citizen File 2637, Record Group 393, NA; Testimony of Joseph Reiter, Court-Martial of Marion D. Erwin, alias Robert St. Clair, Macon, February 14, 1865, Case OO 303, Testimony of Francis Backleiter, Court-Martial of Oscar Davis, Case OO 303, Record Group 153, NA. Like Erwin, Davis claimed he had been too drunk at the time to remember the incident. Davis said his evening in the saloon was just "a little frolic." For contrasting analyses of southwestern humor see Elliott J. Gorn, "Gouge and Bite, Pull Hair and Scratch: The Social Significance of Fighting in the Southern Backcountry," *American Historical Review*, XC (February 1985): 18–43; Michael Fellman, "Alligator Men and Card Sharpers: Deadly Southwestern Humor"; Kenneth S. Lynn, *Mark Twain and Southwestern Humor* (Boston: Little, Brown, 1960); and Arthur K. Moore, *The Frontier Mind* (Lexington: University of Kentucky Press, 1957).

94. Henry H. Twining to his Dear Friend Hattie, Big River Bridge, December 25, 1861, Bond-Fentriss Family Papers, UNC. Dave Garver to his Sister, forty miles west of St. Louis, October 26, 1861, David Garver Letters, UNC.

95. W. C. Quantrill to William W. Scott, Olathe, Kansas Territory, January 22, 1858, Spencer Research Library, Lawrence, reprinted in William E. Connelley, *Quantrill and the Border Wars*, 172. On hunting in the South see Dickson D. Bruce, Jr., *Violence and Culture in the Antebellum South* (Austin: University of Texas Press, 1979), 196–211; and Clarence Gohdes (ed.), *Hunting in the Old South: Original Narratives of the Hunters* (Baton Rouge: Louisiana State University Press, 1967).

96. Captain Eli J. Crandall to Brigadier General Clinton B. Fisk, Brunswick, November 18, 1864, *OR*, XLI (4): 607; Colonel Chester Harding to Colonel H. V. Colburn, St. Joseph, June 6, 1863, Letters Sent File 567, Record Group 393, NA.

97. Lieutenant David M. Freeman to General I. V. Pratt, Carrollton, May 27, 1865, *OR*, XLVIII (1): 293.

98. Major H. Hilliard to Brigadier General Clinton B. Fisk, Weston, August 23, 1864, *OR,* XLI (2): 824; Colonel John F. Phillips to Captain James H. Steger, Warrensburg, July 14, 1864, *OR,* XLI (1): 67.

99. Entries for April 16, May 6, 8, 20, October 20, 1863, Diary of George Titcomb, Huntington. A similar mood was conveyed by A. J. McRoberts, Marshall militiaman, in a letter to his wife Mary in Circleville, Ohio, September 12, 1862. "The immortal squad has been going on their own hook. We came on a parcel of bushwhackers the other eavening down in the bottom and we charged them and put them to skedadling in good earnest. I run so close that one of them jumped off his horse, took to the bush and I got his horse. I fired at them but my horse was running at full speed and I missed them." A. J. McRoberts Collection, JC.

100. Entry for May 28, 1862, Sardius Smith Diary, Ill.SHL.

101. [A Soldier in the 3rd Iowa Cavalry] to the Keokuk *Weekly Gate City,* for February 12, 1862, written in Fulton on January 25, 1862. Most frequently deer were the quarry analogous to guerrillas. In many folk tales, perhaps because of their liquid eyes, deer are especially anthropomorphic animals, and often humans have been turned into deer in legend. Although I would argue that this hunting imagery is essentially dehumanizing, the deer is the most beautiful and nearly human game and hence the noblest object of the hunt.

102. "H. H." [1st Iowa Cavalry] to the Des Moines, *Daily State Register,* Sedelia, April 11, 1862.

103. Brigadier General M. Jeff Thompson to General Gideon J. Pillow, Camp Whitewater, August 12, 1861, *OR,* III: 132.

104. Captain John R. Kelso to Captain H. D. Moore, Neosho, June 2, 1864, *OR,* XXXIV (1): 957–58. A few soldiers wrote personal letters in such a vein, particularly Phineas M. Savery, an especially romantic southern officer and gentleman who on November 20, 1861 wrote to his wife back home near the Missouri River from Sarcoxie in the southeast of the state, about "our mighty army whose serried ranks of Cavalry, Artillery & Infantry are arrayed in hostile attitude against the invaders of our noble state. We are now in reality members of the Confederate States of America and we hope soon to be able to say, the fight is over." Phineas M. Savery Papers, Duke.

105. Dr. H. P. Strong to his wife Sarah, Alton, January 22, 1863, Dr. H. P. Strong Correspondence, Wis.SHS; Henry Crawford to Friends, Sededia, August 8, 1862, H. C. and W. H. Crawford Letters, JC.

106. Henry _____ to General Thomas E. Ewing, Jr., Steamer Marcella, November 3, 1864, Thomas E. Ewing Family Papers, LC. Henry was quoting from a letter to him from a Mr. Alexander of Greenville, Wayne County. Entry for August 12, 1864, Jefferson City, Diary of Charles C. Curtiss, CHS; Captain J. H. Little to Colonel James McFerran, Germantown, March 31, 1864, *OR,* XXXIV (1): 857.

107. Charles P. Taylor to Captain Kemper, near Liberty, reprinted in the Liberty *Tribune,* July 8, 1864; William Coleman to Colonel S. N. Wood, n.p., April 3, 1862, Samuel N. Wood Papers, KSHS. On dueling in the South see Bruce, *Violence and Culture . . . ,* 21–43; Bertram Wyatt-Brown,

Southern Honor (New York: Oxford University Press, 1982), 350–61; Jack K. Williams, *Dueling in the Old South* (College Station: Texas A & M University Press, 1980).

108. George S. Avery to his wife Lizzie, Palmyra, January 15, 1862, George S. Avery Letters, CHS; Entry for April 18, 1862, Cassville, Henry Dysart Diary, Iowa SHS.

109. George Wolz to his brother, Newton County, June 19, 1863, Civil War Papers, MHS—St. L.

110. Edwin H. Harris to his wife, Johnson County, Arkansas, November 24, 1862; Samuel W. Richie to Mrs. Edwin H. Harris, Horse Head, Arkansas, November 25, 1862, both in the Bland Collection, JCHS.

111. Brigadier General Egbert B. Brown to Major Oliver D. Greene, Jefferson City, November 4, 1863; Lieutenant Colonel T. A. Switzler to Brown, Warsaw, August 11, 1863, *OR*, XXII (2): 446, 694.

112. Brigadier General Thomas E. Ewing Jr., to Commanding Officer, Cape Girardeau, St. Louis, June 7, 1864, *OR*, XXXIV (4): 260–61; Brigadier General Clinton B. Fisk to Lieutenant Colonel Daniel M. Draper, Macon, April 18, 1864, *OR*, XXXIV (3): 216; Entry for October 20, 1864, Diary of Webster W. Moses, KSHS.

113. Charley Buford to his Wife, Scott, Kentucky, August 3, 1864, Charles Buford Papers, LC.

114. Entry for February 2, 1863, Forseyth, Diary of Timothy Phillips, Wis.SHS.

115. Entry for June 27, 1861, Osage, Diary of Dr. Joseph T. Trego, KSHS. The story narrating the torture of Gustavas Trout was clipped from the St. Charles newspaper and forwarded by the men's commander, Major A. Krekel, to Colonel Sanderson, the provost marshal in St. Louis on September 19, 1864, with a request that the men be put on trial. They denied the torture and claimed the prisoner had been shot while attempting to escape.

116. Colonel W. R. Pennick to Brigadier General Benjamin Loan, Independence, January 11, 1863, Letters Received File 2593, Record Group 393, NA; Loan passed the report to General Samuel R. Curtis from his post in Jefferson City on January 27, 1863, *OR*, XXII (2): 80; Major Emory S. Foster to Lieutenant D. A. Thatcher, Warrensburg, June 18, 1862, *OR*, XIII: 125; Lieutenant Colonel Daniel M. Draper to Brigadier General C. B. Fisk, Sturgeon, September 29, 1864, *OR*, XLI (1): 440.

117. The report of rings and charms made from human bones is in the letter of Albert J. Rockwell to his Father, Camp Curtis, November 26, 1862, Civil War Letters, Wis.SHS; Major Austin A. King to Brigadier General Clinton B. Fisk, Fayette, September 14, 1864, *OR*, XLI (3): 194; *Missouri Statesman*, August 5, 1864. Concerning scalping, the most sophisticated discussion is James Axtell, "The Unkindest Cut, or Who Invented Scalping? A Case Study," reprinted in Axtell, *The European and the Indian: Essays in Ethnohistory of North America* (New York: Oxford University Press, 1981), 16–35. For a survey on scalping in the Trans-Mississippi West, see Wayne Gard, *Frontier Justice* (Norman: University of Oklahoma Press, 1949), 3–21.

118. Glenn Grey, *The Warriors;* also see William Barry Gault, "Some Remarks on Slaughter," *American Journal of Psychiatry* (October 1971), 450–54;

William Goldsmith and Constantine Cretekos, "Unhappy Odysseys: Psychiatric Hospitalizations among Vietnam Returnees," *Archives of General Psychiatry,* XXX (January 1969): 78–83; Sarah A. Haley, "When the Patient Reports Atrocities: Specific Considerations of the Vietnam Veteran," *Archives of General Psychiatry* (February 1974), 191–96; Joel Yager, "Personal Violence in Infantry Combat," *Archives of General Psychiatry* (February 1975), 257–61. Americans learned a great deal about the mutilation of the Other through their dealings with the Indians. See especially Richard Slotkin, *Regeneration Through Violence: The Mythology of the American Frontier, 1600–1860* (Middletown: Wesleyan University Press, 1973). Even earlier, British suppression of the Irish conditioned them to treat the Indians as they did when they arrived in North America. See Nicholas P. Canny's brilliant essay, "The Ideology of English Colonization: From Ireland to America," *William and Mary Quarterly,* 3d Series, XXX (October 1973): 575–98.

119. Entries for July 4, 5, 10, 1862, July 11, August 4, 21, 24, September 26, October 1, 4, 1863, September 20, 1865, Diary of Sherman Bodwell, KSHS. After the war, Bodwell, a bachelor, served as sheriff of Shawnee County, Kansas. He died in 1871 at age thirty-six. See "Bodwell Family Genealogy," KSHS.

CHAPTER 5. WOMEN AS VICTIMS AND PARTICIPANTS

1. Adelia A. Allen to Dan Holmes, Princeton, Illinois, December 29, 1862, in Daniel B. Holmes Letters, CHS.
2. Lizzie Brannock to Dear Brother Edwin, Chapel Hill, January 13, 1864, Lizzie Brannock Letters, JC. General William S. Rosecrans wrote in 1864 that on both sides the guerrilla war "involved every man and woman in the State (for the females used their magic influence to degenerate men)." This was domestic power turned upside down morally. Orders of William S. Rosecrans, Jefferson City, July 8, 1864, *OR,* XLI (2): 87.
3. Lucy Thurman to Larkin Adamsay, Pine Oak, July 1, 1862, Civil War Papers, MHS—St.L.
4. Court-Martial of Mrs. Mary Jackson, Miss Sue Jackson, and Miss Bettie Jackson, Marshall, Missouri, October 6, 1862, Case LL 1229, Record Group 153, NA. The Jacksons were convicted and banished from Missouri, a sentence suspended by General John M. Schofield, commander of the district, who offered no explanation for his action.
5. 1st Lieutenant J. C. Lindsay to Mrs. Garrison, August 25, 1863, John W. Hudson Family Papers, JCHS.
6. George Spratt to Friend Mary, Paola, Kansas, April 15, 186?, George Spratt Papers, Wis.SHS.
7. Statement of Susan Vaughan et al., Office of the Provost Marshal General of the Department of the Missouri, St. Louis, March 29, 1865, Two or More Citizen File 2637, Record Group 393, NA.
8. Entries for September 29, December 8, 1862, Hiram C. Crandall Diary, Ill.SHL, emphasis in the original. An interesting analysis of the ideological

development of the notion of women's domestically based claims for moral superiority is Mary P. Ryan, *The Empire of the Mother: American Writing About Domesticity, 1830–1860* (New York: Haworth Press, 1982).

9. Daniel R. Smith to his Parents, Jefferson City, August 28, 1861, Daniel R. Smith Papers, Ill.SHL.

10. Captain W. J. Leeper to Brigadier General C. B. Fisk, Patterson, February 1, 1864, *OR*, XXXIV (2): 213.

11. Edwin F. Noyes to Mr. Stephenson, Camp Benton, August 21, 1861, Nathaniel Wright Family Papers, LC. Such tongue lashings administered by women to Union troops were common. Cavalry Captain William B. Ballew and seven of his men visited the Spencer family near Warrensburg, entered their house, and asked for bread. The Spencers' four grown daughters replied, "they could not get it; that their dogs needed it, and they should have it; that they would feed no Black Republicans; but said that they had and would again feed their grub to bushwhackers when they wanted to, and even dared the soldiers to molest a thing about the premises; if so they would report them at Warrensburg." Captain William B. Ballew to Colonel J. F. Phillips, Warrensburg, July 2, 1864, *OR*, XXXIV (1): 1058. Either the Spencer girls had good connections in the Union army, or a large amount of cheek.

12. Charles E. Calkins to his Mother, Otterville, February 10, 1862, Charles E. Calkins Papers, Ill.SHL.

13. Captain James A. Ewing to Colonel _____, Charleston, February 17, 1864, *OR*, XXXIV (1): 145. Another Union detachment merely burned the house jammed with stolen goods of a woman who screamed at them that she paid $2,000 per year to the Confederacy, that her two sons were bushwhackers, "and she cheard for Jef Davis said she did not cair [about the fire] for her sons could make it up in a short time out of the yankey sons of bitches." Sarah and Ruth Bonds were arrested after saying "that they had fed bushwhackers and they would do it in spite of hell they didn't ask the Feds any odds." All these cases demonstrated considerable male restraint as well as the degree of the risk many women permitted themselves to take in their anger. Hugh Sloan to My Dear Wife, Fort Scott, Kansas, May 20, 1864, Hugh Sloan Collection, Wis.SHS; deposition of Henry Jenkins, Jefferson City, April 11, 1864, Two or More Citizen File 2637, Record Group 393, NA.

14. Barton Bates to Edward Bates, St. Louis, October 10, 1861, Edward Bates Collection, MHS—St.L.

15. Brigadier General E. A. Carr to Major H. Z. Curtis, Searcy Landing, Arkansas, May 27, 1862, *OR*, XIII: 86.

16. Entry for Sept. 20, 1862, Timothy Phillips Diary, Wis.SHS.

17. Jonathan Dwight Stevens to My Dear Wife, Cross Hollows, Arkansas, October 28, 1862, Jonathan Dwight Stevens Letters, Wis.SHS. Sgt. Warren Day of Kansas, campaigning in northern Arkansas at the same time as Stevens, made the same empathetic juxtaposition. "I am seeing the sufferings which exist here among the women and children and to hear from you and my darling boy, that you are enjoying health and comfort made me shed tears of joy." Warren Day to Mary, Washington, Arkansas,

November 9, 1862, Correspondence of Warren and Mary Day, KSHS. Sylvester G. Beckwith of Illinois wrote to his wife how much he reviled those soldiers who would rob "the innocent little children of the last mouthful" and "would rob a dead woman of her burning clothes. . . . I hope that all those who do so may receive their reward." He noted that none of his company had taken to such heartless thieving. Thus his homicidal wish was projected onto troops he did not know personally. Nevertheless his sense of outrage was clear. S. G. Beckwith to my Dear Wife, Camp Patterson, January 5, 1862, Sylvester G. Beckwith Papers, Ill.SHL.

18. S. S. Marrett to Dear Companion, Camp near Batesville, Arkansas, June 15, 1862, S. S. Marrett Papers, Duke.

19. S. S. Marrett to Dear Companion, Camp near Red River, Arkansas, May 31, 1862, S. S. Marrett Papers, Duke.

20. L. R. Webber to Mrs. John Stillman Brown, May 24, 1863, John Stillman Brown Family Papers, KSHS.

21. Entries for July 11, August 4, October 1, 1863, Sherman Bodwell Diary, KSHS.

22. Testimony of Lucy Jane McManus, November 9, 1863, Provost Marshal File, Charges of Disloyalty File 2792, Record Group 393, NA.

23. Samuel S. Hildebrand, *Autobiography of Samuel S. Hildebrand* (Jefferson City: State Times Printing Office, 1870), 145.

24. Sophia L. Bissell to Cousin, Lawrence, Kansas, September 8, 1863, Sophia L. Bissell Letters, CHS. Chivalric honor is placed in interesting contexts in Bertram Wyatt-Brown, *Southern Honor* (New York: Oxford University Press, 1982), and in Dickson S. Bruce, Jr., *Violence and Culture in the Antebellum South* (Austin: University of Texas Press, 1979).

25. W. Anderson to the editor of the two papers in Lexington, to the citizens and the community at large, General Brown, and Colonel McFerran and to his petty hirelings, such as Captain Burris, the friend of Anderson, July 7, 1864, in *OR*, XLI (2): 76–77.

26. See for example the postwar apologia of one guerrilla, William H. Gregg Manuscripts, JC, at p. 67.

27. Charles Monroe Chase to the editor of the Sycamore, Illinois, *True Republican and Sentinel,* Independence, August 12, 1863, reprinted in *The Kansas Historical Quarterly,* XXVI (Summer 1960): 124.

28. N. F. Carter to Jud Waldo, Camp Bragg, Arkansas, November 26, 1863, Bland-Harris Collection, JC. This was a report of Carter's fears concerning Osceola, Missouri.

29. Captain John M. Richardson to Colonel Chester Hardin, Springfield, February 26, 1862, *OR*, VIII: 72.

30. Entry for Feb. 14, 1862 in Margaret Mendenhall Frazier and James W. Goodrich, (eds.), " 'Life is Uncertain . . .' Willard Hall Mendenhall's 1862 Civil War Diary," *MHR*, LXXVII (July 1984): 444.

31. M. G. Singleton to Colonel James S. Rollins, Centralia, February 9, 1863, James S. Rollins Papers, JC.

32. Deposition of Mrs. Mary Hall, Franklin County, May 11, 1865, Letters Received File 2593, Record Group 393, NA. Hall made this deposition

five days after the event to a Union provost marshal, of what she called "this Horrid Barbarity."

33. Entry for May 22, 1862, Sardius Smith Diary, Ill.SHL; Entry for May 22, 1862, Henry Dysart Diary, Iowa, SHS.

34. Court-Martial of James Johnson, Jefferson City, May 18, 1863, Case MM 1021, Record Group 153, NA.

35. Mrs. J. R. Roberts to General James B. Long, Quincy, Ill., April 7, 1864, Provost Marshal File Letters Received File 2786, Record Group 393, NA.

36. Entry for February 25, 1863, Forseyth, Arkansas, Timothy Phillips Diary, Wis.SHS.

37. Entry for May 22, 1862, Dr. Joseph H. Trego Diary, KSHS.

38. Brigadier General James A. Pile to Major General W. S. Rosecrans, St. Louis, February 23, 1864, Letters Received File 2593, Record Group 393, NA.

39. Captain Louis F. Green to Alexander Calhoun, Independence, February 14, 1864, Odon Guitar Papers, JC.

40. Report of First Lieutenant James D. Cannon, First Infantry, New Mexico Volunteers, Fort Lyon, Colorado Territory, January 16, 1865, OR, XLI (1): 970–71. Cannon was temporarily attached to the Colorado regiment. His denunciation of Chivington was corroborated by two others outraged enough to turn on their comrades. The massacre became the subject of two investigations; Joint Committee on the Conduct of the War, Massacre of the Cheyenne Indians, 38th Congress, 2nd Session (Washington, 1865), and Report of the Secretary of War, 29th Congress, 2nd Session. Senate Executive Document 26 (Washington, 1867), which are partially reprinted in John M. Carroll (ed.), *The Sand Creek Massacre: A Documentary History* (New York: Sol Lewis, 1973). Also see Stan Hoig, *The Sand Creek Massacre* (Norman: University of Oklahoma Press, 1961).

41. Of course the origins of scalping and mutilation of women and children were attributed to Indian "savages." It is unclear who these men thought they were when they themselves acted this way. Of the immense literature on white extermination of Indians, see Richard Slotkin, *Regeneration Through Violence: The Mythology of the American Frontier, 1600–1860* (Middletown: Wesleyan University Press, 1973). At Drogheda who were the Irish to Cromwell and his men, conscience-stricken Puritans that they were? See L. P. Curtis, Jr., *Anglo-Saxons and Celts: A Study of Anti-Irish Prejudice in Victorian England* (Bridgeport, Conn.: Conference on British Studies, 1968), and Curtis, *Apes and Angels: The Irishman in Victorian Culture* (Washington: Smithsonian Institution, 1971), and Nicholas P. Canny, "The Ideology of English Colonization: From Ireland to America," *William and Mary Quarterly,* 3rd Series, XXX (October 1973): 575–98.

42. Major Jeremiah Hackett to Lt. Colonel Hugh Cameron, Cassville, June 15, 1864, OR, XXXIV (1): 993; entry for April 19, 1862, Henry Dysart Diary, Iowa SHS.

43. Entries for April 20, 1862, July 9, 1863, Sardius Smith Diary, Ill.SHL.

44. Entry for October 19, 1862, James H. Guthrie Diary, Iowa SHS.

45. Entry for July 9, 1863, Sardius Smith Diary, Ill.SHL.

46. James W. Goodrich, "Robert Ormsby Sweeny: Some Civil War Sketches," *MHR,* LXXVII (January 1983): 167.

47. Colonel John Van Densen Dubois to his Father, Springfield, July 28, 1861, John Van Densen Dubois Collection, Beinecke. For an analysis of northern and eastern images of such rural types see Michael Fellman, "Alligator Men and Card Sharpers: Deadly Southwestern Humor."

48. Charles W. Falker to His Wife, near Warrensburg, April 5, 1865, Charles W. Falker Letters, Wis.SHS.

49. Entries for April 6, Harrisonville; April 15, south of Springfield; April 19, Berryville, Arkansas; April 28, in northern Arkansas, Anne E. Hemphill (ed.), "The 1864 Diary of Seth Kelly," *Kansas History,* I (Autumn 1978): 189–210, at 194, 196, 197.

50. K. Veatch to James Veatch, Chariton County, January 15, 1863, Simon Veatch Family Letters, Iowa SHS.

51. Theodore Ritsmiller to his Wife, Benton Barracks, August 31, 1862, Theodore Ritsmiller Letters, Duke.

52. Entry for May 29, 1862, Dr. Joseph H. Trego Diary, KSHS.

53. Entry for January 24, 1865, Diary of W. W. Moses, KSHS. Moses or someone else glued a piece of paper over this diary entry sometime after the war.

54. Entry for May 31, 1863, Diary of Charles L. Lothrop, Iowa, SHS.

55. Bazel F. Lazear to his Wife, Harrisonville, April 29, 1863; Warrensburg, May 13, May 27, 1863; Lexington, June 22, 1863; Jefferson City, July 27, 1863, Bazel F. Lazear Collection, JC. An expurgated version of most of these letters was edited by Vivian Kirkpatrick McLarty, "The Civil War Letters of Colonel Bazel F. Lazear." *MHR,* XLIV (April, July 1950): 254–73; 387–401; XLV (October 1950): 47–63.

56. Investigation of the St. Charles Street prison for Women, St. Louis, January 5, 1864, Two or More Name File 2635, Record Group 393, NA.

57. Entry for March 19, 1863, Diary of Timothy Phillips, Wis.SHS.

58. Mollie McRoberts to A. J. McRoberts, Circleville, Ohio, July 17, 1863; A. J. to Mollie McRoberts, Saline County, July 12, 1863, A. J. McRoberts Papers, JC.

59. Mrs. Edwin H. Harris to her Husband, Paris, Texas, August 12, September, 7, 1862; Edwin H. Harris to his Wife, St. Clair, October 3, 1862, Bland Collection, JCHS.

60. Brigadier General John B. Sanborn to Mrs. Sarah M. Scott, Springfield, February 1, 1865, *OR,* XLVIII (1): 716–17. Also see John B. Sanborn "Reminiscence of the War in the Department of the Missouri" (St. Paul, 1886), pamphlet in the Huntington Library.

61. Phineas M. Savery to his Wife, Springfield, February 1, 1862; Oxford, Mississippi, November 28, 1863; Memphis, Tennessee, June 10, September 1, November 12, 1865; Amanda Savery to her husband, Smithfield, June 15, July 1, August 1, 1865, Phineas M. Savery Papers, Duke.

62. Minerva Blow to her daughter, Susie, St. Louis, March 8, 1861, Blow Family Papers, MHS—St.L. Emphasis in the original. Minerva's husband Henry was appointed U.S. minister to Venezuela in 1861 by Lincoln, and was elected to Congress in 1862. The rest of the Blow family, which came from Alabama, were proslavery Democrats, including Taylor Blow, some-

time owner of Dred Scott. See John A. Bryan, "The Blow Family and Their Slave Dred Scott," *Bulletin of the Missouri Historical Society,* IV (July 1948): 223–31; V (October 1948): 19–33.

63. Mary Hall to Mrs. Venetia Colcord Page, Independence, May 6, 1863, Jacob Hall Family Papers, JCHS.

64. Bethiah Pyatt McKown to John D. McKown, St. Louis, June 4, 1863; February 29, 1864, in James W. Goodrich (ed.), "The Civil War Letters of Bethiah Pyatt McKown," *MHR,* LXVII (January, April 1973): 227–52; 351–70, at 357–58, 362.

65. Charles E. Calkins to his Mother, Otterville, January 5, 1862, Charles E. Calkins Papers, Ill.SHL.

66. John A. Higgins to Nancy Higgins, Greenville, Arkansas, August 4, 1862, John A. Higgins Papers, Ill.SHL.

67. For far less bowdlerized analysis of narcissism see Sigmund Freud, "On Narcissism: An Introduction" (1914) in James Strachey (ed.), *The Standard Edition of the Complete Works of Sigmund Freud,* vol. XIV (London: Hogarth, 1957): 67–102; Heinz Kohut, *The Analysis of the Self* (New York: International Universities Press, 1971).

68. Henry J. Traber to his Family, St. Louis, November 19, 1864, Henry J. Traber Letters, Wis.SHS.

69. George S. Avery to Lizzie Avery, Palmyra, March 12, 1862, George S. Avery Letters, CHS.

70. Charles W. Falker to his Wife, Warrensburg, April 5, 1865; Fort Scott, Kansas, April 18, 1865, Charles W. Falker Letters, Wis.SHS.

71. Two studies which began the discussion of separate gender spheres in America are Carroll Smith-Rosenberg, "The Female World of Love and Ritual: Relations between Women in Nineteenth-Century America," *Signs,* I (Spring 1975): 1–30; and Nancy F. Cott, *The Bonds of Womanhood: "Women's Sphere" in New England, 1780–1835* (New Haven: Yale University Press, 1977). Also see John Mack Faragher, *Women and Men on the Overland Trail* (New Haven: Yale University Press, 1979).

CHAPTER 6. AFTER THE WAR

1. Sarah P. Harlan to her Brother, Haynesville, April 12, 19, May 3, 1865; Harlan to her Mother and Father, June 9, 1865, Bond-Fentriss Family Papers, UNC. What I have found about the absence of catharsis in Missouri confirms Eric L. McKitrick's fascinating analysis of the symbolic inconclusiveness of the peace achieved in 1865: *Andrew Johnson and Reconstruction* (Chicago: University of Chicago Press, 1960), 21–41.

2. Major General Grenville M. Dodge to Captain W. J. Clarke, St. Louis, May 12, 1865; Dodge to Brigadier General R. B. Mitchell, Ft. Scott, Kansas, May 19, 1865; Captain John W. Younger to Brigadier General Clinton B. Fisk, Liberty, May 29, 1865, *OR,* XLVIII (2): 423, 513, 669. Lieutenant General E. Kirby Smith officially surrendered the Trans-Mississippi Department on May 26, the last Confederate commander to give up. By that date, almost all his army had already deserted.

3. Maddie Perkins to Benjamin Cocke, Fayette, October 10, 1865, Bland-Harris Collection, JC. In the same manuscript collection is the journal of Mrs. Edwin E. Harris, kept from September 25 to October 23, 1865, as the Harris family traveled back from Texas to Osceola, meeting up with a caravan of fellow-returning Missourian exiles accompanied by their former slaves.

4. William Crawford to his Son, Trenton, March 13, 1865, H. C. and W. H. Crawford Letters, JC.

5. [Mrs Benton S. Stout] to her Husband, Lafayette County, May 7, 1865, Benton S. Stout Papers, Ill.SHL.

6. W. W. Moses to his Wife, Centerville, May 7, 1865, Webster W. Moses Collection, KSHS.

7. Petition of thirty-five loyal citizens of McDonald County to Governor Thomas C. Fletcher, Newtonia, July 10, 1865, Letters Received File 367, Record Group 393, NA.

8. Mayor E. Grovenor and the Councilmen of Lawrence to Major General Grenville M. Dodge, Lawrence, March 15, 1866; Dodge to Major General John Pope, Ft. Leavenworth, March 24, 1866. On March 17, in Topeka, Kansas Governor S. J. Crawford had endorsed the Lawrence letter to Dodge in even more frightened terms, writing that the *"heartless and merciless fiends"* were by his *"reliable* information" already gathering at Waverly to "re-enact the butchery . . . of 1863." This correspondence is in the Letters Received File 367, Record Group 393, NA.

9. Charles S. Bryan to William S. Bryan, Smith City, September 21, 1866, William Shepard Bryan Papers, UNC; William S. Miller to Colonel James S. McFerran, Spring Hill, September 12, 1866, Letters Received File 2593, Record 393, NA.

10. Captain C. E. Rogers to Colonel J. H. Baker, Warrensburg, July 1, 1865, Provost Marshal Letters Received File 2786, Record Group 393, NA.

11. Richard Huston to Dr. John F. Snyder, Ashland, September 4, 1865, John F. Snyder Papers, Ill.SHL.

12. William E. Hill to Bettie Redding Hill, Chariton County, February 21, 1866, Hill Letters, JC. Old Dave acted on all his resentments. William Walker, alias John Carley, spouted off in the taverns of Idaho City, Idaho Territory, that during the war he had served under Price, Quantrill, and "on his own hook," and that, according to the Idaho City sheriff, he "bragged of taking numbers of persons out of their houses and shooting them down in their own yards, when their wives would be screaming for them." He said he intended to return to Stoddard County where his father's farm had been confiscated and sold, "so that he can kill the man that bought it." The sheriff wrote to the St. Louis army command to find out whether to arrest Walker and to inquire about possible reward money. Walker may or may not have intended to act upon his smoldering resentments, as Old Dave had done with so little success. One can presume that more men bore grudges than acted them out. However, unresolved resentments contained damages of their own. Sheriff of Idaho City to Henry Atkins, March 27, 1867, Letters Received File 2593, Record Group 393, NA.

13. William E. Hill to Bettie Redding Hill, Chariton County, December 3, 1865, Hill Letters, JC.
14. Deposition of Richard Parks, S. Gudgell, J. T. Jennings, and James Anderson, Livingston County, September 1, 1866, Two or More Name File 2635, Record Group 393, NA. For a full analysis of long-term vigilantism in post-Civil War Missouri see David Thelan, *Paths of Resistance: Tradition and Dignity in Industrializing Missouri* (New York: Oxford University Press, 1986), 57–99.
15. James F. Hardin to Major General Winfield S. Hancock, St. Louis, September 15, 1866, Letters Received File 2593, Record Group 393, NA.
16. William F. Leftwich, *Martyrdom in Missouri*, 2 vols. (St. Louis: Southwestern Book & Publishing Company, 1870); I. J. Steig to his Brother James, Granville, August 26, 1866, Samuel S. Steig Papers, Duke; Joseph King Autobiography, JCHS. Concerning the widespread Unionist attacks on the southern-leaning ministry see William E. Parrish, *Missouri Under Radical Rule, 1865–1870* (Columbia: University of Missouri Press, 1965), 68–75; Thomas L. Barclay, "The Test Oath for the Clergy in Missouri," *MHR*, XVIII (April 1924): 59–108.
17. Sheriff J. A. Patterson to Governor Thomas C. Fletcher, Springfield, August 30, 1866, Letters Received File 2593, Record Group 393, NA.
18. James W. Jones and four others to Major General William Hoffman, Liberty, November 11, 1866; F. M. Fulkerson and twenty-six others to Governor Thomas C. Fletcher, Sedelia, October 9, 1866; C. W. Howard to Fletcher, August 6, 1866, all in Letters Received File 2593, Record Group 393, NA.
19. Sheriff Thomas Adamson to Governor Thomas C. Fletcher, Lexington, November 8, 1866; Captain W. P. Wilson to Major General W. S. Hancock, Jefferson City, November 15; Captain W. P. Wilson to Hancock, Lexington, December 3; First Lieutenant James R. Kelly to Brigadier General C. McKeever, Lexington, December 12; Richard C. Vaughan to Hancock, Richmond, December 21; J. A. Berry to Colonel Robert Nugent, Lexington, December 21; Report of Captain Robert Servant, Lexington, December 21, 1866, all in Letters Received File 2593, Record Group 393, NA. Using coercive means to gain power did not mean that radicals were bad governors. The energy, efficiency, and relative honesty of radical rule in Missouri is stressed by William E. Parrish, *Missouri Under Radical Rule, 1865–70* (Columbia: University of Missouri Press, 1965).
20. The case of Missouri confirms much of the positive reevaluation of radical state governance in Kenneth Stampp, *The Era of Reconstruction* (New York: Knopf, 1965). For a firsthand picture of Missouri in 1867 from the point of view of a land-hungry Pennsylvanian see James W. Goodrich and Donald B. Oster (eds.), " 'Few Men But Many Widows . . .': The Daniel B. Fogle Letters, August 8–September 4, 1867," *MHR*, LXXX (April 1986): 273–303. Fogle observed whole counties deserted, countless war orphans, the absence of young men, and cheap land rendered insecure by the real possibility that the former landowners would return from the South to reclaim their farms by violent means.
21. Most of this discussion of the economic and demographic impact of the

Civil War and Reconstruction in Missouri was compiled from the *Seventh, Eighth* and *Ninth Censuses of the United States* (Washington: Government Printing Office). A useful overview is William E. Parrish, *A History of Missouri, Vol. III, 1860–75* (Columbia: University of Missouri Press, 1973). For comparisons with antebellum economic and demographic growth see Walter F. Ryle, *Missouri: Union or Secession* (Nashville: George Peabody College for Teachers, 1931), 1–55. Wyatt W. Belcher, in *The Economic Rivalry between St. Louis and Chicago, 1850–1880* (New York: Columbia University Press, 1947), argues that the Civil War so damaged trade in St. Louis that Chicago gained an insuperable commercial lead during this period. However, Belcher focuses on railroads and commerce, ignoring industrial growth. An excellent analysis of the rise and decline of the hemp industry, one broader than the title of the book suggests, is James F. Hopkins, *A History of the Hemp Industry in Kentucky* (Lexington: University of Kentucky Press, 1951).

22. Patrick O'Brien, *The Economic Effects of the American Civil War*, (Atlantic Highlands, N.J.: Humanities Press International, 1988), is an excellent summary of the debate over the impact of the Civil War on economic growth. Also see Stanley L. Engerman, "The Economic Impact of the Civil War," *Explorations in Entrepreneurial History*, 2d Series, III (1966): 179–99, reprinted in Robert E. Fogel and Stanley L. Engerman (eds.), *The Reinterpretation of American Economic History* (New York: Harper & Row, 1971), 369–79; Harry N. Scheiber, "Economic Change in the Civil War Era: An Analysis of Recent Studies," *Civil War History*, XI (December 1965): 396–411. Also see Ralph Andreano (ed.), *The Economic Impact of the American Civil War* 2d ed. (Cambridge, Mass.: Schenkman, 1967); and David Gilcrest and W. David Lewis (eds.), *Economic Change in the Civil War Era* (Greenville, Del.: Elutherian Mills–Hagley Foundation, 1965). For agricultural developments see Paul W. Gates, *Agriculture and the Civil War* (New York: Knopf, 1965).

23. In *Paths of Resistance,* David Thelan presents an alternative analysis, arguing that the traditionalists staved off the new order with considerable cultural and political success.

24. "Poems," June 1864, in the M. Jeff Thompson Letters, CHS.

25. A Missourian, "The Missourian's Feelings Before the Surrender at Schreveport, La." This poem was copied by William H. Sanders, Johnson County, on July 7, 1866, and presented to Miss Mollie Jones; manuscript in JCHS.

26. John N. Edwards, *Noted Guerrillas, or the Warfare on the Border* (St. Louis: Bryan, Brand, 1877), 149, 31, 19–20, 14, 300, 14, 158, 176.

27. Kent Ladd Steckmesser, *The Western Hero in History and Legend* (Norman: University of Oklahoma Press, 1965); William A. Settle, Jr., *Jesse James Was His Name* (Columbia: University of Missouri Press, 1966).

28. N.d., Warren W. Welsh Diary, JCHS.

29. James W. Evans and A. Wendell Keith, *Autobiography of Samuel S. Hildebrand: The Renowned Missouri Bushwhacker and Unconquerable Rob Roy, Being His Complete Confession, Recently Made to the Writers* (Jefferson City: State Times Book Co., 1870), 28, 54, 74, 107–8, 266, 286–87, 42, 49, 58–59, 62–63, 70–71. Hildebrand was illiterate. In Kentucky, an-

other lone wolf Confederate guerrilla mass murderer was brought to trial for war crimes and hanged after the war. See Thurman Sensing, *Champ Ferguson: Confederate Guerrilla* (Nashville: Vanderbilt University Press, 1942).

30. "William H. Gregg Manuscript," JC, p. 9; Captain Kit Dalton, *Under the Black Flag* (Memphis: Lockhard Publishing Company [1914]), 8; John McCorkle, as written by O. S. Barton, *Three Years with Quantrill* (Armstrong, Texas: Armstrong Herald [1915]), 78.

31. William H. Gregg, "The Lawrence Raid," JC, p. 3.

32. *Autobiography of Samuel S. Hildebrand,* 76.

33. "William H. Gregg Manuscript," 4; McCorkle, *Three Years with Quantrill,* 76–77; Quantrill's story of his murdered brother appears among other places in "Gregg Manuscript," 2–3; McCorkle, 25; John B. Burch, *Charles W. Quantrell as Told by Captain Harrison Trow* (Vega, Texas: J. P. Burch, 1923), 15.

34. Jim Cummins, *Jim Cummins's Book* (Denver: Reed, 1903), 72.

35. "William H. Gregg Manuscript," 59.

36. "William H. Gregg Manuscript," 48–49.

37. Dalton, *Under the Black Flag,* 30.

38. B. James George, Jr., "The Gregg Biography," manuscript in JC, pp. 163–81; newspaper story of September 27, 1901, reprinted in the *Jackson County Democrat,* October 26, 1961, attached to "The Gregg Biography."

39. Mrs. W. H. Gregg, "Can Forgive, But Never Forget"; Mrs. N. M. Harris, "Atrocities upon the Missouri Border," in Missouri Division, United Daughters of the Confederacy, *Women of Missouri During the Sixties* (Jefferson City: Hugh Stephens Printing Company [1901]), 26–27, 214–15.

40. Mrs. R. T. Bass, "Recollections of Quantrill," in *Women of Missouri During the Sixties,* 234–37.

41. Clement A. Evans (ed.), *Confederate Military History,* 12 vols. (Atlanta: Confederate Publishing Company, 1899), IX: 186–88. It is noteworthy that the guerrillas received only three pages of attention in twelve fat volumes. The compilers accepted the ex-guerrilla justifications, but evidently they were not interested in elaborating the whole affair.

42. "The Call of Quantrell" and "The Guerrilla Boy" were reprinted and analyzed by Henry M. Belden, in *Ballads and Songs Collected by the Missouri Folk-Lore Society,* 2d ed. (Columbia: University of Missouri Press, 1955), 353–54, 374–75. The Ozark variant of "The Guerrilla Boy" appears in Vance Randolph, *Ozark Folksongs,* 4 vols. (Columbia: University of Missouri Press, 1946–50), IV: 356–58. A "Navy" was the design on the 1853 Colt six-shooter favored by the guerrillas. "Quantrill," the third ballad discussed, was reprinted in Charles J. Finger, *Frontier Ballads* (Garden City, N.Y.: Doubleday, Page & Co., 1927), 64–65.

43. John N. Edwards, *Noted Guerrillas,* 450–51; Edwards, "The Killing of Jesse James," from the Sedelia *Democrat,* April 1882, reprinted in Jennie Edwards, *John N. Edwards: A Biography, Memoirs, Reminiscences and Recollections* (Kansas City: Jennie Edwards, 1889), 163–65.

44. Editorial in the Sedelia *Weekly Democrat,* October 14, 1882, reprinted in Settle, *Jesse James Was His Name,* 135.

45. *Journal of the House,* Twenty-eighth General Assembly of Missouri, Regular Session, 1875, pp. 1084, 1176, reprinted in Settle, pp. 81, 83. Settle demonstrates convincingly how much political influence the Jameses had both within the Democratic party and among rural Missourians in general. After Frank James's voluntary surrender, the grand jury would not indict him. On the other hand, Robert Ford became American folklore's greatest betraying villain, and Governor Thomas T. Crittenden, who had put the price on Jesse's head, destroyed himself politically by the accomplishment of the killing, despite his later pardon of Frank James. As Settle demontrates, the "modernizers" in Missouri were embarrassed by a roaming outlaw presence which they believed impeded eastern investment in the state. The "traditionalists" backed the James brothers against outside "monopolists."

46. Coleman Younger, *The Story of Cole Younger by Himself* (Chicago: The Hennebury Company, 1903), 76–77; Letter to the Kansas City *Times,* October 15, 1872, quoted in Kent L. Steckmesser's excellent essay, "Robin Hood and the American Outlaw," *Journal of American Folklore,* LXXIX (April–June 1966): 350. Also see Steckmesser, *The Western Hero in History and Legend.*

47. A 1948 Alabama rendition of this story is reprinted in Margaret Gillis Figh, "Nineteenth–Century Outlaws in Alabama Folklore," *Southern Folklore Quarterly,* XXV (June 1961): 130.

48. In a brilliant analysis, Orrin E. Klapp places Jesse James in the context of folk heroes the world over, "The Folk Hero," *Journal of American Folklore,* LXII (January-March 1949): 17–25. Of the enormous literature on Robin Hood see in particular, W. E. Simone, "Robin Hood and Some Other Outlaws," *Journal of American Folklore* (January-March 1958): 23–33; Maurice Keen, *The Outlaws of Medieval England* (London: Routledge and Kegan Paul, 1961).

49. Richard White, "Outlaw Groups of the Middle Border: American Social Bandits," *The Western Historical Quarterly,* XII (October 1981): 387–408. The modern discussion of social banditry owes a great deal to E. J. Hobsbawm, *Primitive Rebels: Studies in Archaic Forms of Social Movement in the Nineteenth and Twentieth Centuries* (New York: Pantheon, 1965), and Hobsbawm, *Bandits,* rev. ed., (New York: Pantheon, 1981). Hobsbawm's picture of social bandits has come under severe attack for its literalness and its somewhat romantic political stance in Anton Blok, "The Peasant and the Brigand: Social Banditry Reconsidered," *Comparative Studies in History and Society,* CIV (September 1972): 494–503. I stress the legendary aspects of the social bandit tradition, not arguing over degrees of literal fact in bandit behavior.

50. McCorkle, *Three Years with Quantrill,* 157.

51. John B. Sanborn, "Reminiscences of the War in the Department of the Missouri" (St. Paul, Minnesota, 1886), 20–21, 30–31. On Sanborn's banishment order see above, p. 127. Sanborn quoted the King James version of the Bible, 2 Samuel 23:3.

52. Matthew 10:34.

ARCHIVAL SOURCE LIST

NATIONAL ARCHIVES, WASHINGTON, D.C.

Archival Source	Source Group
Record Group 153	Judge Advocate General–General Court-Martial Records
Record Group 393	Records of U.S. Army Continental Commands 1821–1920. Dept. of the Missouri
File 367	District of Missouri, Letters Received
File 567	N.W. Missouri, Letters Sent, 1863
File 2593	Letters Received, St. Louis
File 2635	Two or More Name File
File 2636	Citizen File
File 2637	Two or More Name Citizen File
File 2748	Judge Advocate General, Register of Proceedings
File 2751	Register of Courts–Martial
File 2786	Provost Marshal File, Letters Received
File 2792	Provost Marshal File, Charges of Disloyalty
File 2798	Provost Marshal File, Statements of Property Stolen
File 2909	Missouri State Militia, Letters Received
File 2912	Missouri State Militia, Confiscated Property

NATIONAL ARCHIVES, KANSAS CITY

Criminal Case Record, Central Division of Missouri, Jefferson City

Official Record of Confiscation Cases, District of Kansas

Slave Compensation Records, Records of U.S. District Court for District of Kansas

LIBRARY OF CONGRESS

Anderson-Moler Family Papers
Charles Buford Papers
Thomas Ewing Family Papers
Vinnie Ream Hoxie Family Papers
John G. Nicolay Papers

Thomas C. Reynolds Papers
John McAllister Schofield Papers
Samuel B. Treat Papers
Nathaniel Wright Family Papers

JOINT COLLECTION, UNIVERSITY OF MISSOURI, WESTERN HISTORICAL MANUSCRIPT COLLECTION, STATE HISTORICAL SOCIETY OF MISSOURI MANUSCRIPTS

Alvold Collection
David R. Atchison Papers
Bedford Family Papers
Lizzie Brannock Letters
William W. Branson Diary
E. A. Christy Letter
Civil War Letter
Dennis H. Connoway Papers
H. C. & W. H. Crawford Letters
Francis Marion Emmons Civil War
  Letters
John Forbes and Diana Benjamin
  Letters
Charles B. France Papers
Freshour Family Papers
B. James George Collection
William H. Gregg Manuscripts
Odon Guitar Papers

Dr. Glen O. Hardeman Collection
Bland-Harris Collection
William E. and Bettie Redding Hill
  Letters
Waldo Porter Johnson Letters
Bazel F. Lazear Papers
Abiel Leonard Collection
Daniel Burdette Leroy Diary
William C. Long Papers
A. J. McRoberts Papers
John Poyntz Order
James A. Price Letters
James Sidney Rollins Papers
Sheppard Family Papers
Pauline H. Stratton Papers
Lizzie Thompson Letter
Robert T. Van Horn Papers
Woods-Holman Family Papers

Newspapers: (Columbia) Missouri
              Statesman
            (Liberty) *Tribune*

MISSOURI HISTORICAL SOCIETY, ST. LOUIS

Badger Collection
Edward Bates Collection
Blow Family Papers
James O. Broadhead Papers
Civil War Papers
Dorsey Family Papers

Hamilton R. Gamble Papers
Kennett Family Papers
William McCoy Papers
Thomas C. Reynolds Papers
Franklin D. Swap Papers

JACKSON COUNTY HISTORICAL SOCIETY, INDEPENDENCE, MISSOURI

Bland Collection
W. L. Bone Letters
W. A. Brannock Family Letters
David J. Caldwell Diary
Daniel DeWitt Papers
Jacob Hall Family Papers
Walter Harves Collection
Margaret J. Hayes Collection
John W. Hudson Family Papers
J. C. Iserman Letters

Jarbec-Johnston Correspondence
William T. Johnson Recollections
Joseph King Autobiography
"The Missourian's Feelings Before the
  Surrender at Schreveport [*sic*]"
Jacob T. Palmer Autobiography
Annie Hickman Payne Letters
Quantrill Collection
Francis Coleman Smith Recollections
Warren W. Welch Diary

KANSAS CITY PUBLIC LIBRARY

William A. Lyman Letters

Van Horn Papers

KANSAS STATE HISTORICAL SOCIETY, TOPEKA

Samuel Ayres Collection
Sherman Bodwell Diary
David P. Bond Collection
Augustus Bondi Diary
David R. Braden Diary
John Stillman Brown Family Papers
  (Microfilm 567)
Lassel Cain Collection
Campbell Family Collection
Orren A. Curtis Letters (Microfilm
  960)
Warren and Mary Day Correspon-
  dence (Microfilm 175)
Fifth Kansas Cavalry Papers
W. H. Gregg Letters
Hiram Hill Collection
Richard J. Hinton Diary
John J. Ingalls Collection
John A. Martin Letters (Microfilm
  221)

Josephine Blakely Martin Papers
H. Miles Moore Papers
Webster W. Moses Collection
New England Aid Company Papers
Stutely Nichols Papers
Wm. C. Quantrill Collection
Samuel J. Reader Diary
S. Riggs Collection
Charles and Sara Robinson Papers
  (Microfilm 640)
Mary Savage Papers
Thomas C. Stevens Papers
Dr. Joseph H. Trego Diary
  (Microfilm 1008)
Roland S. H. Trego Diary
  (Microfilm 1008)
John D. Walker Collection
Webb Scrapbooks
Samuel N. Wood Papers

KANSAS COLLECTION, KANSAS UNIVERSITY, LAWRENCE

(Gov.) Thomas Carney Correspondence
The Josiah Miller Letters

The Wm. C. Quantrill Collection
The John Vansickle Letters

ILLINOIS STATE HISTORICAL LIBRARY, SPRINGFIELD

Newton Bateman Papers
Sylvester G. Beckwith Papers
Charles E. Calkins Papers
Hiram C. Crandall Diary
Joseph M. Fifer Papers
John A. Higgins Papers
Edwin C. Sackett Papers

Daniel R. Smith Papers
Sardius Smith Diary
John F. Snyder Papers
Rev. Francis Springer Journal
Benton S. Stout Papers
Philip Welsheimer Papers
William Wilson Diary

CHICAGO HISTORICAL SOCIETY

Henry Asbury Collection
George S. Avery Letters
Sophia L. Bissell Letters
Broadside Collection
Lucian B. Case Letters
Charles C. Curtiss Diary

Daniel B. Holmes Correspondence
Warwick Hough Papers
Adolphus S. Hubbard Papers
William C. Quantrill Letters
George Sawin Letters
M. Jeff Thompson Letters

IOWA STATE HISTORICAL DEPARTMENT

M. S. Andrews Diary
Henry Dysart Diary
James H. Guthrie Diary
Letters of 1st Iowa Cavalry
Letters of 3rd Iowa Cavalry
Charles L. Lothrop Letters

John W. Noble Diary
George and William A. Richardson
  Letters
Shedd Family Papers
Simon Veatch Family Letters
Peter Wilson Manuscripts

WISCONSIN STATE HISTORICAL SOCIETY

Charles E. Beecham Letters
John F. Benjamin Letters
Edmund F. and Henry Bennett
  Collection
Coleman C. Chubb Diary
Civil War Letters
Uriah Eberhart Letters
Charles W. Falker Letters
Stanley E. Lathrop Correspondence
Henry J. Marsh Diary
Edmond D. Newton Papers

Timothy Phillips Diaries
Albert J. Rockwell Letters
Hugh Sloan Collection
George Spratt Papers
Jonathan Dwight Stevens Letters
Dr. H. P. Strong Letters
Samuel G. Swain Letters
Jeremiah D. Swart Letters
Henry J. Traber Letters
Henry H. Twining Letters
Charles D. Waldo Diary

LOUISIANA STATE UNIVERSITY, DEPARTMENT OF ARCHIVES AND MANUSCRIPTS

Sarah Cockrell Letters
Banjamin Franklin Cook Letters
Edward Theodor Hansen Diary

R. W. Hinson Letters
John Reid Collection
R. H. Walden Letters

SOUTHERN HISTORICAL COLLECTION, UNIVERSITY OF NORTH CAROLINA LIBRARY

Bond-Fentriss Family Papers
William Shepard Bryan Papers

David Garver Letters
James Lorenzo Morgan Papers

WILLIAM R. PERKINS LIBRARY, DUKE UNIVERSITY

Will Kennedy Papers
S. S. Marrett Papers
Missouri Militia Papers
Philip D. Riggs Papers
Theodore Ritsmiller Letters

Phineas M. Savery Papers
W. W. Scott Papers
Abby E. Stafford Papers
Samuel S. Steig Papers

BEINECKE LIBRARY, YALE UNIVERSITY

Samuel Ryan Curtis Papers
(Col.) John Van Densen Dubois
 Collection

Henry Miles Moore Diary

HUNTINGTON LIBRARY

Samuel R. Curtis Manuscripts
Eldridge Collection
Charles G. Halpine Collection

Richard J. Mohr Letters
George Titcomb Diary

INDEX